THE BEGGARS' BUSH
& OTHER PLAYS

MORE WILDSIDE CLASSICS

Dacobra, or The White Priests of Ahriman, by Harris Burland
The Nabob, by Alphonse Daudet
Out of the Wreck, by Captain A. E. Dingle
The Elm-Tree on the Mall, by Anatole France
The Lance of Kanana, by Harry W. French
Amazon Nights, by Arthur O. Friel
Caught in the Net, by Emile Gaboriau
The Gentle Grafter, by O. Henry
Raffles, by E. W. Hornung
Gates of Empire, by Robert E. Howard
Tom Brown's School Days, by Thomas Hughes
The Opium Ship, by H. Bedford Jones
The Miracles of Antichrist, by Selma Lagerlof
Arsène Lupin, by Maurice LeBlanc
A Phantom Lover, by Vernon Lee
The Iron Heel, by Jack London
The Witness for the Defence, by A.E.W. Mason
The Spider Strain and Other Tales, by Johnston McCulley
Tales of Thubway Tham, by Johnston McCulley
The Prince of Graustark, by George McCutcheon
Bull-Dog Drummond, by Cyril McNeile
The Moon Pool, by A. Merritt
The Red House Mystery, by A. A. Milne
Blix, by Frank Norris
Wings over Tomorrow, by Philip Francis Nowlan
The Devil's Paw, by E. Phillips Oppenheim
Satan's Daughter and Other Tales, by E. Hoffmann Price
The Insidious Dr. Fu Manchu, by Sax Rohmer
Mauprat, by George Sand
The Slayer and Other Tales, by H. de Vere Stacpoole
Penrod (Gordon Grant Illustrated Edition), by Booth Tarkington
The Gilded Age, by Mark Twain
The Blockade Runners, by Jules Verne
The Gadfly, by E.L. Voynich

Please see www.wildsidepress.com for a complete list!

THE BEGGARS' BUSH & OTHER PLAYS

by

FRANCIS BEAUMONT
&
JOHN FLETCHER

WILDSIDE PRESS

A LOST LEADER

This edition published in 2007 by Wildside Press, LLC.
www.wildsidepress.com

BEGGARS' BUSH.

Beggars Bush.

In the folios 1647, 1679.

The second folio adds " *A Comedy.*"

The Beggars Bush. Written by
Francis Beavmont, ⎫
And ⎬ *Gentlemen.*
John Fletcher, ⎭
You may speedily expect those other Playes, which Kirkman and his Hawkers have deceived the buyers withall, selling them at treble the value, that this and the rest will be sold for, which are the onely Originall and corrected copies, as they were first purchased by us at no mean rate, and since printed by us. London, Printed for Humphrey Robinson, and Anne Mosely, at the three Pigeons, and at the Princes Arms in Saint Pauls Church-yard, 1661. 4*to*,—is a reprint of *The Beggars' Bush* from the first folio, with a very few trivial variations, and with the addition of the *Dramatis Personæ*. At the end of this 4to we find " The Prologue " and " The Epilogue ", which, in fact, belong to *The Captain ;* in the first folio they occupy the leaf before *The Beggars' Bush ;* and hence the editor or printer of the 4to supposed that they belonged to the latter play.

OF this comedy Fletcher may certainly be regarded as the sole author; and, as we learn that it was performed at court during Christmas 1622, "upon St. Johns daye at night by the kings players" (see Malone's *Shakespeare* by Boswell, iii. 146), we may conclude that it had been originally acted, and with success, during the course of that year.

A droll taken from *Beggar's Bush*, and entitled *The Lame Commonwealth*, which was played during the suppression of the theatres, may be found in Kirkman's collection, *The Wits, or Sport upon Sport, Part First*, 1672, p. 28 (see vol. i. 200 of the present work). After the Restoration, *Beggar's Bush* was a popular comedy. Three alterations of it have, at different times, been produced. viz. *The Royal Merchant, or, The Beggar's Bush*, by H. N. (supposed to be Henry Norris the comedian), 1706,—a piece which I have not seen: Baker, in *The Companion to the Play-house*, 1764, mentions that it "is now frequently performed." *The Royal Merchant: an Opera. Founded on Beaumont and Fletcher. As it is performed at the Theatre Royal in Covent Garden* (by Thomas Hull the actor), 1768. *The Merchant of Bruges; or, Beggar's Bush; with considerable alterations and additions* by the Honourable Douglas Kinnaird, was brought out at Drury-lane Theatre in 1815, and had a run of many nights, Kean, who played Florez, being then a great attraction.

DRAMATIS PERSONÆ.

WOLFORT, usurper of the earldom of Flanders.

HEMSKIRK, a captain under him.

HUBERT, a nobleman.

HERMAN, a courtier.

FLOREZ, the rightful Earl of Flanders; a supposed merchant, under the name of GOSWIN.

GERRARD, a gentleman, father to FLOREZ[a] by the deceased Countess of Flanders; disguised as a beggar, under the name of CLAUSE.

ARNOLD, a nobleman, disguised as a beggar, under the name of GINKS.

COSTIN, a nobleman, disguised as a beggar.

HIGGEN,
FERRET[b],
PRIG,   } beggars.
SNAP,
and others,

VANDUNK, burgomaster of Bruges.

VANLOCK, a merchant.

Merchants.

Boors.

A Sailor, Soldiers, Attendants.

BERTHA, daughter to the Duke of Brabant; supposed daughter to VANDUNK, and niece to HEMSKIRK, under the name of GERTRUDE.

JACQUELINE, daughter to GERRARD; disguised as a beggar, under the name of MINCHE.

MARGARET, wife to VANDUNK.

FRANCES, daughter to VANLOCK.

SCENE—*During part of the first act, Ghent; afterwards, Bruges and the neighbourhood.*

---

[a] *father to Florez*] In the *Dram. Pers.* of the second folio Gerrard is called "*father-in-law* to Florez",—an error noticed by Mason, who was not aware that in the list prefixed to the 4to he is rightly termed "*father* to Florez." The first folio has no *Dram. Pers.*

[b] *Ferret*] In the *Dram. Pers.* of the second folio is described as "a gentleman disguised": but in the list prefixed to the 4to he is rightly ranked among the real beggars.

BEGGARS' BUSH.

ACT I.

SCENE I.—*Ghent.*—*Before the palace of* WOLFORT.

Enter a Merchant *and* HERMAN.

Mer. Is he, then, taken?
Her. And brought back even now, sir.
Mer. He was not in disgrace?
Her. No man more lov'd,
Nor more deserv'd it, being the only man
That durst be honest in this court.
Mer. Indeed,
We have heard abroad, sir, that the state hath suffer'd
A great change, since the countess' death.
Her. It hath, sir.
Mer. My five years' absence hath kept me a stranger
So much to all the occurrents of my country,
As you shall bind me [a] for some short relation,
To make me understand the present times.
Her. I must begin, then, with a war was made,
And seven years with all cruelty continu'd,
Upon our Flanders by the Duke of Brabant.
The cause grew thus: during our earl's minority,
Wolfort, who now usurps, was employ'd thither,
To treat about a match between our earl

---

[a] *bind me*] "i. e. oblige me." WEBER.

And the daughter and heir of Brabant: during which treaty,
The Brabander pretends, this daughter was
Stoln from his court by practice ᵇ of our state;
Though we are all confirm'd ᶜ 'twas a sought quarrel,
To lay an unjust gripe upon this earldom,
It being here believ'd the Duke of Brabant
Had no such loss. This war upon 't proclaim'd,
Our earl being then a child, although his father
Good Gerrard liv'd, yet (in respect he was
Chosen by the countess' favour for her husband,
And but a gentleman, and Florez holding
His right unto this country from his mother)
The state thought fit in this defensive war,
Wolfort being then the only man of mark,
To make him general.
   Mer. Which place we have heard
He did discharge with honour.
   Her. Ay, so long,
And with so blest successes, that the Brabander
Was forc'd (his treasures wasted, and the choice
Of his best men of arms tir'd or cut off)
To leave the field, and sound a base retreat
Back to his country: but so broken, both
In mind and means, e'er to make head again,
That hitherto he sits down by his loss,
Not daring, or for honour or revenge,
Again to tempt his fortune. But this victory
More broke our state, and made a deeper hurt
In Flanders, than the greatest overthrow
She ever receiv'd; for Wolfort, now beholding
Himself and actions in the flattering glass
Of self-deservings, and that cherish'd by
The strong assurance of his power, for then
All captains of the army were his creatures,
The common soldier too at his devotion,
Made so by full indulgence to their rapines,

ᵇ *practice*] i. e. artful contrivance, stratagem.
ᶜ *confirm'd*] "i. e. convinced." WEBER.

And secret bounties; this strength too well known,
And what it could effect soon put in practice,
As further'd by the childhood of the earl,
And their improvidence that might have pierc'd
The heart of his designs, gave him occasion
To seize the whole: and in that plight you find it.

Mer. Sir, I receive the knowledge of thus much,
As a choice favour from you.

Her. Only I must add,
Bruges holds out.

Mer. Whither, sir, I am going;
For there last night I had a ship put in,
And my horse waits me.

Her. I wish you a good journey. [*Exeunt severally.*

SCENE II.—*The same.—An apartment in the palace of* WOLFORT.

Enter WOLFORT, HUBERT, *and* Attendants.

Wol. What! Hubert stealing from me!—Who disarm'd him?
It was more than I commanded.—Take your sword;
I am best guarded with it in your hand;
I have seen you use it nobly.

Hub. And will turn it
On mine own bosom, ere it shall be drawn
Unworthily or rudely.

Wol. Would you leave me
Without a farewell, Hubert? fly a friend
Unwearied in his study to advance you?
What have I e'er possess'd which was not yours?
Or rather [d] did not court you to command it?
Who ever yet arriv'd to any grace,
Reward, or trust from me, but his approaches
Were by your fair reports of him preferr'd?
And what is more, I made myself your servant,
In making you the master of those secrets

---

[d] *rather*] The correction of the Editors of 1778 (in which they were anticipated by Heath, *MS. Notes*).—Old eds. " either "; and so Seward.

Which not the rack of conscience could draw from me,
Nor I, when I ask'd mercy, trust my prayers with:
Yet, after these assurances of love,
These ties and bonds of friendship, to forsake me!
Forsake me as an enemy! Come, you must
Give me a reason.
   Hub. Sir, and so I will;
If I may do't in private, and you hear it.
   Wol. All leave the room.   [*Exeunt* Attendants.
You have your will: sit down,
And use the liberty of our first friendship.
   Hub. Friendship! when you prov'd traitor first, that vanish'd;
Nor do I owe you any thought but hate.
I know my flight hath forfeited my head;
And, so I may make you first understand
What a strange monster you have made yourself,
I welcome it.
   Wol. To me this is strange language.
   Hub. To you! why, what are you?
   Wol. Your prince and master,
The Earl of Flanders.
   Hub. By a proper title!
Rais'd to it by cunning, circumvention, force,
Blood, and proscriptions!
   Wol. And in all this, wisdom:
Had I not reason, when, by Gerrard's plots,
I should have first been call'd to a strict account,
How and which way I had consum'd that mass
Of money, as they term it, in the war;
Who under-hand had by his ministers
Detracted my great actions [e], made my faith
And loyalty suspected [f]; in which failing,
He sought my life by practice [g]?
   Hub. With what forehead

---

  [e] *actions*] Old eds. "action". We have previously (p. 6) had,—
        "For *Wolfort,* now beholding
          Himself and *actions* in the flattering glass ", &c.

  [f] *loyalty suspected*] So the second folio.—The first folio and the 4to "*loyalty* so *suspected.*"

  [g] *practice*] See note, p. 6.

Do you speak this to me, who (as I know 't)
Must and will say 'tis false?
  Wol. My guard there!
  Hub. Sir,
You bade me sit, and promis'd you would hear;
Which I now say you shall: not a sound more!
For I, that am contemner of mine own,
Am master of your life; then here's a sword
                              [*Draws his sword.*
Between you and all aids, sir. Though you blind
The credulous beast, the multitude, you pass not
These gross untruths on me.
  Wol. How! gross untruths!
  Hub. Ay, and it is favourable g language:
They had been in a mean man lies, and foul ones.
  Wol. You take strange licence.
  Hub. Yes; were not those rumours
Of being call'd unto your answer spread
By your own followers? and weak Gerrard wrought
(But by your cunning practice) to believe
That you were dangerous; yet not to be
Punish'd by any formal course of law,
But first to be made sure, and have your crimes
Laid open after? which your quaint train h taking,
You fled unto the camp, and there crav'd humbly
Protection for your innocent life, and that,
Since you had scap'd the fury of the war,
You might not fall by treason; and for proof
You did not for your own ends make this danger,
Some, that had been before by you suborn'd,
Came forth, and took their oaths they had been hir'd
By Gerrard to your murder. This once heard,
And easily believ'd, th' enragèd soldier,
Seeing no further than the outward man,
Snatch'd hastily his arms, ran to the court,
Kill'd all that made resistance, cut in pieces

---

g *is favourable*] Seward silently printed "*is a favourable*".
h *train*] i. e. artifice, stratagem.

Such as were servants, or thought friends to Gerrard,
Vowing the like to him.
   Wol. Will you yet end?
   Hub. Which he foreseeing, with his son, the earl,
Forsook the city, and by secret ways,
As you give out, and we would gladly have it,
Escap'd their fury; though 'tis more than fear'd
They fell among the rest. Nor stand you there,
To let us only mourn the impious means
By which you got it; but your cruelties since
So far transcend your former bloody ills,
As, if compar'd, they only would appear
Essays of mischief. Do not stop your ears;
More are behind yet.
   Wol. Oh, repeat them not!
'Tis hell to hear them nam'd.
   Hub. You should have thought,
That hell would be your punishment when you did them:
A prince in nothing but your princely lusts
And boundless rapines!
   Wol. No more, I beseech you.
   Hub. Who was the lord of house or land, that stood
Within the prospect of your covetous eye?
   Wol. You are in this to me a greater tyrant
Than e'er I was to any.
   Hub. I end thus
The general grief. Now to my private wrong,
The loss of Gerrard's daughter Jacqueline:
The hop'd-for partner of my lawful bed
Your cruelty hath frighted from mine arms;
And her I now was wandering to recover.
Think you that I had reason now to leave you,
When you are grown so justly odious,
That even my stay here, with your grace and favour,
Makes my life irksome? Here, surely take it [1];
                                    [*Offers his sword.*

---

[1] *Here, surely take it*] Seward printed "*Here*, sir, freely *take it.*" Sympson proposed to read "*Here*, securely *take it*"; which was adopted by the Editors of

And do me but this fruit of all your friendship,
That I may die by you, and not your hangman.

Wol. Oh, Hubert, these your words and reasons have
As well drawn drops of blood from my griev'd heart,
As these tears from mine eyes! despise them not:
By all that's sacred, I am serious, Hubert!
You now have made me sensible, what Furies,
Whips[j], hangmen, and tormentors, a bad man
Does ever bear about him: let the good
That you this day have done be ever number'd
The first of your best actions. Can you think
Where Florez is, or Gerrard, or your love,
Or any else, or all, that are proscrib'd?
I will resign what I usurp, or have
Unjustly forc'd: the days I have to live
Are too, too few to make them satisfaction
With any penitence; yet I vow to practise
All of a man[k].

Hub. Oh, that your heart and tongue
Did not now differ!

Wol. By my griefs, they do not!
Take the good pains to search them out; 'tis worth it.
You have made clean a leper,—trust me, you have,—
And made me once more fit for the society,
I hope, of good men.

Hub. Sir, do not abuse
My aptness to believe.

Wol. Suspect not you
A faith that's built upon so true a sorrow:

1778. The old reading is doubtless right: "*surely*," as Mason observes, "implies, not only with security, but with certainty."

[j] *what Furies, Whips*, &c.] The poet had here perhaps an eye to Juvenal;

"Cur tamen hos tu
Evasisse putes, quos diri conscia facti
Mens habet attonitos, et surdo verbere cædit,
Occultum quatiente animo tortore flagellum?"

Sat. xiii. 192.

[k] *All of a man*] i. e. All that man can do.

Make your own safeties; ask them[1] all the ties
Humanity can give: Hemskirk too shall
Along with you to this so-wish'd discovery,
And in my name profess all that you promise:
And I will give you this help to't; I have
Of late receiv'd certain intelligence
That some of them are in or about Bruges
To be found out; which I did then interpret
The cause of that town's standing out against me;
But now am glad it may direct your purpose
Of giving them their safety and me peace.
  Hub. Be constant to your goodness, and you[m] have it.
                              [*Exeunt severally.*

SCENE III.—*Bruges.—The Exchange.*

Enter three Merchants.

  First Mer. 'Tis much that you deliver of this Goswin.
  Sec. Mer. But short of what I could, yet have the country
Confirm[n] it true, and by a general oath,
And not a man hazard his credit in it.
He bears himself with such a confidence,
As if he were the master of the sea,
And not a wind upon the sailors' compass
But from one part or other was his factor,
To bring him in the best commodities
Merchant e'er ventur'd for.
  First Mer. 'Tis strange.
  Sec. Mer. And yet
This does in him deserve the least of wonder,
Compar'd with other his peculiar fashions,
Which all admire: he's young, and rich, at least
Thus far reputed so, that, since he liv'd
In Bruges, there was never brought to harbour

---

  [1] *them*] i.e. (as Weber saw) for your safeties.—Silently altered by Seward to "thee"; and so the Editors of 1778.
  [m] *you*] Altered by Seward to "you'll."
  [n] *Confirm*] Seward's correction.—Old eds. "Confirm'd"; and so Weber.

So rich a bottom but his bill would pass
Unquestion'd for her lading.
    Third Mer. Yet he still
Continues a good man°.
    Sec. Mer. So good, that but
To doubt him would be held an injury,
Or rather malice, with the best that traffic:
But this is nothing; a great stock, and fortune
Crowning his judgment in his undertakings,
May keep him upright that way; but that wealth
Should want the power to make him dote on it,
Or youth teach him to wrong it, best commends
His constant temper. For his outward habit,
'Tis suitable to his present course of life;
His table furnish'd well, but not with dainties
That please the appetite only for their rareness
Or their dear price; nor given to wine or women,
Beyond his health, or warrant of a man,
I mean, a good one^p; and so loves his state^q,
He will not hazard it at play, nor lend
Upon the assurance of a well-penn'd letter,
Although a challenge second the denial,
From such as make the opinion of their valour
Their means of feeding.
    First Mer. These are ways to thrive,
And the means^r not curs'd.
    Sec. Mer. What follows this
Makes^s many venturers with him in their wishes

    ° *a good man*] i. e. a man able to fulfil engagements, a wealthy man (a mercantile expression, as in vol. vii. 102).
    ^p *a good one*] i. e. (as Mason observes) a virtuous man.—Here the Editors of 1778 explained "*good*"—"in credit"! (which is the meaning of the word a little before.)
    ^q *state*] i. e. estate.
    ^r *And the means*] Seward silently printed "*And* yet *the means*"; and so the Editors of 1778.
    ^s *What follows this*
    Makes, &c.] i. e. "The consequence of this economy, which enables him to be generous when proper objects present themselves to his notice, makes many wish for his welfare, in which they are themselves so nearly interested". *Ed.* 1778.—The punctuation of the first folio and of the 4to is,—

For his prosperity; for when desert
Or reason leads him to be liberal,
His noble mind and ready hand contend
Which can add most to his free courtesies,
Or in their worth or speed to make them so.
Is there a virgin of good fame wants dower?
He is a father to her; or a soldier,
That, in his country's service, from the war
Hath brought home only scars and want? his house
Receives him, and relieves him with that care
As if what he possess'd had been laid up
For such good uses, and he steward of it.
But I should lose myself to speak him further,
And stale[t], in my relation, the much good
You may be witness of, if your remove
From Bruges be not speedy.

First Mer. This report,
I do assure you, will not hasten it;
Nor would I wish a better man to deal with
For what I am to part with.

Third Mer. Never doubt it,
He is your man and ours; only I wish
His too-much forwardness to embrace all bargains
Sink him not in the end.

Sec. Mer. Have better hopes;
For my part, I am confident. Here he comes.

" What follows this,
Makes," &c.

That of the second folio is,—

" What follows, this
Makes," &c.

which was adopted by Weber, who says that that " pointing has exactly the same meaning " as Mason's (see below). Seward made " What follows?" a portion of the preceding speech, and then gave,—

" 2 *Mer.* This
Makes," &c.

Mason would point the passage thus;

" What follows?—this
Makes," &c.

[t] *stale*] i. e. make stale, flat; deprive of zest.

Enter GOSWIN *and* Fourth Merchant.

Gos. I take it at your own rates, your wine of Cyprus;
But, for your Candy sugars, they have met
With such foul weather, and are priz'd so high,
I cannot save in them.

Fourth Mer. I am unwilling
To seek another chapman: make me offer
Of something near my price, that may assure me
You can deal for them.

Gos. I both can and will,
But not with too much loss: your bill of lading
Speaks of two hundred chests, valu'd by you
At thirty thousand gilders; I will have them
At twenty-eight; so, in the payment of
Three thousand sterling, you fall only in
Two hundred pound.

Fourth Mer. You know, they are so cheap——

Gos. Why, look you, I'll deal fairly. There's in prison,
And at your suit, a pirate, but unable
To make you satisfaction, and past hope
To live a week, if you should prosecute
What you can prove against him: set him free,
And you shall have your money to a stiver,
And present payment.

Fourth Mer. This is above wonder,
A merchant of your rank, that have at sea
So many bottoms in the danger of
These water-thieves, should be a means to save 'em;
It more importing you, for your own safety,
To be at charge to scour the sea of them,
Than stay the sword of justice, that is ready
To fall on one so conscious of his guilt
That he dares not deny it.

Gos. You mistake me,
If you think I would cherish in this captain
The wrong he did to you or any man.
I was lately with him (having first, from others'
True testimony, been assur'd a man

Of more desert never put from the shore);
I read his letters of mart[u], from this state granted
For the recovery of such losses as
He had receiv'd in Spain; 'twas that he aim'd at,
Not at three tuns of wine, biscuit, or beef,
Which his necessity made him take from you.
If he had pillag'd you near, or sunk your ship,
Or thrown your men o'erboard, then he deserv'd
The law's extremest rigour: but, since want
Of what he could not live without compell'd him
To that he did (which yet our state calls death),
I pity his misfortune[s], and, to work you
To some compassion of them, I come up
To your own price: save him, the goods are mine;
If not, seek elsewhere, I'll not deal for them.
 Fourth Mer. Well, sir, for your love, I will once be led
To change my purpose.
 Gos. For your profit rather.
 Fourth Mer. I'll presently make means for his discharge;
Till when, I leave you.   [*Exit.*
 Sec. Mer. What do you think of this?
 First Mer. As of a deed of noble pity, guided
By a strong judgment.
 Sec. Mer. Save you, Master Goswin!
 Gos. Good day to all.
 Sec. Mer. We bring you the refusal
Of more commodities.
 Gos. Are you the owners
Of the ship that last night put into the harbour?
 First Mer. Both of the ship and lading.
 Gos. What's the fraught[v]?
 First Mer. Indigo, cochineal, choice China stuffs—
 Third Mer. And cloth of gold brought from Cambal.
 Gos. Rich lading;
For which I were your chapman, but I am
Already out of cash.

  [u] *letters of mart*] i. e. letters of marque: see Nares's *Gloss.*

  [v] *fraught*] Seward printed "fraight"; the Editors of 1778 and Weber "freight."

First Mer. I'll give you day
For the moiety of all.
  Gos. How long?
  Third Mer. Six months.
  Gos. 'Tis a fair offer; which, if we agree
About the prices, I, with thanks, accept of,
And will make present payment of the rest:
Some two hours hence I'll come aboard.
  First Mer. The gunner
Shall speak you welcome.
  Gos. I'll not fail.
  Third Mer.[w] Good morrow.   [*Exeunt* Merchants.
  Gos. Heaven grant my ships a safe return before
The day of this great payment; as they are
Expected three months sooner; and my credit
Stands good with all the world.

Enter CLAUSE.

  Clause. Bless my good master!
The prayers of your poor beadsman ever shall
Be sent up for you.
  Gos. God 'a mercy, Clause!
There's something to put thee in mind hereafter
To think of me.   [*Gives money.*
  Clause. May he that gave it you
Reward you for it with increase, good master!
  Gos. I thrive the better for thy prayers.
  Clause. I hope so.
This three years have I fed upon your bounties,
And by the fire of your blest charity warm'd me;
And yet, good master, pardon me, that must,
Though I have now receiv'd your alms, presume
To make one suit more to you.
  Gos. What is't, Clause?
  Clause. Yet do not think me impudent, I beseech you,
Since hitherto your charity hath prevented

---

[w] *Third Mer.*] Ought perhaps to be "*Merchants*"; for the prefix of the old eds., "3 *Mer.*", (though earlier it is put for *Third Merchant,*) may here mean *Three Merchants.*

VOL. IX.   C

My begging your relief; 'tis not for money,
Nor clothes, good master, but your good word for me.
   Gos. That thou shalt have, Clause; for I think thee honest.
   Clause. To-morrow, then, dear master, take the trouble
Of walking early unto Beggars' Bush[x];
And, as you see me, among others, brethren
In my affliction, when you are demanded
Which you like best among us, point out me,
And then pass by, as if you knew me not.
   Gos. But what will that advantage thee?
   Clause. Oh, much, sir!
'Twill give me the pre-eminence of the rest,
Make me a king among 'em, and protect me
From all abuse such as are stronger might
Offer my age. Sir, at your better leisure
I will inform you further of the good
It may do to me.
   Gos. Troth, thou mak'st me wonder:
Have you a king and commonwealth among you?
   Clause. We have; and there are states are govern'd worse.
   Gos. Ambition among beggars?
   Clause. Many great ones
Would part with half their states[y], to have the place
And credit to beg in the first file, master.
But shall I be so much bound to your furtherance
In my petition?
   Gos. That thou shalt not miss of,
Nor any worldly care make me forget it:
I will be early there.
   Clause. Heaven bless my master!   [*Exeunt severally.*

---

   [x] *Beggars' Bush*] "*This is the way to Beggers-bush.* It is spoken of such, who use dissolute and improvident courses, which tend to poverty. *Beggers-bush* being a tree notoriously known, on the left hand of the London road from Huntington to Caxton." Ray's *Proverbs*, p. 244, ed. 1768.

   [y] *states*] "i. e. estates." WEBER.

ACT II.

SCENE I.—*The Beggars' Bush, in the woods near Bruges.*

Enter HIGGEN, FERRET, PRIG, CLAUSE, SNAP[z], GINKS, *and other* Beggars.

Hig. Come, princes of the ragged regiment;
You o' the blood, Prig, my most Upright-lord,
And these, what name or title e'er they bear,
Jarkman, or Patrico, Crank, or Clapper-dudgeon,
Frater, or Abram-man[a]; I speak to all

[z] *Clause, Snap*] Old eds. " *Clause*, Jaculine," *Snap*,"—by mistake, for they have afterwards (p. 32) " *Enter Jaculine* " ; and so the modern editors.— Throughout the play, both in the stage-directions and prefixes, the modern editors follow the old copies in giving to this lady her real name *Jacqueline* (or, as they put it, *Jaculin*, though that barbarous spelling is found only in some places of the old eds.). But, if her companions are distinguished by their assumed names, it is an impropriety that Jacqueline should retain her real one.

[a] *most Upright-lord,*
- - - - - - - - -
Jarkman, or Patrico, Crank, or Clapper-dudgeon,
Frater, or Abram-man] The following passages (a portion only of which were cited here by Weber) will fully explain these seven cant terms.

" An *Vpright-man* is a sturdy big-bonde knaue, that neuer walkes but (like a Commander) with a short troncheon in his hand, which hee cals his *Filchman*. At Markets, Fayres, and other meetings his voice amongst Beggers is of the same sound that a Constables is of, it is not to be controld. He is free of all the shiers in England, but neuer stayes in any place long ; the reason is, his profession is to be idle, which being looked into, he knowes is punishable, and therfore to auoid the whip he wanders. If hee come to a Farmers doore, the almes hee begs is neither meate nor drinke, but onely money : if any thing else be offered to him, he takes it with disdaine, and laies it vnder a hedge for any that come next ; but, in reuenge of this, if hee spy any geese, hennes, ducks, or such like walking spirits haunting the house, with them he coniures about midnight, vsing them the next morning like traytors, either behedding them or quartering them in pieces ; for which purpose, this band of *Vpright-men* seldome march without fiue or six in a company, so that country people rather giue them mony for feare then out of any deuotion [i. e. charity : see note, vol. viii. 10]. After this bloudy massacre of the poore innocent pullen, the Actors in their bloudy tragedy repaire to their *Stalling-kennes*, and those are tipling houses, which will lend money vpon any stolne goods, and vnto which none but such guests as these resort : there the spits go round, and the cannes walke vp and downe ; there haue they

That stand in fair election for the title

their *Morts* and their *Doxyes* [old ed., by a misprint, *Dopyes :* for explanations of these two terms, see notes, p.p. 25, 29], with whome (after they haue Bowsed profoundly) they lye (in store [stead] of fetherbeds) vppon litters of cleane strawe, to increase the Generation of Rogues and Beggers : for these *Vpright-men* stand so much vppon their reputation that they scorne any *Mort* or *Doxye* should be seene to walke with them ; and indeede what neede they care for them, when he may commaund any Doxye to leaue another man and to lye with him, the other not daring to murmure against it. An *Vpright-man* will seldome complaine of want, for whatsoeuer any one of his profession doth steale, he may challenge a share of it, yea, and may command any inferiour Roague to fetch in booty to serue his tourne. These cary the shapes of soldiers, and can talke of the Low countries, though they neuer were beyond Douer." Dekker's *Belman of London*, &c., sig. c 3, ed. 1608.

" And because no common wealth can stand without some Learning in it, therefore are there some in this Schoole of Beggers that practise writing and reading, and those are called *Jarkmen* [old ed., by a misprint, *Jackmen*] : yea, the *Jarkman* is so cunning sometimes that he can speake Latine ; which learning of his lifts him vp to aduancement, for by that means he becomes Clarke of their Hall, and his office is to make counterfet licences, which are called *Gybes*, to which hee puts seales, and those are termed *Jarkes*." *Id.* sig. D 3. " These counterfeit *Jarkes* (or seales) are grauen with the point of a knife vpon a stickes end, whose roundnesse may well be perceiued from the circle of a common turn'd seale : these for the most part bearing the ilfauoured shape of a *Buffars Nab* or a *Prancers Nab* (a dogs head or a horses), and sometimes an Vnicorns, and such like ; the counterfeit Jarke hauing no circle about the edges. Besides, in the Passe-port you shall lightly [i. e. commonly] find these words, viz. ' For Salomon saith, Who giueth the poore, lendeth the Lord ', &c. ; and that Constables shall helpe them to lodgings, and that Curats shall perswade their parishioners, &c." Dekker's *English Villanies*, &c. sig. M., ed. 1632,—where previously we are told that " they who are Counterfeiters of Passe-ports are called *Ben-fakers*, that is to say, Good-makers," and that " in S. dwelt " a *Ben-faker*, " who tooke two shillings and six pence (two *Boords* and vi *winnes*), or two *Boords* and a *Flag* [i. e. groat], for euery Passeport that went out of his beggerly Office : he counterfeited the Seale of L. D."

" A *Patrico* amongst Beggers is their priest, euery hedge beeing his parish, euery wandring harlot and rogue his parishioners ; the seruice he sayes is onely the marrying of couples, which he does in a wood vnder a tree, or in the open field, and the solemnity of it is thus. The parties to be wedded find out a dead horse or any other beast, and standing one on the one side and the other on the other, the *Patrico* bids them to liue together till death them part; and so shaking hands, the wedding dinner is kept at the next Ale-house they stumble into, where the musick is nothing but knocking with kannes, and their dances none but drunken Brawles." Dekker's *Belman of London*, &c. sig. D 3, ed. 1608.

" Baser in habit, and more vile in condition, than the *Whip-iack*, is the *Counterfet cranke ;* who in all kind of weather going halfe naked, staring wildly with his eyes, and appearing distracted by his lookes, complayning onely that he is troubled with the falling sicknes : albeit you giue them cloathes, they wil weare

Of King of Beggars, with the command adjoining;

none, but rather wish those rags which they haue hanging about them should bee made lothsome by myre, or their naked bosome and armes to appeare full of bruses, and to be bloudy with falling, therby to kyndle in men the greater compassion : to cause that foaming in their mouthes, which is fearefull to behold by the standers by, they haue this trick, priuily to conuey a peece of white soape into one corner of their jawes, which causeth that froth to come boyling forth. These *Crankes* haue likewise there meetings and there wenches at command." *Id*. sig. D 2.

" A *Palliard* comes next into my minde, and he likewise is cal'd a *Clapperdugeon*: his vpper garment is an old cloake made of as many pieces patch'd together as there be villanies in him. This *Palliard* neuer goes without a Mort at his heeles, whom he calles his wife : being either in the streete of a citty or in a country village, they diuide themselues, and beg almes at seuerall doores, but whatsoeuer is gotten (be it bread, cheese, malt, or wooll), they sell it to some Rogue or other, and with the money are merry at a *Bowsing-Ken* [i. e. ale-house]. A *Palliard* carryes about him (for feare of the worst) a Certificate (vnder a ministers hand with the parishes name, which shall be sure to stand farre enough) where this Mort and he were marryed, when all is but forged : many Irishmen are of this lowsie Regiment, and some Welchmen : and the better either to draw pitty from men, as also to giue cullor to their lame wandring, with Sperewort or Arsenick will they in one night poyson their leg, be it neuer so sound, and raise a blister which at their pleasure they can take off againe." *Id*. sig. D. " A *Clapperdogeon* is in English a Begger borne : some call him a *Pallyard*: of which sorts there are two ; first, Naturall, secondly, Artificiall. This fellow (aboue al other that are in the Regiment of Rogues) goeth best armed against the cruelty of winter : he should be wise, for he loues to keepe himselfe warme, wearing a patched *Castor* (a Cloake) for his vpper Robe ; vnder that, a *Togmans* (a Gowne), with high *Stampers* (shooes), the soles an inch thicke, pegged, or else patches at his Girdle ready to clap on ; a great *Scue* (a browne dish) hanging at his girdle, and a tassel of Thrums to wipe it ; a brace of greasie Night-caps on his head, and ouer them (lest he should catch a knauish cold) a hat (or *Nab-cheat*) ; a good *Filch* (or staffe) in his hand, hauing a little yron pegge in the end of it ; a *Bugher* (a little dog) following him, with a smugge *Doxy*, attyred fit for such a Roguish Companion." Dekker's *English Villanies*, &c., sig. M, ed. 1632. The term *Clapper-dudgeon* would seem to have been derived from the wooden dish with a moueable cover,—the *clap-dish* with a *clapper*,—which was carried by beggars (see note on act iv. sc. 4.), and perhaps originally by the *Clapper-dudgeon*.

" A *Frater* is a brother of as damnd a broode as the rest : his office is to trauell with a long wallet at his backe, and a blacke box at his girdle, wherein is a pattent to beg for some Hospitall or Spittle house ; many of which pattents (especially if they be in paper or parchment without the Great Seale) are counterfeit ; and those that are not so, serue the Bearers of them but as instruments to play the Knaues by, for though they get neuer so much, the poore creatures for whome they beg receiue little of it ; they lye soaking with a *Doxye* in a typling house, whilst the spittle wretches are ready to starue for sustenance at home. Let country women returning from Markets, if they be alone and in a dangerous place, take heede of these Proctors, for they haue the Art to vnhorse

Higgen, your orator, in this inter-regnum,

them, and a conscience to send them packing without any peny in their purses." Dekker's *Belman of London*, &c. sig. D, ed. 1608.

" Of all the mad rascalls (that are of this wing) the *Abraham-man* is the most phantastick. The fellow (quoth this old Lady of the Lake vnto me) that sat halfe naked (at table to day) from the girdle upward, is the best *Abraham-man* that euer came to my house, and the notablest villaine. He sweares he hath bin in Bedlam, and will talke frantickly of purpose : you see pinnes stuck in sundry places of his naked flesh, especially in his armes, which paine hee gladly puts himselfe to (beeing indeede no torment at all, his skin is either so dead with some fowle disease, or so hardned with weather), onely to make you beleeue he is out of his wits : he calls himselfe by the name of *Poore Tom*, and comming neere any body, cryes out, ' *Poore Tom* is a cold.' [Here the reader will recollect Shakespeare's Edgar in *King Lear*.] Of these *Abraham-men* some be exceeding mery, and doe nothing but sing songs fashioned out of their owne braines ; some will dance ; others will doe nothing but either laugh or weepe ; others are dogged, and so sullen both in looke and speech, that, spying but small company in a house, they boldly and bluntly enter, compelling the seruants through feare to giue them what they demaund, which is commonly bacon or some thing that will yeelde ready mony. The *Vpright-man* and the *Rogue* are not terribler enemies to poultry ware than *Poore Tom* is ; neither does any man shift cleane lynnen oftner than he does his wenches." *Id*. sig. D 2. " The *Abram Coue* is a lusty strong Rogue, who walketh with a *Slade* about his *Quarrons* (a sheete about his body,) *Trining* (hanging) to his hammes, bandeleere-wise, for al the world as Cutpurses and Theeues weare their sheetes to the Gallowes, in which their Truls are to bury them. Oftentimes (because he scornes to follow any fashions of hose) he goes without breeches ; a cut Jerkin with hanging sleeues (in immitation of our Gallants), but no Sattin or Chamlet Elbowes, for both his legs and armes are bare ; hauing no *Commission* to couer his body, that is to say, no shirt : a face staring like a Sarisin ; his haire long and filthily knotted, for he keepes no Barber ; a good *Filch* (or staffe) of grown Ash, or else Hazel, in his *Fambler* (in his hand), and sometimes a sharpe sticke, on which he hangeth *Ruffe-pecke* (Bakon). These, walking vp and downe the Countrey, are more terrible to women and children then the name of Raw-head and Bloody-bones, Robbin Good-fellow, or any other Hobgoblin. Crackers tyed to the dogs tayle make not the poore Curre runne faster then these *Abram Ninnies* do the sillie villagers of the Countrey, so that when they come to any doore a begging, nothing is denied them. Some of these *Abrams* haue the Letters E. and R. vpon their armes ; some haue crosses, and some other Marke, all of them carying a blue colour ; some weare a yron ring, &c, which marks," though made by themselves, they will tell you are those " of Bedlam."... " And to colour his villany the better, euery one of these *Abrams* hath a seuerall gesture in playing his part : some make an horrid noyse, hollowly sounding ; some whoope, some hollow, some shew only a kind of wild distracted vgly looke, vttering a simple kind of *Mawnding*, with these additions of words (*well and wisely*). Some dance (but keepe no measure) ; others leape vp and downe and fetch Gambals ; all their actions shew them to be as drunke as Beggars ; for, not to bely them, what are they but drunken Beggers? all that they beg being either *Lowre* or *Bowse* (money or drinke)." Then follows a description

SCENE I.] BEGGARS' BUSH. 23

That whilom[b] was your Dommerer[c], doth beseech you
All to stand fair, and put yourselves in rank,
That the first comer may, at his first view,
Make a free choice, to say up the question[d].

Fer. ⎱
Prig. ⎰ 'Tis done, Lord Higgen.

Hig. Thanks to Prince Prig, Prince Ferret.

Fer. Well, pray, my masters all, Ferret be chosen;
Ye 're like to have a merciful mild prince of me.

---

of "*Their Mawnd or Begging.*" Dekker's *English Villanies,* &c., Sig. L 3, ed. 1632.—In Shakespeare's *Romeo and Juliet,* act ii. sc. 1, Mr. Knight gives, with the old copies,

"Young *Abraham* Cupid, he that shot so trim";

and says that "the 'Abraham' Cupid is the cheat—the 'Abraham man'—of our old statutes": but will any one, after reading the above extracts, be disposed to think that he is right?

[b] *whilom*] i. e. formerly.

[c] *Dommerer*] "Equall to the *Cranck* in dissembling is the *Dummerar,* for as the other takes vpon him to haue the falling sicknesse, so this counterfets *Dumbnes;* but let him be whipped well, and his tongue (which he doubles in his mouth, and so makes a horrid and strange noise in stead of speech) will walke as fast as his handes doe when hee comes where any booty is." Dekker's *Belman of London,* &c., sig. D 3, ed. 1608. "The Bel-man tooke his markes amisse in saying that a *Dommerar* is equall to the *Cranke,* for of these *Dommerars* I neuer met but one, and that was at the house of one M. L. of L. This *Dommerars* name was W. He made a strange noise, shewing, by fingers acrosse, that his tongue was cut out at Chalke-hill. In his hand he carryed a sticke, aboute a foote in length, and sharpe at both ends, which he would thrust into his mouth, as if he meant to shew the stumpe of his tongue. But, in doing so, hee did of purpose hit his tongue with the sticke, to make it bleede, which, filling vp his mouth, you could not for blood perceiue any tongue at all, because hee had turned it vpwards, and with his sticke thrust it into his throat. But I caused him to be held fast by the strength of men, vntill such time that, opening his teeth with the end of a small cudgell, I pluckt forth his tongue, and made him speake." Dekker's *English Villanies,* sig. M, ed. 1632. (The latter passage is cited by Weber.)

[d] *to say up the question*] Seward printed "*to save us further question*"!! The Editors of 1778 followed the old eds., observing that, "though '*to say up*' is uncouth and obscure, it may signify—deciding the *question* by *saying* which he (the first comer) thinks the honestest of them." So too Weber. I once conjectured "*to say* upon *the question,*" i. e. to speak upon the question being asked: but I now believe that the reading of the old eds. is right, and that "*to say up*" means—to decide: compare the following passage at p. 26;

"Now, 'cause we thought
We ne'er should 'gree on 't ourselves, because indeed
'Tis hard to *say,* we all dissolv'd to put it
To him that should come next", &c.

Prig. A very tyrant I, an arrant tyrant,
If e'er I come to reign (therefore look to 't,)
Except you do provide me hum^e enough,
And lour to bouse with^f: I must have my capons
And turkeys brought me in, with my green geese,
And ducklings i' the season; fine fat chickens;
Or, if you chance where an eye of tame pheasants^g
Or partridges are kept, see they be mine:
Or straight I seize on all your privilege,
Places, revenues, offices, as forfeit,
Call in your crutches, wooden legs, false bellies,
Forc'd eyes and teeth^h, with your dead arms; not leave you
A dirty clout to beg with o' your heads,
Or an old rag with butter, frankincense,
Brimstone and rosin, birdlime, blood, and cream,
To make you an old soreⁱ; not so much soap
As you may foam with i' the falling-sickness^j;
The very bag you bear, and the brown dish,
Shall be escheated; all your daintiest dells too

^e *hum*] See note, vol. viii. 148.

^f *lour to bouse with*] i. e. money to drink with. "*Lowre*, money." *The Canters Dictionary* in Dekker's *English Villanies*, &c. sig. N 4, ed. 1632. I know not what Weber could be thinking of when he here explained the *verb* " *bouse* " to mean—strong drink.

^g *an eye of tame pheasants*] "An Eye of Pheasants, *Phasianorum fœtura*." Coles's *Dict.*

^h *Forc'd eyes and teeth*] Altered by Seward to " *Forc'd eyes and* tongues"; and so the Editors of 1778. "Seward supposes, that by '*forc'd eyes*' is meant eyes so distorted as to shew only the white, so that the person appears to be blind; and also says, that it is common for beggars to *force* their *tongues* into their throats, in order that they may appear to have been cut off. On those reasons he founds his amendment, and the Editors [of 1778] adopt it; but they all forget, that it was not in the power of Prig, however tyrannical, to prevent their making what use they pleased of their own features: what he threatens to call in, are the artificial implements of imposture, which beggars employ for the purpose of appearing blind or deformed. The word *forced* certainly implies distorted; but, for the reason I have mentioned, it must be applied to false eyes and false teeth, not to natural ones." MASON.

ⁱ *To make you an old sore*] "Dekker gives a long receipt how the artificial sores are produced, but it is too disgusting to be repeated here. The ingredients recommended by him are unslaked lime and soap [with the rust of old iron]. ' A browne paper with butter and waxe being applied, they are cured'. *English Villanies*, &c. Sig. L 4, ed. 1632." WEBER.

^j *foam with i' the falling sickness*] See note concerning the *Counterfeit crank*, p. 20.

I will deflower, and take your dearest doxies [k]
From your warm sides; and then, some one cold night,
I'll watch you what old barn you go to roost in,
And there I'll smother you all i' the musty hay.
  Hig. This is tyrant-like, indeed. But what would Ginks,
Or Clause be here, if either of them should reign?
  Clause. Best ask an ass, if he were made a camel,
What he would be; or a dog, an he were a lion.
  Ginks. I care not what you are, sirs; I shall be
A beggar still, I am sure; I find myself there [1].

[k]   *all your daintiest dells too*
  I will deflower, and take your dearest doxies, &c.] " A *Dell* is a yong wench - - - but as yet not spoyled of her maidenhead: these *Dells* are reserued as dishes for the *Vpright-men,* for none but they must haue the first tast of them; and after the *Vpright-men* have deflowred them (which commonly is when they are very yong), then are they free for any of the brother-hood, and are called *Dells* no more, but *Doxies* [old ed., by a misprint, *Dopers*]. Of these *Dells* some are termed *Wilde Dells,* and those are such as are borne and begotten vnder a hedge; the other are yong wenches that either by death of parents, the villanie of Executors, or the crueltie of maisters and mistresses, fall into this infamous and damnable course of life. When they haue gotten the title of *Doxies,* then are they common for any, and walke for the most part with their betters (who are a degree aboue them) called *Morts,* but whensoeuer an *Vpright-man* is in presence, the *Doxye* is onely at his command. These *Doxyes* will for good victuals or a small peice of money prostitute there bodies to seruingmen, if they can get into any conuenient corner about their maisters houses, and to ploughmen in barnes, haylofts, or stables: they are common pick-pockets, familiars with the baser sorts of cut-purses, and oftentimes secret murtherers of those infants which are begotten of their bodies. These *Doxyes* haue one especial badge to be knowne by, for most of them goe working of laces and shirt-stringes, or such like stuffe, only to giue colour to their idle wandring." Dekker's *Belman of London,* &c. Sig. D 3, ed. 1608. " At her backe she [the *Clapperdudgeon's Doxy*] carrieth a great pack, couered with a patched saue-guard, vnder which she conueieth all such things as she filcheth. Her skil sometimes is to tell Fortunes, to helpe the diseases of women and children. As she walkes, she makes bals or shirt-strings, (but now commonly they knit,) and weares in her hat a needle, with a thread at it. An excellent Angler she is; for, when her *Coue Mawnds* [i.e. begs] at any doore, if any Poultry ware be picking vp their crummes neere them, she feedeth them with bread, and hath a threed tyed to a hooked pin, baited for the nonce, which the Chickin swallowing, is choaked, and conueied vnder the *Castor* [cloak]. Chickins, linnen, woollen, or any thing that is worth the catching, comes into her net " Dekker's *English Villanies,* &c. sig. M, ed. 1632. (A portion of what I have just cited was given by Weber.)

[1] *I find myself there*] " i. e. I find it the fittest condition for me, and that a beggar's is my proper station. Ginks speaks this merely in the character of a beggar who did not aspire to the crown." MASON (the words having been wrongly explained by Seward).

Snap. Oh, here a judge comes!
Hig. Cry, a judge, a judge!

Enter GOSWIN.

Gos. What ail you, sirs? what means this outcry?
Hig. Master,
A sort[m] of poor souls met, God's fools, good master,
Have had some little variance amongst ourselves
Who should be honestest of us, and which lives
Uprightest in his call[n]: now, 'cause we thought
We ne'er should 'gree on't ourselves, because indeed
'Tis hard to say, we all dissolv'd[o] to put it
To him that should come next, and that's your mastership,
Who, I hope, will 'termine it as your mind serves you,
Right, and no otherwise we ask it.   Which,
Which does your worship think is he? sweet master,
Look over us all, and tell us: we are seven of us,
Like to the Seven Wise Masters[p], or the planets.
Gos. I should judge this the man, with the grave beard;
And, if he be not——
Clause. Bless you, good master, bless you!
Gos. I would he were. There's something too amongst you,
To keep you all honest.   [*Gives money, and exit.*
Snap. King of Heaven go with you!
All. Now good reward him;

---

[m] *sort*] "i. e. company." WEBER.

[n] *call*] i. e. calling. So the first folio and the 4to.—The second folio "calling"; and so Seward and the Editors of 1778.

[o] *dissolv'd*] "Mr Seward alters '*dissolv'd*' to 'resolv'd'; but Higgen speaks barbarously here, because, on the appearance of a stranger, he assumes the style of a beggar, *e. g.* ''termine it', in the next line but one.   So afterwards (and it is acknowledged to be part of their table of laws) to
       'keep afoot
   The humble and the common phrase of begging,
   Lest men discover us'." *Ed.* 1778.
"So, in the *maund* or begging phrase of the *Clapperdogeons;* 'Ah, the Vrship of God! looke out with your mercifull eyne, one pittifull looke vpon sore, lame, grieued, and *impudent* (for *impotent*) people,' &c. Dekker's *English Villanies*, &c., sig. M 2, ed. 1632.   That the mistake in the text was an intended one, cannot, therefore, be doubted." WEBER.

[p] *the Seven Wise Masters*] See Ellis's Introd. to the tale so called, in his *Spec. of Early Engl. Metr. Romances*, vol. iii.

May he never want it, to comfort still the poor,
In a good hour!
 Fer. What is't? see: Snap has got it.
 Snap. A good crown, marry.
 Prig. A crown of gold.
 Fer. For our new king; good luck.
 Ginks. To the common treasury with it; if't be gold,
Thither it must.
 Prig. Spoke like a patriot, Ginks[q]!——
King Clause, I bid God save thee first, first, Clause,
After this golden token of a crown.——
Where's orator Higgen with his gratuling[r] speech now,
In all our names?
 Fer. Here he is, pumping for it.
 Ginks. H'as cough'd the second time; 'tis but once more,
And then it comes.
 Fer. So, out with all!—Expect now!
 Hig. That thou art chosen, venerable Clause,
Our king and sovereign, monarch o' the maunders[s],
Thus we throw up our nab-cheats[t] first, for joy,
And then our filches[u]; last, we clap our fambles[x];

---

 [q] *Ginks*] Seward's correction.—All the old eds. "Ferret".

 [r] *gratuling*] "So the old copies [the two folios]. Modern editors alter the word, unnecessarily, to 'gratulating'." WEBER. The 4to has "gratulating"—wrongly.

 [s] *maunders*] "i. e. beggars." WEBER. See note, p. 30.

 [t] *nab-cheats*] "i. e. hats or caps. Dekker's *English Villanies*, &c. sig. N 2, ed. 1632." WEBER.

 [u] *filches*] "'Euery one of them carries a short staffe in his hand, which is called a *Filch*, hauing in the *Nab* or head of it a *Ferme*, (that is to say, a hole,) into which, vpon any piece of seruice, when hee goes a *Filching*, he putteth a hooke of yron, with which hooke hee angles at a window, in the dead of night, for shirts, smockes, or any other linnen or woollen ; and for that reason is the staffe tearmed a *Filch*. So that it is as certaine that hee is an Angler for *Duds* [i.e. clothes] who hath a *Ferme* in the *Nab* of his *Filch*, as that he is a theefe who, vpon the highway, cryes ' stand', and takes a purse. This staffe serueth to more vses then either the Crosse-staffe or the Jacobs, but the vses are not so good nor so honest ; for this *Filching-staffe*, being artificially handled, is able now and then to *Mill* a *Grunter*, a *Bleating Cheate*, a *Red-shanke*, a *Tib of the Buttery*, and such like, or to *Fib a Coues Quarrons in the Rome-pad, for his Loure in his Bung*, that is to say, to kill a Pigge, a Sheepe, a Ducke, a Goose, and such like, or to beate a man by the highway for the money in his purse.' *Id.* sig. M 3." WEBER.

 [x] *fambles*] "i. e. hands. *Id.* sig. N 4." WEBER.

Three subject signs we do it without envy;
For who is he here did not wish thee chosen,
Now thou art chosen? ask 'em; all will say so,
Nay, swear 't; 'tis for the king; but let that pass.
When last in conference at the bousing-ken[y],
This other day, we sate about our dead prince
Of famous memory (rest go with his rags!),
And that I saw thee at the table's end
Rise mov'd, and, gravely leaning on one crutch,
Lift the other like a sceptre at my head,
I then presag'd thou shortly wouldst be king;
And now thou art so. But what need presage
To us, that might have read it in thy beard,
As well as he that chose thee? by that beard
Thou wert found out, and mark'd for sovereignty:
Oh, happy beard! but happier prince, whose beard
Was so remark'd as markèd out our prince,
Not bating us a hair! long may it grow,
And thick and fair, that who lives under it
May live as safe as under Beggars' Bush,
Of which this is the thing, that but the type!

All. Excellent, excellent orator! forward, good Higgen!—
Give him leave to spit.—The fine well-spoken Higgen!

Hig. This is the beard, the bush, or bushy beard,
Under whose gold and silver reign, 'twas said,
So many ages since, we all should smile:
No[a] impositions, taxes, grievances,
Knots in a state, and whips unto a subject,
Lie lurking in this beard, but all kemb'd[z] out.
If now the beard be such, what is the prince
That owes[b] the beard? a father? no, a grandfather,
Nay, the great-grandfather of you his people:
He will not force away your hens, your bacon,
When you have ventur'd hard for 't, nor take from you

---

[y] *bousing-ken*] "i. e. ale-house. *Id.* sig. N 3. From *bouse*, to drink, and *ken*, a house." WEBER.

[z] *kemb'd*] "i. e. combed." REED.

[a] *No*] Old eds. "On."

[b] *owes*] "i. e. owns." SEWARD.

SCENE I.] BEGGARS' BUSH. 29

The fattest of your puddings: under him,
Each man shall eat his own stoln eggs and butter [b],
In his own shade or sun-shine, and enjoy
His own dear dell, doxy, or mort [c], at night,
In his own straw, with his own shirt or sheet
That he hath filch'd that day; ay, and possess
What he can purchase, back or belly-cheats [d],

[b] *under him,*
Each man shall eat his own stoln eggs and butter, &c] A parody on the words of Cranmer concerning Q. Elizabeth in Shakespeare's *Henry the Eighth*, act v. sc. 4;
"In her days every man shall eat in safety,
Under his own vine, what he plants, and sing
The merry songs of peace to all his neighbours."

[c] *dell, doxy, or mort*] The two first terms have been already explained: see note, p. 25. " Of *Morts* there be two kindes, that is to say, A *Walking Mort* and an *Autem-mort*. The *Walking Mort* is of more antiquitie than a *Doxye* [old ed.], by a misprint, *Dopye*], and therefore of more knauerie: they both are vnmarried, but the *Doxy* professes herselfe to bee a maide (if it come to examination), and the *Walking Mort* says shee is a widow whose husband dyed either in the Portugall voyage, was slaine in Ireland or the Low Countries, or come to his end by some other misfortune, leauing her so many small infants on her hand in debt, whome not being able by her honest labour to maintaine, she is compelled to begge. These *Walking Morts* trauell from Country to Countrie, making laces (vpon staues) and small purses, and now and then white vallance for beds. Subtile queanes they are, hard-harted, light-fingerd, cunning in dissembling, and dangerous to be met if any *Rufler* or *Roague* bee in their company. They feare neither God nor good lawes, but onely are kept in aw by the *Vpright-men,* who often times spoyle them of all they haue; which to preuent, the *Walking Morts* vse this pollicy,—they leaue their money (sometime fiue shillings, sometimes ten shillings) in seuerall shires with some honest farmers wife or others whom they know they may trust, and when they trauell that way againe, at halfe yeares end or a quarters, fetch it to serue their turnes; but dare neuer goe in good clothes, least the *Vpright-men* either strip them into rags, or else starke naked, as they vse to doe. An *Autem-Mort* is a woman married (for *Autem* in the Beggers language is a Church): these *Morts* seldome keepe with their husbands, but are from them sometimes a moneth or two, yet neuer walke they without a man in their company, and boyes and girles at their heeles of ten or twelue yeares old, whome they imploy at windowes of houses in the night time or earely in the mornings to pilfer away any thing that is worth the carying away, which in their tongue they call *Milling* [old ed., by a misprint, *Nilling*] *of the Ken.* These *Autem-morts* walke with wallets on their shoulders, and *Slates* (or sheetes) at their backes, in which they vse to lie. Their husbands commonly are *Rufflers, Vpright-men,* or *Wilde Rogues,* and their companions of the same breede ". Dekker's *Belman of London,* &c. Sig. D 4, ed. 1608 (Here Weber gave only short explanations).

[d] *back or belly-cheats*] "i.e.," says Theobald, "raiment or food stolen,"—wrongly,

To his own prop [e] : he will have no purveyors [f]
For pigs and poultry.
 Clause. That we must have, my learnèd orator;
It is our will; and every man to keep
In his own path and circuit.
 Hig. Do you hear?
You must hereafter maund on your own pads [g], he says.
 Clause. And what they get there is their own: besides,
To give good words.
 Hig. Do you mark? to cut bene whids [h];
That is the second law.
 Clause. And keep afoot
The humble and the common phrase of begging,
Lest men discover us.
 Hig. Yes, and cry sometimes,
To move compassion. Sir, there is a table,
That doth command all these things, and enjoins 'em
Be perfect in their crutches, their feign'd plasters,
And their torn passports, with the ways to stammer,
And to be dumb, and deaf, and blind, and lame:
There all the halting paces are set down
I' the learnèd language.
 Clause. Thither I refer them;
Those you at leisure shall interpret to them:
We love no heaps of laws, where few will serve.

as it appears from Dekker's *English Villanies*, &c. (cited by Weber), where we find "*Belly cheate*, an Apron." Sig. N 2, ed. 1632: therefore *back-cheats* must mean—clothing for the back.

 [e] *To his own prop*] "i. e. either, to his own support, or else, by abbreviation, to his own property". THEOBALD. The latter, as Weber observes, seems to be the right explanation.

 [f] *purveyors*] "i. e. officers sent out to provide victuals for the monarch, chiefly when on a progress through the country. They were extremely oppressive, and of course frequently exclaimed against, and satirized in contemporary authors. Osborne relates a singular anecdote of a purveyor in Queen Elizabeth's reign. See his *Works*, edit. 1811. p. 53." WEBER.

 [g] *maund on your own pads*] "i. e. beg on your own roads, which are assigned to you." WEBER. *Pad* is properly—high-way. To *maund* is properly—to mutter or whine out supplications for charity (perhaps originally from begging with a *maund*,—a basket to receive the dole).

 [h] *to cut bene whids*] "*To cut bene whiddes*, to speake good words." *The Canters Dictionary* in Dekker's *English Villanies*, &c. Sig. N 3, ed. 1632.

All. Oh, gracious prince! Save, save the good King Clause!
Hig. A song to crown him!
Fer. Set a sentinel out first.
Snap. The word?
Hig. "A cove [i] comes", and "fumbumbis [k]" to it.

[*Exit* SNAP.

SONG.

Cast our caps and cares away!
This is beggars' holiday:
At the crowning of our king,
Thus we ever dance and sing.
In the world look out and see,
Where so happy a prince as he?
Where the nation live [l] so free,
And so merry as do we?
Be it peace, or be it war,
Here at liberty we are,
And enjoy our ease and rest:
To the field we are not prest;
Nor are call'd into the town,
To be troubled with the gown:
Hang all offices [m], we cry,
And the magistrate too, by!
When the subsidy's increas'd,
We are not a penny sess'd;
Nor will any go to law
With the beggar for a straw.
All which happiness, he brags,
He doth owe unto his rags.

---

[i] *cove*] "The word *Coue*, or *Cofe*, or *Cuffin*, signifies a man, a fellow, &c. but differs something in his property, according as it meets with other words; for a Gentleman is called a *Gentry Coue* or *Cofe*; a good fellow is a *Bene cofe*", &c. *Id.* sig. N 2.

[k] *fumbumbis*] "Is explained by Theobald, probably without any authority but the context, 'to your guard and postures'. But I think with the last editors [Gloss. at the end of the play] that it was 'rather a fancied watch-word than a cant term'." WEBER. I may notice, that in a MS. collection of poetical pieces, most of them written during the reign of Charles the Second, and some of them later, I find a ballad entitled "*Fumbumbis*, or The North Country Mayor."— After this speech, the old eds. have a stage-direction, "*Strike*".

[l] *nation live*] Silently altered by Seward to "nations *live*"; by the Editors of 1778 and Weber to "*nation* lives".

[m] *offices*] So the first folio and the 4to.—The second folio "officers"; and so Seward.

Re-enter SNAP.

Snap. A cove! fumbumbis [n]!
Prig. To your postures! arm!

Enter HUBERT *and* HEMSKIRK, *both disguised.*

Hub. Yonder's the town : I see it.
Hem. There's our danger,
Indeed, afore us, if our shadows [o] save not.
Hig. Bless your good worships!——
Fer. One small piece of money——
Prig. Amongst us all poor wretches——
Clause. Blind and lame——
Ginks. For his sake that gives all——
Hig. Pitiful worships!——
Snap. One little doit——

Enter MINCHE [p].

Minche. King, by your leave, where are you?
Fer.[q] To buy a little bread——
Hig. To feed so many
Mouths, as will ever pray for you.
Prig. Here be seven of us.
Hig. Seven, good master; oh, remember seven!
Seven blessings——
Fer. Remember, gentle worship——
Hig. 'Gainst seven deadly sins——
Prig. And seven sleepers [r].

[n] *A cove ! fumbumbis*] So the first folio and the 4to.—The second folio "*A cove* comes : *Fumbumbis* " (that the present speech might agree exactly with that of Higgen before the song) ; and so Seward.

[o] *shadows*] "i. e. disguises." *Ed.* 1778.

[p] *Minche*] See note, p. 19.

[q] *Fer.*] So the second folio.—The first folio and the 4to " Ger." : but Gerrard (Clause), we may suppose, has his attention occupied by Minche.

[r] *seven sleepers*] An allusion to a celebrated legend. When the emperor Decius persecuted the Christians, seven noble youths of Ephesus concealed themselves in the cavern of an adjacent mountain. There they were doomed to perish by the tyrant, who commanded that the entrance should be secured by a pile of stones. They immediately fell into a deep slumber, which continued during 187 years. At the end of that time, the cave being opened by the possessor of the mountain, they awoke. The bishop of Ephesus, the clergy, the magistrates, and, it is said, the emperor Theodosius himself, hastened to the cave to visit the Seven Sleepers, who, having bestowed their benediction, and related their story, immediately expired. See Gibbon's *Decline and Fall*, &c., vol. iii. 350, ed. 4to.

Hig. If they be hard of heart, and will give nothing——
Alas, we had not a charity this three days!
Hub. There's amongst you all. [*Gives money.*
Fer. Heaven reward you!
Prig. Lord reward you!
Hig. The prince of pity bless thee!
Hub. Do I see? or is't my fancy that would have it so?
Ha! 'tis her face [*Aside*].—Come hither, maid.
Minche. What ha' you,
Bells for my squirrel? I ha' given bun [h] meat.
You do not love me, do you? Catch me a butterfly,
And I'll love you again: when? can you tell?
Peace, we go a-birding: I shall have a fine thing. [*Exit.*
Hub. Her voice too says the same; but, for my head,
I would not that her manners were so chang'd.— [*Aside.*
Hear me, thou honest fellow; what's this maiden,
That lives amongst you here?
Ginks. Ao, ao, ao, ao.
Hub. How! nothing but signs?
Ginks. Ao, ao, ao, ao.
Hub. This is strange:
I would fain have it her, but not her thus. [*Aside.*
Hig. He is de-de-de-de-de-de-deaf, and du-du-dude-dumb,
 sir.   [*Exeunt all the* Beggars *except* SNAP.
Hub. 'Slid, they did all speak plain even now, methought.—
Dost thou know this same maid?
Snap. Whi-whi-whi-whi-which, Gu-Gu-Gu-Gu-God's fool?[i]
She was bo-bo-bo-bo-born at the barn yonder, by Be-Be-Be-
  Be-Beggars' Bush Bo-Bo-Bush:
Her name is Mi-Mi-Mi-Mi-Mi-Minche[j]; so was her mo-mo-
  mo-mother's too-too.

[h] *bun*] Seems to mean—rabbit; or perhaps by this term Minche designates her squirrel.

[i] *God's fool*] Compare, p. 26,—

"A sort of poor souls met, *God's fools*, good master."

[j] *-Minche*] Old eds. " -match "; and so Seward.—" We at first thought '*match*' to be a corruption of '*Madge*'; but as Jaculin [Jacqueline] is in other parts of the play called *Minche*, we suppose it merely a typographical error." *Ed.* 1778. This speech was reduced to prose by Weber: but, when read without the stammering additions, it is blank verse.

Hub. I understand no word he says.—How long
has she been here?

Snap. Lo-lo-long enough to be ni-ni-niggled [k], an she ha'
go-go-go-good luck.

Hub. I must be better inform'd than by this way:
Here was another face too, that I mark'd—
Oh [l], the old man's: but they are vanish'd all
Most suddenly. I will come here again:
Oh, that I were so happy as to find it,
What I yet hope it is, put on [m]! [*Aside.*

Hem. What mean you, sir,
To stay there with that stammerer?

Hub. Farewell, friend.— [*Exit* SNAP.
It will be worth return, to search [*Aside*].—Come;
Protect us our disguise now! Prithee, Hemskirk,
If we be taken, how dost thou imagine
This town will use us, that hath stood so long
Out against Wolfort?

Hem. Even to hang us forth
Upon their walls a-sunning, to make crows' meat.
If I were not assur'd o' the burgomaster,
And had a pretty 'scuse [n] to see a niece there,
I should scarce venture.

Hub. Come, 'tis now too late
To look back at the ports. Good luck, and enter!
[*Exeunt.*

SCENE II.—*Bruges.—The Exchange.*

Enter GOSWIN.

Gos. Still blow'st thou there? and, from all other parts,
Do all my agents sleep, that nothing comes?
There's a conspiracy of winds and servants,

---

[k] *niggled*] "'*Niggling*, companying with a woman'. *The Canter's Dict.* in Dekker's *English Villanies*, &c. sig. N 4, ed. 1632." WEBER.

[l] *Oh*] So the first folio and the 4to.—The second folio "Of"; and so the modern editors.

[m] *put on*] "i. e. assumed". WEBER,—who, like the other modern editors, points these words most improperly.

[n] '*scuse*] i. e. excuse. So the first folio ("*skuys*") and the 4to ("*scuce*").— The second folio "excuse"; and so Seward and the Editors of 1778.

If not of elements, to ha' me break.
What should I think? unless the seas and sands
Had swallow'd up my ships, or fire had spoil'd
My warehouses, or death devour'd my factors,
I must ha' had some returns.

Enter a Merchant.

Mer. Save you, sir!
Gos. Save you!
Mer. No news yet o' your ships?
Gos. Not any yet, sir.
Mer. 'Tis strange.
Gos. 'Tis true, sir [*Exit* Merchant].—What a voice was
   here now!
This was one passing-bell; a thousand ravens
Sung in that man now, to presage my ruins.

Enter Second Merchant.

Sec. Mer. Goswin, good day. These winds are very
   constant.
Gos. They are so, sir,—to hurt.
Sec. Mer. Ha' you had no letters
Lately from England, nor from Denmark?
Gos. Neither.
Sec. Mer. This wind brings them. Nor no news over land,
Through Spain, from the Straits?
Gos. Not any.
Sec. Mer. I am sorry, sir. [*Exit.*
Gos. They talk me down; and, as 'tis said of vultures,
They scent a field fought, and do smell the carcasses
By many hundred miles, so do these my wrecks,
At greater distances. Why, thy will, Heaven,
Come on, and be! yet, if thou please preserve me
But in my own adventure here at home,
Of my chaste love, to keep me worthy of her,
It shall be put in scale 'gainst all ill fortunes:
I am not broken yet°; nor should I fall,
Methinks, with less than that that ruins all. [*Exit.*

   ° *I am not broken yet,* &c.] "Goswin means to say, that the hour of his
bankruptcy was not yet arrived; and his resources were such that nothing

SCENE III.—*The same.*—*A room in the house of* VANDUNK.

Enter VANDUNK, HUBERT, HEMSKIRK, *and* MARGARET [p].

Vand. Captain, you are welcome; so is this your friend,
Most safely welcome; though our town stand out
Against your master, you shall find good quarter:
The troth is, we not love him.—Meg [q], some wine.—
    [*Exit* MARGARET, *who presently re-enters with wine.*
Let's talk a little treason, if we can
Talk treason 'gain the traitors: by your leave, gentlemen,
We here in Bruges think he does usurp,
And therefore I am bold with him.

Hub. Sir, your boldness
Haply becomes your mouth, but not our ears,
While we are his servants; and, as we come here,
Not to ask questions, walk forth on your walls,
Visit your courts of guard, view your munition,
Ask of your corn-provisions, nor inquire
Into the least, as spies upon your strengths;
So let's entreat, we may receive from you
Nothing in passage or discourse, but what
We may with gladness, and our honesties, hear;
And that shall seal our welcome.

Vand. Good: let's drink, then.—
Madge, fill out.—I keep mine old pearl still, captain.

Marg. I hang fast, man.

Hem. Old jewels commend their keeper, sir.

Vand. Here's to you with a heart, my captain's friend,
With a good heart! and, if this make us speak
Bold words anon, 'tis all under the rose,
Forgotten: drown all memory, when we drink!

---

ought to sink him but a general ruin. I cannot agree with the Editors [of 1778] in thinking that he alludes to Gertrude in these two lines, though he does in those which precede them." MASON.

[p] *Margaret*] The old eds. add (by some mistake) "*Boors*"; and so the modern editors.

[q] *Meg*] So the first folio and the 4to.—The second folio "Margaret"; and so Seward.

Hub. 'Tis freely spoken, noble burgomaster:
I 'll do you right.
　　Hem. Nay, sir, Mynheer Vandunk
Is a true statesman.
　　Vand. Fill my captain's cup, there.—Oh, that your master
　　　　Wolfort
Had been an honest man!
　　Hub. Sir?
　　Vand. Under the rose.
　　Hem. Here's to you, Marget [r].
　　Marg. Welcome, welcome, captain.
　　Vand. Well said, my pearl, still!
　　Hem. And how does my niece?
Almost a woman, I think. This friend of mine
I drew along with me, through so much hazard,
Only to see her: she was my errand [s].
　　Vand. Ay, a kind uncle you are,—fill him his glass,—
That in seven years could not find leisure——
　　Hem. No,
It 's not so much.
　　Vand. I 'll bate you ne'er an hour on 't:
It was before the Brabander 'gan his war
For moonshine i' the water there, his daughter
That never was lost; yet you could not find time
To see a kinswoman: but she is worth the seeing, sir,
Now you are come. You ask if she were a woman?
She is a woman, sir,—fetch her forth, Margy [t],—
And a fine woman, and has suitors.　　　[*Exit* MARGARET.
　　Hem. How!
What suitors are they?
　　Vand. Bachelors, young burghers;
And one a gallant; the young prince of merchants
We call him here in Bruges.
　　Hem. How! a merchant!

---

　　[r] *Marget*] So the first folio and the 4to.—The second folio " Margaret "; and so Seward.
　　[s] *errand*] Seward silently printed " *errand* here."
　　[t] *Margy*] So the first folio (" *Margee* "). — The 4to and the second folio " Marget ".—Seward printed " Margaret ".

I thought, Vandunk, you had understood me better,
And my niece too, so trusted to you by me,
Than to admit of such in name of suitors.

Vand. Such! he is such a such, as, were she mine,
I'd give him thirty thousand crowns with her.

Hem. But the same things, sir, fit not you and me. [*Exit.*

Vand. Why, give's some wine, then; this will fit us all.
[*Drinks.*
Here's to you still, my captain's friend, all out!
And still would Wolfort were an honest man!
Under the rose I speak it.—But this merchant
Is a brave boy: he lives so, i' the town here,
We know not what to think on him: at some times
We fear he will be bankrupt; he does stretch,
Tenter his credit so ᵘ; embraces all;
And, to't, the winds have been contrary long:
But then, if he should have all his returns,
We think he would be a king, and are half sure on't.—
Your master is a traitor, for all this,
Under the rose,—here's to you,—and usurps
The earldom from a better man.

Hub. Ay, marry, sir,
Where is that man?

Vand. Nay, soft: an I could tell you,
'Tis ten to one I would not. Here's my hand;
I love not Wolfort: sit you still with that.
Here comes my captain again, and his fine niece;
And there's my merchant; view him well.—Fill wine here!

Re-enter HEMSKIRK *and* MARGARET, *with* GERTRUDE *and* GOSWIN.

Hem. You must not only know me for your uncle
Now, but obey me: you, go cast yourself
Away, upon a dunghill here! a merchant!
A petty fellow! one that makes his trade
With oaths and perjuries!

Gos. What is that you say, sir?

ᵘ *Tenter his credit so*] "i. e. stretch it to the utmost extent, as cloth is expanded upon tenter-hooks." WEBER.

If it be me you speak of, as your eye
Seems to direct, I wish you would speak to me, sir.
  Hem. Sir, I do say, she is no merchandize:
Will that suffice you?
  Gos. Merchandize, good sir!
Though you be kinsman to her, take no leave thence
To use me with contempt: I ever thought
Your niece above all price.
  Hem. And do so still, sir:
I assure you, her rate's at more than you are worth.
  Gos. You do not know what a gentleman's worth, sir,
Nor can you value him.
  Hub. Well said, merchant!
  Vand. Nay,
Let him alone, and ply your matter.
  Hem. A gentleman!
What, o' the wool-pack? or the sugar-chest?
Or lists of velvet? which is't, pound or yard,
You vent your gentry by?
  Hub. Oh, Hemskirk, fie!
  Vand. Come, do not mind 'em; drink.—He is no Wolfort,
Captain, I advise you.
  Hem. Alas, my pretty man,
I think't be angry, by its look! come hither,
Turn this way a little: if it were the blood
Of Charlemagne, as't may, for aught I know,
Be some good botcher's issue [v], here in Bruges——
  Gos. How!
  Hem. Nay, I'm not certain of that; of this I am,
If it once buy and sell, its gentry is gone.
  Gos. Ha, ha!
  Hem. You are angry, though you laugh.
  Gos. No, now 'tis pity
Of your poor argument. Do not you, the lords
Of land, (if you be any,) sell the grass,
The corn, the straw, the milk, the cheese——
  Vand. And butter:
Remember butter; do not leave out butter.

---

[v] *botcher's issue*] A *botcher* is a mender of old clothes.

Gos. The beefs and muttons, that your grounds are stor'd
with?
Swine, with the very mast, beside the woods?
Hem. No; for those sordid uses we have tenants,
Or else our bailiffs.
Gos. Have not we, sir, chapmen
And factors, then, to answer these? Your honour[v],
Fetch'd from the heralds' A B C, and said over,
With your court-faces, once an hour, shall never
Make me mistake myself. Do not your lawyers
Sell all their practice, as your priests their prayers?
What is not bought and sold? the company
That you had last, what had you for 't, i' faith?
Hem. You now grow saucy.
Gos. Sure[w], I have been bred
Still with my honest liberty, and must use it.
Hem. Upon your equals, then.
Gos. Sir, he that will
Provoke me first doth make himself my equal.
Hem. Do you hear? no more!
Gos. Yes, sir, this little, I pray you,
And 't shall be aside; then, after, as you please.
You appear the uncle, sir, to her I love
More than mine eyes; and I have heard your scorns
With so much scoffing, and [with] so much shame,
As each strive[s] which is greater: but, believe me,
I suck'd not in this patience with my milk.
Do not presume, because you see me young;
Or cast despites on my profession,
For the civility and tameness of it:
A good man bears a contumely worse
Than he would do an injury. Proceed not
To my offence: wrong is not still successful;
Indeed, it is not. I would approach your kinswoman
With all respect done to yourself and her.
      [*Takes hold of* GERTRUDE's *hand.*

 [v] *honour*] So the second folio.—The first folio and the 4to " errour."
 [w] *Sure*] Was altered by Seward to " Sir ", because the old reading " would make him doubt whether he had been bred with an honest liberty or no."— " '*Sure*' does not imply *doubt*, but *affirmation*." *Ed.* 1778.

Hem. Away, companion[x]! handling her? take that!
[*Strikes him.*
Gos. Nay, I do love no blows, sir: there's exchange!
[*Gets* HEMSKIRK'S *sword, cuts him on the head with it,
and then throws it off the stage.*
Hub. Hold, sir!
Marg. Oh, murder!
Gert. Help my Goswin!
Marg. Man[y]!
Vand. Let 'em alone. My life for one!
Gos. Nay, come,
If you have will.
Hub. None to offend you I, sir.
Gos. He that had, thank himself!—Not hand her? yes, sir,
And clasp her, and embrace her; and (would she
Now go with me) bear her through all her race,
Her father, brethren, and her uncles, arm'd,
And all their nephews, though they stood a wood
Of pikes, and wall of cannon.—Kiss me, Gertrude;
Quake not, but kiss me.
Vand. Kiss him, girl; I bid you.—
My merchant royal! Fear no uncles: hang 'em,
Hang up all uncles! Are we not in Bruges,
Under the rose here?
Gos. In this circle, love,
Thou art as safe as in a tower of brass.
Let such as do wrong, fear.
Vand. Ay, that's good:
Let Wolfort look to that.
Gos. Sir, here she stands,
Your niece, and my belov'd. One of these titles
She must apply to: if unto the last,
Not all the anger can be sent unto her,
In frown or voice, or other art[z], shall force her,

---

[x] *companion*] Equivalent to—fellow.

[y] *Man*] "i. e. husband, with which signification it is still used in Scotland."
WEBER.

[z] *other art*] "Mr. Theobald altered the last word to 'act.' But, as Mr Mason observes, 'ancient dramatic writers frequently use these two words to

Had Hercules a hand in 't.—Come, my joy,
Say thou art mine aloud, love, and profess it.
 Vand. Do; and I drink to it.
 Gos. Prithee, say so, love.
 Gert. 'Twould take away the honour from my blushes;—
Do not you play the tyrant, sweet;—they speak it.
 Hem. I thank you, niece.
 Gos. Sir, thank her for your life;
And fetch your sword within.
 Hem. You insult too much
With your good fortune, sir.
 [*Exeunt* GOSWIN *and* GERTRUDE.
 Hub. A brave clear spirit!—
Hemskirk, you were to blame: a civil habit
Oft covers a good man; and you may meet,
In person of a merchant, with a soul
As resolute and free, and all ways worthy,
As else in any file of mankind. Pray you,
What meant you so to slight him?
 Hem. 'Tis done now;
Ask no more of it; I must suffer. [*Exit.*
 Hub. This
Is still the punishment of rashness—sorrow.
Well, I must to the woods, for nothing here
Will be got out. There I may chance to learn
Somewhat to help my inquiries further. [*Aside.*
 Vand. Ha!
A looking-glass[a]!

---

express the same idea.' The editors of the edition of 1750 introduced, and those of 1778 continued the same alteration in the following passage of *The Custom of the Country:*

'Though my desires were loose, from unchaste *art*,
 Heaven knows, I am free.'" WEBER.

In the present passage, I think, Theobald's alteration is not required: in that just cited from *The Custom of the Country* (see vol. iv. 493) it is absolutely necessary.

[a] *A looking-glass*] "Does not Vandunk here, now grown quite fuddled, call for an utensil at this day known among drinkers by the name of a *looking-glass?*" *Ed.* 1778. "The interpretation of the editors is certainly right, as the word is used with the same meaning in the old English translation of *Drunken Barnaby's Journal*, edit. 1805, p. 41." WEBER.

Hub. How now, brave burgomaster?
Vand. I love no Wolforts, and my name's Vandunk.
Hub. Van-drunk it's rather. Come, go sleep within.
Vand. Earl Florez is right heir; and this same Wolfort,—
Under the rose I speak it——
Hub. Very hardly[b].
Vand. Usurps; and a rank traitor, as ever breath'd,
And all that do uphold him. Let me go;
No man shall hold me [up][c], that upholds him.
Do you uphold him?
Hub. No.
Vand. Then hold me up. [*Exeunt.*

SCENE IV.—*Before the house of* VANDUNK.

Enter GOSWIN *and* HEMSKIRK.

Hem. Sir, I presume you have a sword of your own,
That can so handle another's.
Gos. Faith, you may, sir.
Hem. And you have made me have so much better thoughts
  of you,
As I am bound to call you forth.
Gos. For what, sir?
Hem. To the repairing of mine honour and hurt here.
Gos. Express your way.
Hem. By fight, and speedily.
Gos. You have your will. Require you any more?
Hem. That you be secret, and come single.
Gos. I will.
Hem. As you are the gentleman you would be thought!
Gos. Without the conjuration : and I'll bring
Only my sword, which I will fit to yours.
I'll take his[d] length within.

[b] *Very hardly*] "i. e. you speak it with great difficulty." WEBER.
[c] *hold me* [*up*]] The last word was rightly inserted by Seward (who states, erroneously, that the old copies read " *hold* he ").
[d] *his*] Silently altered to "its" by Seward ; and so his successors.

Hem. Your place now, sir?
Gos. By the sand-hills.
Hem. Sir, nearer to the woods,
If you thought so, were fitter.
Gos. There, then.
Hem. Good.
Your time?
Gos. 'Twixt seven and eight.
Hem. You'll give me, sir,
Cause to report you worthy of my niece,
If you come like your promise.
Gos. If I do not,
Let no man think to call me unworthy first:
I'll do't myself, and justly wish to want her.
[*Exeunt severally.*

ACT III.

SCENE I.—*Before a tavern in the outskirts of Bruges.*

Enter three or four Boors.

First Boor. Come, English beer, hostess, English beer by the belly^e!
Sec. Boor. Stark^f beer, boy, stout and strong beer!—So; sit down, lads,
And drink me upsey-Dutch^g: frolic, and fear not.

^e *by the belly*] Seward, at Sympson's suggestion, printed " *by th'* barrel"; and so his successors. But that the old reading is right, there can be no doubt. We find a similar expression in *The Knight of the Burning Pestle*, act ii. sc. 2. vol. ii. 157, "here's money and gold *by th' eye*, my boy"; and in Marlowe's *Jew of Malta*, act iii,

"Assure thyself thou shalt have broth *by the eye*."

Both "*by the belly*" and "*by the eye*" seem equivalent to—in abundance.
^f *Stark*] "i. e. Strong" WEBER. So the second folio.—The first folio and the 4to "Start."
^g *upsey-Dutch*] According to Gifford, "a thick and heady kind of beer, the common beverage of the Low Countries, was much drunk in England about this time; and familiarly known by the name of *opzee* (over sea). As it was of a stupifying nature, to be *upsee Dutch* was synonymous with being in a state of perfect inebriation, dull, lifeless, &c. *Upsee Freeze* (Friesland beer) is a phrase of similar

Enter HIGGEN *disguised as a sow-gelder, singing as follows.*

Have ye any work for the sow-gelder, ho ?
My horn[g] goes to high, to low, to high, to low !
Have ye any pigs, calves, or colts,
Have ye any lambs in your holts,[h]
To cut for the stone ?
Here comes a cunning one.
Have ye any braches[i] to spade,
Or e'er a fair maid
That would be a nun ?
Come, kiss me, 'tis done.
Hark, how my merry horn doth blow
To high, to low, to high, to low !

First Boor. Oh, excellent !—Two-pence a-piece, boys, two-pence a-piece !—Give the boy[j] some drink there !—Piper, wet[k] your whistle. Canst tell me a way now how to cut off my wife's concupiscence ?

Hig. I'll sing you a song for't.   [*Sings.*

Take her, and hug her,
And turn her, and tug her,
And turn her again, boy, again :
Then, if she mumble,
Or if her tail tumble,
Kiss her amain, boy, amain !

---

import, and occurs very frequently in the writers of Jonson's age. To *drink upsee Dutch* or *upsee Freeze* was to drink swinishly, like a Dutchman, &c. A strong kind of malt liquor, made here in imitation of the Friesland or Oversea beer, was called *upsee English.*" Note on Jonson's *Works*, iv. 150. See also the *Glossary* of Nares, who doubts if we have yet had the true explanation of the origin of the phrase.

[g] *My horn,* &c.] So in *Cornu-Copiæ, Pasquils Night-cap,* &c. (attributed to Rowlands), 1612 ;

"And so much credit now attends it [the horn] daily,
That euery common Crier, Petie Baily,
Swine-heards and braue *Sow-golders* [sic], *in a pride*
Doe beare a horne low dangling by their side." P. 108.

[h] *holts*] Generally signifies—woods, forests (as in vol. ii. 54),—sometimes, wooded hills, high grounds : see Chalmers's Gloss. to Sir D. Lyndsay's *Works*, and *Promptorium Parvulorum*, ed. Camden. Here Fletcher evidently used the word for the sake of a rhyme, and probably intended it to mean simply—pastures.

[i] *braches*] i. e. bitches : see note, vol. iii. 9.

[j] *boy*] Seward's correction, adopted by his successors,—" *boy* " meaning either the tavern-boy who brings the drink (compare the first line of the second speech in this scene), or else Higgen.

[k] *wet*] Seward chose to print " whet" ; and so his successors !!

> Do thy endeavour
> To take off her fever,
> Then her disease no longer will reign.
> If nothing will serve her,
> Then thus, to preserve her,
> Swinge her amain, boy, amain!
>
> Give her cold jelly,
> To take up her belly,
> And once a day swinge her again.
> If she stand all these pains,
> Then knock out her brains;
> Her disease no longer will reign.

First Boor. More excellent, more excellent, sweet sow-gelder!

Sec. Boor. Three-pence a-piece, three-pence a-piece!

Hig. Will you hear a song how the devil was gelded?

Third Boor. Ay, ay; let's hear the devil roar, sow-gelder.

SONG[1] by HIGGEN.

> He ran at me first in the shape of a ram,
> And over and over the sow-gelder came:
> I riss[m], and I halter'd him fast by the horn;
> I pluck'd out his stones, as you'd pick out a corn.
>   Baa! quoth the devil, and forth he slunk,
>   And left us a carcass of mutton that stunk.
>
> The next time, I rode a good mile and a half,
> Where I heard he did live in disguise of a calf:
> I bound and I gelt him, ere he did any evil;
> He was here at his best but a sucking devil[n].
>   Maa! yet he cried, and forth he did steal,
>   And this was sold after for excellent veal.
>
> Some half a year after, in the form[o] of a pig,
> I met with the rogue, and he look'd very big:

---

[1] *Song*] Found only in the second folio.

[m] *riss*] i. e. rose. Here the old copy has "rise": but see before, vol. iv. 7, 97, vol. vi. 435, vol. vii. 19.—A periodical critic, while reviewing some of the earlier volumes of the present work, objected to my retaining this archaism: I have, however, the sanction of Gifford for doing so: See Jonson's *Works*, iv. 259.

[n] *a sucking devil*] Seward silently printed "*a young sucking devil*"; and so the Editors of 1778,—a reading borrowed from Durfey's *Pills to Purge Melancholy*, where (vol. v. 330) the three stanzas in our text (considerably varied) and two additional ones, make up a ballad called *The Gelding the Devil*.

[o] *in the form*] Seward silently printed "*in form*"; and so the Editors of 1778.

I catch'd at his leg, laid him down on a log;
Ere a man could fart twice, I had made him a hog.
Owgh! quoth the devil, and forth gave a jerk,
That a Jew was converted, and eat of the perk [p].

First Boor. Groats a-piece [q], groats a-piece, groats a-piece!—
There, sweet sow-gelder.   [*Gives money.*

    Enter PRIG *disguised as a juggler, and* FERRET *as his man.*

Prig. Will ye see any feats of activity,
Some slight of hand, leger-de-main? hey, pass,
Presto, be gone there?
    Sec. Boor. Sit down, juggler.
    Prig. Sirrah, play you your art well [*Aside to* FERRET].—
    Draw near, piper [r].—   [*To* HIGGEN.
Look you, my honest friends, you see my hands;
Plain-dealing is no devil. Lend me some money;
Twelve-pence a-piece will serve.
    First and Sec. Boor. There, there.   [*Giving money.*
    Prig. I thank you,
Thank ye heartily. When shall I pay ye?
    All the Boors. Ha, ha, ha! by the mass, this was a fine trick.
    Prig. A merry slight toy. But now I'll shew your worships
A trick indeed.
    Hig. Mark him well now, my masters.
    Prig. Here are three balls: these balls shall be three bullets.
One, two, and three! *ascentibus, malentibus!*
Presto, be gone! They are vanish'd: fair play, gentlemen.
Now, these three, like three bullets, from your three noses
Will I pluck presently. Fear not; no harm, boys.
Tityre, tu patulæ.
    [*Pulls the* Boors' *noses, while* HIGGEN *and* FERRET *pick their pockets, and remove some of their cloaks.*

---

[p] *perk*] "i. e. pork, for the rhyme's sake." WEBER. Seward silently printed "pork."

[q] First Boor. *Groats a-piece,* &c.] This speech was omitted by Weber!!!

[r] *Draw near, piper*] Weber, supposing that "*piper*" meant Ferret, gave in the stage-direction above, "*Enter Prig and Ferret, disguised as a juggler and a piper.*" But Higgen is the "*piper*": see p. 45, where the First Boor says to him, "*Piper,* wet your whistle."

First Boor. Oh, oh, oh!
Prig. Recubans sub jermine fagi.
Sec. Boor. You pull too hard; you pull too hard!
Prig. Stand fair, then.
Silvertram[r] trim-tram.
Third Boor. Hold, hold, hold!
Prig. Come aloft, bullets three, with a whim-wham!—
Have ye their moneys? [*Aside to* HIGGEN *and* FERRET.
Hig. Yes, yes.
First Boor. Oh, rare juggler!
Sec. Boor. Oh, admirable juggler!
Prig. One trick more yet.
Hey, come aloft! *sa, sa, flim, flum, taradumbis!*
East, west, north, south, now fly like Jack with a *bumbis!*
Now all your money's gone: pray, search your pockets.
First Boor. Humh!
Sec. Boor. He!
Third Boor. The devil a penny's here!
Prig. This was a rare trick.
First Boor. But 'twould be a far rarer to restore it.
Prig. I'll do ye that too. Look upon me earnestly,
And move not any ways your eyes from this place,
This button here.
 [*While the* Boors *look at* PRIG, *counters are put into their pockets by* HIGGEN *and* FERRET.
Pow, whir, whiss! Shake your pockets.
First Boor. By the mass, 'tis here again, boys.
Prig. Rest ye merry:
My first trick has paid me.
All the Boors. Ay, take it, take it,
And take some drink too.
Prig. Not a drop now, I thank you.—
Away! we are discover'd else.
 [*Exit with* HIGGEN *and* FERRET.

---

[r] *Silvertram*] So both the folios.—The 4to has "Silvestram": but probably the learned Prig rejects Virgil's word ("*Silvestrem*"), with a sly allusion to the *silver* which is now vanishing from the Boors' pockets.

SCENE I.] BEGGARS' BUSH.

Enter CLAUSE *disguised as a blind aquavitæ-man, and a* Boy *who sings as follows:*

Bring out your cony-skins[s], fair maids, to me,
And hold 'em fair, that I may see ;
Grey, black, and blue : for your smaller skins,
I 'll give ye looking-glasses, pins ;
And for your whole cony,
Here's ready, ready money.
Come, gentle Joan, do thou begin
With thy black, black, black cony-skin ;
And Mary then, and Jane will follow,
With their silver-hair'd skins and their yellow.
The white cony-skin I will not lay by,
For, though it be faint, 'tis fair to the eye ;
The grey, it is warm ; but yet, for my money,
Give me the bonny, bonny black cony.
Come away, fair maids ; your skins will decay :
Come and take money, maids ; put your ware away.
Cony-skins, cony-skins ! have ye any cony-skins ?
I have fine bracelets, and fine silver pins.

Clause. Buy any brand-wine[t], buy any brand-wine ?

Boy. Have ye any cony-skins ?

Sec. Boor. My fine canary-bird, there's a cake for thy worship.

First Boor. Come, fill, fill, fill, fill, suddenly. Let's see, sir; what's this ?[u]

Clause. A penny, sir.

First Boor. Fill till 't be six-pence, And there 's my pig[v].

Boy. This is a counter, sir.

First Boor. A counter ! Stay you : what are these, then ?— Oh, execrable juggler ! oh, damn'd juggler !—— Look in your hose[w], ho ! this comes of looking forward.

Third Boor. Devil a Dunkirk ! what a rogue 's this juggler, This hey-pass, re-pass ! h' as repass'd us sweetly.

Sec. Boor. Do ye call these tricks ?

---

[s] *Bring out your cony-skins,* &c.] This song (with some variations) is found in Durfey's *Pills to Purge Melancholy,* vol. v. 303.

[t] *brand-wine*] "*Brandy,* and other spirits, are called *brand wine* in the Low Countries and Germany." WEBER (after Reed).

[u] *What 's this?*] i. e. what is the price of the quantity of spirits now poured out for me ?

[v] *pig*] " i. e. sixpence." THEOBALD.

[w] *hose*] i. e. breeches.

VOL. IX.   E

Re-enter HIGGEN, *disguised as a gold-end-man* [w].

Hig. Have ye any ends of gold or silver?

Sec. Boor. This fellow comes to mock us.—Gold or silver! cry copper!

First Boor. Yes, my good friend,
We have e'en an end of all we have.

Hig. 'Tis well, sir;
You have the less to care for.—Gold and silver! [*Exit.*

Re-enter PRIG, *disguised as an old-clothes-man.*

Prig. Have ye any old cloaks to sell, have ye any old cloaks to sell? [*Exit.*

First Boor. Cloaks!—Look about ye, boys; mine's gone!

Sec. Boor. A [pox] [x] juggle 'em!
[Pox] o' their prestoes! mine's gone too!

Third Boor. Here's mine yet.

First Boor. Come, come, let's drink, then.—More brand-wine!

Boy. Here, sir.

First Boor. If e'er I catch your sow-gelder, by this hand, I'll strip him.
Were ever fools so ferk'd? [y] We have two cloaks yet,
And all our caps: the devil take the flincher!

All the Boors. Yaw, yaw, yaw, yaw!

Enter HEMSKIRK.

Hem. Good den,[z] my honest fellows:
You are merry here, I see.

---

[w] *Re-enter Higgen, disguised as a gold-end-man*] The old eds. have merely "*Enter Higgen*"; and so the modern editors,—except Weber, who gave "*Enter Higgen, disguised as a buyer of old gold and silver lace*",—wrongly.—"A gold-end-man is one who buys broken pieces of gold and silver, an itinerant jeweller. In the *Beggars' Bush*, Higgen enters, crying 'Have ye any *ends of gold or silver?*' words which might be heard every day in the streets of London." Gifford's note on Jonson's *Works*, iv. 79. Compare a copy of verses among the Commendatory Poems prefixed to the first vol. of the present work, p. liii;

"Thus *ends-of-gold-and-silver-men* are made,
As th' use to say, goldsmiths of his own trade."

[x] [*pox*] Here, and in the next line, the old eds. have a break.

[y] *ferk'd*] "i. e. cheated, fobbed." *Ed.* 1778. See note, vol. iv. 216.

[z] *Good den*] A corruption of *good e'en*, good evening.—Old eds. "*Good* do'n."—Seward silently printed "*Good* ev'n."

Third Boor. 'Tis all we have left, sir.
Hem. What hast thou? aquavitæ?
Boy. Yes.
Hem. Fill out, then;
And give these honest fellows round.
All the Boors. We thank you.
Hem. May I speak a word in private to ye?
All the Boors. Yes, sir.
Hem. I have a business for you, honest friends,
If you dare lend your help, shall get you crowns.
Clause. Ha!
Lead me a little nearer, boy. [*Aside to* Boy.
First Boor. What is 't, sir?
If it be any thing to purchase money
(Which is our want), command us.
All the Boors. All, all, all, sir.
Hem. You know the young spruce merchant in[a] Bruges?
Sec. Boor. Who, Master Goswin?
Hem. That: he owes me money,
And here in town there is no stirring of him.
Clause. Say you so? [*Aside.*
Hem. This day, upon a sure appointment,
He meets me a mile hence, by the chase-side,
Under the row of oaks: do you know it?
All the Boors. Yes, sir.
Hem. Give 'em more drink.—There, if you dare but venture,
When I shall give the word, to seize upon him,
Here's twenty pound.
Third Boor. Beware the juggler!
Hem. If he resist, down with him, have no mercy.
First Boor. I warrant you, we'll hamper him.
Hem. To discharge you,
I have a warrant here about me.
Third Boor. Here's our warrant;
This carries fire i' the tail. [*Shewing his cudgel.*
Hem. Away with me, then! the time draws on.—

[a] *merchant in*] Seward silently printed "*merchant* here *in*".

I must remove so insolent a suitor,
And, if he be so rich, make him pay ransom
Ere he see Bruges' towers again. Thus wise men
Repair the hurts they take by a disgrace,
And piece the lion's skin with the fox's case[a]. [*Aside.*
Clause. I am glad I have heard this sport yet. [*Aside.*
Hem. There's for thy drink.—Come, pay the house within,
 boys,
And lose no time.
 Clause. Away with all our haste too!
  [*Exeunt, on one side,* HEMSKIRK, *followed by the*
   Boors; *on the other,* CLAUSE *and* Boy.

SCENE II.—*A chase bordering on the woods near Bruges.*
 Enter GOSWIN.
Gos. No wind blow fair yet? no return of moneys,
Letters, nor any thing to hold my hopes up?
Why, then, 'tis destin'd that I fall, fall miserably,
My credit I was built on sinking with me.
Thou boisterous North-wind, blowing my misfortunes,
And frosting all my hopes to cakes of coldness,
Yet stay thy fury! give the gentle South
Yet leave to court those sails that bring me safety!
And you, auspicious fires [b], bright twins in heaven,
Dance on the shrouds! He blows still stubbornly,
And on his boisterous rack [c] rides my sad ruin.
There is no help, there can be now no comfort;

---

[a] *case*] i. e. skin.

[b] *And you, auspicious fires*, &c.] " The bright twins in heaven are Castor and Pollux, who were supposed to have been converted into stars, and form the constellation Gemini. When certain electrical exhalations appeared in a storm about the shrouds of a ship, it was formerly considered as a fortunate omen, and attributed to the presence of Castor and Pollux." MASON. " The same superstition prevails still in the Mediterranean ; only the auspicious Pagan twins have been converted into the Christian San Elmo, whose proper name is said to have been San Pedro Gonzales Telmo. The same lights are also denominated Corpo Santo." WEBER.

[c] *rack*] i. e. collection of thin vapoury clouds.—"The present passage ", says Weber, " supports Mr. Malone's interpretation of this word strongly ; 'A body of clouds, or rather the *course of clouds in motion.*' " But see note, vol. ii. 120.

To-morrow, with the sun-set, sets my credit.
Oh, misery! thou curse of man, thou plague,
In the midst of [c] all our strength, thou strikest us!
My virtuous love is lost too: all, what I have been,
No more hereafter to be seen than shadow.
To prison now! Well, yet there's this hope left me;
I may sink fairly under this day's venture,
And so to-morrow's cross'd, and all those curses.
Yet manly I'll invite my fate: base Fortune
Shall never say, she has cut my throat in fear.
This is the place his challenge call'd me to,
And was a happy one at this time for me;
For let me fall before my foe i' the field,
And not at bar before my creditors!

Enter HEMSKIRK.

H'as kept his word [*Aside*].—Now, sir, your sword's tongue
   only,
Loud as you dare; all other language——
  Hem. Well, sir,
You shall not be long troubled. Draw.
  Gos. 'Tis done, sir;
And now, have at you!
  Hem. Now!

Enter Boors, *who attempt to seize* GOSWIN.

  Gos. Betray'd to villains!—Slaves, ye shall buy me bravely!—
And thou, base coward——

Enter CLAUSE *and other* Beggars *disguised, who assail* HEMSKIRK *and the* Boors.

  Clause. Now upon 'em bravely!
Conjure 'em soundly, boys!
  Boors. Hold, hold!
  Clause. Lay on still!
Down with that gentleman-rogue, swinge him to syrup!—
                      [HEMSKIRK *runs off.*
Retire, sir, and take breath.—Follow, and take him;
Take all; 'tis lawful prize.   [*Exeunt some of the* Beggars.

---

    [c] *of*] So the 4to and the second folio.—Omitted in the first folio.

Boors. We yield.
Clause. Down with 'em!
Into the wood, and rifle 'em, tew^d 'em, swinge 'em!
Knock me their brains into their breeches!
Boors. Hold, hold!   [*Exeunt all except* GOSWIN.
Gos. What these men are I know not; nor for what cause
They should thus thrust themselves into my danger
Can I imagine—but, sure, Heaven's hand was in 't—
Nor why this coward knave should deal so basely,
To eat me up with slaves: but, Heaven, I thank thee!
I hope thou hast reserv'd me to an end
Fit for thy creature, and worthy of thine honour.
Would all my other dangers here had ^e suffer'd!
With what a joyful heart should I go home, then!
Where now, Heaven knows, like him that waits his sentence,
Or hears his passing-bell—but there's my hope still ^g.

Re-enter CLAUSE.

Clause. Blessing upon you, master!
Gos. Thank you. Leave me;
For, by my troth, I have nothing now to give thee.
Clause. Indeed, I do not ask, sir; only it grieves me
To see you look so sad. Now, goodness keep you
From troubles in your mind!
Gos. If I were troubled,
What could thy comfort do? prithee, Clause, leave me.
Clause. Good master, be not angry; for what I say
Is out of true love to you.
Gos. I know thou lov'st me.
Clause. Good master, blame that love, then, if I prove so
    saucy
To ask you why you are sad.

^d *tew*] i.e. work, dress,—drub : see note, vol. iv. 140.
^e *had*] Heath (*MS. Notes*) would read " I 'd."
^g *Where now, Heaven knows, like him that waits his sentence,*
   Or hears his passing-bell—but there's my hope still] "'*Where*', i.e. Whereas."
WEBER.—"This is obscure; but we apprehend the meaning to be, that Goswin still hopes for assistance from Heaven." *Ed.* 1778. Such is doubtless the meaning of the passage (and so it had been explained, at an earlier date, by Heath in his *MS. Notes*).

Gos. Most true, I am so;
And such a sadness I have got will sink me.
  Clause. Heaven shield it, sir!
  Gos. Faith, thou must lose thy master.
  Clause. I had rather lose my neck, sir. Would I knew——
  Gos. What would the knowledge do thee good (so miserable
Thou canst not help thyself), when all my ways,
Nor all the friends I have——
  Clause. You do not know, sir,
What I can do: cures, sometimes, for men's cares,
Flow where they least expect 'em.
  Gos. I know thou wouldst do:
But, farewell, Clause, and pray for thy poor master.
  Clause. I will not leave you.
  Gos. How!
  Clause. I dare not leave you, sir [g], I must not leave you,
And, till you beat me dead, I will not leave you.
By what you hold most precious, by Heaven's goodness,
As your fair youth may prosper, good sir, tell me!
My mind believes yet something's in my power
May ease you of this trouble.
  Gos. I will tell thee.
For a hundred thousand crowns, upon my credit,
Taken up of merchants to supply my traffics,
The winds and weather envying of my fortune,
And no return to help me off yet shewing,
To-morrow, Clause, to-morrow, which must come,
In prison thou shalt find me poor and broken [h].
  Clause. I cannot blame your grief, sir.
  Gos. Now, what say'st thou?
  Clause. I say, you should not shrink; for he that gave you,
Can give you more; his power can bring you off, sir;
When friends and all forsake you, yet he sees you.
  Gos. There's [i] all my hope.

[g] *I dare not leave you, sir,* &c.] So the second folio.—The first folio and the 4to have;
  " *I dare not leave ye,*
    And till ye beate me dead, I must *not leave ye.*"
[h] *broken*] "i. e. bankrupt." WEBER.
[i] *There's*] So the second folio.—The first folio and the 4to " That's ". Compare p. 54, *l.* 16.

Clause. Hope still, sir. Are you tied
Within the compass of a day, good master,
To pay this mass of money?
  Gos. Even to-morrow.
But why do I stand mocking of my misery?
Is 't not enough the floods and friends forget me?
  Clause. Will no less serve?
  Gos. What if it would?
  Clause. Your patience:
I do not ask to mock you. 'Tis a great sum,
A sum for mighty men to start and stick at;
But not for honest. Have you no friends left you,
None that have felt your bounty, worth this duty?
  Gos. Duty! thou know'st it not.
  Clause. It is a duty,
And, as a duty, from those men have felt you,
Should be return'd again. I have gain'd by you;
A daily alms these seven years you have shower'd on[j] me.
Will half supply your want?
  Gos. Why dost thou fool me?
Canst thou work miracles?
  Clause. To save my master,
I can work this.
  Gos. Thou wilt make me angry with thee.
  Clause. For doing good?
  Gos. What power hast thou?
  Clause. Inquire not,
So I can do it, to preserve my master.
Nay, if it be three parts——
  Gos. Oh, that I had it!
But, good Clause, talk no more; I feel thy charity,
As thou hast felt mine: but, alas——
  Clause. Distrust not;
'Tis that that quenches you: pull up your spirit,
Your good, your honest, and your noble spirit;
For, if the fortunes of ten thousand people
Can save you, rest assur'd. You have forgot, sir,
The good you did, which was the power you gave me:

---

[j] *on*] So the second folio.—Omitted in the first folio and in the 4to.

You shall now know the King of Beggars' treasure;
And let the winds blow as they list[k], the seas roar,
Yet here to-morrow you shall find your harbour.
Here fail me not, for, if I live, I'll fit you.
  Gos. How fain I would believe thee!
  Clause. If I lie, master,
Believe no man hereafter.
  Gos. I will try thee:
But He knows, that knows all.
  Clause. Know me to-morrow,
And, if I know not how to cure you, kill me.
So, pass in peace, my best, my worthiest master!
                                     [*Exeunt severally.*

    SCENE III.—*The interior of the woods near Bruges.*
       Enter HUBERT *disguised as a huntsman.*
  Hub. Thus have I stoln away disguis'd from Hemskirk,
To try these people; for my heart yet tells me
Some of these beggars are the men I look for.
Appearing like myself, they have no reason
(Though my intent is fair, my main end honest)
But to avoid me narrowly. That face too,
That woman's face, how near it is! Oh, may it
But prove the same, and, Fortune, how I'll bless thee!
Thus, sure, they cannot know me, or suspect me,
If to my habit I but change my nature,
As I must do. This is the wood they live in;
A place fit for concealment; where, till fortune
Crown me with that I seek, I'll live amongst 'em.   [*Exit.*

      SCENE IV.—*Another part of the woods.*
Enter HIGGEN, PRIG, FERRET, GINKS, *and other* Beggars, *with
                the* Boors.
  Hig. Come, bring 'em out, for here we sit in justice.
Give to each one a cudgel, a good cudgel:—
And now attend your sentence. That you are rogues,

---

    [k] *list*] So the second folio.—The first folio and the 4to " please."

And mischievous base rascals,—there's the point now,—
I take it, is confess'd.

Prig. Deny it if you dare, knaves!

Boors. We are rogues, sir.

Hig. To amplify the matter, then; rogues as [k] ye are,
(And lamm'd [l] ye shall be ere we leave ye)—

Boors. Yes, sir.

Hig. And to the open handling of our justice,—
Why did ye this upon the proper person
Of our good master? were you drunk when you did it?

Boors. Yes, indeed, were we.

Prig. You shall be beaten sober.

Hig. Was it for want you undertook it?

Boors. Yes, sir.

Hig. You shall be swinged abundantly.

Prig. And yet, for all that,
You shall be poor rogues still.

Hig. Has not the gentleman,—
Pray, mark this point, brother Prig,—that noble gentleman,
Reliev'd ye often, found ye means to live by,
By employing some at sea, some here, some there,
According to your callings?

Boors. 'Tis most true, sir.

Hig. Is not the man an honest man?

Boors. Yes, truly.

Hig. A liberal gentleman? and, as ye are true rascals,
Tell me but this,—have ye not been drunk, and often,
At his charge?

Boors. Often, often.

Hig. There's the point, then:
They have cast themselves, brother Prig.

Prig. A shrewd point, brother.

Hig. Brother, proceed you now; the cause is open;
I am somewhat weary.

Prig. Can you do these things,
You most abominable stinking rascals,
You turnip-eating rogues?

---

[k] *as*] Silently omitted by Seward; and so his successors.
[l] *lamm'd*] i. e. beaten.

Boors. We are truly sorry.

Prig. Knock at your hard hearts, rogues, and presently
Give us a sign you feel compunction:
Every man up with's cudgel, and on his neighbour
Bestow such alms, till we shall say sufficient,
(For there your sentence lies,) without partiality,
Either of head or hide, rogues, without sparing,
Or we shall take the pains to beat you dead else.
You know [m] your doom.

Hig. One, two, and three! about it! [*Boors beat one another.*

Prig. That fellow in the blue has true compunction;
He beats his fellow[n] bravely.—Oh, well struck, boys!

Enter CLAUSE.

Hig. Up with that blue breech! now plays he the devil!—
So; get ye home, drink small beer, and be honest.
[*Exeunt* Boors.
Call in the gentleman.

Clause. Do, bring him presently;
His cause I'll hear myself.   [*Exeunt some of the* Beggars.

Hig. Prig. With all due reverence,
We do resign, sir.

Re-enter Beggars *with* HEMSKIRK.

Clause. Now, huffing sir, what's your name?

Hem. What's that to you, sir?

Clause. It shall be, ere we part.

Hem. My name is Hemskirk.
I follow the earl, which you shall feel.

Clause. No threatening,
For we shall cool you, sir. Why didst thou basely
Attempt the murder of the merchant Goswin?

Hem. What power hast thou to ask me?

Clause. I will know it,
Or flay thee till thy pain discover it.

[m] *You know*] Old eds. "*You* shall *know*". The Editors of 1778 very properly threw out "shall", seeing that it "had been copied by mistake from the preceding line." Weber, however, replaced it in the text.

[n] *fellow*] Old eds. "fellowes" and "fellows".

Hem. He did me wrong, base wrong.
Clause. That cannot save you.
Who sent you hither? and what further villanies
Have you in hand?
Hem. Why wouldst thou know? what profit,
If I had any private way, could rise
Out of my knowledge, to do thee commodity º?
Be sorry for what thou hast done, and make amends, fool:
I'll talk no further to thee, nor these rascals.
Clause. Tie him to that tree.   [*They tie him to a tree.*
Hem. I have told you whom I follow.
Clause. The devil you should do, by your villanies.—
Now he that has the best way, wring it from him.
Hig. I undertake it. Turn him to the sun, boys:
Give me a fine sharp rush.—Will you confess yet?
Hem. Ye have robb'd me already; now you'll murder me.
Hig. Murder your nose a little. Does your head purge, sir?
To it again; 'twill do you good.
Hem. Oh,
I cannot tell you any thing!
Clause. Proceed, then.   [*To* HIGGEN.
Hig. There's maggots in your nose; I'll fetch 'em out, sir.
Hem. Oh, my head breaks!
Hig. The best thing for the rheum, sir,
That falls into your worship's eyes.
Hem. Hold, hold!
Clause. Speak, then.
Hem. I know not what.
Hig. It lies in 's brain yet;
In lumps it lies: I'll fetch it out the finest!
What pretty faces the fool makes! heigh!
Hem. Hold,
Hold, and I'll tell ye all! Look in my doublet,
And there, within the lining, in a paper,
You shall find all.
Clause. Go fetch that paper hither,
And let him loose for this time. [*They untie him.—Exit* FERRET.

º *commodity*] i.e. benefit.

Enter HUBERT *disguised as before.*

Hub. Good even, my honest friends.
Clause. Good even, good fellow.
Hub. May a poor huntsman, with a merry heart,
A voice shall make the forest ring about him,
Get leave to live amongst ye ? true as steel, boys;
That knows all chases, and can watch all hours,
And with my quarter-staff, though the devil bid stand,
Deal such an alms shall make him roar again;
Prick ye the fearful hare through cross-ways, sheep-walks,
And force the crafty Reynard climb the quicksets;
Rouse ye the lofty stag, and with my bell-horn
Ring him a knell, that all the woods shall mourn him,
Till, in his funeral tears, he fall before me?
The pole-cat, martern [p], and the rich-skinn'd lucern [q],
I know to chase; the roe, the wind outstripping;
Isgrin [r] himself, in all his bloody anger,
I can beat from the bay; and the wild sounder [s]

[p] *martern*] Or *marten*,—" a large species of the weesel, the fur of which is held in high estimation." *Ed.* 1778.

[q] *lucern*] " This animal is nearly the size of a wolf. It is covered with an exceeding rich fur, the colour between red and brown, and something mailed like a cat, intermixed with black spots." *Ed.* 1778. " A luzarne. *Loup cervier.*" Cotgrave's *Dict.*

[r] *Isyrin*] Silently altered to " Isgrim " by the Editors of 1778 ; and so Weber. " The reader need not be told that Isgrim, or Isengrin, is the name of the wolf, and Reynard that of the fox, in the romance which bears the name of the latter, and which has now enjoyed an uninterrupted popularity for six centuries past." WEBER.

[s] *and the wild sounder*
Single, and with my arm'd staff turn the boar, &c.] Seward, according to " the only dictionary in which he could find the word," explained " *sounder*" to be another term for wild boar ; and so his successors : he also, because " the mention of both in the same sentence was a tautology," preposterously altered the passage thus,—
" *and the wild sounder*
Single, and with my boar-staff arm'd, thus *turn,*" &c.
But "*sounder*" is—a herd of wild swine : " To beginne," says Turbervile, " with the termes that are proper for the companies of beasts : you shall vnderstand that Huntsmen vse to saye, *An Heard of Harts* and *Hindes, Buckes* and *Does ; and A Trippe of Gotes* and *Geates ; A beauie of Rowes; A Sounder of Swine,*" &c. *The Noble Art of Venerie,* &c., 1611, p. 237 : and " *single the wild sounder*" means—separate or divide the wild sounder : Turbervile (speaking of the hart) tells us, " When he is hunted, and doth first leaue the heard, we say that he is

Single, and with my arm'd staff turn the boar,
Spite of his foamy tushes, and thus strike him,
Till he fall down my feast.
>   *Clause.* A goodly fellow!
>   *Hub.* What mak'st thou here, ha? [*Aside.*
>   *Clause.* We accept thy fellowship.
>   *Hub.* Hemskirk, thou art not right, I fear; I fear thee.
>   [*Aside.*

>   *Re-enter* FERRET, *with a paper.*

>   *Fer.* Here is the paper; and, as he said, we found it.
>   *Clause.* Give me it.—I shall make a shift yet, old as I am,
To find your knavery. [*Reads*] You are sent here, sirrah,
To discover certain gentlemen, a spy-knave,
And, if ye find 'em, if not by persuasion
To bring 'em back, by poison to despatch 'em.
>   *Hub.* By poison! ha! [*Aside.*
>   *Clause.* Here is another, Hubert:
What is that Hubert, sir?
>   *Hem.* You may perceive there.
>   *Clause.* I may perceive a villany, and a rank one.
Was he join'd partner of thy knavery?
>   *Hem.* No;
He had an honest end (would I had [t] had so!);
Which makes him scape such cut-throats.
>   *Clause.* So it seems;
For here thou art commanded, when that Hubert
Has done his best and worthiest service this way,
To cut his throat; for here he's set down dangerous.
>   *Hub.* This is most impious. [*Aside.*
>   *Clause.* I am glad we have found you.
Is not this true?

Singled or *emprymed.*" *Ibid.,* p. 244: compare also a passage in Sir P. Sidney's *Arcadia;*

" Deadlie wounds inward bleed; each sleight sore mattereth;
    Hardlie they heard [herd] which by good hunters *singled* be."
                                                    Lib. i. p. 74. ed. 1598.

Nares (*Gloss.* in v. *Sounder*), having missed the meaning of "*single,*" proposed, very unnecessarily, to read,
            " from *the wild sounder*
        Single," &c.

[t] *had*] So the 4to and the second folio.—The first folio " have ".

Hem. Yes; what are you the better?
Clause. You shall perceive, sir, ere you get your freedom.—
Take him aside.—And, friend, we take thee to us,
Into our company. Thou dar'st be true unto us?
Hig. Ay, and obedient too?
Hub. As you had bred me.
Clause. Then, take our hand; thou art now a servant to
us.——
Welcome him, all.
Hig. Stand off, stand off: I'll do it.—
We bid you welcome three ways; first, for your person,
Which is a promising person; next, for your quality [t],
Which is a decent and a gentle quality;
Last, for the frequent means you have to feed us:
You can steal, 'tis to be presum'd?
Hub. Yes, venison,
Or, if I want—— [u]
Hig. 'Tis well; you understand right,
And shall practise [v] daily. You can drink too?
Hub. Soundly.
Hig. And you dare know a woman from a weather-cock?
Hub. Yes, if I handle her.
Clause. Now swear him [w].
Hig. I crown thy nab [x] with a gage of bene-bowse,

[t] *quality*] i.e. occupation.

[u] *Or, if I want*—] So the first folio and the 4to.—The second folio " And *if* you *want*—— "; and so Seward.

[v] *practise*] So the second folio.—The first folio and the 4to "learne"; and so Weber.

[w] *Now swear him*] " There is here a great confusion in the first folio [and in the 4to]. The " stalling" of Hubert and the subsequent explanation of the cant terms are transferred from the present place to the end of the speech of Hubert, on page 65,

'Be not so stubborn : I shall swinge you soundly,
An you play tricks with me';—

and the words of Clause, " *Now swear him* ", are there repeated. The present regulation was introduced into the second folio, and proves what has been asserted before, that considerable pains were taken with that edition, and that manuscripts of the plays were on many occasions consulted ". WEBER.

[x] *I crown thy nab* &c.] " i.e. literally,—'I crown thy head with a quart-pot of good drink, and ordain thee by the beggars' oath (—" *Salomon*, a altar or masse." *Cant terms* at the end of Harman's *Caveat for Common Cursetors*, ed. 1573—)

And stall thee by the salmon into the clowes;
To maund on the pad, and strike all the cheats,
To mill from the ruffmans commission and slates,
Twang dells i' the strommel, and let the queer-cuffin
And harmanbecks trine, and trine to the ruffin!
Clause. Now interpret this unto him.
Hig. I pour on thy pate a pot of good ale,
And by the rogues' oath a rogue thee instal;
To beg on the way, to rob all thou meets,
To steal from the hedge both the shirt and the sheets,
And lie with thy wench in the straw till she twang,
Let the constable, justice, and devil go hang!—
You are welcome, brother!
All. Welcome, welcome, welcome!—
But who shall have the keeping of this fellow?
Hub. Thank ye, friends:
And I beseech ye, if ye dare ʸ but trust me

into the company of rogues; to beg on the road, and rob all you meet, to steal from the hedges shirt and sheets, lie with maids (see note on "*dells,*" p. 25) in the straw, and let the justice and constables hang, and go to the devil!' Old eds. have "gag", "benbouse", "stiromell", and "Herman (and Hermon) Beck strine": the spelling of these words was rectified by the Editors of 1778; who also printed "salomon", but unnecessarily, for we find in the *Canting Rithmes* in Dekker's *English Villanies,* &c. sig. N. 3. ed. 1632,

'Cyarum, by *Salmon,* and thou shalt pek my jere.'"
WEBER (the note altered)

At the commencement of this speech, Higgen is supposed to empty the pot of drink on Hubert's head: "This done, the Grand Signior called for a *Gage* of *Bowse,* which belike signified a quart of drinke; for presently a pot of Ale being put into his hand, hee made the yong Squire kneele downe, and, powring the full pot on his pate, vttered these wordes, 'I doe stall thee,'" &c. Dekker's *Belman of London,* &c. sig. C. ed. 1608.

ʸ All. *Welcome, welcome, welcome!—*
But who shall have the keeping of this fellow?
Hub. Thank ye, friends:
And I beseech ye, if ye dare, &c.] So the first folio and the 4to.—The second folio;
  "*All.* Welcom, welcom, welcom, but who shall have the keeping
  Of this fellow?
  Hub. Sir, if you dare," &c.
and so Seward.—The Editors of 1778 printed;
  "*All.* Welcome, welcome, welcome!
  Hub. Thank ye, friends.
  Clause. But who shall have the keeping of this fellow?
  Hub. I do beseech ye, if ye dare", &c.

(For I[z] have kept wild dogs and beasts for wonder,
And made 'em tame too), give into my custody
This roaring rascal: I shall hamper him,
With all his knacks and knaveries, and, I fear me,
Discover yet a further villany in him:
Oh, he smells rank o' the rascal!
   Clause. Take him to thee;
But, if he scape——
   Hub. Let me be even hang'd for him.—
Come [a], sir, I 'll tie you to my leash.
   Hem. Away, rascal!
   Hub. Be not so stubborn: I shall swinge you soundly,
An you play tricks with me.
   Clause. So, now come in:
But ever have an eye, sir, to your prisoner.
   Hub. He must blind both mine eyes, if he get from me.
   Clause. Go, get some victuals and some drink, some good
        drink;
For this day we 'll keep holy to good fortune.
Come, and be frolic with us.
   Hig. You are a stranger, brother; I pray, lead;
You must, you must, brother [b].   [*Exeunt.*

SCENE IV.—*Bruges. A room in the house of* VANDUNK.

Enter GOSWIN *and* GERTRUDE.

   Gert. Indeed you 're welcome: I have heard your scape;
And therefore give her leave, that only loves you,
Truly and dearly loves you, give her joy leave
To bid you welcome. What is 't makes you sad, man?

But, as Weber remarks, Clause would not ask who should have the keeping of Hemskirk, the power to determine it being in himself.
  [z] *For I*] Old eds. " *For if I.*"
  [a] *Come*] So the second folio.—The first folio and the 4to " Roome ".
  [b] *You are a stranger, brother; I pray, lead;
You must, you must, brother*] So the second folio.—The first folio and the 4to have merely " *Ye are a stranger* ".

Why do you look so wild? is't I offend you?
Beshrew my heart, not willingly.
   Gos. No, Gertrude.
   Gert. Is't the delay of that you long have look'd for,—
A happy marriage? Now I come to urge it;
Now when you please to finish it.
   Gos. No news yet?   [*Aside.*
   Gert. Do you hear, sir?
   Gos. Yes.
   Gert. Do you love me?
   Gos. Have I liv'd
In all the happiness fortune could seat me,
In all men's fair opinions——   [*Aside.*
   Gert. I have provided
A priest, that's ready for us.
   Gos. And can the devil,
In one ten days, that devil Chance, devour me?   [*Aside.*
   Gert. We'll fly to what place you please.
   Gos. No star prosperous?
All at a swoop?   [*Aside.*
   Gert. You do not love me, Goswin;
You will not look upon me.
   Gos. Can men's prayers,
Shot up to Heaven with such a zeal as mine are,
Fall back like lazy mists, and never prosper?
Gyves I must wear, and cold must be my comfort;
Darkness, and want of meat. Alas, she weeps too!
Which is the top of all my sorrows [*Aside*].—Gertrude!
   Gert. No, no, you will not know me; my poor beauty,
Which has been worth your eyes——
   Gos. The time grows on still;
And, like a tumbling wave, I see my ruin
Come rolling over me.   [*Aside.*
   Gert. Yet will you know me?
   Gos. For a hundred thousand crowns——   [*Aside.*
   Gert. Yet will you love me?
Tell me but how I have deserv'd your slighting?
   Gos. For a hundred thousand crowns——   [*Aside.*
   Gert. Farewell, dissembler!—

Gos. Of which I have scarce ten! oh, how it starts me!
[*Aside.*
Gert. And may the next you love, hearing my ruin——
Gos. I had forgot myself. Oh, my best Gertrude,
Crown of my joys and comforts!
Gert. Sweet, what ail [b] you?
I thought you had been vex'd with me.
Gos. My mind, wench,
My mind, o'erflow'd with sorrow, sunk my memory.
Gert. Am I not worthy of the knowledge of it?
And cannot I as well affect your sorrows
As your delights? You love no other woman?
Gos. No, I protest.
Gert. You have no ships lost lately?
Gos. None that I know of.
Gert. I hope you have spilt no blood, whose innocence
May lay this on your conscience.
Gos. Clear, by Heaven!
Gert. Why should you be thus, then?
Gos. Good Gertrude, ask not;
Even by the love you bear me.
Gert. I am obedient.
Gos. Go in, my fair; I will not be long from you—
Nor long, I fear me [c], with thee [*Aside*].—At my return,
Dispose me as you please.
Gert. The good gods guide you! [*Exit.*
Gos. Now for myself [d], which is the least I hope for,
And, when that fails, for man's worst fortune, pity! [*Exit.*

[b] *what ail*] So the first folio and the 4to.—The second folio "*what* ails"; and so the modern editors: but the other reading is the more usual phraseology of the time.

[c] *me*] Weber chose to omit this word.

[d] *myself*] Heath would read "his help," i. e. "the help promised him by Clause, upon which, it was plain by what Goswin had said at the end of the second scene of this act, he had very little dependence." *MS. Notes.* But the old text is, I think, right.

ACT IV.

SCENE I.—*Bruges. The Exchange.*

Enter Goswin *and four* Merchants.

Gos. Why, gentlemen, 'tis but a week more I entreat you,
But seven short days; I am not running from ye;
Nor, if you give me patience, is it possible
All my adventures fail. You have ships abroad
Endure the beating both of wind and [e] weather:
I am sure 'twould vex your hearts to be protested:
Ye are all fair merchants.

First Mer. Yes, and must have fair play;
There is no living here else: one hour's failing
Fails us of all our friends, of all our credits.
For my part, I would stay, but my wants tell me,
I must wrong others in 't.

Gos. No mercy in ye?

Sec. Mer. 'Tis foolish to depend on others' mercy:
Keep yourself right, and even cut your cloth, sir,
According to your calling. You have liv'd here
In lord-like prodigality, high, and open,
And now you find what 'tis: the liberal spending
The summer of your youth, which you should glean in,
And, like the labouring ant, make use and gain of,
Has brought this bitter stormy winter on you,
And now you cry.

Third Mer. Alas, before your poverty,
We were no men, of no mark, no endeavour!
You stood alone, took up all trade, all business
Running through your hands, scarce a sail at sea
But loaden with your goods: we, poor weak pedlars,
When by your leave, and much entreaty to it,
We could have stowage for a little cloth
Or a few wines, put off [f], and thank['d] your worship.

---

[e] *and*] So the second folio.—The first folio and the 4to "or".
[f] *put off*] "i. e. pulled off our hats." Mason.

Lord, how the world's chang'd with you! Now, I hope, sir,
We shall have sea-room.

Gos. Is my misery
Become my scorn too? have ye no humanity?
No part of men left? are all the bounties in me
To you, and to the town, turn'd my reproaches?

Fourth Mer. Well, get your moneys ready: 'tis but two hours;
We shall protest you else, and suddenly.

Gos. But two days!

First Mer. Not an hour. You know the hazard.
[*Exeunt* Merchants.

Gos. How soon my light's put out! Hard-hearted Bruges!
Within thy walls may never honest merchant
Venture his fortunes more! Oh, my poor wench too!

Enter CLAUSE.

Clause. Good fortune, master!

Gos. Thou mistak'st me, Clause;
I am not worth thy blessing.

Clause. Still a sad man?
No belief, gentle master?—Come, bring it in, then.—

Enter HIGGEN *and* PRIG, *disguised as porters, bringing in bags of money.*

And now believe your beadsman.

Gos. Is this certain?
Or dost thou work upon my troubled sense?

Clause. 'Tis gold, sir;
Take it, and try it.

Gos. Certainly, 'tis treasure.
Can there be yet this blessing?

Clause. Cease your wonder:
You shall not sink for ne'er a sous'd flap-dragon [g],
For ne'er a pickled pilcher [h] of 'em all, sir.

---

[g] *flap-dragon*] Was a raisin, a plum, &c. (and sometimes even the end of a candle), made to float in a shallow dish, or glass, of brandy or other liquor, from which, when set on fire, it was to be snatched by the mouth, and swallowed.

[h] *pilcher*] i. e. pilchard.

'Tis there; your full sum, a hundred thousand crowns:
And, good sweet master, now be merry. Pay 'em,
Pay the poor pelting [h] knaves that know no goodness;
And cheer your heart up handsomely.
   Gos. Good Clause,
How cam'st thou by this mighty sum? if naughtily,
I must not take it of thee; 'twill undo me.
   Clause. Fear not; you have it by as honest means
As though your father gave it. Sir, you know not
To what a mass the little we get daily,
Mounts in seven years: we beg it for Heaven's charity,
And to the same good we are bound to render it.
   Gos. What great security?
   Clause. Away with that, sir!
Were not you more than all the men in Bruges,
And all the money, in my thoughts——
   Gos. But, good Clause,
I may die presently.
   Clause. Then this dies with you.
Pay when you can, good master; I'll no parchments:
Only this charity I shall entreat you,—
Leave me this ring.
   Gos. Alas, it is too poor, Clause!
   Clause. 'Tis all I ask; and this withal, that when
I shall deliver this back, you shall grant me
Freely one poor petition.
   Gos. There; I confirm [i] it;   [*Gives ring.*
And may my faith forsake me when I shun it!
   Clause. Away! your time draws on.—Take up the money,
And follow this young gentleman.
   Gos. Farewell, Clause,
And may thy honest memory live ever!
   Clause. Heaven bless you, and still keep you! farewell,
     master.
           [*Exeunt, on one side,* Goswin, Higgen, *and* Prig;
              on the other, Clause.

---

  [h] *pelting*] i.e. paltry, contemptible.
  [i] *confirm*] So the second folio.—The first folio and the 4to "confesse."

SCENE II.—*The woods near Bruges.*

Enter HUBERT, *disguised as before.*

Hub. I have lock'd my youth up, close enough for gadding,
In an old tree, and set watch over him.

Enter MINCHE [j].

Now for my love, for sure this wench must be she;
She follows me [*Aside*].—Come hither, pretty Minche.
Minche. No, no, you 'll kiss.
Hub. So I will.
Minche. I' deed, la!
How will you kiss me, pray you?
Hub. Thus [*Kisses her*]—Soft as my love's lips! [*Aside.*
Minche. Oh!
Hub. What's your father's name?
Minche. He's gone to heaven.
Hub. Is it not Gerrard, sweet?
Minche. I 'll stay no longer:
My mother's an old woman, and my brother
Was drown'd at sea with catching cockles.—Oh, love!
Oh, how my heart melts in me! how thou fir'st me! [*Aside.*
Hub. 'Tis certain she [*Aside*].—Pray, let me see your hand,
  sweet.
Minche. No, no, you 'll bite it.
Hub. Sure, I should know that gimmal [k].
Minche. 'Tis certain he: I had forgot my ring too.
Oh, Hubert, Hubert! [*Aside.*
Hub. Ha! methought she nam'd me.— [*Aside.*
Do you know me, chick?
Minche. No, indeed; I never saw you;
But, methinks, you kiss finely.
Hub. Kiss again, then.—
By Heaven, 'tis she! [*Aside.*

---

[j] *Minche*] See note, p. 19.

[k] *gimmal*] i. e. a sort of double ring, curiously constructed (*Gimmal* rings, though originally double, were also made triple, and even quadruple; yet the name remained unchanged). See Nares's *Gloss.* in. v.

Minche. Oh, what a joy he brings me! [*Aside.*
Hub. You are not Minche?
Minche. Yes, pretty gentleman;
And I must be married to-morrow to a capper[1].
Hub. Must you, my sweet? and does the capper love you?
Minche. Yes, yes; he'll give me pie, and look in mine eyes thus.——
'Tis he; 'tis my dear love! oh, blest fortune! [*Aside.*
Hub. How fain she would conceal herself, yet shew[s] it!— [*Aside.*
Will you love me, and leave that man? I'll serve—[m]
Minche. Oh, I shall lose myself! [*Aside.*
Hub. I'll wait upon you,
And make you dainty nosegays.
Minche. And where will you stick 'em?
Hub. Here in thy bosom; and[n] make a crown of lilies
For your fair head.
Minche. And will you love me, 'deed la?
Hub. With all my heart.
Minche. Call me to-morrow, then,
And we'll have brave cheer, and go to church together.
Give you good even, sir.
Hub. But one word, fair Minche!
Minche. I must be gone a-milking.
Hub. You shall presently.
Did you never hear of a young maid call'd Jacqueline?
Minche. I am discover'd [*Aside*].—Hark in your ear; I'll tell you:
You must not know me; kiss, and be constant ever.
Hub. Heaven curse me else! [*Exit* JACQUELINE.
'Tis she; and now I am certain
They are all here. · Now for my other project! [*Exit.*

---

[1] *a capper*] "One who makes or sells caps." *Ed.* 1778 (from Johnson's *Dict.*).
[m] *I'll serve*—] "So the old eds. The modern copies, '*I'll serve* you.'" WEBER.
[n] *in thy bosom; and*] The first folio and the 4to " *in bosome, and.*"—The second folio " *in* my *bosom,* Sweet*, and.*"—The modern editors print "*in thy bosom,* sweet ; *and.*"

SCENE III.—*Bruges.*—*The Exchange.*

Enter GOSWIN, *four* Merchants; HIGGEN *and* PRIG, *disguised as before, with bags of money.*

First Mer. Nay, if 'twould do you courtesy—
Gos. None at all, sir:
Take it, 'tis yours; there's your ten thousand for you;
Give in my bills.—Your sixteen.
Third Mer. Pray, be pleas'd, sir,
To make a further use.
Gos. No.
Third Mer. What I have, sir,
You may command. Pray, let me be your servant.
Gos. Put your hats on: I care not for your courtesies;
They are most untimely done, and no truth in 'em.
Sec. Mer. I have a fraught ° of pepper——
Gos. Rot your pepper!
Shall I trust you again? There's your seven thousand.
Fourth Mer. Or, if you want fine sugar, 'tis but sending.
Gos. No, I can send to Barbary; those people,
That never yet knew faith, have nobler freedoms.—
These carry to Vanlock, and take my bills in;
To Peter Zuten these; bring back my jewels.—
Why are these pieces? [*Guns fired within.*

Enter Sailor.

Sail. Health to the noble merchant!
The Susan is return'd.
Gos. Well?
Sail. Well, and rich, sir,
And now put in.
Gos. Heaven, thou hast heard my prayers!
Sail. The brave Rebecca too, bound from the Straits,
With the next tide is ready to put after.
Gos. What news o' the fly-boat?

° *fraught*] So the 4to; and so Seward.—Both the folios "frought."—The Editors of 1778 and Weber "freight."

Sail. If this wind hold till midnight,
She will be here, and wealthy; escap'd[p] fairly.
  Gos. How, prithee, sailor?
  Sail. Thus, sir: she had fight,
Seven hours together, with six Turkish galleys,
And she fought bravely, but at length was boarded,
And overlaid with strength; when presently
Comes boring up the wind Captain Vannoke,
That valiant gentleman you redeem'd from prison:
He knew the boat, set in, and fought it bravely;
Beat all the galleys off, sunk three, redeem'd her,
And, as a service to you, sent her home, sir.
  Gos. An honest noble captain, and a thankful!
There's for thy news: go, drink the merchant's health, sailor.
        [*Gives money.*
  Sail. I thank your bounty, and I'll do it to a doit, sir.
        [*Exit.*
  First Mer. What miracles are pour'd upon this fellow!
  Gos. This year, I hope, my friends, I shall scape prison,
For all your cares to catch me.
  Sec. Mer. You may please, sir,
To think of your poor servants in displeasure,
Whose all they have, goods, moneys, are at your service.
  Gos. I thank you;
When I have need of you, I shall forget you.
You are paid, I hope?
  Merchants. We joy in your good fortunes. [*Exeunt.*

                Enter VANDUNK.

  Vand. Come, sir, come, take your ease; you must go
          home with me;
Yonder is one weeps and howls.
  Gos. Alas, how does she?
  Vand. She will be better soon, I hope.
  Gos. Why soon, sir?

---

[p] *escap'd*] Old eds. "scap't" and "'scap'd."—The modern editors silently print, for the metre, "she 'scap'd": but, though our poets generally write "scape" and "scap'd", they sometimes have "*escape*" (as at p. 93 l. 21) and "*escap'd*" (as at p. 10 l. 7).

Vand. Why, when you have her in your arms: this night,
   my boy,
She is thy wife.
   Gos. With all my heart I take her.
   Vand. We have prepar'd; all thy friends will be there,
And all my rooms shall smoke to see the revel.
Thou hast been wrong'd, and no more shall my service
Wait on the knave her uncle: I have heard all,
All his baits for my boy; but thou shalt have her.
Hast thou despatch'd thy business?
   Gos. Most.
   Vand. By the mass, boy,
Thou tumblest now in wealth, and I joy in it;
Thou art the best boy that Bruges ever nourish'd.
Thou hast been sad: I'll cheer thee up with sack,
And, when thou art lusty, I'll fling thee to thy mistress:
She'll hug thee, sirrah.
   Gos. I long to see it.—
I had forgot you: there's for you, my friends;
         [*To* HIGGEN *and* PRIG, *giving them money.*
You had but heavy burdens. Commend my love
To [Clause]; my best love, all the love I have [q],
To honest Clause; shortly I will thank him better.
                     [*Exit with* VANDUNK.
   Hig. By the mass, a royal merchant! gold by the handful!
Here will be sport soon, Prig.
   Prig. It partly seems so;
And here will I be in a trice.
   Hig. And I, boy.
Away apace! we are look'd for.

<blockquote>
q   *Commend my love*
   To [Clause]; my best love, all the love I have, &c.] Seward printed;
         '*Commend my love,*
   Commend *my best love, all the love I have,*" &c.
The Editors of 1778 gave;
         '*Commend my love*
   To my best friend, *my best love, all the love I have,*' &c.
Weber thus;
         "*Commend my love,*
   My best love, all the love I have," &c.
</blockquote>

Prig. Oh, these bak'd meats!
Methinks I smell them hither.
Hig. Thy mouth waters. [*Exeunt.*

SCENE IV.—*The woods near Bruges.*

Enter HUBERT *disguised as before, and* HEMSKIRK.

Hub. I must not.
Hem. Why? 'tis in thy power to do it,
And in mine to reward thee to thy wishes.
Hub. I dare not, nor I will not.
Hem. Gentle huntsman,
Though thou hast kept me hard, though in thy duty,
Which is requir'd to do it, thou'st us'd me stubbornly,
I can forgive thee freely.
Hub. You the earl's servant?
Hem. I swear, I am near as his own thoughts to him;
Able to do thee——
Hub. Come, come, leave your prating.
Hem. If thou dar'st but try——
Hub. I thank you heartily; you will be
The first man that will hang me; a sweet recompense!
I could do ['t] (but I do not say I will)
To any honest fellow that would think on 't,
And be a benefactor.
Hem. If it be not recompens'd, and to thy own desires;
If, within these ten days, I do not make thee——
Hub. What? a false knave?
Hem. Prithee, prithee, conceive me rightly; any thing
Of profit or of place that may advance thee——
Hub. Why, what a goosecap wouldst thou make me! do
not I know
That men in misery will promise any thing,
More than their lives can reach at?
Hem. Believe me, huntsman,
There shall not one short[r] syllable that comes from me pass
Without its full performance.

---

[r] *short*] Perhaps this word was foisted in by the transcriber or printer. Seward took his usual liberties with the passage.

Hub. Say you so, sir?
Have you e'er a good place for my quality[s]?
Hem. A thousand; chases, forests, parks; I'll make thee
Chief ranger over all the games.
Hub. When?
Hem. Presently.
Hub. This may provoke me: and yet, to prove a knave
too——
Hem. 'Tis to prove honest; 'tis to do good service,
Service for him thou art sworn to, for thy prince:
Then, for thyself that good. What fool would live here,
Poor, and in misery, subject to all dangers
Law and lewd[t] people can inflict, when bravely,
And to himself, he may be law and credit?
Hub. Shall I believe thee?
Hem. As that thou hold'st most holy.
Hub. You may play tricks.
Hem. Then let me never live more.
Hub. Then you shall see, sir, I will do a service
That shall deserve indeed.
Hem. 'Tis well said, huntsman,
And thou shalt be well thought of.
Hub. I will do it:
'Tis not your setting[u] free, for that's mere nothing,
But such a service, if the earl be noble,
He shall for ever love me.
Hem. What is't, huntsman?
Hub. Do you know any of these people live here?
Hem. No.
Hub. You are a fool, then: here be those, to have 'em,
I know the earl so well, would make him caper.
Hem. Any of the old lords that rebell'd?
Hub. Peace! all:
I know 'em every one, and can betray 'em.
Hem. But wilt thou do this service?
Hub. If you'll keep
Your faith and free word to me.

---

[s] *my quality*] i. e. (as before, p. 63) my occupation, a person of my occupation (a huntsman).   [t] *lewd*] Equivalent here to—rude, barbarous.

[u] *setting*] So the second folio.—The first folio and the 4to "letting"; and so the Editors of 1778 and Weber.

Hem. Wilt thou swear me?
Hub. No, no, I will believe you. More than that too,
Here's the right heir.
Hem. Oh, honest, honest huntsman!
Hub. Now, how to get these gallants, there's the matter.
You will be constant? 'tis no work for me else.
Hem. Will the sun shine again?
Hub. The way to get 'em!
Hem. Propound it, and it shall be done.
Hub. No slight [v]
(For they are devilish crafty, it concerns 'em),
Nor reconcilement [w] (for they dare not trust neither),
Must do this trick.
Hem. By force?
Hub. Ay, that must do it;
And with the person of the earl himself:
Authority, and mighty, must come on 'em,
Or else in vain: and thus I would have you do it.
To-morrow night be here; a hundred men will bear 'em,
So he be there, for he's both wise and valiant,
And with his terror will strike dead their forces:
The hour be twelve o'clock: now, for a guide
To draw ye without danger on these persons,
The woods being thick and hard to hit, myself,
With some few with me, made unto our purpose,
Beyond the wood, upon the plain, will wait ye
By the great oak.
Hem. I know it. Keep thy faith, huntsman,
And such a shower of wealth——
Hub. I warrant you:
Miss nothing that I tell you.
Hem. No.
Hub. Farewell.
You have your liberty; now use it wisely,
And keep your hour. Go closer [x] about the wood there,
For fear they spy you.
Hem. Well.

[v] *slight*] i.e. artifice.
[w] *reconcilement*] "i. e. *pretended* reconcilement." *Ed.* 1778.
[x] *closer*] Silently altered to "close" by the Editors of 1778; and so Weber.

Hub. And bring no noise with you.
Hem. All shall be done to the purpose. Farewell, huntsman. [*Exeunt severally.*

SCENE V.—*Another part of the woods.*

Enter CLAUSE, HIGGEN, PRIG, GINKS, SNAP, *and* FERRET.

Clause. Now, what's the news in town?
Ginks. No news, but joy, sir;
Every man wooing of the noble merchant,
Who has [y] his hearty commendations to you.
Fer. Yes, this is news; this night he's to be married.
Ginks. By the mass, that's true; he marries Vandunk's daughter,
The dainty black-ey'd dell [z].
Hig. I would my clapper [a]
Hung in his baldrick [b]! what [c] a peal could I ring!

---

[y] *has*] Altered to " sends " by Seward, who thought that, with the old reading, the sentence was imperfect!

[z] *dell*] See note, p. 25. The correction of Theobald and Sympson, approved by Mason, who observes that " Ginks [though a nobleman in disguise] conforms to the language of his assumed profession."—Old eds. " bell ".—The Editors of 1778 and Weber print " belle ".

[a] *clapper*]—Used here with a quibble—was the cover of the *clap-dish* or *clack-dish*, which was carried by sturdy beggars for the purpose of receiving alms, and which they opened and shut with a loud clap to excite the pity of the charitable or the fear of the hard-hearted. Weber, in a note on this passage, wrongly explains the *clapper* to be the *clap-dish* itself; but he afterwards rightly observes that the *clap-dish* was originally appropriated to lepers (—see Gifford's note on Massinger's *Works*, ii. 257, ed. 1813—), and adds, " upon the continent, I have frequently seen old women come out of alms-houses on the road (which probably were once allotted to lepers), with such dishes, striking the cover down, and begging for their hospitals ". Nares (*Gloss.* in v.) says, that a sort of *clap-dish* is still used on particular days by a society of widows, who subsist in alms-houses, without the gate of York called *Mickle-gate Bar*.—(In an earlier note on this play, p. 21, I have expressed myself with seeming inaccuracy in stating that the *clap-dish* " was perhaps originally carried by the *Clapper-dudgeon*" : I meant to say, that, *after it had been borrowed by the beggars from the lepers*, it was perhaps first carried by the *Clapper-dudgeon*.)

[b] *baldrick*] i. e. belt.

[c] *what*] So the first folio and the 4to.—The second folio " a *what*."—The modern editors " ah, *what*."

Clause. Married!

Ginks. 'Tis very true, sir. Oh, the pies,
The piping-hot mince-pies!

Prig. Oh, the plum-pottage!

Hig. For one leg of a goose now would I venture a limb,
  boys:
I love a fat goose, as I love allegiance;
And, [pox [c]] upon the boors, too well they know it,
And therefore starve their poultry.

Clause. To be married
To Vandunk's daughter! [*Aside.*

Hig. Oh, this precious merchant!
What sport he will have! But, hark you, brother Prig;
Shall we do nothing in the foresaid [d] wedding?
There's money to be got, and meat, I take it:
What think you of a morris?

Prig. No, by no means;
That goes no further than the street, there leaves us:
Now, we must think of something that must [e] draw us
Into the bowels of it, into the buttery,
Into the kitchen, into the cellar; something
That that old drunken burgomaster loves:
What think you of a wassail [f]?

Hig. I think worthily.

Prig. And very fit it should be: thou, and Ferret,
And Ginks, to sing the song; I for the structure,
Which is the bowl.

Hig. Which must be upsey-English[g],
Strong lusty London beer. Let's think more of it.

Clause. He must not marry. [*Aside.*

Enter HUBERT, *disguised as before.*

Hub. By your leave, in private,
One word, sir, with you. Gerrard! do not start me[h]:

  [c] [*pox*] A break here in the old eds.

  [d] *foresaid*] "Modern editors read 'aforesaid'." WEBER.

  [e] *must*] Silently altered to "may" by Seward; and so his successors.

  [f] *a wassail*] i. e. a merry-making with the *wassail-bowl* (see note, vol. ii. 100) and singing (see the following speeches).

  [g] *upsey-English*] See note, p. 44.

  [h] *do not start me*] "Mr. Seward, concurring with Mr. Theobald in opinion,

I know you, and he knows you, that best loves you:
Hubert speaks to you, and you must be Gerrard;
The time invites you to it.
  Clause. Make no show, then.
I am glad to see you, sir; and I am Gerrard.
How stand affairs?
  Hub. Fair, if you dare now follow.
Hemskirk I have let go, and these my causes
I 'll tell you privately, and how I have wrought him:
And then, to prove me honest to my friends,
Look upon these directions; you have seen his. [*Gives a paper.*
  Hig. Then will I speak a speech, and a brave speech,
In praise of merchants. Where's the ape?
  Prig. [Pox[i]] take him!
A gouty bear-ward[j] stole him the other day.
  Hig. May his bears worry him! That ape had paid it:
What dainty tricks,—([pox] o' that whoreson[k] bear-ward!)—
In his French doublet, with his blister'd bullions [l],
In a long stock tied up! Oh, how daintily
Would I have made him wait, and change [m] a trencher,
Carry a cup of wine! Ten thousand stinks
Wait on thy mangy hide [n], thou lousy bear-ward!
  Clause. [*To* HUBERT] 'Tis passing well; I both believe
            and joy in 't,
And will be ready. Keep you here the mean while,
And keep this in.—I must a while forsake ye:
Upon mine anger, no man stir this two hours.

---

reads, '*do not start,* MAN'. The old lection seems to us perfect sense; meaning, '*do not be alarmed* AT *me*'; as we familiarly say, '*do not fly me*', for '*do not fly* FROM *me.*' Goswin says above, speaking of his distressful situation, '*Oh, how it starts me!*' " *Ed.* 1778.

  [i] [*Pox*] Here, and in the next line but two, the old eds. have a break.

  [j] *bear-ward*] i. e. bear-keeper.

  [k] *whoreson*] So the first folio and the 4to.—The second folio "bursen"; and so Seward.

  [l] *blister'd bullions*] See note, vol. vii. 291. So the second folio.—The first folio has "baster'd (the 4to "bastar'd") *bullions*",—in consequence of which Weber gave "bastard *bullions*".

  [m] *change*] So the first folio and the 4to.—The second folio "shift"; and so Seward.

  [n] *hide*] So the second folio.—The first folio and the 4to "soule".

Hig. Not to the wedding, sir?
Clause. Not any whither.
Hig. The wedding must be seen, sir: we want meat too;
We be monstrous [n] out of meat.
Prig. Shall it be spoken,
Fat capons shak'd their tails at 's in defiance?
And turkey-tombs [o], such honourable monuments?
Shall pigs, sir, that the parson's self would envy,
And dainty ducks——
Clause. Not a word more! obey me. [*Exit.*
Hig. Why, then, come, doleful death [p]! This is flat tyranny;
And, by this hand——
Hub. What?
Hig. I'll go sleep upon't. [*Exit.*
Prig. Nay, an there be a wedding, and we wanting,
Farewell, our happy days!—We do obey, sir. [*Exeunt.*

SCENE VI.—*Bruges.*—*Before the house of* VANDUNK.

Enter two young Merchants.

First Mer. Well met, sir: you are for this lusty wedding?
Sec. Mer. I am so; so are you, I take it.
First Mer. Yes;
And it much glads me, that to do him service,
Who is the honour of our trade and lustre,
We meet thus happily.
Sec. Mer. He's a noble fellow,
And well becomes a bride of such a beauty.
First Mer. She is passing fair indeed. Long may their loves
Continue like their youths, in spring of sweetness!
All the young merchants will be here, no doubt on't;
For he that comes not to attend this wedding,

---

[n] *We be monstrous*] So the first folio and the 4to.—The second folio "*We* are horrible"; and so the modern editors.

[o] *turkey-tombs*] "i. e. turkey-pies." SEWARD.

[p] *Why, then, come, doleful death!*] A quotation, it would seem, from some play or ballad.

The curse of a most blind one fall upon him,
A loud wife, and a lazy!—Here's Vanlock.

Enter VANLOCK *and* FRANCES.

Vanl. Well overtaken, gentlemen : save ye!
First Mer. The same to you, sir.—Save you, fair Mistress
Frances!
I would this happy night might make you blush too.
Vanl. She dreams apace.
Fran. That's but a drowsy fortune.
Sec. Mer. Nay, take us with ye too ; we come to that end :
I am sure ye are for the wedding.
Vanl. Hand and heart, man,
And what these feet [q] can do ; I could have tript it
Before this whoreson gout.

Enter CLAUSE.

Clause. Bless ye, masters!
Vanl. Clause! how now, Clause? thou art come to see thy
master
(And a good master he is to all poor people)
In all his joy; 'tis honestly done of thee.
Clause. Long may he live, sir! but my business now is,
If you would please to do it, and to him too—

Enter GOSWIN.

Vanl. He's here himself.
Gos. Stand at the door, my friends!
I pray, walk in. Welcome, fair Mistress Frances!
See what the house affords : there's a young lady
Will bid you welcome.
Vanl. We joy your happiness.

---

[q] *these feet*] Mason's correction, and obviously necessary : " Vanlock means to say, that he will dance as well as his feet will permit ; but, before that whoreson gout, he could have done it nimbly."—Old eds. " their *feet* " ; and so the modern editors,—Weber pointing the passage thus,

" And what their feet can do, I could have ", &c.

and explaining " their *feet* "—" the feet of others " !

Gos. I hope it will be so.

[*Exeunt all except* GOSWIN *and* CLAUSE.

Clause, nobly welcome!
My honest, my best friend, I have been careful
To see thy moneys——
   Clause. Sir, that brought not me.
Do you know this ring again?
   Gos. Thou hadst it of me.
   Clause. And do you well remember yet the boon you gave me,
Upon return of this?
   Gos. Yes, and I grant it,
Be it what it will: ask what thou canst, I'll do it,
Within my power.
   Clause. You are not married yet?
   Gos. No.
   Clause. Faith, I shall ask you that that will disturb you;
But I must put you to your promise.
   Gos. Do;
And, if I faint and flinch in 't——
   Clause. Well said, master!
And yet it grieves me too: and yet it must be.
   Gos. Prithee, distrust me not.
   Clause. You must not marry:
That's part of the power you gave me; which to make up,
You must presently depart, and follow me.
   Gos. Not marry, Clause!
   Clause. Not, if you keep your promise,
And give me power to ask.
   Gos. Prithee, think better:
I will obey, by Heaven!
   Clause. I have thought the best, sir.
   Gos. Give me thy reason: dost thou fear her honesty?
   Clause. Chaste as the ice, for any thing I know, sir.
   Gos. Why shouldst thou light on that, then? to what purpose?
   Clause. I must not now discover.
   Gos. Must not marry!

Shall I break now, when my poor heart is pawn'd?
When all the preparation——
  Clause. Now, or never.
  Gos. Come, 'tis not that thou wouldst; thou dost but
    fright me.
  Clause. Upon my soul, it is, sir; and I bind you.
  Gos. Clause, canst thou be so cruel?
  Clause. You may break, sir;
But never more in my thoughts appear honest.
  Gos. Didst ever see her?
  Clause. No.
  Gos. She is such a thing,—
Oh, Clause, she is such a wonder! such a mirror,
For beauty and fair virtue, Europe has not!
Why hast thou made me happy to undo me?
But look upon her; then, if thy heart relent not,
I'll quit her presently.—Who waits there?
  Serv. [*within*] Sir?
  Gos. Bid my fair love come hither, and the company.—
Prithee, be good unto me: take a man's heart,
And look upon her truly; take a friend's heart,
And feel what misery must follow this.
  Clause. Take you a noble heart, and keep your promise:
I forsook all I had, to make you happy.
Can that thing, call'd a woman, stop your goodness?

    Enter GERTRUDE *and* VANDUNK, *with the* Merchants [r].

  Gos. Look, there she is: deal with me as thou wilt now:
Didst ever see a fairer?
  Clause. She is most goodly.
  Gos. Pray you, stand still.
  Gert. What ails my love?
  Gos. Didst thou ever,
By the fair light of Heaven, behold a sweeter?
Oh, that thou knew'st but love, or ever felt him!
Look well, look narrowly upon her beauties.
  First Mer. Sure, h'as some strange design in hand, he
    starts so.

---

[r] *with the Merchants*] Perhaps Vanlock and Frances ought to re-enter also.

Sec. Mer. This beggar has a strong power over his pleasure.
Gos. View all her body.
Clause. 'Tis exact and excellent.
Gos. Is she a thing, then, to be lost thus lightly?
Her mind is ten times sweeter, ten times nobler;
And but to hear her speak, a paradise;
And such a love she bears to me, a chaste love,
A virtuous, fair, and fruitful love! 'tis now too
I am ready to enjoy it; the priest ready, Clause,
To say the holy words shall make us happy:
This is a cruelty beyond man's study:
All these are ready, all our joys are ready,
And all the expectation of our friends:
'Twill be her death to do it.
   Clause. Let her die, then.
   Gos. Thou canst not; 'tis impossible.
   Clause. It must be.
   Gos. 'Twill kill me too; 'twill murder me. By Heaven, Clause,
I'll give thee half I have! come, thou shalt save me.
   Clause. Then you must go with me,—I can stay no longer,—
If you be true and noble.
   Gos. Hard heart, I'll follow!   [*Exit* CLAUSE.
Pray ye, all go in again, and, pray, be merry:
I have a weighty business—Give my cloak there!—

      Enter Servant, *with a cloak.*

Concerns my life and state—make no inquiry—
This present hour befaln me: with the soonest
I shall be here again. Nay, pray, go in, sir,
And take them with you.—'Tis but a night lost, gentlemen.
   Vand. Come, come in; we will not lose our meat yet,
Nor our good mirth; he cannot stay long from her,
I am sure of that.
   Gos. I will not stay, believe, sir.
        [*Exit* VANDUNK *with* Merchants *and* Servant.
Gertrude, a word with you.
   Gert. Why is this stop, sir?

Gos. I have no more time left me, but to kiss thee,
And tell thee this,—I am ever thine: farewell, wench. [*Exit.*
  Gert. And is that all your ceremony? is this a wedding?
Are all my hopes and prayers turn'd to nothing?
Well, I will say no more, nor sigh, nor sorrow—
Oh me [r]!—till to thy face I prove thee false. [*Exit.*

ACT V.

SCENE I.—*A plain adjoining to the woods near Bruges.*

Enter GERTRUDE *masked, and a* Boor *with a torch.*
  Gert. Lead, if thou think'st we are right. Why dost thou make
These often stands? thou said'st thou knew'st the way.
  Boor. Fear nothing; I do know it.—Would 'twere homeward!   [*Aside.*
  Gert. Wrought from me by a beggar! at the time
That most should tie him! 'Tis some other love,
That hath a more command on his affections;
And he that fetch'd him a disguisèd agent,
Not what he personated, for his fashion
Was more familiar with him, and more powerful,
Than one that ask'd an alms: I must find out
One, if not both. Kind darkness, be my shroud,
And cover love's too-curious search in me!
For yet, suspicion, I would not name thee.   [*Aside.*
  Boor. Mistress, it grows somewhat pretty and dark.
  Gert. What then?
  Boor. Nay, nothing. Do not think I am afraid,
Although perhaps you are.
  Gert. I am not. Forward!
  Boor. Sure, but you are. Give me your hand; fear nothing.
There's one leg in the wood: do not pull backward [s].

---

  [r] *Oh me*] In the second folio, this exclamation is placed at the end of the line (rightly, perhaps); and so Seward and the editors of 1778, who silently print "Ah *me!*"
  [s] *pull backward*] So the first folio and the 4to.—The second folio "*pull* me *backward*"; and so Seward.

What a sweat one on's are in, you or I!
Pray God it do not prove the plague! yet, sure,
It has infected me; for I sweat too;
It runs out at my knees: feel, feel, I pray you.
   Gert. What ails the fellow?
   Boor. Hark, hark, I beseech you!
Do you hear nothing?
   Gert. No.
   Boor. List! a wild hog;
He grunts: now 'tis a bear; this wood is full of 'em:
And now a wolf, mistress; a wolf, a wolf;
It is the howling of a wolf.
   Gert. The braying
Of an ass, is it not?
   Boor. Oh, now one has me!
Oh, my left ham!——Farewell.
   Gert. Look to your shanks;
Your breech is safe enough; the wolf's a fern-brake.
   Boor. But see, see, see! there is a serpent in it;
It has eyes as broad as platters; it spits fire;
Now it creeps towards us: help me to say my prayers:
It hath swallow'd me almost; my breath is stopt;
I cannot speak: do I speak, mistress? tell me.
   Gert. Why, thou strange [s] timorous sot, canst thou perceive
Any thing i' the bush but a poor glow-worm?
   Boor. It may be 'tis but a glow-worm now; but 'twill
Grow to a fire-drake [t] presently.
   Gert. Come thou from it.
I have a precious guide of you, and a courteous,
That gives me leave to lead myself the way thus.
   [*Within.* Holla [u] !]
   Boor. It thunders: you hear that now?
   Gert. I hear one holla.
   Boor. 'Tis thunder, thunder: see, a flash of lightning!
Are you not blasted, mistress? pull your mask off:
It has play'd the barber with me here; I have lost

---

   [s] *strange*] So the second folio.—Omitted in the first folio and the 4to.

   [t] *fire-drake*] i. e. fiery dragon, fiery serpent.

   [u] [*Within. Holla*] Not in the old eds., which have, however, later in this scene, a stage-direction, "*Holla again*".

My beard, my beard: pray God you be not shaven!
'Twill spoil your marriage, mistress.
  Gert. What strange wonders
Fear fancies in a coward!
  Boor. Now the earth opens.
  Gert. Prithee, hold thy peace.
  Boor. Will you on, then?
  Gert. Both love and jealousy have made me bold:
Where my fate leads me I must go.
  Boor. God be with you, then!   [*Exit* GERTRUDE.

    Enter WOLFORT *and* HEMSKIRK *with* Soldiers.
  Hem. It was the fellow, sure, he that should guide me,
The huntsman, that did holla us.
  Wol. Best make a stand,
And listen to his next.—Ha!
  Hem. Who goes there?
  Boor. Mistress, I am taken.
  Hem. Mistress!—Look forth, soldiers.   [*Exeunt Soldiers.*
  Wol. What are you, sirrah?
  Boor. Truly, all is left
Of a poor boor by day-light; by night, nobody.
You might have spar'd your drum, and guns, and pikes too,
For I am none that will stand out, sir, I:
You may take me in [u] with a walking-stick,
Even when you please, and hold me with a pack-thread.
  Hem. What woman was't you call'd to?
  Boor. Woman! none, sir.
  Wol. None! did you not name mistress?
  Boor. Yes, but she's
No woman yet: she should have been this night,
But that a beggar stole away her bridegroom,
Whom we were going to make hue and cry after.
I tell you true, sir; she should ha' been married to-day,
And was the bride and all; but in came Clause,
The old lame beggar, and whipt [v] up Master Goswin
Under his arm, away with him; as a kite,
Or an old fox, would swoop away a gosling.

  [u] *take me in*] i. e. conquer me.
  [v] *whipt*] So the 4to.—Both the folios " whips" ; and so the modern editors.

Re-enter Soldiers *with* GERTRUDE.

Hem. 'Tis she, 'tis she, 'tis she!—Niece!
Gert. Ha!
Hem. She, sir!
This was a noble entrance to your fortune,
That, being on the point thus to be married,
Upon her venture here, you should surprise her.
Wol. I begin, Hemskirk, to believe my fate
Works to my ends.
Hem. Yes, sir; and this adds trust
Unto the fellow our guide, who assur'd me Florez
Liv'd in some merchant's shape, as Gerrard did
I' the old beggar's, and that he would use
Him for the train ʷ to call the other forth;
All which we find is done.
[*Within.* Holla!]
Hem. That's he again.
Wol. Good we sent ˣ out to meet him.
Hem. Here's the oak.
Gert. Oh, I am miserably lost, thus faln
Into my uncle's hands from all my hopes!
No matter now ʸ, whe'r ᶻ thou be false or no,
Goswin; whether thou love another better,

ʷ *train*] Artifice, stratagem (of enticement).

ˣ *sent*] Mason would read "set".

ʸ *Oh, I am miserably lost, thus faln*
Into my uncle's hands from all my hopes!
No matter now, &c.] The first folio and the 4to, thus;
  " O I am miserably lost, thus falne
  Into my vncles hands from all my hopes,
  Can I not thinke away my selfe and dye ?
  O I am miserably lost ; thus fallen
  Into my Uncles hands, from all my hopes :
  No matter now," &c.
(the third of the lines just cited being also repeated as the concluding one of the speech). The second folio has only,—
  "I am miserably lost, thus faln
  Into my Uncles hands from all my hopes,
  Can I not think away my self and dye ?"
(the rest of the speech perhaps, as Weber suggests, having been rejected by the author on a revisal of the text); and so Seward; so too the Editors of 1778 (printing "Oh, *I am*", &c.).

ᶻ *whe'r*] "i. e. whether." WEBER.

Or me alone ; or whe'r thou keep thy vow
And word, or that thou come or stay; for I
To thee from henceforth must be ever absent,
And thou to me. No more shall we come near,
To tell ourselves how bright each other ['s] eyes were,
How soft our language, and how sweet our kisses,
Whilst we made one our food, th' other our feast ;
Not mix our souls by sight, or by a letter,
Hereafter; but as small relation have,
As two new gone to inhabiting a grave.
Can I not think away myself and die [a] ?

Enter HUBERT *disguised as before,* HIGGEN, PRIG, FERRET, SNAP,
and GINKS, *disguised as* Boors.

Hub. I like your habits well; they are safe ; stand close.
Hig. But what's the action we are for now, ha ?
Robbing a ripper [b] of his fish ?
Prig. Or taking
A poulterer prisoner, without ransom, bullies ?
Hig. Or cutting off a convoy of butter?
Fer. Or surprising a boor's ken, for grunting-cheats [c] ?

[a] *and die*] After these words the Editors of 1778 inserted "*Exeunt*" ; and so Weber. But Hemskirk has previously said (p. 90), " Here's the oak ", meaning the oak beside which Hubert had promised to meet him—

("myself,
With some few with me, made unto our purpose,
Beyond the wood, upon the plain, will wait ye
By the great oak". p. 78) ;

and he now remains at the back of the stage with his party, waiting the arrival of Hubert.

[b] *a ripper*] " *Ripper,* properly *ripier,* from the Latin *ripa,* is a word still used in the northern counties, and signifies a kind of travelling fishmonger, who carries fish from the coast, to sell in the inland parts. "*Ed.* 1778. Some etymologists derive the word from *ripp,* the basket in which the fish is carried.

[c] *ken, for grunting-cheats,* &c.] Theobald's correction.—Old eds. " *ken, for granting cheates* &c."—" *Ken,* a house [Dekker's *English Villanies,* sig. N 2. ed. 1632].—*Grunting-cheats,* pigs [*Id. ibid*].—*Cackling-cheats,* cocks or capons [*Id. ibid*].—*Margery-praters,* hens [*Id.* sig. N 4].—*Rogers* and *Tibs of the buttery* are both words for geese, according to Dekker [*Id. ibid,* and Harman's *Caveat for Common Cursetors,* ed. 1573], but *The English Rogue* [a work of no authority] explains the former by cloak-bag." WEBER.

Prig. Or cackling-cheats?
Hig. Or Margery-praters, Rogers,
And Tibs o' the buttery?
Prig. Oh, I could drive a regiment
Of geese afore me, such a night as this,
Ten leagues, with my hat and staff, and not a hiss
Heard, nor a wing of my troops disorder'd!
Hig. Tell us,
If it be milling of a lag of duds[e],
The fetching off a buck[f] of clothes, or so?
We are horribly out of linen.
Hub. No such matter.
Hig. Let me alone for any farmer's dog,
If you have a mind to the cheese-loft; 'tis but thus—
And he is a silenc'd mastiff, during pleasure.
Hub. Would it would please you to be silent!
Hig. Mum[g].
Wol. Who's there?
Hub. A friend; the huntsman.
Hem. Oh, 'tis he.
Hub. I have kept touch[h], sir. Which is the earl, of these?
Will he[i] know a man now?
Hem. This, my lord, 's the friend
Hath undertook the service.
Hub. If 't be worth
His lordship's thanks, anon, when it is done,
Lording, I'll look for 't. A rude woodman, I
Know how to pitch my toils, drive in my game;
And I have done 't; both Florez and his father
Old Gerrard, with Lord Arnold of Benthuisen,

---

[e] *milling of a lag of duds*] " i. e. stealing a buck of clothes, Dekker,—*id.* sig. N. 3. (as it is explained in the next line)." WEBER (the note altered).

[f] *buck*] Old eds. "back."

[g] *Mum*] After this word the Editors of 1778 inserted "*Enter Wolfort, Hemskirk, Gertrude, Boor*, &c."; and so Weber ("*Re-enter Wolfort*" &c.): but see first note in the preceding page.

[h] *kept touch*] " To keep touch, *Facere quod dixeris.*" Coles's *Dict.*

[i] *he*] So the second folio.—The first folio and the 4to "ye".

Costin[j], and Jacqueline, young Florez' sister:
I have 'em all.
  Wol. Thou speak'st too much, too happy,
To carry faith with it.
  Hub. I can bring you
Where you shall see, and find 'em.
  Wol. We will double
Whatever Hemskirk then hath promis'd thee.
  Hub. And I'll deserve it treble. What horse ha' you?
  Wol. A hundred.
  Hub. That is well. Ready to take
Upon surprise of 'em?
  Hem. Yes.
  Hub. Divide, then,
Your force into five squadrons; for there are
So many out-lets, ways thorough the wood,
That issue from the place where they are lodg'd;
Five several ways; of all which passages
We must possess ourselves, to round 'em in;
For by one starting-hole they'll all escape else.
I, and four boors here to me[k], will be guides:
The squadron where you are myself will lead;
And, that they may be more secure, I'll use
My wonted whoops and hollas, as I were
A hunting for 'em; which will make them rest
Careless of any noise, and be a direction
To the other guides how we approach 'em still.
  Wol. 'Tis order'd well, and relisheth the soldier.—
Make the division, Hemskirk.—You are my charge,
Fair one; I'll look to you.
  Boor. Shall nobody need
To look to me. I'll look unto myself.
                              [*Aside, and then runs off.*
  Hub. 'Tis but this, remember.
  Hig. Say, 'tis done, boy.   [*Exeunt.*

---

[j] *Costin*] "Old copies read 'Cozen.' He is, however, afterwards called by the name adopted in the text." WEBER.

[k] *to me*] "i. e. in addition to me." WEBER. The 4to has "*to* ye",—wrongly.

SCENE II.—*The interior of the woods near Bruges.*

Enter CLAUSE *and* GOSWIN[1].

Clause. By this time, sir, I hope you want no reasons
Why I broke off your marriage; for, though I
Should as a subject study you my prince
In things indifferent, it will not therefore
Discredit you to acknowledge me your father,
By hearkening to my necessary counsels.
   Gos. Acknowledge you my father! sir, I do;   [*Kneels.*
And may impiety, conspiring with
My other sins, sink me, and suddenly,
When I forget to pay you a son's duty
In my obedience, and that help'd forth[m]
With all the cheerfulness——
   Clause. I pray you, rise;   [FLOREZ *rises.*
And may those powers that see and love this in you
Reward you for it! Taught by your example,
Having receiv'd the rights due to a father,
I tender you th' allegiance of a subject;
Which, as my prince, accept of.   [*Kneels.*
   Gos. Kneel to me!   [*Raises him.*
May mountains first fall down beneath their valleys,
And fire no more mount upwards, when I suffer
An act in nature so preposterous!
I must o'ercome in this; in all things else
The victory be yours. Could you here read me,
You should perceive how all my faculties
Triumph in my blest fate, to be found yours:
I am your son, your son, sir! and am prouder

---

[1] *Clause and Goswin*] From this place to the end of the play, Weber, in the stage-directions and prefixes, gave the real names of these personages,—*Gerrard* and *Florez;* yet he inconsistently retained the false names, *Gertrude* and *Ginks.*—So too the Editors of 1778,—who, besides, designated Gerrard by his real name, after p. 80, where Hubert says, "*Gerrard!* do not start me," &c.—Seward, in these particulars, followed the old eds. throughout.

[m] *and that help'd forth*] Altered by Seward to "*and that* too held *forth*"!! In this line, as the Editors of 1778 saw, "*obedience*" is a quadrisyllable.

To be so[n], to the father to such goodness,
(Which Heaven be pleas'd I may inherit from you!)
Than I shall ever of those specious titles
That plead for my succession in the earldom
(Did I possess it now) left by my mother.
   Clause. I do believe it: but——
   Gos. Oh, my lov'd father,
Before I knew you were so, by instinct
Nature had taught me to look on your wants,
Not as a stranger's! and, I know not how,
What you call'd charity, I thought the payment
Of some religious debt Nature stood bound for:
And, last of all, when your magnificent bounty,
In my low ebb of fortune, had brought in
A flood of blessings, though my threatening wants,
And fear of their effects, still kept me stupid,
I soon found out it was no common pity
That led you to it.
   Clause. Think of this hereafter,
When we with joy may call it to remembrance;
There will be a time, more opportune than now,
To end your story, with all circumstances.
I add this only: when we fled from Wolfort,
I sent you into England, and there plac'd you
With a brave Flanders merchant, call'd rich Goswin,
A man supplied by me unto that purpose,
As bound by oath never to discover you;
Who, dying, left his name and wealth unto you,
As his reputed son, and yet receiv'd so.
But now, as Florez, and a prince, remember,
The country's and the subject's general good
Must challenge the first part in your affection;
The fair maid, whom you chose to be your wife,
Being so far beneath you, that your love
Must grant she's not your equal.
   Gos. In descent,
Or borrow'd glories from dead ancestors:

---

[n] *To be so,* &c.] Heath (*MS. Notes*) would read, unnecessarily,—
   " *To be so to* a *father* of *such goodness.*"

But for her beauty, chastity, and all virtues
Ever remember'd in the best of women,
A monarch might receive from her, not give,
Though she were his crown's purchase : in this only
Be an indulgent father; in all else
Use your [n] authority.

Enter HUBERT *disguised as before*, HEMSKIRK, WOLFORT, GER-
TRUDE, *and* Soldiers.

Hub. Sir, here be two of 'em,
The father and the son; the rest you shall have
As fast as I can rouze them. [*Exit.*
Clause. Who's this ? Wolfort ?
Wol. Ay, cripple; your feign'd crutches will not help you,
Nor patch'd disguise, that hath so long conceal'd you;
It's now no halting : I must here find Gerrard,
And in this merchant's habit one call'd Florez,
Who would be an earl.
Clause. And is, wert thou a subject.
Gos. Is this that traitor Wolfort ?
Wol. Yes; but you
Are they that are betray'd.—Hemskirk!
Gert. My Goswin
Turn'd prince! Oh, I am poorer by this greatness,
Than all my former jealousies or misfortunes!
Gos. Gertrude!
Wol. Stay, sir; you were to-day too near her:
You must no more aim at those easy accesses,
'Less [o] you can do 't in air, without a head;
Which shall be suddenly tried.
Gert. Oh, take my heart first!
And, since I cannot hope now to enjoy him,
Let me but fall a part of his glad ransom.
Wol. You know not your own value that entreat——
Clause. So proud a fiend as Wolfort!

---

[n] *your*] So the second folio.—The first folio and the 4to "my". (The preceding speeches of Goswin seem to prove that the author did not write "thy".)
[o] *'Less*] "i. e. unless." WEBER.

Wol. For so lost
A thing as Florez.
 Gos. And that would be so,
Rather than she should stoop again to thee:
There is no death, but 's sweeter than all life,
When Wolfort is to give it.—Oh, my Gertrude,
It is not that, nor princedom, that I go from;
It is from thee; that loss includeth all!
 Wol. Ay, if my young prince knew his loss, he would say so;
Which, that he yet may chew on, I will tell him.
This is no Gertrude, nor no Hemskirk's niece,
Nor Vandunk's daughter: this is Bertha, Bertha!
The heir of Brabant, she that caus'd the war,
Whom I did steal, during my treaty there,
In º your minority, to raise myself;
I then foreseeing 'twould beget a quarrel;
That, a necessity of my employment;
The same employment make me master of strength;
That strength, the lord of Flanders; so of Brabant,
By marrying her: which had not been to do, sir,
She come of years, but that the expectation,
First, of her father's death, retarded it;
And since, the standing-out of Bruges; where
Hemskirk had hid her, till she was near lost:
But, sir, we have recover'd her: your merchant-ship
May break; for this was one of your best bottoms,
I think.
 Clause. Insolent devil!

 Re-enter HUBERT, *with* MINCHE, GINKS, *and* COSTIN.

 Wol. Who are these, Hemskirk?
 Hem. More, more, sir.
 Gos. How they triumph in their treachery!
 Hem. Lord Arnold of Benthuisen ᴾ, this Lord Costin,
This Jacqueline, the sister unto Florez.
 Wol. All found! Why, here's brave game; this was
 sport royal,

º *In*] So the second folio.—The first folio and the 4to " For."
ᴾ *Benthuisen*] Here the old eds. have " Benthusin "; but see p. 92, last line.

VOL. IX.   H

98   BEGGARS' BUSH.   [ACT V.

And puts me in thought of a new kind of death for 'em.
Huntsman, your horn: first, wind me Florez' fall;
Next, Gerrard's; then, his daughter Jacqueline's.
Those rascals, they shall die without their rites ᑫ:
Hang 'em, Hemskirk, on these trees. I'll take
The assay of these myself ʳ.
   Hub. Not here, my lord:
Let 'em be broken up upon a scaffold;
'Twill shew the better when their arbor's made ˢ.

   ᑫ *Those rascals, they shall die without their rites*] Weber was correct in his observation that "rascals" is used here with a quibble, the word meaning, in huntsmen's language,—deer that are lean and out of season: but he certainly was wrong in retaining the spelling of the old eds., "rights."

   ʳ   *I'll take
The assay of these myself*] See note, vol. i. 266.

   ˢ *when their arbor's made*] In a note on Jonson's *Works* (vi. 270), Gifford observes that "*the making of the arbor* means, in plain English, the cutting up of the game"; but he gives no further explanation. The phrase is fully illustrated by the following curious extract from a piece of considerable rarity :—"*How you shall vndoe, or breake-vp a Hart.* After the fall of the Hart or Stag, and that the huntsmen are come in together, and haue winded the death of the Hart, you shal lay him vpright vpon his hornes, which is called suing of the Hart: then let the best man in the company, or some personage of account, take the assay before the assembly: which done, then first cut off the cods, then begin at the jawes, and slit him downe to the assay, and so directly downe to the cods: which being done, begin first to slit the left leg before, and next the left leg behinde, which you must not forget in any hand before you goe to the right side, which you must performe next in the same manner: the which being done, begin at the cheeke on the left side, from which directly take off the skinne downe to the breast, and so downe to the assay, and to the place of the end: then begin at the other side, and doe the same in like manner, but cut not the tayle of the beast (which we call the single) alway in any hand, but cutting off the skin, let it remayne to the hanches: then spreading the skin abroad, let the bodie be laid vpon the same, very open, and begin first *to make the Arbor, which is the conduit which leadeth vnto the stomacke, guts and bag,* and must be made fast and close by a round knot: then cut out the shoulders, which must be done with a very long broad-poynted knife, wherein you must obserue to keepe the outside of the inner skin whole, and lay it close to the side: then open the belly, and take out the sewet, which is most excellent and needfull for Surgions: then putting in your hand vnder the breast-bone, pul downe *the Arbor,* and turning out the panch, take away the rate, filling it with the bloud and sewet, hauing a needle and a thread ready to sow it vp with: then searching into the small guts, take out the maw, and next the liuer, laying them vpon the skin: next after these take out the bladder: then going to the vmbles, first loosen the aduancers which do leane to the necke, and taking the throat or wessand, loosen the fillets very circumspectly, which fals to the vmbles, and must be gathered

Clause. Wretch, art thou not content thou hast betray'd us,
But mock ['st] us too?

Ginks. False Hubert, this is monstrous!

Wol. Hubert!

Hem. Who? this?

Clause. Yes, this is Hubert, Wolfort;
I hope he has help'd himself to a tree.

Wol. The first,
The first of any,—and most glad I have you, sir:
I let you go before, but for a train [u].
Is't you have done this service?

Hub. As your huntsman;
But now as Hubert—save yourselves—I will——
The Wolf's afoot! let slip! kill, kill, kill, kill!

Enter, with a drum, VANDUNK, *Merchants,* HIGGEN, PRIG,
FERRET, *and* SNAP.

Wol. Betray'd!

Hub. No, but well catch'd; and I the huntsman.

Vand. How do you, Wolfort? rascal! good knave Wolfort!
I speak it now without the rose!—and Hemskirk,
Rogue Hemskirk! you that have no niece: this lady
Was stoln by you, and ta'en by you, and now
Resign'd by me to the right owner here.—
Take her, my prince!

Gos. Can this be possible?—
Welcome, my love, my sweet, my worthy love!

---

and stripped vpon the wessand with the same, with the naues and sewet, and the flesh along the midriff from both the sides, and so like a huntsman make vp the vmbles with all these together, only keepe the lights vpon the skin: this being done, slit the skin wherein the Hart is infolded, and take away the haires which grow about the same: and in caruing the Hart you shal find a bone therein, which hath the vertue to cure the malady called the passion of the heart: then cutting away the loose skirts, fil them with bloud to saue the melting of the grease: then cut away the necke from both the sides, and take the head away from the neck, taking out the tongue and the braine, laying them with the lights, the small guts, and the bloud, vpon the skinne, to reward the hounds, which is called the Querrie. The left shoulder of the Hart is his fee which dresseth him, and so is the skin and the right shoulder the Forresters fee." *A Jewell for Gentrie, &c.* (by T. S.), ed. 1614, sig. F 2 [G 2].

[u] *train*] See note, p. 90.

Vand. I ha' given you her twice: now keep her better;
　　and thank
Lord Hubert, that came to me in Gerrard's name,
And got me out, with my brave boys, to march
Like Cæsar, when he bred his Commentaries;
So I, to breed[t] my chronicle, came forth
Cæsar Vandunk, *et veni, vidi, vici.*—
Give me my bottle, and set down the drum.—
You had your tricks, sir, had you? we ha' tricks too:
You stole the lady?
　　Hig. And we led your squadrons
Where they ha' scratch'd their legs a little with brambles,
If not their faces.
　　Prig. Yes, and run their heads
Against trees.
　　Hig. 'Tis Captain Prig, sir.
　　Prig. And Colonel Higgen.
　　Hig. We have fill'd a pit with your people, some with legs,
Some with arms broken, and a neck or two
I think be loose.
　　Prig. The rest too, that escap'd,
Are not yet out o' the briars.
　　Hig. And your horses, sir,
Are well set up in Bruges all by this time.
You look as you were not well, sir, and would be
Shortly let blood: do you want a scarf?
　　Vand. A halter!
　　Clause. 'Twas like yourself, honest and noble Hubert!—
Canst thou behold these mirrors all together
Of thy long, false, and bloody usurpation,
Thy tyrannous proscription, and fresh treason;
And not so see thyself as to fall down,
And, sinking, force a grave, with thine own guilt,
As deep as hell, to cover thee and it?
　　Wol. No, I can stand, and praise the toils that took me;
And laughing in them die: they were brave snares.
　　Gos. 'Twere truer valour, if thou durst repent
The wrongs thou'st done, and live.

---

[t] *breed*] So the second folio ("*bread*").—The first folio and the 4to "end."

Wol. Who? I repent,
And say I am sorry? Yes, 'tis the fool's language,
And not for Wolfort.
Vand. Wolfort, thou art a devil,
And speak'st his language.—Oh, that I had my longing!
Under this row of trees now would I hang him.
Gos. No, let him live until he can repent;
But banish'd from our state:—that is thy doom.
Vand. Then hang his worthy captain here, this Hemskirk,
For profit of th' example.
Gos. No; let him
Enjoy his shame too, with his conscious life
To shew how much our innocence contemns
All practice ^u, from the guiltiest, to molest us.
Vand. A noble prince!
Clause. Sir, you must help to join
A pair of hands, as they have done their ^v hearts here,
And to their loves wish ^w joy.
Gos. As to mine own.—
My gracious sister! worthiest brother!
Vand. I'll go afore, and have the bonfire made,
My fireworks, and flap-dragons ^x, and good backrack ^y;
With a peck of little fishes, to drink down
In healths to this day. [*Exit.*

^u *practice*] See note, p. 6.
^v *their*] The modern editors silently print " of."
^w *wish*] Seward's correction.—Old eds. " with."
^x *flap-dragons*] See note, p. 69.
^y *backrack*]—Which the Editors of 1778 supposed to mean—salt-fish!—was rightly explained by Mason to be a celebrated Rhenish wine, so named from a town in the Lower Palatinate.—The wine of *Baccharach*, observes Henderson, "is placed by Sachs at the head of all the growths of the Rhine ; but from what can be learned concerning its history, there is some difficulty in believing that it ever could have merited this distinction. The vineyards of the Rhinegau had been for several centuries in a high state of cultivation ; but most of them being the property of ecclesiastical dignitaries and monks, their choicest produce would seldom come into the market. At Baccharach, however, there may have been a general depot for the wines of the adjacent territories, as was afterwards the case at Bingen ; and in this way several of the better sorts may have passed under that name, though they did not grow in the immediate vicinity of the place from which they received their denomination."—*Hist. of Anc. and Mod. Wines,* p. 312.

Hig. 'Slight, here be changes!
The bells ha' not so many, nor a dance, Prig.
  Prig. Our company's grown horrible thin by it.—
What think you, Ferret?
  Fer. Marry, I do think
That we might all be lords now, if we could stand for 't.
  Hig. Not I, if they should offer it: I'll dislodge first,
Remove the Bush to ˣ another climate.
  Clause. Sir, you must thank this worthy burgomaster.
Here be friends ʸ ask to be look'd on too,
And thank'd; who, though their trade and course of life
Be not so perfect but it may be better'd,
Have yet us'd me with courtesy, and been true
Subjects unto me, while I was their king;
A place I know not well how to resign,
Nor unto whom. But this I will entreat
Your grace; command them follow me to Bruges;
Where I will take the care on me to find
Some manly, and more profitable course,
To fit them as a part of the republic.
  Gos. Do you hear, sirs? do so.
  Hig. Thanks to your good grace!
  Prig. To your good lordship!
  Fer. May you both live long!
  Clause. Attend me at Vandunk's, the burgomaster's.
      [*Exeunt all except* HIGGEN, PRIG, FERRET, *and* SNAP.
  Hig. Yes, to beat hemp, and be whipt twice a week,
Or turn the wheel for Crab the rope-maker;
Or learn to go along with him his course;
That's a fine course now, i' the commonwealth.—Prig,
What say you to it?
  Prig. It is the backward'st course
I know i' the world.
  Hig. Then Higgen will scarce thrive by it,
You do conclude?
  Prig. Faith, hardly, very hardly.
  Hig. Troth, I am partly of your mind, Prince Prig:
And therefore, farewell, Flanders! Higgen will seek

ˣ *to*] Seward silently printed " unto "; the Editors of 1778 " into."
ʸ *Here be friends*] Seward silently printed " *Here be* more *friends*."

Some safer shelter, in some other climate,
With this his tatter'd colony. Let me see;
Snap, Ferret, Prig, and Higgen, all are left
O' the true blood: what, shall we into England?
Prig. Agreed.
Hig. Then bear up bravely with your Brute[z], my lads!
Higgen hath prigg'd the prancers[a] in his days,
And sold good penny-worths: we will have a course;
The spirit of Bottom is grown bottomless[b].
Prig. I'll maund[c] no more, nor cant.
Hig. Yes, your sixpenny-worth
In private, brother: sixpence is a sum
I'll steal you any man's dog for.
Prig. For sixpence more
You'll tell the owner where he is.

[z] *with your Brute*] i. e. with your Brutus,—with him who will lead you into England as Brutus, the descendant of Æneas, is said to have led thither his Trojan companions.—The Editors of 1778 rightly explained the passage as alluding to *Brute* or *Brutus:* yet Mason (who must have been seized with a fit of mental blindness) was unable to "perceive the allusion", and proposed to read "'*with your* brutes',—meaning—their horses"!!!

[a] *prigg'd the prancers*] " A *Prigger of Prancers* is a horse-stealer, for to *Prig* signifies in the Canting language to steale, and *Prancer* signifies a horse. These walke (in frieze or lether Jerkins) with a wand in their hands, watching in what pasture [are] any horses fit for their turne, and those within three or foure nights after are conueyd away at the least 60 miles from the place: if they meete the Owners in their ground, they haue shifts to auoide his suspition by feigning they haue lost their way to such a towne. These Hackney-men that let out horses will request seruice at gentlemens houses, their skill being to keepe a Gelding well; and, if they get entertainment, they stand to their word, for they keepe the Gelding so well, that his Maister shall neuer finde fault with any disease he hath, vnlesse it be that he had the dizzynes in his head, which made him reele out of his stable to bee sold forty miles off at a fayre. These haue their female spyes that suruey medowes and closes, and long onely for horseflesh". Dekker's *Belman of London*, &c., sig. D, ed. 1608.

[b] *The spirit of Bottom is grown bottomless*] " At the conclusion of Beaumont and Fletcher's *Beggars' Bush*," says Steevens, " there seems to be a sneer at this character of Bottom [in Shakespeare's *Midsummer-Night's Dream*]; but I do not very clearly perceive its drift. . . . It may mean, that either the public grew indifferent to bad actors, to plays in general, or to characters, the humour of which consisted in blunders." Note on *Midsummer-Night's Dream*, act v. sc. 1. Whatever be the meaning of the passage, I do not believe that Steevens has hit it by any of his conjectures.

[c] *maund*] See note, p. 30.

Hig. 'Tis right:
Higgen must practise, so must Prig, to eat;
And write the letter, and gi' the word.——

But now
No more, as either of these——
 Prig. But as true beggars
As e'er we were——
 Hig. We stand here for an epilogue.
Ladies, your bounties first! the rest will follow;
For women's favours are a leading alms:
If you be pleas'd, look cheerly, throw your eyes
Out at your masks.
 Prig. And let your beauties sparkle.
 Hig. So may you ne'er want dressings, jewels, gowns,
Still i' the fashion!
 Prig. Nor the men you love,
Wealth nor discourse to please you!
 Hig. May you, gentlemen,
Never want good fresh suits, nor liberty!
 Prig. May every merchant here see safe his ventures!
 Hig. And every honest citizen his debts in!
 Prig. The lawyers gain good clients!
 Hig. And the clients
Good counsel!
 Prig. All the gamesters here, good fortune!
 Hig. The drunkards, too, good wine!
 Prig. The eaters, meat
Fit for their tastes and palates!
 Hig. The good wives,
Kind husbands!
 Prig. The young maids, choice of suitors!
 Hig. The midwives, merry hearts!
 Prig. And all, good cheer!
 Hig. As you are kind unto us and our Bush!
We are the beggars, and your daily beadsmen,
And have your money; but the alms we ask,
And live by, is your grace: give that, and then
We'll boldly say, our word is, *Come agen!* [*Exeunt.*

LOVE'S CURE;

OR,

THE MARTIAL MAID.

Loves Cure, or, The Martial Maid.

In the folios, 1647, 1679.
The second folio adds " *A Comedy.*"

THIS comedy appears to have been written wholly by Fletcher, the Epilogue mentioning only a single author: the Prologue, which gives Beaumont a share in the composition, is of no authority, as it was spoken at a revival of the play.

The date of the original representation of *Love's Cure* is uncertain. If Weber be right in supposing that a passage in act ii. sc. 2,—

" did the cold Muscovite beget thee,
That lay here lieger in the last great frost ?"—

refers to the Russian ambassador who was in England in 1622 (see note *ad l.*), the comedy was perhaps produced towards the end of that year, or in 1623.

PROLOGUE,

AT THE REVIVING OF THIS PLAY.

Statues and pictures challenge price and fame,
If they can justly boast and prove they came
From Phidias or Apelles. None deny,
Poets and painters hold a sympathy;
Yet their works may decay, and lose their grace,
Receiving blemish in their limbs or face;
When the mind's art has this preeminence,
She still retaineth her first excellence.
Then why should not this dear piece be esteem'd
Child to the richest fancies that e'er teem'd?
When not their meanest off-spring that came forth
But bore the image of their fathers' worth,
Beaumont's and Fletcher's, whose desert out-weighs
The best applause, and their least sprig of bays
Is worthy Phœbus; and who comes to gather
Their fruits of wit, he shall not rob the treasure.
Nor can you ever surfeit of the plenty,
Nor can you call them rare, though they be dainty:
The more you take, the more you do them right;
And we will thank you for your own delight.

DRAMATIS PERSONÆ.

PEDRO DE VITELLI.
LAMORAL, } his friends.
ANASTRO,
FERNANDO DE ALVAREZ.
LUCIO, his son.
SAAVEDRA, friend to ALVAREZ.
PIORATO, a swordsman.
Assistente.
Alguazier.
Herald.
PACHIECO ALASTO, a cobbler.
LAZARILLO, his servant.

MENDOZA PEDICULO DE VERMINI, a botcher.
METALDI DE FORGIO, a smith.
BOBADILLA SPINDOLA ZANCHO, servant to EUGENIA, and afterwards steward to ALVAREZ.
STEPHANO, Servants, Pages, Watch, Guard, Spectators.

EUGENIA, wife to ALVAREZ.
CLARA, her daughter.
GENEVORA, sister to VITELLI.
MALRODA, mistress to VITELLI.

SCENE—*Seville.*

LOVE'S CURE;

OR,

THE MARTIAL MAID.

ACT I.

SCENE I.—*A street.*

Enter VITELLI, LAMORAL, *and* ANASTRO.

Vit. Alvarez pardon'd!
Anas. And return'd.
Lam. I saw him land
At St. Lucar's; and such a general welcome
Fame, as harbinger to his brave actions,
Had with the easy people prepar'd for him,
As if by his command alone, and fortune,
Holland, with those Low Provinces that hold out
Against the Arch-duke, were again compell'd
With their obedience to give up their lives
To be at his devotion.
    Vit. You amaze me;
For, though I have heard that, when he fled from Seville
To save his life (then forfeited to law
For murdering Don Pedro my dear uncle),
His extreme wants enforc'd him to take pay
In th' army, sat down then before Ostend;
'Twas never yet reported, by whose favour
He durst presume to entertain a thought
Of coming home with pardon.

 Anas. 'Tis our nature
Or not to hear, or not to give belief
To what we wish far from our enemies.
 Lam. Sir, 'tis most certain, the Infanta's letters,
Assisted by the Arch-duke's, to king Philip,
Have not alone secur'd him from the rigour
Of our Castilian justice, but return'd him
A free man, and in grace.
 Vit. By what curs'd means
Could such a fugitive arise unto
The knowledge of their highnesses? much more,
(Though known) to stand but in the least degree
Of favour with them?
 Lam. To give satisfaction
To your demand (though to praise him I hate
Can yield me small contentment), I will tell you,
And truly; since, should I detract his worth,
'Twould argue want of merit in myself.
Briefly to pass his tedious pilgrimage
For sixteen years, a banish'd guilty man,
And to forget the storms, the affrights, the horrors,
His constancy, not fortune overcame,
I bring him, with his little son, grown man,
(Though 'twas said here he took a daughter with him,)
To Ostend's bloody siege [a], that stage of war,
Wherein the flower of many nations acted,
And the whole Christian world spectators were:
There by his son (or were he by adoption
Or nature his) a brave scene was presented,
Which I make [b] choice to speak of, since from that
The good success of Alvarez had beginning.
 Vit. So I love virtue in an enemy,
That I desire, in the relation of
This young man's glorious deed, you 'd keep yourself
A friend to truth and it.
 Lam. Such was my purpose.

---

 [a] *Ostend's bloody siege,* &c.] See note, vol. iii. 154.
 [b] *make*] Weber chose to print " made ".

The town being oft assaulted, but in vain,
To dare the proud defendants to a sally,
Weary of ease, Don Inigo Peralta,
Son to the general of our Castile forces,
All arm'd, advanc'd within shot of their walls,
From whence the musketeers play'd thick upon him;
Yet he, brave youth, as careless of the danger
As careful of his honour, drew his sword,
And waving it about his head, as if
He dar'd one spirited like himself to trial
Of single valour, he made his retreat,
With such a slow, and yet majestic pace,
As if he still call'd loud, "Dare none come on?"
When suddenly from a postern of the town
Two gallant horsemen issu'd, and o'ertook him,
The army looking on, yet not a man
That durst relieve the rash adventurer;
Which Lucio, son to Alvarez, then seeing,
As in the vant-guard he sat bravely mounted,
(Or were it pity of the youth's misfortune,
Care to preserve the honour of his country,
Or bold desire to get himself a name)
He made his brave horse like a whirlwind bear him
Among the combatants; and in a moment
Discharg'd his petronel^c with such sure aim,
That of the adverse party from his horse
One tumbled dead; then wheeling round, and drawing
A falchion, swift as lightning he came on
Upon the other, and with one strong blow,
In view of the amazèd town and camp,
He strake him dead, and brought Peralta off
With double honour to himself.

 Vit. 'Twas brave:
But the success of this?

 Lam. The camp receiv'd him
With acclamations of joy and welcome;
And, for addition to the fair reward

_c *petronel*] " A small gun used by the cavalry." W<small>EBER</small>.

(Being a massy chain of gold given to him
By young Peralta's father,) he was brought
To the Infanta's presence, kiss'd her hand,
And from that lady (greater in her goodness
Than her high birth) had this encouragement:
" Go on, young man: yet, not to feed thy valour
With hope of recompense to come from me,
For present satisfaction of what's past,
Ask any thing that's fit for me to give
And thee to take, and be assur'd of it."
   Anas. Excellent princess!
   Vit. And styl'd worthily
The heart-blood, nay, the soul of soldiers.
But what was his request?
   Lam. That the repeal
Of Alvarez makes plain: he humbly begg'd
His father's pardon, and so movingly
Told the sad story of your uncle's death,
That the Infanta wept; and instantly
Granting his suit, working the Arch-duke to it,
Their letters were directed to the king,
With whom they so prevail'd, that Alvarez
Was freely pardon'd.
   Vit. 'Tis not in the king
To make that good.
   Anas. Not in the king! what subject
Dares contradict his power?
   Vit. In this I dare,
And will; and not call his prerogative
In question, nor presume to limit it.
I know he is the master of his laws,
And may forgive the forfeits made to them,
But not the injury done to my honour:
And since, forgetting my brave uncle's merits,
And many services under Duke D'Alva,
He suffers him to fall, wresting from Justice
The powerful sword that would revenge his death,
I'll fill with this Astræa's empty hand,
And in my just wreak make this arm the king's.

My deadly hate to Alvarez and his house,
Which as I grew in years hath still increas'd
(As if it call'd on Time to make me man),
Slept while it had no object for her fury
But a weak woman and her talk'd-of daughter;
But now, since there are quarries worth her flight [d],
Both in the father and his hopeful son,
I'll boldly cast her off, and gorge her full
With both their hearts. To further which, your friendship
And oaths will your assistance: let your deeds
Make answer to me [e]: useless are all words,
Till you have writ performance with your swords. [*Exeunt.*

SCENE II.—*A room in the house of* ALVAREZ.

Enter BOBADILLA, *and* LUCIO *in woman's clothes.*

Lucio. Go, fetch my work. This ruff was not well starch'd;
So tell the maid; 't has too much blue in it:
And look you that the partridge and the pullen
Have clean meat and fresh water, or my mother
Is like to hear on 't.

Bob. Oh, good St. Jaques, help me! Was there ever such an hermaphrodite heard of? would any wench living, that should hear and see what I do, be wrought to believe that

---

[d] *quarries worth her flight*]—quarries, i. e. game, prey : see note, vol. ii. 554.—Both the folios "*quarries, worth her* sight".—" The correction in the text is Sympson's, and there can be no doubt of its propriety, as these lines are a continued chain of metaphors from falconry." WEBER.

[e]   *To further which, your friendship*
And oaths will your assistance : let your deeds
Make answer to me] So the passage was pointed by Sympson, and, no doubt, rightly (Mason observes that the word "*will*" is used in a similar sense at p. 119,—
            "Send for music,
    And *will* the cooks to use their best of cunning", &c.).
The Editors of 1778 printed,—
            " To further which, your friendship,
        And oaths ! Will your assistance let your deeds
            Make answer to me ?"
and so Weber.

the best of a man lies under this petticoat, and that a codpiece were far fitter here than a pinned placket [f]?

Lucio. You had best talk filthily, do; I have a tongue
To tell my mother, as well as ears to hear
Your ribaldry.

Bob. Nay, you have ten women's tongues that way, I am sure. Why, my young master, or mistress, madam, don, or what you will, what the devil have you to do with pullen or partridge? or to sit pricking on a clout all day? You have a better needle, I know, and might make better work, if you had grace to use it.

Lucio. Why, how dare you speak this before me, sirrah?

Bob. Nay, rather, why dare not you do what I speak? [Pox][g], though my lady, your mother, for fear of Vitelli and his faction, hath brought you up like her daughter, and has kept you this twenty year (which is ever since you were born) a close prisoner within doors; yet, since you are a man, and are as well provided as other men are, methinks you should have the same motions of the flesh as other cavaliers of us are inclined unto.

Lucio. Indeed, you have cause to love those wanton motions,
They having holp[h] you to an excellent whipping,
For doing something (I but put you in mind of it)
With the Indian maid the governor sent my mother
From Mexico.

Bob. Why, I but taught her a Spanish trick in charity, and holp the king to a subject, that may live to take Grave Maurice[i] prisoner; and that was more good to the state

---

[f] *placket*] See note, vol. vi. 508.

[g] [*Pox*] A break here in both the folios.

[h] *holp*] Theobald's correction.—Both the folios "hope".

[i] *Grave Maurice*] Sympson printed "grave" without a capital letter, at the suggestion of Seward, who observed that "it is an epithet only, and a characteristic of prince Maurice of Nassau, who, after performing great actions against the Spaniards, is said to have died of grief on account of the siege of Breda", &c.; and so the Editors of 1778!!!—" *Grave* is Dutch, and *graaf* German (not for *prince* or count, as Mason has it, but simply) for *count;* and the Nassau family, one branch of which were elected *Stadtholders*, being counts of the empire, were consequently denominated *Grave* Maurice, *Grave* Henry, &c. So in Dekker's *Guls Hornbook*, ' You may discourse how honourably your *Grave* used you; observe that you call your *Grave Maurice* your *Grave* '." WEBER.

than a thousand such as you are ever like to do: and I will tell you, (in a fatherly care of the infant, I speak it,) if he live (as, bless the babe, in passion I remember him!) to your years, shall he spend his time in pinning, painting, purling, and perfuming, as you do? No; he shall to the wars, use his Spanish pike, though with the danger of the lash, as his father has done; and, when he is provoked, as I am now, draw his Toledo desperately, as——

Lucio. You will not kill me? Oh!

Bob. I knew this would silence him: how he hides his eyes! If he were a wench now, as he seems, what an advantage had I, drawing two Toledos, when one can do this! But, oh me, my lady! I must put up [*Aside*].—Young master, I did but jest.—Oh, Custom, what hast thou made of him! [*Aside.*

Enter EUGENIA *and* STEPHANO [j].

Eug. For bringing this, be still my friend; no more
A servant to me.

Bob. What's the matter?

Eug. Here,
Even here, where I am happy to receive
Assurance of my Alvarez' return,
I will kneel down; and may those holy thoughts
That now possess me wholly, make this place
A temple to me, where I may give thanks
For this unhop'd-for blessing Heaven's kind hand
Hath pour'd upon me!

Lucio. Let my duty, madam,
Presume, if you have cause of joy, to entreat
I may share in it.

Bob. 'Tis well he has forgot how I frighted him yet [k].
[*Aside.*

Eug. Thou shalt: but first kneel with me, Lucio,
No more Posthumia now: thou hast a father,

---

[j] *Stephano*] Both the folios "Servants" (a mistake for "Servant").

[k] *how I frighted him yet*] "The word '*yet*' at the end of this line offends Sympson; but it is frequently used in all these plays in the sense of *however* or "*nevertheless*". MASON. See Gifford's note on Jonson's *Works*, ii. 239.

A father living to take off that name,
Which my too-credulous fears that he was dead
Bestow'd upon thee. Thou shalt see him, Lucio,
And make him young again by seeing thee,
Who only hadst a being in my womb
When he went from me, Lucio. Oh, my joys
So far transport me, that I must forget
The ornaments of matrons, modesty,
And grave behaviour! But let all forgive me,
If in th' expression of my soul's best comfort,
Though old, I do a while forget mine age,
And play the wanton in the entertainment
Of those delights I have so long despair'd of.
   Lucio. Shall I, then, see my father?
   Eug. This hour, Lucio;
Which reckon the beginning of thy life,
I mean that life in which thou shalt appear
To be such as I brought thee forth, a man.
This womanish disguise, in which I have
So long conceal'd thee, thou shalt now cast off,
And change those qualities thou didst learn from me
For masculine virtues; for which seek no tutor,
But let thy father's actions be thy precepts.—
And for thee, Zancho, now expect reward
For thy true service.
   Bob. Shall I?—You hear, fellow Stephano? learn to know me more respectively[1]. How dost thou think I shall become the steward's chair? ha? will not these slender haunches shew well with a gold chain and a night-cap[m] after supper, when I take the accounts?
   Eug. Haste, and take down those blacks, with which my
     chamber

---

[1] *respectively*] i. e. respectfully; as in vol. iii. 494, vol. v. 376 (so the adjective *respective* was formerly common in the sense of respectful; as in the concluding speech of the 4th act of Shakespeare's *Two Gentlemen of Verona*, where Mr. Knight wrongly explains the word).

[m] *with a gold chain and a night-cap*] Both the folios "*with a chaine, and a gold night-cap*"; and so Sympson (though he proposed the right reading in a note), and Weber. That in great families, a gold chain was worn by stewards, appears from innumerable passages of our early writers.

Hath, like the widow, her sad mistress, mourn'd,
And hang up for it the rich Persian arras
Us'd on my wedding-night; for this to me
Shall be a second marriage: send for music,
And will the cooks to use their best of cunning [n]
To please the palate.

Bob. Will your ladyship have a potato-pie [o]? 'tis a good stirring dish for an old lady after a long Lent.

Eug. Begone, I say! why, sir, you can go faster?

Bob. I could, madam; but I am now to practise the steward's pace; that's the reward I look for: every man must fashion his gait according to his calling.—You, fellow Stephano, may walk faster to overtake preferment; so, usher me. [*Exit, preceded by* STEPHANO.

Lucio. Pray, madam, let the waistcoat I last wrought
Be made up for my father: I will have
A cap and boot-hose [p] suitable to it.

Eug. Of that
We'll think hereafter, Lucio; our thoughts now
Must have no object but thy father's welcome;
To which, thy help!

Lucio. With humble gladness, madam. [*Exeunt.*

SCENE III.—*A hall in the same.*

Enter ALVAREZ, *and* CLARA *in man's clothes.*

Alv. Where lost we Saavedra?

Clara. He was met,
Entering the city, by some gentlemen,
Kinsmen, as he said, of his own, with whom,
For compliment-sake (for so I think he term'd it),
He was compell'd to stay; though I much wonder
A man that knows to do, and has done well

---

[n] *cunning*] i. e. skill.

[o] *potato-pie*] "It has been already observed that potatoes were considered as strong provocatives." WEBER. See vol. vi. 69, vol. viii. 333.

[p] *boot-hose*] See note, vol. iv. 150.

In the head of his troop, when the bold foe charg'd home,
Can learn so suddenly to abuse his time
In apish entertainment. For my part,
By all the glorious rewards of war,
I had rather meet ten enemies in the field,
All sworn to fetch my head, than be brought on
To change an hour's discourse with one of these
Smooth city-fools or tissue-cavaliers,
(The only gallants, as they wisely think,)
To get a jewel, or a wanton kiss
From a court-lip, though painted.
   Alv. My love Clara [q],
(For Lucio is a name thou must forget,
With Lucio's bold behaviour,) though thy breeding
I' the camp may plead something in the excuse
Of thy rough manners, custom having chang'd
(Though not thy sex) the softness of thy nature,
And Fortune, then a cruel step-dame to thee,
Impos'd upon thy tender sweetness burdens
Of hunger, cold, wounds, want, such as would crack
The sinews of a man not born a soldier;
Yet, now she smiles, and like a natural mother
Looks gently on thee, Clara, entertain
Her proffer'd bounties with a willing bosom:
Thou shalt no more have need to use thy sword;
Thy beauty (which even Belgia hath not alter'd)
Shall be a stronger guard to keep my Clara,
Than that has been (though never us'd but nobly):
And know thus much——
   Clara. Sir, I know only that
It stands not with my duty to gainsay you
In any thing: I must and will put on
What fashion you think best, though I could wish
I were what I appear.
   Alv. Endeavour rather
To be what you are, Clara; entering here,
As you were born, a woman.   [*Music.*

---

[q] *love Clara*] I suspect, with Sympson and Seward, that the poet wrote "lov'd *Clara*".

Enter EUGENIA, LUCIO, *and* Servants.

Eug. Let choice music,
In the best voice that e'er touch'd human ear,
(For joy hath tied my tongue up,) speak your welcome!
Alv. My soul (for thou giv'st new life to my spirit),
Myriads of joys, though short in number of
Thy virtues, fall on thee! Oh, my Eugenia,
The assurance that I do embrace thee, makes
My twenty years of sorrow but a dream;
And by the nectar which I take from these
I feel my age restor'd, and, like old Æson,
Grow young again!
Eug. My lord, long-wish'd-for, welcome!
'Tis a sweet briefness; yet in that short word
All pleasures which I may call mine begin;
And may they long increase, before they find
A second period! Let mine eyes now surfeit
On this so-wish'd-for object, and my lips,
Yet modestly, pay back the parting kiss
You trusted with them, when you fled from Seville
With little Clara my sweet daughter: lives she?
Yet I could chide myself, having you here,
For being so covetous of all joys at once,
To inquire for her; you being, alone, to me
My Clara, Lucio, my lord, myself,
Nay, more than all the world.
Alv. As you to me are.
Eug. Sit down, and let me feed upon the story
Of your past dangers, now you are here in safety:
It will give relish and fresh appetite
To my delights, if such delights can cloy me.
Yet do not, Alvarez: let me first yield you
Account of my life in your absence, and
Make you acquainted how I have preserv'd
The jewel left lock'd up in my womb, when you,
In being forc'd to leave your country, suffer'd
A civil death.

Alv. Do, my Eugenia;
'Tis that I most desire to hear.
 Eug. Then know——   [*Clashing of swords within.*
 Alv. What noise is that?
 Saav. [*within*] If you are noble enemies,
Oppress me not with odds, but kill me fairly!
 Vit. [*within*] Stand off! I am too many of myself.

Enter BOBADILLA.

 Bob. Murder, murder, murder! Your friend, my lord, Don Saavedra, is set upon in the streets by your enemies, Vitelli and his faction: I am almost killed with looking on them.
 Alv. I'll free him, or fall with him! Draw thy sword,
And follow me!   [*Exit.*
 Clara. Fortune, I give thee thanks
For this occasion once more to use it!   [*Exit.*
 Bob. Nay, hold not me, madam: if I do any hurt, hang me.
 Luc. Oh, I am dead with fear! Let's fly into
Your closet, mother.
 Eug. No hour of my life
Secure of danger! Heaven be merciful,
Or now at once despatch me!

Enter VITELLI, pursued by ALVAREZ and SAAVEDRA; and CLARA beating off ANASTRO.

 Clara. Follow him:
Leave me to keep these off.
 Alv. Assault my friend,
So near my house!
 Vit. Nor in it will spare thee,
Though 'twere a temple; and I'll make it one,
I being the priest, and thou the sacrifice
I'll offer to my uncle.
 Alv. Haste thou to him,
And say I sent thee!   [*They fight.*
 Clara. 'Twas put bravely by——
And that—and yet[r] comes on, and boldly—rare!

---

 [r] *and yet*] Sympson silently printed "*yct* he"; and so his successors.

In the wars, where emulation and example
Join to increase the courage, and make less
The danger, valour and true resolution
Never appear'd so lovely—brave again!
Sure, he is more than man; and, if he fall,
The best of virtue, fortitude, would die with him:
And can I suffer it? forgive me, duty!
So I love valour as I will protect it
Against my father, and redeem it, though
'Tis forfeited by one I hate.
 Vit. Come on!
All is not lost yet: you shall buy me dearer
Before you have me.—Keep off.
 Clara. Fear me not:
Thy worth has took me prisoner, and my sword
For this time knows thee only for a friend,
And to all else I turn the point of it.
 Saav. Defend your father's enemy!
 Alv. Art thou mad?
 Clara. Are you men rather? Shall that valour, which
Begot you lawful honour in the wars,
Prove now the parent of an infamous bastard,
So foul, yet so long-liv'd, as murder will
Be to your shames? Have each of you, alone,
With your own dangers only, purchas'd glory
From multitudes of enemies, not allowing
Those nearest to you to have part in it,
And do you now join, and lend mutual help
Against a single opposite? Hath the mercy
Of the great king but newly wash'd away
The blood that with the forfeit of your life
Cleav'd to your name and family, like an ulcer,
In this again to set a deeper dye upon
Your infamy? You'll say he is your foe,
And by his rashness call'd on his own ruin:
Remember yet, he was first wrong'd, and honour
Spurr'd him to what he did; and next, the place
Where now he is, your house, which by the laws
Of hospitable duty should protect him;
Have you been twenty years a stranger to it,

To make your entrance now in blood? or think you
Your countryman, a true-born Spaniard, will be
An offering fit to please the Genius of it?
No; in this I 'll presume to teach my father,
And this first act of disobedience shall
Confirm I am most dutiful.
   Alv. I am pleas'd
With what I dare not give allowance ˢ to.—   [*Aside.*
Unnatural wretch, what wilt thou do?
   Clara. Set free
A noble enemy: come not on! by [Heaven ᵗ],
You pass to him through me!—The way is open:
Farewell: when next I meet you, do not look for
A friend, but a vow'd foe; I see you worthy,
And therefore now preserve you for the honour
Of my sword only.
   Vit. Were this man a friend,
How would he win me, that, being my vow'd foe,
Deserves so well! [*Aside.*]—I thank you for my life;
But how I shall deserve it, give me leave
Hereafter to consider.   [*Exit.*
   Alv. Quit thy fear;
All danger is blown over: I have letters
To the governor, in the king's name, to secure us
From such attempts hereafter; yet we need not,
That have such strong guards of our own, dread others;
And, to increase thy comfort, know, this young man,
Whom with such fervent earnestness you eye,
Is not what he appears, but such a one
As thou with joy wilt bless, thy daughter Clara.
   Eug. A thousand blessings in that word!
   Alv. The reason
Why I have bred her up thus, at more leisure
I will impart unto you. Wonder not
At what you have seen her do, it being the least
Of many great and valiant undertakings
She hath made good with honour.

   ˢ *allowance*] i. e. approbation.
   ᵗ [*Heaven*] A break here in both the folios.

Eug. I'll return
The joy I have in her with one as great
To you, my Alvarez. You, in a man,
Have given to me a daughter; in a woman,
I give to you a son: this was the pledge
You left here with me, whom I have brought up
Different from what he was, as you did Clara,
And with the like success; as she appears,
Alter'd by custom, more than woman, he,
Transform'd by his soft life, is less than man.
   Alv. Fortune in this gives ample satisfaction
For all our sorrows past.
   Lucio. My dearest sister!
   Clara. Kind brother!
   Alv. Now our mutual care must be
Employ'd to help wrong'd Nature to recover
Her right in either of them, lost by custom:
To you I give my Clara, and receive
My Lucio to my charge; and we'll contend,
With loving industry, who soonest can
Turn this man woman, or this woman man.   [*Exeunt.*

ACT II.

SCENE I.—*A street.*

Enter PACHIECO *and* LAZARILLO.

   Pach. Boy, my cloak and rapier: it fits not a gentleman of my rank to walk the streets in querpo[u].

   Laz. Nay, you are a very rank gentleman, signior. I am very hungry: they tell me in Seville here, I look like an eel with a man's head; and your neighbour the smith here hard by would have borrowed me th' other day to have fished with me, because he had lost his angle-rod.

---

   [u] *in querpo*] i. e. in close habit, without a cloak,—in an undress. (Sp. *cuerpo*, the body).

Pach. Oh, happy thou, Lazarillo, being the cause of other men's wits, as in thine own! Live lean and witty still: oppress not thy stomach too much: gross feeders, great sleepers; great sleepers, fat bodies; fat bodies, lean brains. No, Lazarillo; I will make thee immortal, change thy humanity into deity, for I will teach thee to live upon nothing.

Laz. Faith, signior, I am immortal then already, or very near it, for I do live upon little or nothing. Belike that's the reason the poets are said to be immortal; for some of them live upon their wits, which is indeed as good as little or nothing. But, good master, let me be mortal still, and let's go to supper.

Pach. Be abstinent; shew not the corruption of thy generation: he that feeds shall die; therefore, he that feeds not shall live.

Laz. Ay, but how long shall he live? there's the question.

Pach. As long as he can without feeding. Didst thou read of the miraculous maid in Flanders——

Laz. No, nor of any maid else; for the miracle of virginity now-a-days ceases ere the virgin can read virginity.

Pach. She that lived three year without any other sustenance than the smell of a rose?

Laz. I heard of her, signior; but they say her guts shrunk all into lutestrings, and her nether parts clinged together like a serpent's tail; so that though she continued a woman still above the girdle, beneath yet [v] she was monster.

Pach. So are most women, believe it.

Laz. Nay all women, signior, that can live only upon the smell of a rose.

Pach. No part of the history is fabulous.

Laz. I think rather, no part of the fable is historical. But for all this, sir, my rebellious stomach will not let me be immortal: I will be as immortal as mortal hunger will suffer. Put me to a certain stint, sir; allow me but a red herring a-day.

Pach. O, de Dios! wouldst thou be gluttonous in thy delicacies?

---

[v] *beneath yet*] Sympson silently printed "*yet beneath*".—Qy. "*beneath* it" (the MS. having had "yt")?

Laz. He that eats nothing but a red herring a-day shall ne'er be broiled for the devil's rasher: a pilcher[v], signior, a surdiny[w], an olive, that I may be a philosopher first, and immortal after.

Pach. Patience, Lazarillo; let contemplation be thy food a while: I say unto thee, one pease was a soldier's provant[x] a whole day at the destruction of Jerusalem.

Laz. Ay, an it were any where but at the destruction of a place, I'll be hanged.

Enter METALDI *and* MENDOZA.

Met. Signior Pachieco Alasto, my most ingenious cobbler of Seville, the *buenas noches* to your signiory!

Pach. Signior Metaldi de Forgio, my most famous smith and man of metal, I return your courtesy ten-fold, and do humble my bonnet beneath the shoe-sole of your congie.— The like to you, Signior Mendoza Pediculo de Vermini[y], my most exquisite hose-heeler.

Laz. Here's a greeting betwixt a cobbler, a smith, and a botcher! they all belong to the foot, which makes them stand so much upon their gentry. [*Aside.*

Mend. Signior Lazarillo!

Laz. Ah, signior, *sì!* Nay, we are all signiors here in Spain, from the jakes-farmer to the grandee or adelantado[z]. —This botcher looks as if he were dough-baked; a little butter now, and I could eat him like an oaten cake: his father's diet was new cheese and onions, when he got him: what a scallion-faced[a] rascal 'tis! [*Aside.*

Met. But why, Signior Pachieco, do you stand so much on the priority and antiquity of your quality[b] (as you call it) in comparison of ours?

---

[v] *pilcher*] i. e. pilchard.

[w] *surdiny*] "A sardella, sardina, i. e. anchovy." WEBER. The sardine and the anchovy are distinct fishes, though often confounded with each other.

[x] *provant*] "i. e. provision, ration." WEBER.

[y] *Vermini*] Both the folios "Vermim".

[z] *adelantado*] i. e. the king's lieutenant of a country, or deputy in any important place of charge.

[a] *scallion-faced*] "A scallion is a kind of small onion [a shallot]." WEBER.

[b] *quality*] "i. e. profession or calling." WEBER.

Mend. Ay; your reason for that?

Pach. Why, thou iron-pated smith, and thou woollen-witted hose-heeler, hear what I will speak indifferently, and according to antient writers, of our three professions; and let the upright Lazarillo be both judge and moderator.

Laz. Still am I the most immortally hungry that may be.

Pach. Suppose thou wilt derive thy pedigree, like some of the old heroes (as Hercules, Æneas, Achilles), lineally from the gods, making Saturn thy great-grandfather, and Vulcan thy father: Vulcan was a god——

Laz. He'll make Vulcan your godfather by-and-by.

Pach. Yet, I say, Saturn was a crabbed blockhead; and Vulcan a limping horn-head, for Venus his wife was a strumpet, and Mars begat all her children: therefore, however, thy original must of necessity spring from bastardy. Further, what can be a more deject spirit in man, than to lay his hands under every one's horse's feet, to do him service, as thou dost?—For thee, I will be brief: thou dost botch, and not mend; thou art a hider of enormities, *viz.* scabs, chilblains, and kibed heels; much prone thou art to sects and heresies, disturbing state and government; for how canst thou be a sound member in the commonwealth, that art so subject to stitches in the ancles?—Blush and be silent, then, oh, ye mechanics! compare no more with the politic cobbler; for cobblers in old time have prophesied: what may they do now, then, that have every day waxed better and better? Have we not the length of every man's foot? are we not daily menders? yea, and what menders? not horse-menders——

Laz. Nor manners-menders.

Pach. But sole-menders: oh, divine cobblers! Do we not, like the wise man, spin our own threads (or our wives for us)? do we not, by our sewing the hide, reap the beef? are not we of the gentle-craft, whilst both you are but craftsmen? You will say, you fear neither iron nor steel, and what you get is wrought out of the fire: I must answer you again though, all this is but forgery. You may likewise say, a man's a man that has but a hose on his head: I must likewise answer, that man is a botcher that has a heeled hose on his head. To conclude, there can be no comparison with the cobbler, who is all in all in the commonwealth, has his politic eye and ends on every man's steps that walks, and whose course shall be lasting to the world's end.

Met. I give place: the wit of man is wonderful: thou hast hit the nail on the head, and I will give thee six pots for 't, though I ne'er clinch shoe again.

Enter VITELLI *and* ALGUAZIER.

Pach. Who 's this? oh, our Alguazier[e]; as arrant a knave as e'er wore one head under two offices; he is one side Alguazier.

Met. The other side Sergeant.

Mend. That 's both sides carrion, I am sure.

Pach. This is he apprehends whores in the way of justice, and lodges 'em in his own house in the way of profit. He with him is the grand don Vitelli, 'twixt whom and Fernando Alvarez the mortal hatred is: he is indeed my don's bawd, and does at this present lodge a famous courtezan of his, lately come from Madrill [f].

Vit. Let her want nothing, signior, she can ask:
What loss or injury you may sustain
I will repair, and recompense your love:
Only that fellow's coming I mislike,
And did forewarn her of him. Bear her this,
With my best love; at night I 'll visit her. [*Gives money.*

Alg. I rest your lordship's servant.

Vit. Good even, signior [g].—
Oh, Alvarez, thou hast brought a son with thee
Both brightens and obscures our nation,
Whose pure strong beams on us shoot like the sun's
On baser fires. I would to Heaven my blood

---

[e] *Alguazier*] " This should be more correctly, *Alguazil* ". WEBER. In a former play we have had " Algazeirs": see vol. viii. 481.

[f] *Madrill*] i. e. Madrid. This form of the name (which occurs again in the present work) was very common : see, for instance, Middleton and Rowley's *Spanish Gipsy*,—Middleton's *Works*, iv. 104, 118, &c. ed. Dyce. So the first folio.—The second folio " Madrid"; and so the modern editors.

[g] *Signior*] Both folios " signiors"; and so the modern editors : but assuredly Vitelli (—compare his preceding speech—) is addressing the Alguazier only.

Had never stain'd thy bold unfortunate hand,
That with mine honour I might emulate,
Not persecute such virtue! I will see him,
Though with the hazard of my life; no rest
In my contentious spirits can I find,
Till I have gratified him in like kind. [*Aside, and then exit.*

Alg. I know you not: what are ye? hence, ye base besognios [g]!

Pach. Marry, cazzo, Signior Alguazier! do you not know us? why, we are your honest neighbours, the cobbler, smith, and botcher, that have so often sat snoring cheek by joll with your signiory in rug at midnight.

Laz. Nay, good signior, be not angry; you must understand, a cat and such an officer see best in the dark.

Met. By this hand, I could find in my heart to shoe his head!

Pach. Why, then [we] know you, signior: thou mongrel, begot at midnight, at the gaol-gate, by a beadle on a catchpole's wife, are not you he that was whipt out of Toledo for perjury?

Mend. Next, condemned to the galleys for pilfery, to the bull's pizzle?

Met. And after called to the Inquisition for apostacy?

Pach. Are not you he that, rather than you durst go an industrious voyage, being pressed to the islands, skulked till the fleet was gone, and then earned your royal [h] a-day by squiring punks and punklings up and down the city?

Laz. Are not you a Portuguese born, descended o' the Moors, and came hither into Seville with your master, an arrant tailor, in your red bonnet and your blue jacket, lousy; though now your block-head be covered with the Spanish block [i], and your lashed shoulders with a velvet pee [j]?

[g] *besognios*] i. e. beggars, needy fellows.

[h] *royal*] i. e. spur-royal, or spur-ryal : see note, vol. iii. 9.—The modern editors print "ryal" and "rial".

[i] *block*] i. e. hat (properly, the mould on which the crown is formed).

[j] *velvet pee*] "Is nonsense : we should read ' velvet *peel* ', meaning a coat or covering of velvet." MASON.

Pach. Are not you he that have been of thirty callings, yet ne'er a one lawful? that being a chandler first, professed sincerity, and would sell no man mustard to his beef on the sabbath, and yet sold hypocrisy all your life-time?

Met. Are not you he that were since a surgeon to the stews, and undertook to cure, what the church itself could not, strumpets? that riss [k] to your office by being a great don's bawd?

Laz. That commit men nightly, offenceless, for the gain of a groat a prisoner, which your beadle seems to put up, when you share three-pence?

Mend. Are not you he that is a kisser of men in drunkenness, and a betrayer in sobriety?

Alg. Diablo! they'll rail me into the galleys again.

[*Aside.*

Pach. Yes, signior, thou art even he we speak of all this while. Thou mayest, by thy place now, lay us by the heels, 'tis true: but take heed; be wiser, pluck not ruin on thine own head; for never was there such an anatomy [l], as we shall make thee then; be wise therefore, oh, thou child of the night! be friends, and shake hands. Thou art a proper man, if thy beard were redder [m]: remember thy worshipful function, a constable; though thou turnest day into night, and night into day, what of that? Watch less, and pray more: gird thy bear's skin (*viz.* thy rug-gown) to thy loins; take thy staff in thy hand, and go forth at midnight [n]: let not thy mittens abate the talons of thy authority, but gripe

---

[k] *riss*] i. e. rose. See note, p. 46.—Both the folios "rise".

[l] *anatomy*] See note, vol. iv. 143.

[m] *Thou art a proper man, if thy beard were redder*] "In a preceding note [see vol. v. 41, and vol. viii. 318] it has been observed, that Judas was painted with a red beard, and to this Pachieco may sneeringly allude, as his fellow Mendoza had before said to the *alguacil*—' Are not you he that is a kisser of men in drunkenness, and a betrayer in sobriety?' ", &c. WEBER. But in the present passage, as Nares remarks (*Gloss.* in *Red Beard*), "it is suggested that the Alguaziers beard ought to be more red, doubtless, to strike terror."

[n] *gird thy bear's skin* (viz. *thy rug-gown*) *to thy loins; take thy staff in thy hand, and go forth at midnight*] "These words are found only in the first folio." *Ed.* 1778. "They were probably omitted in folio 1679, as being a profane allusion to scripture." WEBER.

theft and whoredom, wheresoever thou meetest 'em; bear 'em away like a tempest, and lodge 'em safely in thine own house.

Laz. Would you have whores and thieves lodged in such a house?

Pach. They ever do so: I have found a thief or a whore there, when the whole suburbs could not furnish me.

Laz. But why do they lodge there?

Pach. That they may be safe and forth-coming; for in the morning usually the thief is sent to the gaol, and the whore prostrates herself to the justice.

Mend. Admirable Pachieco!

Met. Thou cobbler of Christendom!

Alg. There is no railing with these rogues: I will close with 'em, till I can cry quittance [*Aside*].—Why, signiors, and my honest neighbours, will you impute that as a neglect of my friends, which is an imperfection in me? I have been sand-blind from my infancy: to make you amends, you shall sup with me.

Laz. Shall we sup with you, sir?—O' my conscience, they have wronged the gentleman extremely.

Alg. And, after supper, I have a project to employ you in, shall make you drink and eat merrily this month. I am a little knavish: why, and do not I know all you to be knaves?

Pach. I grant you, we are all knaves, and will be your knaves; but, oh, while you live, take heed of being a proud knave!

Alg. On, then, pass: I will bear out my staff, and my staff shall bear out me.

Laz. Oh, Lazarillo, thou art going to supper! [*Exeunt.*

SCENE II.—*A room in the house of* ALVAREZ. *Arms hanging on the walls.*

Enter LUCIO *in man's clothes, and* BOBADILLA.

Lucio. Pray, be not angry.

Bob. I am angry, and I will be angry. *Diablo!* what should you do in the kitchen? cannot the cooks lick their fingers, without your overseeing? nor the maids make pottage, except your dog's head be in the pot? Don Lucio? Don Quot-quean [n], Don Spinster! wear a petticoat still, and put on your smock a' Monday; I will have a baby o' clouts made for it, like a great girl. Nay, if you will needs be starching of ruffs, and sewing of black-work, I will, of a mild and loving tutor, become a tyrant: your father has committed you to my charge, and I will make a man or a mouse on you.

Lucio. What would you have me do? This scurvy sword
So galls my thigh, I would 'twere burnt! Pish, look,
This cloak will ne'er keep on; these boots too, hide-bound,
Make me walk stiff, as if my legs were frozen;
And my spurs jingle like a morris-dancer:
Lord, how my head aches with this roguish hat!
This masculine attire is most uneasy;
I am bound up in it: I had rather walk
In folio again, loose, like a woman.

Bob. In *foolio*, had you not?
Thou mock to Heaven, and Nature, and thy parents!
Thou tender leg of lamb! Oh, how he walks
As if he had be-piss'd himself, and fleers!
Is this a gait for the young cavalier,
Don Lucio, son and heir to Alvarez?
Has it a corn? or does it walk on conscience,
It treads so gingerly? Come on your ways:
Suppose me now your father's foe, Vitelli,
And spying you i' the street, thus I advance:
I twist my beard, and then I draw my sword.

Lucio. Alas!

Bob. And thus accost thee; "Traitorous brat,
How durst thou thus confront me? impious twig
Of that old stock, dew'd with my kinsman's gore,
Draw! for I'll quarter thee in pieces four."

Lucio. Nay, prithee, Bobadilla, leave thy fooling;
Put up thy sword: I will not meddle with you.

---

[n] *Quot-quean*] " A corruption of *cotquean*, a man who employs himself more in women's affairs than in those befitting a man." WEBER. Gifford was certainly mistaken in asserting that *cotquean* is a corruption of *cuckquean* (note on Jonson's *Works*, ii. 482). They are distinct words: see Richardson's *Dict.*

Ay, justle me, I care not; I'll not draw:
Pray, be a quiet man.

Bob. Do you hear? answer me as you would do Don Vitelli, or I'll be so bold as to lay the pommel of my sword over the hilts of your head.—
" My name's Vitelli, and I'll have the wall."

Lucio. " Why, then, I'll have the kennel: what a coil you keep!
Signior, what happen'd 'twixt my sire and your
Kinsman, was long before I saw the world;
No fault of mine, nor will I justify
My father's crimes: forget, sir, and forgive,
'Tis Christianity: I pray, put up your sword;
I'll give you any satisfaction
That may become a gentleman. However,
I hope you are bred to more humanity
Than to revenge my father's wrong on me,
That crave your love and peace."—La you now, Zancho,
Would not this quiet him, were he ten Vitellis?

Bob. Oh, craven chicken of a cock o' the game! Well, what remedy? Did thy father see this, o' my conscience, he would cut off thy masculine gender, crop thine ears, beat out thine eyes, and set thee in one of the pear-trees for a scarecrow. As I am Vitelli, I am satisfied; but, as I am Bobadilla Spindola Zancho, steward of the house, and thy father's servant, I could find in my heart to lop off the hinder part of thy face, or to beat all thy teeth into thy mouth. Oh, thou whey-blooded milksop! I'll wait upon thee no longer: thou shalt even wait upon me. Come your ways, sir; I shall take a little pains with you else.

Enter CLARA *in woman's clothes.*

Clara. Where art thou, brother Lucio?—Ran tan tan, ta ran tan ran tan tan, ta ran tan tan tan!—Oh, I shall no more see those golden days! These clothes will never fadge with me [o] : a [pox] [p] o' this filthy vardingale, this hip-hape [q] !

---

[o] *fadge with me*] i. e. suit me.

[p] [*pox*] A break here in both the folios.

[q] *hip-hape*] i.e. covering for the hip (to *hap* in the sense of—to cover, is still commonly used in Scotland).

—Brother, why are women's haunches only limited, confined, hooped in, as it were, with these same scurvy vardingales?

Bob. Because women's haunches only are most subject to display, and fly out.

Clara. Bobadilla, rogue, ten ducats, I hit the prepuce of thy cod-piece!

Lucio. Hold, if you love my life, sister! I am not Zancho Bobadilla; I am your brother Lucio. What a fright you have put me in!

Clara. Brother! and wherefore thus?

Lucio. Why, master steward here, Signior Zancho, made me change: he does nothing but misuse me, and call me coward, and swears I shall wait upon him.

Bob. Well, I do no more than I have authority for.— Would I were away though! for she's as much too mannish as he too womanish: I dare not meddle with her; yet I must set a good face on't, if I had it [*Aside*].—I have like charge of you, madam; I am as well to mollify you as to qualify him. What have you to do with armours, and pistols, and javelins, and swords, and such tools? Remember, mistress, Nature hath given you a sheath only, to signify, women are to put up men's weapons, not to draw them. Look you now, is this a fit trot for a gentlewoman? You shall see the court-ladies move like goddesses, as if they trod air; they will swim you their measures [r], like whiting-mops [s], as if their feet were fins, and the hinges of their knees oiled. Do they love to ride great-horses [t], as you do? no; they love to ride great asses sooner. Faith, I know not what to say to ye both: Custom hath turned Nature topsy-turvy in you.

Clara. Nay, but, master steward——

Bob. You cannot trot so fast, but he ambles as slowly.

Clara. Signior Spindle, will you hear me?

Bob. He that shall come to bestride your virginity had better be a-foot o'er the dragon.

---

[r] *measures*] See note, vol. i. 166.

[s] *whiting-mops*] "i. e. young whitings,—commonly used as a term of endearment." WEBER.

[t] *great-horses*] See note, vol. vii. 159.

Clara. Very well!

Bob. Did ever Spanish lady pace so?

Clara. Hold these a little.
  [*Takes down from the wall a truncheon and weapons.*

Lucio. I'll not touch 'em, I.

Clara. First do I break your office o'er your pate,
You dog-skin-fac'd rogue, pilcher ᵗ, you poor-John ᵘ!
Which I will beat to stock-fish. [*Beats him.*

Lucio. Sister—

Bob. Madam—

Clara. You cittern-head ᵛ! who have you talk'd to, ha?
You nasty, stinking, and ill-countenanc'd cur!

Bob. By this hand, I'll bang your brother for this, when I get him alone.

Clara. How!—Kick him, Lucio.—He shall kick you, Bob,
Spite o' thy ʷ nose; that's flat.—Kick him, I say,
Or I will cut ˣ thy head off! [LUCIO *kicks him.*

Bob. Softly, you'd best!

Clara. Now, thou lean, dried, and ominous-visag'd knave,
Thou false and peremptory steward, pray!
For I will hang thee up in thine own chain ʸ.

Lucio. Good sister, do not choke him.

Bob. Murder! murder! [*Exit.*

Clara. Well, I shall meet with you.—Lucio, who bought
  this?
'Tis a reasonable good one: but there hangs one,
Spain's champion ne'er us'd truer; with this staff
Old Alvarez has led up men so close,
They could almost spit in the cannon's mouth;
Whilst I with that, and this, well mounted, scurr'd ᶻ

ᵗ *pilcher*] i. e. pilchard.

ᵘ *poor-John*] "i. e. hake dried and salted." WEBER.

ᵛ *cittern-head*] Equivalent to—ugly fellow, in allusion to the grotesquely carved heads with which citterns (i. e. guitars, see note, vol. iii. 68) were frequently decorated.

ʷ *thy*] Both the folios "the".

ˣ *cut*] Weber chose to print "kick"!!   ʸ *chain*] See note, p. 118.

ᶻ *scurr'd*] i. e. scour'd. So the first folio.—The second folio "scour'd".—Sympson, at Seward's suggestion, printed "skirr'd"; and so his successors.

A horse-troop through and through, like swift Desire,
And seen poor rogues retire, all gore, and gash'd
Like bleeding shads.

Lucio. Bless us, sister Clara,
How desperately you talk! What do you call this gun?
A dag [a]?

Clara. I'll give't thee; a French petronel.
You never saw my Barbary, the Infanta
Bestow'd upon me, as yet, Lucio:
Walk down, and see it.

Lucio. What, into the stable?
Not I; the jades will kick: the poor groom there
Was almost spoil'd the other day.

Clara. Fie on thee!
Thou wilt scarce be a man before thy mother.

Lucio. When will you be a woman?

Clara. Would I were none!
But Nature's privy seal assures me one.

Enter ALVAREZ *with* BOBADILLA.

Alv. Thou anger'st me. Can strong habitual custom
Work with such magic on the mind and manners,
In spite of sex and nature? Find out, sirrah,
Some skilful fighter.

Bob. Yes, sir.

Alv. I will rectify
And redeem either's proper inclination,
Or bray 'em in a mortar, and new-mould 'em.

Bob. Believe your eyes, sir: I tell you, we wash an Ethiop. [*Exit.*

Clara. I strike it, for ten ducats.

Alv. How now, Clara,
Your breeches on still? And your petticoat
Not yet off, Lucio? art thou not gelt?
Or did the cold Muscovite beget thee,
That lay here lieger in the last great frost [b]?

---

[a] *dag*] "i. e. pistol." WEBER.

[b] *Or did the cold Muscovite beget thee,*
   That lay here lieger in the last great frost?] Sympson silently printed " *Or*

Art not thou, Clara, turn'd a man indeed
Beneath the girdle? and a woman thou?
I'll have you search'd; by [Heaven] [c], I strongly doubt!
We must have these things mended. Come, go in. [*Exit.*

Enter VITELLI *with* BOBADILLA.

Bob. With Lucio, say you? there is [d] for you.
Vit. And there is for thee. [*Gives money.*
Bob. I thank you. You have now bought a little advice of me: if you chance to have conference with that lady there, be very civil, or look to your head! she has ten nails, and you have but two eyes: if any foolish hot motions should chance to rise in the horizon, under your equinoctial there, qualify it as well as you can, for I fear the elevation of your pole will not agree with the horoscope of her constitution: she is Bell the Dragon [e], I assure you. [*Exit.*
Vit. Are you the Lucio, sir, that sav'd Vitelli?
Lucio. Not I, indeed, sir; I did never brabble [f]:
There walks that Lucio metamorphosèd.
Vit. Do you mock me? [*Exit* LUCIO.
Clara. No, he does not: I am that
Supposèd Lucio that was, but Clara
That is, and daughter unto Alvarez.
Vit. Amazement daunts me. Would my life were riddles,
So you were still my fair expositor!
Protected by a lady from my death?

---

did not the", &c.: *lieger*, i. e. resident ambassador. "Russian ambassadors were at King James's court in 1617, and in 1622; and as Sir John Finett, in his *Philoxenis*, mentions, that in the latter year, on account of the great frost they [the ambassador] did not stir from their [his] house till June [April], the text probably alludes to the latter embassy, and this fixes the date of the play." WEBER. Finett's words are; "The nine and twentieth of Aprill [1622], the Russian Ambassador having not stirred from his home all the Winter, and being desirous to take the fresh Aire, was by me accompanied to Theobalds," &c. *Philoxenis*, p. 103.

[c] [*Heaven*] A break here in both the folios.

[d] *there is*] i. e. there he is.—The modern editors silently print "there he's" and "there he *is*": but compare the next speech.

[e] *Bell the Dragon*] Sympson silently printed "*Bell* and *the Dragon*"; and so his successors.

[f] *brabble*] i. e. brawl.

Oh, I shall wear an everlasting blush
Upon my cheek from this discovery!
Oh, you, the fairest soldier I e'er saw,
Each of whose eyes, like a bright beamy shield,
Conquers, without blows, the contentious——
    Clara. Sir, guard yourself; you are in your enemy's house,
And may be injur'd.
    Vit. 'Tis impossible :
Foe, nor oppressing odds, dares prove Vitelli,
If Clara side him, and will call him friend.
I would the difference of our bloods were such
As might with any shift be wip'd away!
Or would to Heaven yourself were all your name;
That, having lost blood by you, I might hope
To raise blood from you! But my black-wing'd fate
Hovers aversely over that fond hope;
And he, whose tongue thus gratifies [f] the daughter
And sister of his enemy, wears a sword
To rip the father and the brother up :
Thus you, that sav'd this wretched life of mine,
Have sav'd it to the ruin of your friends.
That my affections should promiscuously
Dart love and hate at once, both worthily!
Pray, let me kiss your hand.
    Clara. You are treacherous,
And come to do me mischief.
    Vit. Speak on still :
Your words are falser, fair, than my intents,
And each sweet accent far more treacherous; for,
Though you speak ill of me, you speak so well
I do desire to hear you.
    Clara. Pray, be gone;
Or kill me, if you please.
    Vit. Oh, neither can I!
For to be gone were to destroy my life;
And to kill you were to destroy my soul.
I am in love; yet must not be in love :

---

[f] *gratifies*] "i. e. makes acknowledgments, returns thanks to." HEATH (*MS. Notes*).

I'll get away apace. Yet, valiant lady,
Such gratitude to honour I do owe,
And such obedience to your memory,
That, if you will bestow something, that I
May wear about me, it shall bind all wrath,
My most inveterate wrath, from all attempts,
Till you and I meet next.
 Clara. A favour, sir?
Why, I will give you good counsel.
 Vit. That already
You have bestow'd;—a ribbon or a glove——
 Clara. Nay, those are tokens for a waiting-maid
To trim the butler with.
 Vit. Your feather——
 Clara. Fie!
The wenches give them to their [g] serving-men.
 Vit. That little ring——
 Clara. 'Twill hold you but by the finger;
And I would have you faster.
 Vit. Any thing
That I may wear, and but remember you.
 Clara. This smile; my good opinion; or myself;
But that, it seems, you like not.
 Vit. Yes; so well,
When any smiles, I will remember yours;
Your good opinion shall in weight poise me
Against a thousand ill; lastly, yourself
My curious eye now figures in my heart,
Where I will wear you till the table [h] break.
So, whitest angels guard you!
 Clara. Stay, sir: I
Have fitly thought to give what you as fitly
May not disdain to wear.
 Vit. What's that?
 Clara. This sword.—
I never heard a man speak till this hour:

  [g] *their*] Sympson silently printed "the"; and so his successors.
  [h] *the table*] "i. e. the picture, or rather, the board on which it is painted—my heart." WEBER (the note shortened).

His words are golden chains; and now, I fear,
The lioness hath met a tamer here:
Fie, how this tongue chimes¹! [*Aside.*]—What was I saying?
Oh, this favour I bequeathe you, which I tie
         [*Ties on the sword.*
In a love-knot, fast, ne'er to hurt my friends;
Yet be it fortunate 'gainst all your foes
(For I have neither friend nor foe, but yours)
As e'er it was to me! I have kept it long,
And value it, next my virginity.
But, good, return it; for I now remember
I vow'd, who purchas'd it should have me too.
 Vit. Would that were possible! but, alas, it is not!
Yet this assure yourself, most honour'd Clara,
I'll not infringe an article of breath
My vow hath offer'd to you; nor from this part
Whilst it hath edge or point, or I a heart. [*Exit.*
 Clara. Oh, leave me living!—What new exercise
Is crept into my breast, that blancheth clean
My former nature? I begin to find
I am a woman, and must learn to fight
A softer sweeter battle than with swords.
I am sick methinks; but the disease I feel
Pleaseth, and punisheth. I warrant, love
Is very like this, that folks talk of so;
I skill not ʲ what it is, yet sure even here,
Even in my heart, I sensibly perceive
It glows, and riseth like a glimmering flame,
But know not yet the essence on't, nor name. [*Exit.*

---

¹ *this tongue chimes*] The correction of Heath (*MS. Notes*), who explains it,
"i. e. her own tongue, which had just uttered two *chiming* or rhyming verses."
—Both the folios "his *tongue chimes*"; and so the modern editors.

ʲ *I skill not*]—Which Weber wrongly explains—I care not,—means—I know
not. "*Skill*, to know, to understand." Brockett's *Gloss. of North Country
Words.*

ACT III.

SCENE I.—*A room in the house of the* Alguazier.

Enter MALRODA *and* Alguazier.

Malr. He must not! nor he shall not! who shall let[j] him?
You, politic Diego[k], with your face of wisdom!
Don Blirt! the [pox up]on[l] your aphorisms,
Your grave and sage ale-physiognomy!
Do not I know thee for the Alguazier,
Whose dunghill all the parish scavengers
Could never rid? Thou comedy to men,
Whose serious folly is a butt for all
To shoot their wits at; whilst thou hast not wit,
Nor heart, to answer, or be angry!
    Alg. Lady——
    Malr. Peace, peace, you rotten rogue, supported by
A staff of rottener office! Dare you check
Any's accesses that I will allow?
Piorato is my friend, and visits me
In lawful sort, to espouse me as his wife;
And who will cross, or shall, our interviews?
You know me, sirrah, for no chambermaid,
That cast her belly and her waistcoat[m] lately.
Thou think'st thy constableship is much: not so;
I am ten offices to thee; ay, thy house,
Thy house and office is maintain'd by me.
    Alg. My house-of-office is maintain'd i' the garden.
Go to! I know you, and I have conniv'd;
You 're a delinquent, but I have conniv'd;

---

[j] *let*] "i. e. hinder." WEBER.

[k] *Diego*] An allusion—as before, vol. iii. 274, vol. vii. 34—to a person who was in very bad *odour*. He is again alluded to at p. 162 of the present comedy, and more particularly in the next play, act ii. sc. 2.

[l] *the* [*pox up*]*on*] So the Editors of 1778 and Weber.

[m] *her waistcoat*] As a low strumpet: see note, vol. i. 39.

A poison, though not in the third degree [n];
I can say, black's your eye, though it be grey;
I have conniv'd at this your friend and you:
But what is got by this connivency?
I like his feature [o] well; a proper man,
Of good discourse, fine conversation,
Valiant, and a great carrier of the business,
Sweet-breasted [p] as the nightingale or thrush:
Yet I must tell you, you forget yourself;
My lord Vitelli's love, and maintenance,
Deserves no other Jack i' the box but he.
What though he gather'd first the golden fruit,
And blew your pigs-coat up into a blister,
When you did wait at court upon his mother,
Has he not well provided for the barn [q]?
Beside, what profit reap I by the other?
If you will have me serve your pleasure, lady,
Your pleasure must accommodate my service;
As good be virtuous and poor, as not
Thrive by my knavery: all the world would be
Good, prosper'd goodness like to villany.
I am the king's vicegerent by my place;
His right lieutenant in mine own precinct.

Malr. Thou art a right rascal in all men's precincts:

[n] *Go to! I know you, and I have conniv'd;*
You 're a delinquent, but I have conniv'd;
A poison, though not in the third degree] Both the folios have;
" Go too, I know you, and I have *contriv'd;*
Y' are a delinquent, but I have *contriv'd*
A poyson, though not in the third degree;"
and so the modern editors.—" The reading of the folios," observes Heath, " is stark nonsense. What had the Alguazier *contrived?* and particularly, what *poison* had he *contrived?*" and, after giving the excellent emendation which I have adopted, he explains it, " You are a delinquent, you are a poison, yet I have connived at all this", adding, " the correction is confirmed by the next line but one,
'I have *conniv'd* at this your friend and you.'
Every one knows that connivancy at offences for the sake of a bribe is one of the grand sources of a corrupt officer's profits; and there is humour in the Alguazier's repeating so often his connivancy." *MS. Notes.*

[o] *feature*] Sympson's correction.—Both the folios " feather".

[p] *Sweet-breasted*] i. e. sweet-voiced: see note, vol. viii. 54.

[q] *barn*]—Or *bairn*—i. e. child.

Yet now, my pair of twins, of fool and knave,
Look, we are friends; there's gold for thee: admit
Whom I will have, and keep it from my don,
And I will make thee richer than thou art wise:
Thou shalt be my bawd and my officer;
Thy children shall eat still, my good night-owl,
And thy old wife sell andirons to the court,
Be countenanc'd by the dons, and wear a hood,
Nay, keep my garden-house [q]; I'll call her mother,
Thee father, my good poisonous red-hair'd dill [r],
And gold shall daily be thy sacrifice,
Wrought from a fertile island of mine own,
Which I will offer, like an Indian queen.
   Alg. And I will be thy devil, thou my flesh,
With which I'll catch the world.
   Malr. Fill some tobacco,
And bring it in. If Piorato come
Before my don, admit him; if my don
Before my love, conduct him, my dear devil.
   Alg. I will, my dear flesh.   [*Exit* MALRODA.
                   First come, first serv'd: well said!—
Oh, equal [s] Heaven, how wisely thou disposest
Thy several gifts! One's born a great rich fool,
For the subordinate knave to work upon;
Another's poor, with wit's addition,
Which, well or ill us'd, builds a living up,—
And that too from the sire oft descends;
Only fair virtue by traduction
Never succeeds [t], and seldom meets success:
What have I, then, to do with't? My free will,
Left me by Heaven, makes me or good or ill.
Now, since vice gets more in this vicious world
Than piety, and my stars' confluence

   [q] *garden-house*] See note, vol. i. 32.
   [r] *dill*] Silently altered by Sympson to "deel"; and so the Editors of 1778: Weber printed "devil" (and, perhaps, rightly; see what follows in the text).— But qy. "drill"? "The Drill (beast), *Satyrus Indicus.*" Coles's *Dict.* "Drill, a Baboon, or over-grown Ape." Kersey's *Dict.*
   [s] *equal*] i. e. just.
   [t] *Never succeeds*] "i. e. never follows by *succession.*" *Ed.* 1778.

Enforce my disposition to affect
Gain and the name of rich, let who will practise
War, and grow that way great; religious,
And that way good. My chief felicity
Is wealth, the nurse of sensuality :
And he that mainly labours to be rich,
Must scratch great scabs, and claw a strumpet's itch.
[*Exit.*

SCENE II.—*A street before the house of the Alguazier.*

Enter PIORATO *and* BOBADILLA.

Pio. To say, sir, I will wait upon your lord,
Were not to understand myself.

Bob. To say, sir,
You will do any thing but wait upon him,
Were not to understand my lord.

Pio. I'll meet him
Some half-hour hence, and doubt not but to render
His son a man again : the cure is easy;
I have done divers.

Bob. Women do you mean, sir?

Pio. Cures I do mean, sir. Be there but one spark
Of fire remaining in him unextinct,
With my discourse I'll blow it to a flame,
And with my practice into action.
I have had one so full of childish fear,
And womanish-hearted, sent to my advice,
He durst not draw a knife to cut his meat.

Bob. And how, sir, did you help him?

Pio. Sir, I kept him
Seven days in a dark room by candle-light,
A plenteous table, spread with all good meats,
Before his eyes, a case of keen broad knives
Upon the board, and he so watch'd he might not
Touch the least modicum, unless he cut it :
And thus I brought him first to draw a knife.

Bob. Good!

Pio. Then for ten days did I diet him
Only with burnt pork, sir, and gammons of bacon;
A pill of caviary now and then,
Which breeds choler adust, you know——
   Bob. 'Tis true.
   Pio. And, to purge phlegmatic humour and cold crudities,
In all that time he drank me *aqua-fortis*,
And nothing else but——
   Bob. Aqua-vitæ, signior ;
For *aqua-fortis* poisons.
   Pio. Aqua-fortis,
I say again : what's one man's poison, signior,
Is another's meat or drink.
   Bob. Your patience, sir ;
By your good patience, h'ad a huge cold stomach.
   Pio. I fir'd it, and gave him then three sweats
In the Artillery-yard, three drilling days :
And now he'll shoot a gun, and draw a sword,
And fight, with any man in Christendom.
   Bob. A receipt for a coward ! I'll be bold, sir,
To write your good prescription.
   Pio. Sir, hereafter
You shall, and underneath it put *probatum*.
Is your chain right [u]?
   Bob. It is both right and just, sir;
For, though I am a steward, I did get it
With no man's wrong.
   Pio. You are witty.
   Bob. So, so.
Could you not cure one, sir, of being too rash
And over-daring ?—there now's my disease—
Fool-hardy, as they say ? for that in sooth
I am.
   Pio. Most easily.
   Bob. How ?
   Pio. To make you drunk, sir,
With small beer once a-day, and beat you twice,

---

[u] *Is your chain right*] See note, p. 118: "*right*, i. e. real gold." WEBER.

Till you be bruis'd all over; if that help not,
Knock out your brains.
　Bob. This is strong physic, signior,
And never will agree with my weak body:
I find the medicine worse than the malady,
And therefore will remain fool-hardy still.
You 'll come, sir?
　Pio. As I am a gentleman.
　Bob. A man o' the sword should never break his word.
　Pio. I 'll overtake you: I have only, sir,
A complimental visitation
To offer to a mistress lodg'd here by.
　Bob. A gentlewoman?
　Pio. Yes, sir.
　Bob. Fair and comely?
　Pio. Oh, sir, the paragon, the nonpareil
Of Seville, the most wealthy mine of Spain
For beauty and perfection.
　Bob. Say you so?
Might not a man entreat a courtesy,
To walk along with you, signior, to peruse
This dainty mine, though not to dig in 't, signior?
Hauh—I hope you 'll not deny me, being a stranger:
Though I am steward, I am flesh and blood,
And frail as other men.
　Pio. Sir, blow your nose!
I dare not, for the world: no; she is kept
By a great don, Vitelli.
　Bob. How!
　Pio. 'Tis true.
　Bob. See, things will veer about! This Don Vitelli
Am I to seek now, to deliver letters
From my young mistress Clara; and, I tell you,
Under the rose, (because you are a stranger
And my [e]special friend,) I doubt there is
A little foolish love betwixt the parties,
Unknown unto my lord.
　Pio. Happy discovery!
My fruit begins to ripen [*Aside*].—Hark you, sir:

I would not wish you now to give those letters;
But home, and ope this to Madonna Clara,
Which when I come I 'll justify, and relate
More amply and particularly.
   Bob. I approve
Your counsel, and will practise it: *beso las manos.*—
Here 's two chewres chewr'd ᵛ: when Wisdom is employ'd,
'Tis ever thus [*Aside*].—Your more acquaintance, signior!
I say not better, lest you think I thought not
Yours good enough.
   Pio. Your servant, excellent steward!
                                  [*Exit* BOBADILLA.
Would all the dons in Spain had no more brains!
Here comes the Alguazier.

               Enter Alguazier.
               Dieu vous garde, monsieur!
Is my cuz stirring yet?
   Aly. Your cuz, good cousin!
A whore is like a fool, a-kin to all
The gallants in the town. Your cuz, good signior,
Is gone abroad, sir, with her other cousin,
My lord Vitelli; since when there hath been
Some dozen cousins here to inquire for her.
   Pio. She 's greatly allied, sir.
   Alg. Marry, is she, sir;
Come of a lusty kindred. The truth is,
I must connive no more; no more admittance
Must I consent to: my good lord has threaten'd me,
And you must pardon.
   Pio. Out upon thee, man!
Turn honest in thine age? one foot i' the grave?
Thou shalt not wrong thyself so for a million.
Look, thou three-headed Cerberus (for wit

   ᵛ *Here 's two chewres chewr'd*] "i. e. here are two businesses despatched."
SYMPSON. *Chewre* is a corrupt form of *char* or *chare*, a turn of work, a job.
The expression in the text is used by very early writers: so in *A New and
Pleasaunt enterlude intituled the Mariage of Witte and Science*, n. d., "This
chayer is chared." Sig. D 4.

I mean), here is one sop, and two, and three;
For every chop a bit. [*Gives money.*]
Alg. Ay, marry, sir!
Well, the poor heart loves you but too well[w]:
We have been talking on you, faith, this hour,
Where, what I said—Go to! she loves your valour;
Oh, and your music most abominably!
She is within, sir, and alone.
[PIORATO *goes to the other side of him.*]
What mean you?
Pio. That is your sergeant's side, I take it, sir:
Now, I endure your constable's much better;
There is less danger in't; for one, you know,
Is a tame harmless monster in the light,
The sergeant, salvage[x] both by day and night.
Alg. I'll call her to you for that.
Pio. No, I will charm her[y].
Alg. She's come.

Enter MALRODA.

Pio. My spirit!
Malr. Oh, my sweet!
Leap hearts to lips, and in our kisses meet!
Pio. [*sings*]

> Turn, turn thy beauteous face away:
> How pale and sickly looks the day,
> In emulation of thy brighter beams!
> Oh, envious light, fly, fly, begone!
> Come, night, and piece two breasts as one!
> When what love does we will repeat in dreams.
> Yet, thy eyes open, who can day hence fright?
> Let but their lids fall, and it will be night.

Alg. Well, I will leave you to your fortitude,
And you to temperance. Ah, ye pretty pair!
'Twere sin to sunder you. Lovers being alone

---

[w] *but too well*] Sympson silently printed "*but too* too *well*"; and so probably the author wrote.

[x] *salvage*] Is the old form of "*savage*," but that Piorato uses it "affectedly" (as Weber asserts) is not so certain.

[y] *I will charm her*] Qy. Ought not Piorato's song to follow immediately after this speech?

Make one of two, and day and night all one.
But fall not out, I charge you, keep the peace;
You know my place else. [*Exit.*

Malr. No, you will not marry;
You are a courtier, and can sing, my love,
And want no mistresses: but yet I care not;
I'll love you still, and when I am dead for you,
Then you'll believe my truth.

Pio. You kill me, fair:
It is my lesson that you speak. Have I
In any circumstance deserv'd this doubt?
I am not like your false and perjur'd don,
That here maintains you, and has vow'd his faith,
And yet attempts in way of marriage
A lady not far off.

Malr. How's that?

Pio. 'Tis so:
And therefore, mistress, now the time is come
You may demand his promise; and I swear
To marry you with speed.

Malr. And, with that gold
Which Don Vitelli gives, you'll walk some voyage,
And leave me to my trade; and laugh, and brag
How you o'er-reach'd a whore, and gull'd a lord.

Pio. You anger me extremely: fare you well.
What should I say to be believ'd? Expose me
To any hazard; or, like jealous Juno,
The incensèd step-mother of Hercules,
Design me labours most impossible [z],
I'll do 'em, or die in 'em; so at last
You will believe me.

---

[z] *labours most impossible*] "Sympson wishes to weaken the expression by reading—'labours '*most* (i. e. almost) impossible'. But the present reading is right, and a bold poetical mode of expression used by Shakespeare as well as by our authors. In *Much Ado about Nothing*, Beatrice says that Benedict amused himself in devising impossible slanders: in *The Merry Wives of Windsor*, Ford says that he would search for Falstaff in impossible places: and in Jonson's *Sejanus*, Silius accuses Aper of malicious and manifold applying, foul arresting, and impossible construction." MASON.

Malr. Come; we are friends; I do:
I am thine; walk in. My lord has sent me outsides,
But thou shalt have 'em; the colours are too sad[a].
Pio. Faith, mistress, I want clothes indeed.
Malr. I have
Some gold, too, for my servant.
Pio. And I have
A better metal for my mistress. [*Exeunt.*

SCENE III.—*A room in the same.*

Enter, from opposite sides, VITELLI *and* Alguazier.

Alg. Undone!—Wit, now or never help me!—My master!
He will cut my throat; I am a dead constable!
And he'll not be hang'd neither; there's the grief.—
[*Aside.*
The party, sir, is here——
Vit. What?
Alg. He was here,—
I cry your lordship mercy,—but I rattled him;
I told him here was no companions
For such debosh'd[b] and poor-condition'd fellows;
I bid him venture not so desperately
The cropping of his ears, slitting his nose,
Or being gelt.
Vit. 'Twas well done.
Alg. Please your honour,
I told him there were stews; and then at last
Swore three or four great oaths she was remov'd,
Which I did think I might in conscience,
Being for your lordship.
Vit. What became of him?
Alg. Faith, sir, he went away with a flea in's ear,
Like a poor cur, clapping his trindle tail[c]
Betwixt his legs.—*A chi ha, a chi ha, a chi ha!*—Now luck!
[*Aside.*

---

[a] *sad*] "i. e. sombre, dark." WEBER.
[b] *debosh'd*] i.e. debauched. So the first folio.—The second folio "debauch'd."
[c] *trindle tail*] Properly *trundle* tail,—i. e. round, curly tail.

Enter MALRODA *and* PIORATO.

Malr. 'Tis he; do as I told thee; bless thee, signior!— Oh, my dear lord!

Vit. Malroda! what, alone?

Malr. She never is alone that is accompanied With noble thoughts, my lord; and mine are such, Being only of your lordship.

Vit. Pretty lass!

Malr. Oh, my good lord, my picture's done; but, faith, It is not like. Nay, this way, sir; the light Strikes best upon it here.

    [*While she shews* VITELLI *the picture,* PIORATO
        steals to the door.

Pio. Excellent wench!   [*Aside, and then exit.*

Alg. I am glad the danger's over.   [*Aside, and then exit.*

Vit. 'Tis wondrous like, But that Art cannot counterfeit what Nature Could make but once.

Malr. All's clear: another tune You must hear from me now [*Aside*].—Vitelli, thou 'rt A most perfidious and a perjur'd man, As ever did usurp nobility.

Vit. What mean'st thou, Mal?

Malr. Leave your betraying smiles, And change the tunes of your enticing tongue To penitential prayers; for I am great, In labour even, with anger; big with child Of woman's rage, bigger than when my womb Was pregnant by thee. Go, seducer, fly Out of the world; let me the last wretch be Dishonour'd by thee: touch me not; I loathe My very heart, because thou lay'st there long. A woman's well help'd up, that's confident In e'er a glittering outside on ᵇ you all! Would I had honestly been match'd to some Poor country swain, ere known the vanity Of court! peace then had been my portion,

    ᵇ *on*] i. e. of.—The modern editors silently print " of."

Nor had been[c] cozen'd by an hour's pomp,
To be a whore unto my dying day.
 Vit. Oh,
The uncomfortable ways such women have!
Their different speech and meaning, no assurance
In what they say or do; dissemblers
Even in their prayers, as if the weeping Greek
That flatter'd Troy a-fire had been their Adam;
Liars, as if their mother had been made
Only of all the falsehood of the man
Dispos'd into that rib! Do I know this,
And more; nay, all that can concern this sex,
With the true end of my creation?
Can I with rational discourse sometimes
Advance my spirit into Heaven, before
'T has shook hands with my body, and yet blindly
Suffer my filthy flesh to master it,
With sight of such fair frail beguiling objects?
When I am absent, easily I resolve
Ne'er more to entertain those strong desires
That triumph o'er me, even to actual sin;
Yet when I meet again those sorcerer's eyes,
Their beams my hardest resolutions thaw,
As if that cakes of ice and July met;
And her sighs, powerful as the violent North,
Like a light feather twirl me round about,
And leave me in mine own low state again.—   [*Aside.*
What ail'st thou? prithee, weep not. Oh, those tears,
If they were true and rightly spent, would raise
A flowery spring i' the midst of January;
Celestial ministers with crystal cups
Would stoop to save 'em for immortal drink!
But from[d] this passion: why all this?
 Malr. Do you ask?
You are marrying: having made me unfit

---

 [c] *had been*] Heath (*MS. Notes*) would read "*had* I *been*": but we find many examples of an ellipsis like the present.

 [d] *from*] i. e. turn from,—have done with.—The modern editors print "*But from this passion—why all this?*"

For any man, you leave me fit for all :
Porters must be my burdens now, to live;
And, fitting me yourself for carts and beadles,
You leave me to 'em : and who, of all the world,
But the virago, your great arch-foe's daughter?
But on! I care not this poor rush[e]! 'twill breed
An excellent comedy; ha! ha! 't makes me laugh;
I cannot choose. The best is, some report
It is a match for fear, not love, o' your side.
   Vit. Why, how the devil knows she that I saw
This lady? are all whores piec'd with some witch?
I will be merry [*Aside*].—Faith, 'tis true, sweetheart,
I am to marry.
   Malr. Are you? you base lord!
By [Heaven][f], I'll pistol thee.
   Vit. A roaring whore!—   [*Aside.*
Take heed: there's a correction-house hard by.
You ha' learn'd this o' your swordman, that I warn'd you of,
Your fencers and your drunkards. But whereas
You upbraid me with oaths, why, I must tell you
I ne'er promis'd you marriage, nor have vow'd,
But said I lov'd[g] you, long as you remain'd
The woman I expected, or you swore:
And how you have fail'd of that, sweetheart, you know.
You fain would shew your power: but, fare you well;
I'll keep no more faith with an infidel.
   Malr. Nor I my bosom for a Turk. Do you hear?
Go; and the devil take me, if ever
I see you more! I was too true.
   Vit. Come; pish!
That devil take the falsest of us two!
   Malr. Amen!
   Vit. You are an ill clerk, and curse yourself:
Madness transports you. I confess, I drew you
Unto my will; but you must know, that must not

   [e] *this poor rush*] Which, we may suppose, she takes up from the floor,—rooms being formerly (before the introduction of carpets) strewed with rushes.
   [f] [*Heaven*] A break here in both the folios.
   [g] *I lov'd*] Sympson and the Editors of 1778 chose to print " I'd love " ; Weber, " *I* love."

Make me dote on the habit of my sin:
I will, to settle you to your content,
Be master of my word. And yet he lied,
That told you I was marrying, but in thought:
But will you slave me to your tyranny
So cruelly, I shall not dare to look
Or speak to other women? make me not
Your smock's monopoly. Come, let's be friends:
Look, here's a jewel for thee: I will come
At night, and——
   Malr. What? i' faith, you shall not, sir.
   Vit. Faith and troth, and verily, but I will.
   Malr. Half-drunk, to make a noise and rail?
   Vit. No, no;
Sober, and dieted for the nonce[g]. I am thine:
I have won the day.
   Malr. The night, though, shall be mine.
                                      [*Exeunt severally.*

SCENE IV.—*A room in the house of* ALVAREZ.

Enter CLARA *and* BOBADILLA.

   Clara. What said he, sirrah?
   Bob. Little, or nothing. Faith, I saw him not,
Nor will not: he doth love a strumpet, mistress,
Nay, keeps her spitefully, under the constable's nose:
It shall be justified by the gentleman,
Your brother's master, that is now within
A-practising. There are your letters [*Gives letters*]: come,
You shall not cast yourself away, while I live;
Nor will I venture my right-worshipful place
In such a business. Here's your mother,—down[h],—
And he that loves you; another-gates fellow, i-wis[i],
If you had any grace——
   Clara. Well, rogue!   [*Sits, and works.*

---

  [g] *for the nonce*] i. e. for the occasion.
  [h] *down*] i. e. sit down to your work.
  [i] *i-wis*] i. e. truly, certainly. Heath's correction (*MS. Notes*).—Both the folios "I wish"; and so the modern editors.

Bob. I'll in,
To see Don Lucio manage: he will make
A pretty piece of flesh, I promise you;
He does already handle his weapon finely.   [*Exit.*

Enter EUGENIA *and* SAAVEDRA.

Eug. She knows your love, sir, and the full allowance
Her father and myself approve it with;
And I must tell you, I much hope it hath
Wrought some impression, by her alteration:
She sighs, and says *forsooth,* and cries *heigh-ho!*
She'll take ill words o' the steward and the servants,
Yet answer affably and modestly;
Things, sir, not usual with her. There she is;
Change some few words.
　Saav. Madam, I am bound to you.—
How now, fair mistress? working?
　Clara. Yes, forsooth;
Learning to live another day.
　Saav. That needs not.
　Clara. No, forsooth? by my truly, but it does;
We know not what we may come to.
　Eug. 'Tis strange.
　Saav. Come, I ha' begg'd leave for you to play.
　Clara. Forsooth,
'Tis ill for a fair lady to be idle.
　Saav. She had better be well busied, I know that.
Turtle, methinks you mourn: shall I sit by you?
　Clara. If you be weary, sir, you had best be gone:
I work not a true stitch, now you're my mate.
　Saav. If I be so, I must do more than side you.
　Clara. Even what you will, but tread me.
　Saav. Shall we bill?
　Clara. Oh, no, forsooth?
　Saav. Being so fair, my Clara,
Why do you delight in black work?
　Clara. Oh, white sir,
The fairest ladies like the blackest men:

I ever lov'd the colour; all black things
Are least subject to change.
   Saav. Why, I do love
A black thing too; and the most beauteous faces
Have oftenest of them, as the blackest eyes,
Jet-archèd brows, such hair. I'll kiss your hand.
   Clara. 'Twill hinder me my work, sir; and my mother
Will chide me, if I do not do my task.
   Saav. Your mother, nor your father, shall chide. You
Might have a prettier task, would you be rul'd,
And look with open eyes.
   Clara. I stare upon you,
And broadly see you; a wondrous proper man!
Yet 'twere a greater task for me to love you,
Than I shall ever work, sir, in seven year.—
[Pox]^j o' this stitching! I had rather feel
Two, than sew one. This rogue has given me a stitch
Clean 'cross my heart [*Aside*].—Good faith, sir, I shall prick
    you.
   Saav. In gooder faith, I would prick you again.
   Clara. Now you grow troublesome: pish, the man is
    foolish!
   Saav. Pray, wear these trifles.
   Clara. Neither you, nor trifles:
You are a trifle; wear yourself, sir, out,
And here no more trifle the time away.
   Saav. Come, you're deceiv'd in me; I will not wake,
Nor fast, nor die for you.
   Clara. Goose, be not you deceiv'd:
I cannot like, nor love, nor live with you,
Nor fast, nor watch, nor pray for you.
   Eug. Her old fit.
   Saav. Sure, this is not the way [*Aside*].—Nay, I will
    break
Your melancholy——

---

j [*Pox*] A break here in both the folios, which the Editors of 1778 and Weber filled up with "Plague", though, in an earlier speech of Clara (p. 134, last line) they supplied "Pox",—a word which was formerly (see, for instance, vol. iv. p. 445, l. 10) not unusual in a lady's mouth.

Clara. I shall break your pate, then.
Away, you sanguine scabbard!
Eug. Out upon thee!
Thou 'lt break my heart, I am sure.
Saav. She's not yet tame.

Enter ALVAREZ; PIORATO *and* LUCIO, *fencing; and* BOBADILLA.

Alv. On, sir! put home! or I shall goad you here
With this old fox[k] of mine, that will bite better.—
Oh, the brave age is gone! in my young days
A chevalier would stock a needle's point [1]
Three times together.—Straight i' the hams!
Or shall I give you new garters?
Bob. Faith, old master,
There's little hope; the linen sure was dank
He was begot in, he's so faint and cold:
Even send him to Toledo, there to study;
For he will never fadge with[m] these Toledos.—
Bear you up your point there, pick his teeth! Oh, base!
Pio. Fie, you are the most untoward scholar! Bear
Your body gracefully; what a posture's there!
You lie too open-breasted.
Lucio. Oh!
Pio. You'd never
Make a good statesman.
Lucio. Pray, no more!
I hope to breathe in peace, and therefore need not
The practice of these dangerous qualities:
I do not mean to live by 't, for I trust
You'll leave me better able.
Alv. Not a button.—
Eugenia, let's go get us a new heir.
Eug. Ay, by my troth, your daughter's as untoward.

---

[k] *fox*] A familiar term for the old English broad-sword, which we have had repeatedly before.

[1] *would stock a needle's point*] " i. e. would hit it with a stoccado, a thrust of his rapier." MASON. The meaning is—would run his sword into the eye of a needle: to *stock* is—to thread.

[m] *fadge with*] See note, p. 134.

Alv. I will break thee bone by bone, and bake thee,
Ere I'll ha' such a wooden son to inherit.—
Take him a good knock; see how that will work.
   Pio. Now for your life, signior!
   Lucio. Oh, alas, I am kill'd!
My eye is out! look, father! Zancho! [Pox],[m]
I'll play the fool no more thus, that I will not.
   Clara. 'Heart, ne'er a rogue in Spain shall wrong my
     brother,
Whilst I can hold a sword.   [*Thrusts at* PIORATO.
   Pio. Hold, madam, madam!
   Alv. Clara——
   Eug. Daughter——
   Bob. Mistress——
   Pio. Bradamante[n]!
Hold, hold, I pray!
   Alv. The devil's in her, o' the other side, sure.—
There's gold for you.—They have chang'd what-ye-call't's.
Will no cure help? Well, I have one experiment,
And, if that fail, I'll hang him: then here's[o] an end on 't.—
Come you along with me; and you, sir.
   Bob. Now are you going to drowning.
      [*Exeunt* ALVAREZ, EUGENIA, LUCIO, *and* BOBADILLA.
   Saav. I'll even along with ye; she's too great a lady
For me, and would prove more than my match.   [*Exit.*
   Clara. You're he spoke of Vitelli to the steward?
   Pio. Yes; and, I thank you, you have beat me for 't.
   Clara. But are you sure you do not wrong him?
   Pio. Sure!
So sure that, if you please venture yourself,
I'll shew you him and his cockatrice together,
And you shall hear 'em talk.
   Clara. Will you? by [Heaven][p], sir,
You shall endear me ever; and I ask
You mercy.

---

[m] [*Pox*] A break here in the first folio.

[n] *Bradamante*] One of Ariosto's heroines (already mentioned, vol. viii. 336).

[o] *here 's*] The modern editors silently print "there's" (Sympson and the Editors of 1778 omitting the preceding word, "*then*").

[p] [*Heaven*] A break here in both the folios.

Pio. You were somewhat boisterous.

Clara. There's gold to make you amends; and for this pains I'll gratify you further. I'll but mask me, And walk along with you. Faith, let's make a night on't.
[*Exeunt.*

SCENE V.—*A street.*

Enter Alguazier, Pachieco, Mendoza, Metaldi, *and* Lazarillo.

Alg. Come on, my brave water-spaniels; you that hunt ducks in the night, and hide more knavery under your gowns than your betters: observe my precepts, and edify by my doctrine. At yond corner will I set you: if drunkards molest the street, and fall to brabbling[q], knock you down the malefactors, and take you up their cloaks and hats, and bring them to me; they are lawful prisoners, and must be ransomed ere they receive liberty. What else you are to execute upon occasion, you sufficiently know, and therefore I abbreviate my lecture.

Met. We are wise enough, and warm enough[r].

Mend. Vice this night shall be apprehended.

Pach. The terror of rug-gowns shall be known, and our bills[s] discharge us of after-reckonings.

Laz. I will do any thing, so I may eat.

Pach. Lazarillo, we will spend no more: now we are grown worse, we will live better; let us follow our calling faithfully.

Alg. Away, then! the commonwealth is our mistress; and who would serve a common mistress, but to gain by her? [*Exeunt.*

[q] *brabbling*] i. e. brawling.

[r] *We are wise enough, and warm enough*] See note, vol. iii. 64; and compare a passage in note, p. 21, l. 26 of the present volume.

[s] *bills*] See note, vol. iii. 141 (used here with a quibble, of course).

ACT IV.

SCENE I.—*A street.*

Enter VITELLI, LAMORAL, GENEVORA, ANASTRO, *and two* Pages *with lights.*

Lam. I pray you, see the masque, my lord.
Ana. 'Tis early night yet.
Gen. Oh, if it be so late, take me along;
I would not give advantage to ill tongues
To tax my being here, without your presence
To be my warrant.
Vit. You might spare this, sister,
Knowing with whom I leave you; one that is,
By your allowance and his choice, your servant,
And, may my counsel and persuasion work it,
Your husband speedily.—For your entertainment
My thanks: I will not rob you of the means
To do your mistress some acceptable service,
In waiting on her to my house.
Gen. My lord——
Vit. As you respect me, without further trouble
Retire, and taste those pleasures prepar'd for you,
And leave me to my own ways.
Lam. When you please, sir.
[*Exeunt, on one side,* LAM., GEN., ANAS., *and Pages; on the other,* VITELLI.

SCENE II.—*A room in the house of the Alguazier, with a gallery.*

Enter MALRODA *and* Alguazier.

Malr. You'll leave my chamber?
Alg. Let us but bill once,
My dove, my sparrow, and I, with my office,
Will be thy slaves for ever.
Malr. Are you so hot?

Alg. But taste the difference of a man in place:
You 'll find that, when authority pricks him forward,
Your don, nor yet your Diego[s], comes not near him,
To do a lady right. No men pay dearer
For their stoln sweets than we; three minutes' trading
Affords to any sinner a protection
For three years after; think on that. I burn:
But one drop of your bounty!
   Malr. Hence, you rogue!
Am I fit for you? is 't not grace sufficient
To have your staff a bolt to bar the door
Where a don enters, but that you 'll presume
To be his taster?
   Alg. Is no more respect
Due to this rod of justice?
   Malr. Do you dispute?
Good doctor of the dungeon, not a word more!
[Pox][t], if you do, my lord Vitelli knows it.
   Alg. Why, I am big enough to answer him,
Or any man.
   Malr. 'Tis well.
   Vit. [*within*] Malroda!
   Alg. How!
   Malr. You know the voice; and now crouch like a cur
Ta'en worrying sheep: I now could have you gelded
For a bawd rampant; but, on this submission,
For once I spare you.
   Alg. I will be reveng'd.   [*Aside.*

           Enter VITELLI.
         My honourable lord!
   Vit. There's for thy care.   [*Gives money.*
   Alg. I am mad, stark mad! proud pagan! scorn her host?
I would I were but valiant enough to kick her!
I 'd wish no manhood else.   [*Aside.*
   Malr. What's that?

---

  [s] *nor yet your Diego*] See note, p. 142. So both the folios.—Sympson printed "*nor your Diego*," stating in a note, most erroneously, that such is the reading of the first folio.

  [t] [*Pox*] A break here in both the folios.

Alg. I am gone.   [*Exit.*

Enter, above, PIORATO *and* CLARA.
Pio. You see I have kept my word.
Clara. But in this object
Hardly deserv'd my thanks.
Pio. Is there aught else
You will command me?
Clara. Only your sword,
Which I must have. Nay, willingly: I yet know
To force it, and to use it.
Pio. 'Tis yours, lady.   [*Gives his sword.*
Clara. I ask no other guard.
Pio. If so, I leave you.—
And now, if that the constable keep his word,
A poorer man may chance to gull a lord.
[*Aside, and then exit above.*
Malr. By this good [light] [u], you shall not!
Vit. By this [light],
I must and will, Malroda! What do you make
A stranger of me[v]?
Malr. I'll be so to you,
And you shall find it.
Vit. These are your old arts,
To endear the game you know I come to hunt for;
Which I have borne too coldly.

---

[u] [*light*] Here, and in the next line, both the folios have a break. I am by no means certain that the word which I have inserted is the true one.—The Editors of 1778 gave "*kiss*"; and so Weber: than which nothing could be more absurdly at variance with the context, Vitelli exclaiming immediately after, " What do you make a stranger of me ?"

[v] *What do you make
A stranger of me?*] i.e., for what, why do you make, &c. So before;
" *What* shall I heap up
Long repetitions?" vol. v. 384.
" *What* do you make so dainty on 't?" vol. vi. 453.
" *What* should I leave my state to pins and poking-sticks," &c. vol. vii. 361.
" *What* dost thou think me mad?" vol. viii. 80.

The last of these passages is cited from the present edition in Churton's *Literary Register* for April, 1845, as an example of "such abominable ignorance of the old phraseology" on my part, as " was never before displayed by any one undertaking the office of editor,"—the reviewer adding, that "*What*" is merely an exclamation, and that the proper pointing of the passage is, " What! dost thou think me mad?"

Malr. Do so still;
For, if I heat you, hang me!
　Vit. If you do not,
I know who'll starve for 't. Why, thou shame of women,
Whose folly or whose impudence is greater
Is doubtful to determine! this to me,
That know thee for a whore?
　Malr. And made me one;
Remember that.
　Vit. Why, should I but grow wise,
And tie that bounty up, which nor discretion
Nor honour can give way to, thou wouldst be
A bawd ere twenty; and, within a month,
A barefoot, lousy, and diseasèd whore,
And shift thy lodgings oftner than a rogue
That's whipt from post to post.
　Malr. Pish! all our college
Know you can rail well in this kind.
　Clara. For me
He never spake so well.　　　　　　　　　　　*[Aside.*
　Vit. I have maintain'd thee
The envy of great fortunes; made thee shine
As if thy name were glorious; stuck thee full
Of jewels, as the firmament of stars;
And in it made thee so remarkable,
That it grew questionable whether Virtue poor,
Or Vice so set forth as it is in thee,
Were even by Modesty's self to be preferr'd:
And am I thus repaid?
　Malr. You are still my debtor:
Can this, though true, be weigh'd with my lost honour,
Much less my faith? I have liv'd private to you,
And but for you had ne'er known what lust was,
Nor what the sorrow for 't.
　Vit. 'Tis false.
　Malr. 'Tis true.
But how return'd by you? thy whole life being
But one continu'd act of lust, and shipwreck
Of women's chastities.

Vit. But that I know
That she that dares be damn'd dares any thing,
I should admire thy tempting me: but presume not
On the power you think you hold o'er my affections;
It will deceive you: yield, and presently,
Or, by the inflamèd blood which thou must quench,
I'll make a forcible entry!
 Malr. Touch me not:
You know I have a throat: [pox]^v, if you do,
I will cry out a rape, or sheathe this here,
Ere I'll be kept, and us'd for julep-water,
To allay the heat which luscious meats and wine,
And not desire, hath rais'd.
 Vit. A desperate devil!
My blood commands my reason: I must take
Some milder way.   [*Aside.*
 Malr. I hope, dear don, I fit you:
The night is mine, although the day was yours:
You are not fasting now. This speeding trick
(Which I would as a principle leave to all
That make their maintenance out of their own Indies,
As I do now) my good old mother taught me:
"Daughter," quoth she, "contest not with your lover,
His stomach being empty; let wine heat him,
And then you may command him": 'tis a sure one.
His looks shew he is coming.   [*Aside.*
 Vit. Come, this needs not,
Especially to me: you know how dear
I ever have esteem'd you——
 Clara. Lost again!   [*Aside.*
 Vit. That any sigh^w of yours hath power to change
My strongest resolution; and one tear
Sufficient to command a pardon from me
For any wrong from you, which all mankind
Should kneel in vain for.
 Malr. Pray you, pardon those
That need your favour, or desire it.

---

 ^v [*pox*] A break here in both the folios; which the editors of 1778 and Weber filled up with "by Heaven."
 ^w *sigh*] Both the folios "sight".

Vit. Prithee,
Be better temper'd. I'll pay, as a forfeit
For my rash anger, this purse fill'd with gold :
Thou shalt have servants, gowns, attires; what not?
Only continue mine.
    Malr. 'Twas this I fish'd for.   [*Aside.*
    Vit. Look on me, and receive it.
    Malr. Well, you know
My gentle nature, and take pride to abuse it.
You see a trifle pleases me : we are friends;
This kiss, and this, confirms it.
    Clara. With my ruin!   [*Aside.*
    Malr. I'll have this diamond and this pearl.
    Vit. They are yours.
    Malr. But will you not, when you have what you came for,
Take them from me to-morrow ? 'tis a fashion
Your[x] lords of late have us'd.
    Vit. But I'll not follow.
    Clara. That any man at such a rate as this
Should pay for his repentance!   [*Aside.*
    Vit. Shall we to bed now?
    Malr. Instantly, sweet. Yet, now I think on't better,
There's something first that in a word or two
I must acquaint you with.
    Clara. Can I cry aim
To this[y], against myself? I'll break this match,
Or make it stronger with my blood. [*Aside, and then exit above.*

Re-*enter* Alguazier, *with* Piorato, Pachieco, Metaldi, Mendoza,
        and Lazarillo, *and stand apart.*

    Alg. I am yours :
A don's not privileg'd here more than yourself:
Win her, and wear her.
    Pio. Have you a priest ready?
    Alg. I have him for thee, lad.—And, when I have
Married this scornful whore to this poor gallant,

---

    [x] *Your*] Heath (*MS. Notes*) would read "You"; but the alteration is not necessary
       [y]   *cry aim*
To this] i. e. give encouragement to this : see note, vol. vi. 305.

She will make suit to me : there is a trick
To bring a high-pric'd wench upon her knees.—
For you, my fine neat harpies, stretch your talons,
And prove yourselves true night-birds.
  Pach. Take my word
For me and all the rest.
  Laz. If there be meat
Or any banquet stirring, you shall see
How I'll bestow myself.
  Alg. When they are drawn,
Rush in upon 'em; all's fair prize you light on.
I must away: your officer may give way
To the knavery of his watch, but must not see it.
You all know where to find me.
  Met. There look for us. [*Exit* Alguazier.
  Vit. Who's that?
  Malr. My Piorato! welcome, welcome!
Faith, had you not come when you did, my lord
Had done I know not what to me.
  Vit. I am gull'd;
First cheated of my jewels, and then laugh'd at!—
Sirrah, what make you here?
  Pio. A business brings me,
More lawful than your own.
  Vit. How's that, you slave?
  Malr. He's such that would continue her a whore,
Whom he would make a wife of.
  Vit. I'll tread upon [*Draws his sword.*
The face you dote on, strumpet!
  Pach. Keep the peace there!
           [*Coming forward with the others.*
  Vit. A plot upon my life too?

    Enter CLARA, *below, with* PIORATO's *sword.*

  Met. Down with him!
  Clara. Shew your old valour, and learn from a woman:
One eagle has a world of odds against
A flight of daws, as these are. [*She beats them off.*

Pio. Get you off;
I'll follow instantly.
 Pach. Run for more help there!
      [*Exeunt all except* VITELLI *and* CLARA.
 Vit. Loss of my gold and jewels, and the wench too,
Afflicts me not so much as the having Clara
The witness of my weakness.   [*Aside.*
 Clara. He turns from me:
And yet I may urge merit, since his life
Is made my second gift.   [*Aside.*
 Vit. May I ne'er prosper,
If I know how to thank her!   [*Aside.*
 Clara. Sir, your pardon
For pressing thus, beyond a virgin's bounds,
Upon your privacies; and let my being
Like to a man, as you are, be the excuse
Of my soliciting that from you, which shall not
Be granted on my part, although desir'd
By any other. Sir, you understand me;
And 'twould shew nobly in you to prevent
From me a farther boldness, which I must
Proceed in, if you prove not merciful,
Though with my loss of blushes and good name.
 Vit. Madam, I know your will, and would be thankful,
If it were possible I could affect
The daughter of an enemy.
 Clara. That fair false one,
Whom with fond dotage you have long pursu'd,
Had such a father; she to whom you pay
Dearer for your dishonour, than all titles
Ambitious men hunt for are worth.
 Vit. 'Tis truth.
 Clara. Yet, with her, as a friend, you still exchange
Health for diseases, and, to your disgrace,
Nourish the rivals to your present pleasures
At your own charge; us'd as a property
To give a safe protection to her lust,
Yet share in nothing but the shame of it.
 Vit. Grant all this so, to take you for a wife

Were greater hazard; for, should I offend you
(As 'tis not easy still to please a woman),
You are of so great a spirit, that I must learn
To wear your petticoat, for you will have
My breeches from me.

Clara. Rather from this hour
I here abjure all actions of a man,
And will esteem it happiness from you
To suffer like a woman. Love, true love
Hath made a search within me, and expell'd
All but my natural softness, and made perfect
That which my parents' care could not begin.
I will shew strength in nothing, but my duty
And glad desire to please you, and in that
Grow every day more able.

Vit. Could this be,
What a brave race might I beget! I find
A kind of yielding; and no reason why
I should hold longer out: she's young, and fair,
And chaste, for sure; but, with her leave, the devil
Durst not attempt her [*Aside*].—Madam, though you have
A soldier's arm, your lips appear as if
They were a lady's.

Clara. They dare, sir, from you
Endure the trial.

Vit. [*Kisses her*] Ha! once more, I pray you.—
The best I ever tasted; and 'tis said
I have prov'd many. 'Tis not safe, I fear,
To ask the rest now. Well, I will leave whoring,
And luck Heaven[z] send me with her! [*Aside*.]—Worthiest
    lady,
I'll wait upon you home, and by the way
(If e'er I marry, as I'll not forswear it)
Tell you, you are my wife.

Clara. Which if you do,
From me all mankind[a] women learn to woo! [*Exeunt.*

[z] *Heaven*] The correction of Heath (*MS. Notes*).—Both the folios "herein";
and so the modern editors.

[a] *mankind*] i. e. masculine, man-like.

SCENE III.—*A street.*

Enter Alguazier, PACHIECO, METALDI, MENDOZA, *and* LAZARILLO.

Alg. A cloak! good purchase[b]: and rich hangers[c]! well:
We'll share ten pistolets a-man.

Laz. Yet still
I am monstrous hungry: could you not deduct
So much out of the gross sum as would purchase
Eight loins of veal and some two dozen of capons?

Pach. Oh, strange proportion for five!

Laz. For five! I have
A legion in my stomach, that have kept
Perpetual fast these ten years: for the capons,
They are to me but as so many black-birds.
May I but eat once, and be satisfied,
Let the Fates call me, when my ship is fraught,
And I shall hang in peace.

Alg. Steal well to-night,
And thou shalt feed to-morrow. So; now you are
Yourselves again, I'll raise another watch
To free you from suspicion: set on any
You meet with boldly; I'll not be far off,
To assist you and protect you. [*Exit.*

Met. Oh, brave officer!

Pach. Would every ward had one but so well given,
And we would watch, for rug, in gowns of velvet[d]!

Enter ALVAREZ, LUCIO, *and* BOBADILLA.

Mend. Stand close; a prize!

Met. Satin and gold lace, lads!

Alv. Why dost thou hang upon me?

Lucio. 'Tis so dark
I dare not see my way: for Heaven-sake, father,
Let us go home!

Bob. No, even here we'll leave you.—
Let's run away from him, my lord.

Lucio. Oh, 'las!

[b] *purchase*] i. e. booty.   [c] *hangers*] See note, vol. iii. 39.
[d] *for rug, in gowns of velvet*] "i. e. in velvet gowns instead of rug gowns."
WEBER.

Alv. Thou hast made me mad, and I will beat thee dead,
Then bray thee in a mortar, and new-mould thee,
But I will alter thee.

Bob. 'Twill never be:
He has been three days practising to drink,
Yet still he sips like to a waiting-woman,
And looks as he were murdering of a fart
Among wild Irish swaggerers.

Lucio. I have still
Your good word, Zancho.—Father——

Alv. Milk-sop, coward!
No house of mine receives thee; I disclaim thee:
Thy mother on her knees shall not entreat me
Hereafter to acknowledge thee.

Lucio. Pray you, speak for me!

Bob. I would, but now I cannot with mine honour.

Alv. There's only one course left that may redeem thee,
Which is, to strike the next man that you meet;
And, if we chance to light upon a woman,
Take her away, and use her like a man,
Or I will cut thy hamstrings.

Pach. This makes for us.

Alv. What dost thou do now?

Lucio. Sir, I am saying my prayers;
For, being to undertake what you would have me,
I know I cannot live.

Enter LAMORAL, GENEVORA, ANASTRO, *and* Pages *with lights.*

Lam. Madam, I fear
You'll wish you had us'd your coach; your brother's house
Is yet far off.

Gen. The better, sir; this walk
Will help digestion after your great supper,
Of which I have fed largely.

Alv. To your task!
Or else you know what follows.

Lucio. I am dying:
Now, Lord have mercy on me!—By your favour,
Sir, I must strike you.

Lam. For what cause?

Lucio. I know not.
And I must likewise talk with that young lady
An hour in private.
　Lam. What you must, is doubtful;
But I am certain, sir, I must beat you. 　　*[Strikes him.*
　Lucio. Help, help!
　Alv. Not strike again?
　Lam. How! Alvarez!
　Anas. This for my lord Vitelli's love!
　　　　　　　　　　　　　　　[Strikes down ALVAREZ.
　Pach. Break out;
And, like true thieves, make prey on either side,
But seem to help the stronger[d].
　Bob. Oh, my lord!
They have beat him on his knees.
　Lucio. Though I want courage,
I yet have a son's duty in me, and
Compassion of a father's danger; that,
That wholly now possesses me. 　　*[Rushes on them.*
　Alv. Lucio,
This is beyond my hope.
　Met. So; Lazarillo,
Take up all, boy. Well done!
　Pach. And now steal off
Closely and cunningly.
　Anas. How! have I found you?—
Why, gentlemen, are you mad, to make yourselves
A prey to rogues?
　Laz.[e] Would we were off!
　Bob. Thieves, thieves!
　Lam. Defer our own contention, and down with them!
　　　　　　[They attack PACH., MET., MEND., *and* LAZ.
　Lucio. I'll make you sure!
　Bob. Now he plays the devil.
　Gen. This place is not for me. 　　*[Exit with* Pages.
　Lucio. I'll follow her:
Half of my penance is past o'er. 　　*[Aside, and then exit.*

　　[d] *stronger*] Both the folios " stranger."
　　[e] *Laz.*] Both the folios " Lam." ; and so the modern editors.

Re-enter, on one side, Alguazier, *with* Watches; *enter, on the other side,* Asistente[f], *who stands apart.*

Alg. What noise,
What tumult's there? keep the king's peace, I charge you!
Pach. I am glad he's come yet.
Alv. Oh, you keep good guard
Upon the city, when men of our rank
Are set upon in the streets!
Lam. The Asistente[g]
Shall hear of't, be assur'd.
Anas. And, if he be
That careful governor he is reported,
You will smart for it.
Alg. Patience, good signiors:
Let me survey the rascals. Oh, I know them,
And thank you for them: they are pilfering rogues
Of Andalusia, that have perus'd
All prisons in Castile. I dare not trust
The dungeon with them; no, I'll have them home
To my own house.
Pach. We had rather go to prison.
Alg. Had you so, dog-bolts[h]? yes, I know you had:
You there would use your cunning fingers on
The simple locks, you would; but I'll prevent you.
Lam. My mistress lost! good night.   [*Exit.*
Bob. Your son's gone too;
What should become of him?
Alv. Come of him what will,
Now he dares fight, I care not: I'll to bed.—
Look to your prisoners, Alguazier.
            [*Exeunt, on one side,* ALVAREZ *and* BOBADILLA;
                on the other, LAMORAL *and* ANASTRO.
Alg. All's clear'd.

[f] *Asistente*] Means properly—as already remarked in a note on *The Spanish Curate*, vol. viii. 431,—the chief officer of justice at Seville. Throughout that comedy the word is Anglicised to *Assistant*, and is used as another term for Judge. In the present play, the stage-directions of the first folio have invariably "*Asistente*"; those of the second folio, in one place "Assistant", in another "*Asistente*"; and the word is equivalent to—Governor.

[g] *Asistente*] The first folio "assistance": the second folio "assistants".

[h] *dog-bolts*] See notes, vol. iii. 149, vol. iv. 137.

Droop not for one disaster: let us hug,
And triumph in our knaveries.
    Asist. This confirms
What was reported of him.   [*Aside.*
    Met. 'Twas done bravely.
    Alg. I must a little glory in the means
We officers have to play the knaves, and safely;
How we break through the toils pitch'd by the law,
Yet hang up them that are far less delinquents:
A simple shopkeeper's carted for a bawd,
For lodging, though unwittingly, a smock-gamester;
Where[1], with rewards and credit, I have kept
Malroda in my house, as in a cloister,
Without taint or suspicion.
    Pach. But suppose
The governor should know it?
    Alg. He! good gentleman,
Let him perplex himself with prying into
The measures in the market, and the abuses
The day stands guilty of: the pillage of
The night is only mine, mine own fee-simple,
Which you shall hold from me, tenants at will,
And pay no rent for 't.
    Pach. Admirable landlord!
    Alg. Now we'll go search the taverns, commit such
As we find drinking, and be drunk ourselves
With what we take from them. These silly wretches,
Whom I for form-sake only have brought hither,
Shall watch without, and guard us.
    Asist. And we will   [*Coming forward.*
See you safe lodg'd, most worthy Alguazier,
With all of you, his comrades.
    Met. 'Tis the governor.
    Alg. We are betray'd.
    Asist. My guard there!

              Enter Guard.
              Bind them fast.—
How men in high place and authority

[1] *Where*] "i. e. Whereas." WEBER.

Are in their lives and estimations wrong'd
By their subordinate ministers! yet such
They cannot but employ; wrong'd Justice finding
Scarce one true servant in ten officers.—
To expostulate with you, were but to delay
Your crimes' due punishment, which shall fall upon you
So speedily and severely, that it shall
Fright others by the example; and confirm,
However corrupt officers may disgrace
Themselves, 'tis not in them to wrong their place.—
Bring them away.
 Alg. We'll suffer nobly yet,
And like to Spanish gallants.
 Pach. And we'll hang so.
 Laz. I have no stomach to it; but I'll endeavour.
[*Exeunt.*

SCENE IV.—*Another street.*

Enter LUCIO *and* GENEVORA.

 Gen. Nay, you are rude; pray you, forbear; you offer now
More than the breeding of a gentleman
Can give you warrant for.
 Lucio. 'Tis but to kiss you;
And think not I'll receive that for a favour
Which was enjoin'd me for a penance, lady.
 Gen. You have met a gentle confessor; and, for once,
(So then you will rest satisfied,) I vouchsafe it.
 Lucio. Rest satisfied with a kiss! why, can a man
Desire more from a woman? is there any
Pleasure beyond it? may I never live,
If I know what it is!
 Gen. Sweet innocence!   [*Aside.*
 Lucio. [*Kisses her*] What strange new motions do I feel!
   my veins
Burn with an unknown fire; in every part
I suffer alteration; I am poison'd,

Yet languish with desire again to taste it,
So sweetly it works on me.
　Gen. I ne'er saw
A lovely man till now.　　　　　　　　　　*[Aside.*
　Lucio. How can this be?
She is a woman, as my mother is,
And her I have kiss'd often, and brought off
My lips unscorch'd: yours are more lovely, lady,
And so should be less hurtful. Pray you, vouchsafe
Your hand, to quench the heat ta'en from your lip:
Perhaps that may restore me.
　Gen. Willingly.
　Lucio. The flame increases. If to touch you burn thus,
What would more strict embraces do? I know not:
And yet, methinks, to die so were to ascend
To Heaven through Paradise.
　Gen. I am wounded too;
Though modesty forbids that I should speak
What ignorance makes him bold in [*Aside*].—Why do you fix
Your eyes so strongly on me?
　Lucio. Pray you, stand still:
There is nothing else that is worth the looking on:
I could adore you, lady.
　Gen. Can you love me?
　Lucio. To wait on you in your chamber, and but touch
What you, by wearing it, have made divine,
Were such a happiness! I am resolv'd,
I'll sell my liberty to you for this glove,
And write myself your slave.

　　　　　　　　　Enter LAMORAL.

　Gen. On easier terms
Receive it, as a friend.　　　　*[Gives him her glove.*
　Lam. How! giving favour?
I'll have it, with his heart.
　　　　　　　[Seizes the glove, and puts it in his hat.
　Gen. What will you do?
　Lucio. As you are merciful, take my life rather!
　　　　　　　　　　　　[Kneels to LAMORAL.

Gen. Will you depart [k] with it so?

Lucio.[l] Does that grieve you?

Gen. I know not; but even now you appear['d] valiant.

Lucio. 'Twas to preserve my father: in his cause
I could be so again.

Gen. Not in your own?
Kneel to thy rival, and thine enemy!
Away, unworthy creature! I begin
To hate myself, for giving entrance to
A good opinion of thee. For thy torment,
If my poor beauty be of any power,
Mayst thou dote on it desperately! but never
Presume to hope for grace, till thou recover
And wear the favour that was ravish'd from thee.

Lam. He wears my head too then. [*Exit.*

Gen. Poor fool, farewell! [*Exit.*

Lucio. My womanish soul, which hitherto hath govern'd
This coward flesh, I feel departing from me;
And in me, by her beauty, is inspir'd
A new and masculine one, instructing me
What's fit to do or suffer. Powerful Love,
That hast with loud and yet a pleasing thunder
Rous'd sleeping manhood in me, thy new creature,
Perfect thy work; so that I may make known,
Nature, though long kept back, will have her own!
[*Exit.*

[k] *depart*] "i. e. part." *Ed.* 1778.
[l] *Lucio*] Both the folios "Lam."

ACT V.

SCENE I.—*A street.*

Enter LAMORAL *and* LUCIO.

Lam. Can it be possible that, in six short hours,
The subject still the same, so many habits
Should be remov'd? or this new Lucio (he
That yesternight was baffled[1] and disgrac'd,
And thank'd the man that did it; that then kneel'd
And blubber'd like a woman) should now dare
On terms of honour seek[m] reparation
For what he then appear'd not capable of?

Lucio. Such miracles men that dare do injuries
Live to their shames to see, for[n] punishment
And scourge to their proud follies.

Lam. Prithee, leave me:
Had I my page or footman here to flesh thee,
I durst the better hear thee.

Lucio. This scorn needs not:
And offer such no more!

Lam. Why, say I should,
You'll not be angry?

Lucio. Indeed, I think I shall.
Would you vouchsafe to shew yourself a captain,
And lead a little further, to some place
That's less frequented——

Lam. He looks pale.

Lucio. If not,
Make use of this.

Lam. There's anger in his eyes too;

---

[1] *baffled*] i. e. ignominiously treated, insulted: see notes, vol. ii. 286, vol. iii. 399.

[m] *honour seek*] Sympson silently printed "*honour to seek*"; and so the Editors of 1778.

[n] *see, for*] Both the folios " *see,* and *for.*"

His gesture, voice, behaviour, all new-fashion'd.
Well, if it does endure in act the trial
Of what in show it promises to make good,
Ulysses' Cyclops, Iö's transformation,
Eurydice fetch'd from hell, with all the rest
Of Ovid's fables, I'll put in my[n] creed;
And, for proof all incredible things may be,
Write down that Lucio, the coward Lucio,
The womanish Lucio, fought.

Lucio. And Lamoral,
The still-employ'd great duellist Lamoral,
Took his life from him.

Lam. 'Twill not come to that, sure:
Methinks the only drawing of my sword
Should fright that confidence.

Lucio. It confirms it rather:
To make which good, know you stand now oppos'd
By one that is your rival; one that wishes
Your name and title greater, to raise his;
The wrong you did less pardonable than it is,
But your strength to defend it more than ever
It was when justice friended it; the lady
For whom we now contend, Genevora,
Of more desert (if such incomparable beauty
Could suffer an addition); your love
To Don Vitelli multiplied, and your hate
Against my father and his house increas'd;
And lastly, that the glove which you there wear,
To my dishonour, (which I must force from you,)
Were dearer to you than your life.

Lam. You'll find
It is, and so I'll guard it.

Lucio. All these meet, then,
With the black infamy to be foil'd by one
That's not allow'd a man, to help your valour;
That, falling by your hand, I may or die,
Or win in this one single opposition

---

[n] *my*] Both the folios "*your*".

My mistress, and such honour as I may
Enrich my father's arms with!
   Lam. 'Tis said nobly:
My life with them are at the stake.
   Lucio. At all, then!
                      [*They fight.* LUCIO *disarms* LAMORAL.
   Lam. She's yours: this, and my life too, follow your
      fortune!   [*Gives up his hat with the glove.*
And give not only back that part the loser
Scorns to accept of.
   Lucio. What's that?
   Lam. My poor life;
Which do not leave me as a further torment,
Having despoil'd me of my sword, mine honour,
Hope of my lady's grace, fame, and all else
That made it worth the keeping.
   Lucio. I take back
No more from you than what you forc'd from me,
And with a worser title. Yet think not
That I'll dispute this, as made insolent
By my success, but as one equal with you,
If so you will accept me. That new courage
(Or call it fortune, if you please), that is
Conferr'd upon me by the only sight
Of fair Genevora, was not bestow'd on me
To bloody purposes; nor did her command
Deprive me of the happiness to see her,
But till I did redeem her favour from you;
Which only I rejoice in, and share with you
In all you suffer else.
   Lam. This courtesy
Wounds deeper than your sword can, or mine own:
Pray you, make use of either, and despatch me.
   Lucio. The barbarous Turk is satisfied with spoil;
And shall I, being possess'd of what I came for,
Prove the more infidel?
   Lam. You were better be so
Than publish my disgrace, as 'tis the custom,
And which I must expect.

Lucio. Judge better on° me:
I have no tongue to trumpet mine own praise
To your dishonour; 'tis a bastard courage
That seeks a name out that way, no true-born one.
Pray you, be comforted; for, by all goodness,
But to her virtuous self (the best part of it),
I never will discover on what terms
I came by these: which yet I take not from you,
But leave you, in exchange of them, mine own,
With the desire of being a friend; which if
You will not grant me, but on further trial
Of manhood in me, seek me when you please,
(And though I might refuse it with mine honour)
Win them again, and wear them. So, good morrow.
[*Gives him his own hat, and exit.*

Lam. I ne'er knew what true valour was till now;
And have gain'd more by this disgrace, than all
The honours I have won: they made me proud,
Presumptuous of my fortune, a mere beast,
Fashion'd by them, only to dare and do,
Yielding no reasons for my wilful actions
But what I stuck on my sword's point, presuming
It was the best revenue. How unequal
Wrongs well maintain'd make us to others, which,
Ending with shame, teach us to know ourselvesᴾ!
I will think more on 't.

Enter VITELLI.

Vit. Lamoral!
Lam. My lord?
Vit. I came to seek you.
Lam. And unwillingly
You ne'er found me till now. Your pleasure, sir?

° *on*] i. e. of.—The modern editors silently print "of".

ᴾ   *How unequal*
Wrongs well maintain'd make us to others, which,
Ending with shame, teach us to know ourselves] "'*Unequal*' in this place means unjust, *iniquus*. '*Wrongs well maintained*' means injuries successfully maintained, not justly." MASON.—Both the folios "makes".

Vit. That which will please thee, friend: thy vow'd love
    to me
Shall now be put in action; means is offer'd
To use thy good sword for me, that which still
Thou wear'st as if it were a part of thee.
Where is it?
    Lam. 'Tis chang'd for one more fortunate:
Pray you, inquire not how.
    Vit. Why, I ne'er thought
That there was magic[q] in it, but ascrib['d]
The fortune of it to the arm.
    Lam. Which is
Grown weaker too. I am not (in a word)
Worthy your friendship: I am one new-vanquish'd,
Yet shame to tell by whom.
    Vit. But I'll tell thee
'Gainst whom thou art to fight, and there redeem
Thy honour lost, if there be any such.
The king, by my long suit, at length is pleas'd
That Alvarez and myself, with either's second,
Shall end the difference between our houses,
Which he accepts of: I make choice of thee;
And, where[r] you speak of a disgrace, the means
To blot it out by such a public trial
Of thy approvèd valour, will revive
Thy ancient courage. If you embrace it, do;
If not, I'll seek some other.
    Lam. As I am,
You may command me.
    Vit. Spoke like that true friend,
That loves not only for his private end!   [*Exeunt.*

---

    [q] *magic*] Sympson's correction.—Both the folios "musick".
    [r] *where*] i. e. whereas.

SCENE II.—*Another street.*

Enter GENEVORA *with a letter, and* BOBADILLA.

Gen. This from Madonna Clara?
Bob. Yes, an't please you.
Gen. Alvarez' daughter?
Bob. The same, lady.
Gen. She
That sav'd my brother's life?
Bob. You are still in the right:
She will'd me wait your walking forth, and, knowing
How necessary a discreet wise man
Was in a business of such weight, she pleas'd
To think on me. It may be, in my face
Your ladyship, not acquainted with my wisdom,
Finds no such matter: what I am, I am:
Thought's free, and think you what you please.
Gen. 'Tis strange——
Bob. That I should be wise, madam?
Gen. No, thou art so.
There's for thy pains; and, prithee, tell thy lady
[*Gives money.*
I will not fail to meet her: I'll receive
Thy thanks and duty in thy present absence.
Farewell, farewell, I say! now thou art wise.
[*Exit* BOBADILLA.
She writes here, she hath something to impart
That may concern my brother's life: I know not;
But general fame does give her out so worthy,
That I dare not suspect her; yet wish Lucio
Were master of her mind: but, fie upon't!
Why do I think on him?

Enter LUCIO.

See, I am punish'd for it
In his unlook'd-for presence! now I must
Endure another tedious piece of courtship
Would make one forswear courtesy. [*Aside.*

Lucio. Gracious madam, [*Kneels.*
The sorrow paid for your just anger towards me,
Arising from my weakness, I presume
To press into your presence, and despair not
An easy pardon.
    Gen. He speaks sense: oh, strange! [*Aside.*
    Lucio. And yet believe, that no desire[s] of mine,
Though all are too strong in me, had the power,
For their delight, to force me to infringe
What you commanded; it being in your part
To lesson your great rigour when you please,
And mine to suffer with an humble patience
What you'll impose upon it.
    Gen. Courtly too! [*Aside.*
    Lucio. Yet hath the poor and contemn'd Lucio, madam,
(Made able only by his hope to serve you,)
Recover'd what with violence, not justice,
Was taken from him; and here at your feet,
With these, he could have laid the conquer'd head
Of Lamoral ('tis all I say of him)
For rudely touching that which, as a relic,
I ever would have worshipp'd, since 'twas yours.
        [*Lays the hat and glove at her feet.*
    Gen. Valiant, and every thing a lady could
Wish in her servant! [*Aside.*
    Lucio. All that's good in me,
That heavenly love, the opposite to base lust,
Which would have all men worthy, hath created;
Which, being by your beams of beauty form'd,
Cherish as your own creature.
    Gen. I am gone
Too far now to dissemble [*Aside*].—Rise, or sure
I must kneel with you too: let this one kiss
Speak the rest for me: 'tis too much I do,
And yet, if Chastity would, I could wish more.
    Lucio. In overjoying me, you are grown sad:
What is it, madam? by [my soul, I swear] [8],

---

[8] [*my soul, I swear*] A break here in both the folios.

There's nothing that's within my nerves (and yet,
Favour'd by you, I should as much as man)
But when you please, now, or on all occasions
You can think of hereafter, but you may
Dispose of at your pleasure!
  Gen. If you break
That oath again, you lose me : yet so well
I love you, I shall never put you to 't;
And yet, forget it not. Rest satisfied
With that you have receiv'd now : there are eyes
May be upon us; till the difference
Between our friends are ended[s], I would not
Be seen so private with you.
  Lucio. I obey you.
  Gen. But let me hear oft from you, and remember
I am Vitelli's sister.
  Lucio. What's that, madam?
  Gen. Nay, nothing. Fare you well : who feels love's fire,
Would ever ask to have means to desire[t].   [*Exeunt.*

SCENE III.—*A court in the Castle of Saint Jago: a scaffolding in the back-ground, filled with spectators.*

  Enter[u] Asistente[v], SAAVEDRA, ANASTRO, Herald, and Attendants.
  Asist. Are they come in?
  Herald. Yes.
  Asist. Read the proclamation,
That all the people here assembled may
Have satisfaction what the king's dear love,
In care of the republic, hath ordain'd.—
Attend with silence.—Read aloud.

---

    [s]   *till the difference*
    Between our friends are ended] Examples of similar phraseology have occurred before : see notes, vol. v. 7, 94, &c.
    [t] *to have means to desire*] " i. e. to have the means to compass his desire." SYMPSON. "Surely, this is wrongly interpreted. The meaning is, 'All who feel the pleasure of love, would wish always to have the means of loving.' *To have means to desire* cannot be construed *means to compass his desire.*" *Ed.* 1778. I incline to believe that Sympson's explanation is the right one.
    [u] *Enter*] Weber gave "*Enter* above"; which is proved to be wrong by a subsequent part of the scene.
    [v] *Asistente*] See note, p. 173.

Herald. [reads] *Forasmuch as our high and mighty master, Philip, the potent and most catholic king of Spain, hath not only in his own royal person been long and often solicited and grieved with the deadly and uncurable hatred sprung up betwixt the two ancient and most honourably-descended houses of these his two dearly and equally-beloved subjects, Don Fernando*^w *de Alvarez and Don Pedro de Vitelli (all which in vain his majesty hath often endeavoured to reconcile and qualify); but that also, through the debates, quarrels, and outrages daily arising, falling, and flowing from these great heads, his public civil government is seditiously and barbarously molested and wounded, and many of his chief gentry (no less tender to his royal majesty than the very branches of his own sacred blood) spoiled, lost, and submerged in the impious inundation and torrent of their still-growing malice; it hath therefore pleased his sacred majesty, out of his infinite affection to preserve his commonwealth and general peace from farther violation (as a sweet and heartily-loving father of his people), and on the earnest petitions of these arch-enemies, to order and ordain, that they be ready, each with his well-chosen and beloved friend, armed at all points like gentlemen, in the Castle of St. Jago, on this present Monday morning, betwixt eight and nine of the clock; where (before the combatants be allowed to commence this granted duel) this to be read aloud for the public satisfaction of his majesty's well-beloved subjects. Save the king!* [*Drums within.*

Saav. Hark, how their drums speak their insatiate thirst
Of blood, and stop their ears 'gainst pious Peace,
Who, gently whispering, implores their friendship!

Asist. Kings nor authority can master Fate.—
Admit 'em, then; and blood extinguish hate!

Enter, severally, ALVAREZ *and* LUCIO, VITELLI *and* LAMORAL.

Saav. Stay: yet be pleas'd to think, and let not daring
(Wherein men now-a-days exceed even beasts,
And think themselves not men else) so transport you
Beyond the bounds of Christianity.

---

^w *Fernando*] Here both the folios "Ferdinando": but see p. 129, sixth speech.

Lord Alvarez, Vitelli, gentlemen,
No town in Spain, from our metropolis
Unto the rudest hovel, but is great
With your assurèd valours' daily proofs :
Oh, will you then, for a superfluous fame,
A sound of honour, which, in these times, all
Like heretics profess (with obstinacy,
But most erroneously), venture your souls ?
'Tis a hard task, thorough a sea of blood
To sail, and land at Heaven.
   Vit. I hope not,
If Justice be my pilot. But, my lord,
You know, if argument, or time, or love,
Could reconcile, long since we had shook hands :
I dare protest, your breath cools not a vein
In any one of us; but blows the fire,
Which nought but blood reciprocal can quench.
   Alv. Vitelli, thou say'st bravely, and say'st right;
And I will kill thee for 't, I love thee so.
   Vit. Ha, ha, old man! upon thy death I'll build
A story with this arm, for thy old wife
To tell thy daughter Clara seven years hence,
As she sits weeping by a winter-fire,
How such a time Vitelli slew her husband
With the same sword his daughter favour'd him,
And lives, and wears it yet.—Come, Lamoral,
Redeem thyself.
   Lam. Lucio, Genevora
Shall on this sword receive thy bleeding heart,
For my presented hat, laid at her feet.
   Lucio. Thou talk'st well, Lamoral : but 'tis thy head
That I will carry to her to thy hat.—
Fie, father! I do cool too much.
   Alv. Oh, boy, thy father's true son !—
Beat drums !—And so, good morrow to your lordship !
                                     [*Drums.*

       Enter, above, EUGENIA, CLARA, *and* GENEVORA.
   Saav. Brave resolutions !
   Anas. Brave, and Spanish right !

Gen. Lucio!
Clara. Vitelli!
Eug. Alvarez!
Alv. How the devil
Got these cats into the gutter? my puss too!
Eug. Hear us!
Gen. We must be heard!
Clara. We will be heard!
Vitelli, look; see, Clara on her knees,
Imploring thy compassion!—Heaven, how sternly
They dart their emulous eyes, as if each scorn'd
To be behind the other in a look!—
Mother, Death needs no sword here!—Oh, my sister,
(Fate fain would have it so,) persuade, entreat!
A lady's tears are silent orators,
Or should be so at least, to move beyond
The honiest-tonguèd[x] rhetorician.—
Why will you fight? why, does an uncle's death,
Twenty-year old, exceed your love to me,
But twenty days? whose forc'd cause and fair manner
You could not understand, only have heard.
Custom, that wrought so cunningly on Nature
In me, that I forgot my sex, and knew not
Whether my body female were or male,
You did unweave, and had the power to charm
A new creation in me, made me fear
To think on those deeds I did perpetrate.
How little power though you allow to me,
That cannot with my sighs, my tears, my prayers,
Move you from your own loss, if you should gain!

   Vit. I must forget you, Clara: till I have
Redeem'd my uncle's blood, that brands my face
Like a pestiferous carbuncle, I am blind
To what you do, deaf to your cries, and marble
To all impulsive exorations.
When on this point I have perch'd thy father's soul,

---

[x] *honiest-tonguèd*] Sympson's proposed emendation.—Both the folios " honest tongu'd ".

I 'll tender thee this bloody reeking hand,
Drawn forth the bowels of that murderer;
If thou canst love me then, I 'll marry thee,
And, for thy father lost, get thee a son;
On no condition else.
   Asist. Most barbarous!
   Saav. Savage!
   Anas. Irreligious!
   Gen. Oh, Lucio,
Be thou more merciful! thou bear'st fewer years,
Art lately wean'd from soft effeminacy;
A maiden's manners, and a maiden's heart,
Are neighbours still to thee: be, then, more mild;
Proceed not to this combat. Be'st thou desperate
Of thine own life? yet, dearest, pity mine!
Thy valour 's not thine own; I gave it thee;
These eyes begot it, this tongue bred it up,
This breast would lodge it: do not use my gifts
To mine own ruin: I have made thee rich;
Be not so thankless to undo me for 't.
   Lucio. Mistress, you know I do not wear a vein
I would not rip for you, to do you service:
Life 's but a word, a shadow, a melting dream,
Compar'd to essential and eternal honour.
Why, would you have me value it beyond
Your brother? If I first cast down my sword,
May all my body here be made one wound,
And yet my soul not find Heaven thorough it!
   Alv. You would be caterwauling too; but, peace!
Go, get you home, and provide dinner for
Your son and me; we 'll be exceeding merry.—
Oh, Lucio, I will have thee cock of all
The proud Vitellis that do live in Spain!
Fie, we shall take cold! Hunch! [pox] [y], I am hoarse
Already.

       [y] [*pox*] A break here in both the folios.

Lam. How your sister whets my spleen!
I could eat Lucio now[z].
  Gen. Vitelli! brother!
Even for your father's soul, your uncle's blood,
As you do love my life; but last, and most,
As you respect your own honour and fame,
Throw down your sword! he is most valiant
That herein yields first.
  Vit. Peace, you fool!
  Clara. Why, Lucio,
Do thou begin: 'tis no disparagement;
He's elder, and thy better, and thy valour
Is in his infancy.
  Gen. Or pay it me,
To whom thou ow'st it. Oh, that constant Time
Would but go back a week! then, Lucio,
Thou wouldst not dare to fight.
  Eug. Lucio, thy mother,
Thy mother begs it! throw thy sword down first.
  Alv. I'll throw his head down after, then.
  Gen. Lamoral,
You have often sworn[a] you'd be commanded by me.
  Lam. Never to this: your spite and scorn, Genevora,
Has lost all power in me.
  Gen. Your hearing for six words!
  Asist. Saav. Anas. Strange obstinacy!
  Alv. Vit. Lucio. Lam. We'll stay no longer.
  Clara. Then, by thy oath, Vitelli,
Thy dreadful oath, thou wouldst return that sword
When I should ask it, give it to me now;
This instant I require it!
  Gen. By thy vow,

---

[z] *I could eat Lucio now*] After these words, the first folio has,—
   "*Gen.* Lamorall: you have often sworne
   You'ld be commanded by me",—
a speech which presently occurs. Perhaps, as Weber observes, the intermediate speeches were omitted in the representation.

[a] *sworn*] Both the folios "swore": but earlier the first folio has "*sworn*"; see the preceding note.

As dreadful, Lucio, to obey my will
In any one thing I would watch to challenge,
I charge thee not to strike a stroke! Now, he
Of our two brothers that loves perjury
Best, and dares first be damn'd, infringe his vow!
   Saav. Excellent ladies!
   Vit. Pish, you tyrannize.
   Lucio. We did equivocate.
   Alv. On!
   Clara. Then, Lucio,
So well I love my husband (for he is so,
Wanting but ceremony), that I pray
His vengeful sword may fall upon thy head
Successfully, for falsehood to his sister!
   Gen. I likewise pray, Vitelli, Lucio's sword
(Who equally is my husband as thou hers)
May find thy false heart, that durst gage thy faith,
And durst not keep it!
   Asist. Are you men, or stone?
   Alv. Men, and we'll prove it with our swords.
   Eug. Your hearing for six words, and we have done!—
Zancho, come forth!—We'll fight our challenge too.—

   Enter, above, BOBADILLA, *with two swords and a pistol.*

Now speak your resolutions.
   Gen. These they are;
The first blow given betwixt you sheaths these swords
In one another's bosoms.
   Eug. And, rogue, look
You at that instant do discharge that pistol
Into my breast: if you start back, or quake,
I'll stick you like a pig.
   Alv. Hold[b]! you are mad.
   Gen. This we [have] said; and, by our hope of bliss,
This we will do! Speak your intents.
   Clara. Gen. Strike!

---

   [b] *Hold*] Before this word, there is a break in both the folios, which Weber filled up with "By Heaven": but no addition is required either for the sense or the metre.

Eug. Shoot!
Alv. Vit. Lucio. Lam. Hold, hold! all friends!
Asist. Come down.
        [*Exeunt, above,* EUGENIA, CLARA, GENEVORA, *and*
            BOBADILLA.
Alv. These devilish women
Can make men friends and enemies when they list.
  Saav. A gallant undertaking, and a happy!
Why, this is noble in you; and will be
A welcomer present to our master Philip
Than the return from his Indies.

Enter, below, EUGENIA, CLARA, GENEVORA, *and* BOBADILLA.

Clara. Father, your blessing!
Alv. Take her. If ye bring not
Betwixt you boys that will find out new worlds,
And win 'em too, I 'm a false prophet.
  Vit. Brother,
There is a sister. Long-divided streams
Mix now at length, by fate.
  Bob. I am not regarded: I was the careful steward that provided these instruments of peace; I put the longest weapon in your sister's hand, my lord, because she was the shortest lady; for likely the shortest ladies love the longest —men. And, for mine own part, I could have discharged it: my pistol is no ordinary pistol; it has two ramming bullets; but, thought I, why should I shoot my two bullets into my old lady? If they had gone, I would not have stayed long after; I would even have died too, bravely, i' faith, like a Roman steward; hung myself in mine own chain [d], and there had been a story of Bobadilla Spindola Zancho for after-ages to lament. Hum; I perceive, I am not only not regarded, but also not rewarded.
  Alv. Prithee, peace!
Shalt have a new chain, next St. Jaques' day,
Or this new-gilt.

---

[d] *chain*] See note, p. 118.

Bob. I am satisfied; let Virtue have her due. And yet I am melancholy upon this atonement[e]: pray Heaven the state rue it not! I would my lord Vitelli's steward and I could meet! they should find it should cost 'em a little more to make us friends. Well, I will forswear wine and women for a year; and then I will be drunk to-morrow, and run a-whoring like a dog with a broken bottle at 's tail; then will I repent next day, and forswear 'em again more vehemently; be forsworn next day again, and repent my repentance; for thus a melancholy gentleman doth and ought to live.

Asist. Nay, you shall dine with me; and afterward
I 'll with ye to the king. But, first, I will
Despatch the castle's business, that this day
May be complete.—Bring forth the malefactors!

Alguazier, PACHIECO, METALDI, MENDOZA, LAZARILLO, PIORATO,
  and MALRODA, *are brought in by the* Guard.

You, Alguazier, the ring-leader of these
Poor fellows, are degraded from your office.
You must restore all stoln goods you receiv'd,
And watch a twelvemonth without any pay:
This if you fail of, (all your goods confiscate,)
You are to be whipt, and sent into the galleys.

Alg. I like all, but restoring; that catholic doctrine
I do dislike. Learn, all ye officers,
By this to live uprightly—if you can!   [*Exit.*

Asist. You, cobbler, to translate your manners new,
Are doom'd to the cloisters of the Mendicants,
With this your brother botcher, there for nothing
To cobble, and heel hose for the poor friars,
Till they allow your penance for sufficient,
And your amendment: then you shall be freed,
And may set up again.

Pach. Mendoza, come:
Our souls have trod awry in all men's sight;
We 'll under-lay 'em, till they go upright.
                    [*Exeunt* PACHIECO *and* MENDOZA.

---

[e] *atonement*] i. e. reconcilement.

Asist. Smith, in those shackles you, for your hard heart,
Must lie by th' heels a year.

Met. I have shod your horse, my lord.

Asist. Away! [*Exit* METALDI.
For you, my hungry white-loaf'd face,
You must to the galleys, where you shall be sure
To have no more bits than you shall have blows.

Laz. Well, though [I] herrings want, I shall have rows.
[*Exit.*

Asist. Signior, you have prevented us, and punish'd
Yourself severelier than we would have done:
You have married a whore; may she prove honest!

Pio. 'Tis better, my lord, than to marry an honest woman
That may prove a whore.

Vit. 'Tis a handsome wench: an thou canst keep her tame,
I'll send you what I promis'd.

Pio. Joy to your lordships!

Alv. Here may all ladies learn to make of foes
The perfect'st friends; and not the perfect'st foes
Of dearest friends, as some do now-a-days.

Vit. Behold the power of Love! lo, Nature lost[f]
By Custom irrecoverably, past the hope
Of friends' restoring, Love hath here retriev'd
To her own habit; made her blush to see
Her so-long monstrous metamorphoses!
May strange affairs never have worse success! [*Exeunt.*

---

[f] *lo, Nature lost*, &c.] Heath's correction (*MS. Notes*).—Both the folios " to *nature lost* ", &c. ; and so Sympson, who proposed in a note " *Nature,* tho' *lost*", &c., which was adopted by the Editors of 1778.—Weber gave Mason's conjecture, " So *Nature lost* ", &c.

EPILOGUE.

Our author fears there are some rebel hearts,
Whose dulness doth oppose Love's piercing darts;
Such will be apt to say there wanted wit,
The language low, very few scenes are writ
With spirit and life: such odd things as these
He cares not for, nor ever means to please;
For, if yourselves, a mistress, or Love's friends,
Are lik'd[g] with this smooth play, he hath his ends.

[g] *lik'd*] "i. e. pleased." Sympson.

THE
MAID IN THE MILL.

The Maid in the Mill.

In the folios, 1647, 1679.
The second folio adds "*A Comedy.*"

WE find from the memoranda of Sir Henry Herbert that this comedy was the joint production of Fletcher and William Rowley [a], that it was licensed August 29, 1623, and acted at the Globe: its success is not to be doubted, for on the same authority we learn that it was performed three times at court, during that year—"Upon Michelmas night att Hampton Court, by the K. Company", " Upon Allhollows night at St. James, the prince being there only, with reformations", and " Upon St. Stevens daye, the king and prince being there, by the K. Company, att Whitehall." See Malone's *Shakspeare* (by Boswell), iii. 226-7.

" The Plot of Antonio, [Martine,] Ismenia, and Aminta, is borrow'd from *Gerardo*, a Romance translated from the Spanish of Don Gonzalo de Cespides and Meneces: see the Story of Don Jayme, pag. 350. As to the Plot of Otrante's seizing Florimel, the Millers supposed Daughter, and attempting her Chastity, 'tis borrow'd from an Italian Novel writ by Bandello, a Translation of which into French the Reader may find in *Les Histoires Tragiques par M. Belleforest*, Tom. i. Hist. 12. The same Story is related by M. Goulart; see *Les Histoires admirables de notre temps*, 8°. Tom. i. p. 212." Langbaine's *Account of Engl. Dram. Poets*, p. 211.

Of the two tales indicated by Langbaine, abridgements were given by Weber, which, with very material alterations, I now subjoin.

i. (*Gerardo* [b], pp. 347—371, ed. 1653.) " Gerardo, having unexpectedly met his friend Don Jayme on the coast of Barbary, and having related to him his own adventures, requested him to mention the cause which led him to so remote a shore. Don Jayme accordingly gave the following narrative. During his residence at Zaragoza, ill-will arose between his uncle Don Julio de Aragon and Don Lisauro; the latter conceiving himself offended by the former. In consequence of this quarrel some serious rencountres occurred, and the nobles ranged themselves into factions on the sides of the two opponents. Don Julio had occasion to take a journey out of town, and his nephew Don Jayme accompanied him. On their return, and when within some three leagues of Zaragoza, they were compelled by a violent storm to seek shelter in ' a good fair house of pleasure, which

---

[a] Of W. Rowley (who played one of the characters in this comedy) some notice will be found in the biographical essay prefixed to the present edition.

[b] Concerning this romance, *vide* introduction to *The Spanish Curate*, vol. viii. 373. When Weber edited that play, he had not seen *Gerardo*.

seemed to belong to some gentleman'; and they reached it just as 'a coach entred in at another Gate, driven (as it might seem) by the same necessity'. After remaining there some time, the old gentleman wished to pursue his way homewards; but Don Jayme, curious to view the females whom he supposed to be in the coach, lifted up one of the boot-lids and looked in, 'when out issued two men, who, laying hold on their swords, as they joyntly blamed this unmannerly act, obliged him to the like, and the rather, he knowing them to be no other than Lisauro and his kinsman Tirso, both his vowed Enemies'. The fray extended to the servants of the parties, and a general scuffle ensued, accompanied by the outcries of the women in the carriage. Don Julio pursued Lisauro, who stumbled and fell: Don Julio had like to have fallen above him; which Tirso observing, attacked Don Julio, tilting at him with his sword; but Don Jayme warded off the thrusts aimed at his uncle. By this time Lisauro had risen; and Don Jayme, 'leaving Don Julio and Tirso to begin again upon even terms', engaged in a combat with Lisauro, disarmed him, and would have followed up his advantage, 'had it not been for the intercession of two Dames, one of which laying hold on his Contrary [c], all blubber'd and afflicted, and the other coming towards Don Jayme, sought to asswage his anger, and to mediate for the disarmed Gentleman. She that spoke to Don Jayme had her face all covered with Tiffany, which serving as a Mask, onely discovered two fair eys, but at this time clouded with some pitifull tears, which, accompanied with sighs and discreet phrase, not onely reined in Don Jayme's unbridled fury, but also (seeing Tirso on one side wounded by his Uncle flie back, and on the other their servants driven up to a corner labour in their defence) made him to second Tirso, and, re-bating Don Julio's blows and his, cried [cry] out to them to hold: and by this time some other indifferent parties came happily in and parted them all. Don Jayme signified to the unknown Dame that her discreet and noble carriage gained him to be her servant as far as the saving her Kinsman or friends life, and should command his own'. With difficulty he persuaded his uncle to mount his horse; and, in the hurry, forgot to take leave of the gentlewomen. When they had returned to Zaragoza, Don Jayme, by the advice of his uncle, withdrew for more than a fortnight to 'a village some days journey off'. The officers of justice having at length pacified the parties, Don Jayme came back, and endeavoured to obtain information who the unknown ladies were and whither they had gone; but without success. After more than two months, as he was one morning going out of his lodging 'to meet some friends who had appointed the venturing of a Rest at Primera,'

[c] *Contrary*] i. e. opponent.

a woman in a mask put a letter into his hand, and saying 'to-morrow morning you shall have me here for the answer', suddenly departed. The letter contained thanks 'for his nobleness not long since to Lisauro' in the fray, and gave some broad hints of the fair writer's affection for himself. In his answer to this epistle Don Jayme let the lady know the search he had made to discover her, urged his desire to see her, and concluded 'with submitting himself to her will, without seeking to know or inquire any thing that might contradict her pleasure'. Next morning he delivered his answer to the masked woman at the appointed place. ''Twas now about the gladsom time of Shrove-tide, more solemnly kept in Zaragosa than any other Citie of Spain ; at which time, with some friends and kinsmen of his own age and condition, clad in colours and Vizards, Don Jayme marched up and down the streets, enjoying many a mirthfull oportunity; for at this time of year the women have full liberty, and dispense with their ordinary reservedness'. During this season, on Sunday night, the friends visited several private houses where revels were kept, and at last entered that of Signior Bellides, one of the opposite faction, 'where all the youth, bravery, and beauty of the Citie was'. There Don Jayme was immediately struck by the charms of a lady next whom he was seated. She discovered who he was, spoke to him by name, and was expressing her great satisfaction at seeing him, when one of the gallants interrupted her by 'inviting her out to a Galliard'; nor was she able, on account of the great crowd in the room, to rejoin Don Jayme during the evening. Don Jayme, having mentioned to one of his friends the impression which the lady's beauty had made upon him, was informed that she was the daughter of Signior Bellides, 'which made him much more wonder at the success, and sorrowfully despairfull least the differences betwixt her friends and his would quite dash the prosecution of that amorous fire which by little and little had wholly seiz'd his heart'. During the Shrovetide sports he again met her several times, but could never obtain a moment's conversation with her. This new passion, however, did not make him forget the lady whom he had seen at the country-house ; and he was greatly surprised and perplexed by receiving from the latter 'a Ticket in which she not onely signified her jealous complaints, but particularized also the most singular acts and signs even to the very Phrase he used to the Dame of the Revels.' He resolved to deny all ; and, in his answer, most earnestly requested to see her. She excused herself from granting this request; and he, 'slackning the return of answers to her Tickets, began to re-prosecute his amorous intents with the spritely Dame of the Revels'; and, having obtained her permission 'that his minde might be signified to her in a Song', he serenaded her about midnight, being heard not only by her, but by the whole neighbourhood. The following day he was upbraided for this want of fidelity in a letter from the country-lady, and invited to an interview with her the ensuing night. He was accordingly conducted into a narrow lane, and left under 'certain ruinous white Walls', while his guide 'by another way returned to give notice to her Mistris'. After a long hour at least, a woman (whom by her voice he knew to be his guide) drew up a neighbouring window, and 'bade him get to the top of the broken Wall, from whence they might conveniently speak to him.' His fair one at last appeared, and (the wall on which he stood well nigh reaching to the iron frame of her bay window, and there being a light in her chamber) proved to be no other than the daughter of Signior Bellides. He was altogether unprepared for such a discovery, and stood mute, till she informed him that she and the country-lady were the same, that her name was Ismenia, and that nothing but the enmity of their parents had prevented her hitherto from giving him an assignation. Don Jayme now 'excused the errour of his inconstancy against the countrey Dame, attributing it to the rare beauty and attractive power of Ismenia'; and he learned from her 'that the reason of her coming with Lisauro and Tirso to the countrey house was to avoid the storm which that afternoon took them as they were going from Zaragosa to a Village, where at the same time her Father lay very sick; for whom, together with her Mother (the fore-mentioned woman in the Fray), they went to bring him more commodiously home; and that afterward returning to the City, inforced, as she said (but more by her own generous condition) by Don Jayme's courtesie, she indeavoured by her trusty Maid to give him notice of her affection'. Day coming on, the lovers parted, after appointing future meetings in the same place. The following night, as Don Jayme was about to mount the old wall, three or four persons entered the lane, whom he heard closely whispering. His trouble was increased by Ismenia appearing at the window and calling upon him to approach. The men drew nearer, and he suddenly 'let fly at them outrageously', and killed one of them. The rest fled, crying out for help; and Don Jayme, thinking it prudent to retire, 'had no sooner slipped out of the Lane, when another Troop of men entered into it, whom afterward he understood to have been all of one party, Officers appointed purposely to apprehend some suspicious persons thereabouts'. Next morning he received a letter from Ismenia excusing her inconsiderateness, and advising him to discontinue their private meetings for a while, watch being kept both within and without her father's house. With her approbation he quitted Zaragoza, but kept up a correspondence with her by letters. After two months, unable to endure a longer absence from her, he returned to Zaragoza; and next night proceeded to the usual place of meeting, accompanied by his friend Don Martin de Urrea. His visits were frequently repeated; and the passion of the enamoured pair increased so violently, that at last, Ismenia 'taking first Heaven and her true servant to witness of his hand and faithfull vow to be her Spouse, consented Don Jayme should by the window enter her Chamber, though, for some necessary respects, the reward of his labours was deferred till the next night'. His restlessness and agitation the following morning were perceived by Don Martin, who drew the secret from him, being considered by the lover as his most faithful friend. Don Martin was easily prevailed on to accompany Don Jayme, whom, under pretence of a more complete disguise, he persuaded to exchange his cloak with him. Don Jayme having mounted the wall, two men rushed into the lane, and suddenly assailed his companion. Don Jayme leapt down, and assisting Don Martin to drive them off, pursued one of them 'somewhat hard, to remove him a good way from his Mistresses danger'. On coming back, he could not find Don Martin; and climbing the wall, he perceived the window closely shut, which he supposed to be in consequence of Ismenia's having heard the clashing of swords, and her dread of a discovery. The next morning her maid brought him a letter, expressing her eagerness to renew the transports of the preceding night. Full of perplexity he went, as night approached, to Don Martin's lodging, but could not gain admittance. From thence he proceeded to his mistress's abode; and, when he had entered her chamber by the usual means, Ismenia upbraided him with his present sadness, as well as with his unwillingness to be seen by her and his utter silence on the preceding night. Don Jayme, finding 'that some other had been his substitute', swooned in her arms; and a purse left under her pillow 'by him that possessed the place and her honour', in which a little book bearing Don Martin's name was enclosed, led to a final detection of his treachery. The maid now confessed that Don Martin had endeavoured to persuade her that Don Jayme had no real love for her mistress, his sole object being to revenge himself on the house of Bellides, and that he 'lived lasciviously' with another woman; that Don Martin declared himself at last so far as to offer the maid some gifts of value, if she would make known his own affection to her mistress; and that, on finding these arts to be unavailing, he pretended that his only purpose had been to try the fidelity of the maid and the constancy of her mistress. Don Jayme did all he could to comfort Ismenia ('who had many a dead traunce in his arms'), and 'with a loving imbrace took leave, promising her faithfully not to be at quiet till her honour were fully satisfied, if not restored'. He lay in wait for his treacherous friend; but learned that Don Martin (who had doubtless missed the purse, and knew that it would betray his guilt) had absconded. He now went frequently to the post-house, and looking over letters from all parts, at last lighted on one addressed to a kinsman of Don Martin: breaking it open, he found that it was written by Don Martin from Oran in Barbary, and contained a request that his relation would send him certain moneys and trunks of apparel to that place. After acquainting Ismenia with this happy discovery, he set out for Oran, 'determined, if he could, to kill his enemy'. Having arrived in a small bark at the port of Massalquibir, he had intelligence from one of the soldiers of the fort that Don Martin was in the city. Giving the soldier some silver, Don Jayme sent him to the town 'to let Don Martin know, that in the Bark (which Don Jayme fained to be his) there came certain Trunks directed to him from Zaragosa, for which he must of necessity come aboard to fetch them at night, because with the first fair winde the Bark was to set sail for Spain'. The messenger brought back word that Don Martin was preparing to come, and only stayed to provide himself with a horse. Don Jayme set out on horseback towards Oran, and, having ridden about half way thither, waited for several hours under some rocks. He began to doubt his messenger's fidelity, when a horseman appeared, who, saluting him, asked whether he travelled towards the city or the port. Don Jayme, recognising the speaker by his voice, exclaimed, 'Thyself, false Don Martin, art the Port and Haven to which I go, at which the satisfaction of my Revenge must safely land; and to no other am I bound; and therefore speedily defend thyself; for know that I have not crossed the stormy Seas to return to the wrong'd Ismenia with less than thy lifes Revenge'. Don Martin answered with a bold defiance: and 'both of them falling back to come on with more force, wheeling about to take field-room enough, began to set spurs to their Horses'. They desperately rushed together, and with the violence of the shock both came to the ground, Don Jayme unhurt, but Don Martin run through the body by his adversary's lance.—Don Jayme concluded his story by saying, 'Of Ismenia's goodness as confident am I, as satisfied with the deserved chastisement of her wrong, which I purpose to solder (since with honour I now may) by accomplishing my wedlock vow. This, Gerardo, is my intent; this resolution carries me for Spain, more joyfull than when I left my Countrey, for I shall not onely comply with my loves obligation, but with a greater, my souls'."

ii. (Bandello—*Alessandro Duca di Firenze fa che Pietro sposa una Mugnaia che hauena rapita, e le fa far molto ricca dote.*) "Pietro, one of the favourites of Alessandro de Medici, endeavoured in vain to gain the love of the beautiful daughter of a miller, who dwelt near his country-seat. At last, with the assistance of two friends, he forcibly brought her to his house, and there gratified his desires. The miller went to Florence, and complained of this violence to the duke, who, promising to redress his wrongs, advised him to return to his mill. Alessandro followed him; and then proceeded on a visit to Pietro, and inspected his house. Pietro excused himself from shewing one of the smaller rooms, pretending that it was in great confusion, and that, his steward being at Florence, he could not find the key. The duke, however, insisting on seeing the apartment, Pietro whispered to him, laughing, 'that he had a young girl concealed there'. This only served to increase the duke's curiosity: the door was opened, and a full discovery took place. The duke declared that Pietro, and his two friends, deserved to lose their heads; but that he pardoned them on condition that Pietro should immediately marry the girl and give her two thousand ducats, while his two accomplices gave her a thousand ducats each. The marriage was then solemnized, the duke having assured Pietro that, if he should at any time use her ill, it would be regarded by him as an injury done to his own sister."

The Maid in the Mill was one of those pieces in which the youthful Betterton displayed his histrionic powers at the Cockpit in Drury-lane, in the company formed by Rhodes on the eve of the Restoration (see vol. vi. 3): and Langbaine (*Account of Engl. Dram. Poets*, p. 211) mentions its having " been reviv'd by the Dukes House."

DRAMATIS PERSONÆ.

PHILIPPO, king of Spain.
OTRANTE, a count.
JULIO, a count [d].
ANTONIO, his nephew.
BELLIDES, a gentleman, and head of the family so called.
LISAURO, his son.
MARTINE, friend to ANTONIO.
TERZO, kinsman to BELLIDES.
GERASTO, friend to OTRANTE.
PEDRO, ⎫
MONCADO, ⎬ courtiers.
GOSTANZO, ⎫
GIRALDO, ⎬ friends to JULIO.
PHILIPPO, ⎭
VERTIGO, a French tailor.

FRANIO, a miller.
BUSTOFA, his son.
PEDRO, a musician.
Lords, Gentlemen, Constable, Officers, Servants; a boy as Cupid, and a man as a Shepherd, in the interlude.

ISMENIA, daughter to BELLIDES.
AMINTA, her cousin.
FLORIMEL, daughter to JULIO, and supposed daughter to FRANIO.
GILLIAN, wife to FRANIO.
Three women as Nymphs in the interlude.

SCENE—*Toledo and the neighbouring country.*

The principal actors were—

Joseph Taylor.   John Thomson.
John Lowin.   Robert Benfield.
John Underwood.   Tho. Pollard.
William Rowley.

Fol. 1679.

---

[d] *Julio, a count*] Towards the end of the play, the king says, "Who? Count Julio?"

THE MAID IN THE MILL.

ACT I.

SCENE I.—*The country, in the immediate neighbourhood of Toledo.*

Enter LISAURO, TERZO, ISMENIA, *and* AMINTA.

Lisauro [*To* Attendants *within*]. Let the coach go round:
we 'll walk along these meadows,
And meet at port[a] again.—Come, my fair sister,
These cool shades will delight you.
  Amin. Pray, be merry:
The birds sing as they meant to entertain you;
Every thing smiles abroad; methinks the river,
As he steals by, curls up his head to view you:
Every thing is in love.
  Ism. You would have it so:
You, that are fair, are easy of belief, cousin;
The theme slides from your tongue.
  Amin. I fair! I thank you:
Mine is but shadow when your sun shines by me.
  Ism. No more of this; you know your worth, Aminta.
Where are we now?
  Amin. Hard by the town, Ismenia.
  Terzo. Close by the gates.
  Ism. 'Tis a fine air.
  Lis. A delicate;
The way so sweet and even, that the coach

---

[a] *at port*] "i. e. at the gate of the city." MASON.

Would be a tumbling trouble to our pleasures.
Methinks I am very merry.
  Ism. I am sad.
  Amin. You are ever so when we entreat you, cousin.
  Ism. I have no reason : such a trembling here,
Over my heart, methinks!
  Amin. Sure, you are fasting,
Or not slept well to-night; some dream, Ismenia?
  Ism. My dreams are like my thoughts, honest and in-
    nocent;
Yours are unhappy[a]. Who are these that coast us?
You told me the walk was private.
  Terzo. 'Tis most commonly.

      Enter ANTONIO *and* MARTINE.

  Ism. Two proper men : it seems they have some business;
With me none, sure. I do not like their faces :
They are not of our company.
  Terzo. No, cousin.—
Lisauro, we are dogg'd.
  Lis. I find it, cousin.
  Ant. What handsome lady[b]——
  Mart. Yes, she's very handsome;
They are handsome both.
  Ant. Martine, stay; we are cozen'd.
  Mart. I will go up : a woman is no wildfire.
  Ant. Now, by my life, she is sweet! Stay, good Martine :
They are of our enemies, the house of Bellides;
Our mortal enemies.
  Mart. Let 'em be devils,
They appear so handsomely, I will go forward :
If these be enemies, I'll ne'er seek friends more.
  Ant. Prithee, forbear : the gentlewomen——
  Mart. That's it, man,
That moves[c] me like a gin[d]: pray you, stand off.—Ladies——

---

    [a] *unhappy*] " i. e. wicked." WEBER.
    [b] *What handsome lady*—] Qy. " *What a handsome lady!* " ?
    [c] *moves*] So the second folio.—The first folio " mopes ".
    [d] *a gin*] " i. e. an engine or instrument." WEBER.

Lis. They are both our enemies, both hate us equally;
By this fair day, our mortal foes!
Terzo. I know 'em;
And come here to affront: how they gape at us!
They shall have gaping work.
            [LIS. *and* TER. *draw their swords.*
Ism. Why your swords, gentlemen?
Terzo. Pray you, stand you off, cousin;
And good now leave your whistling; we are abus'd all.—
Back, back, I say!
Lis. Go back!
Ant. We are no dogs, sir,
To run back on command.
Terzo. We'll make ye run, sir.
Ant. Having a civil charge of handsome ladies,
We are your servants: pray ye, no quarrel, gentlemen;
There's way enough for both.
Lis. We'll make it wider.
Ant. If you will fight, arm'd from[e] this saint, have at ye!
        [ANT. *and* MART. *draw their swords, and fight with*
            LIS. *and* TER.
Ism. Oh, me unhappy!—Are ye gentlemen,
Discreet and civil, and in open view thus——
Amin. What will men think of us! Nay, you may kill us.
Mercy o' me! through my petticoat? what bloody gentlemen!
Ism. Make way through me, ye had best, and kill an innocent:
Brother—why, cousin—by this light, I'll die too!—
This gentleman is temperate; be you merciful—
Alas, the swords!
Amin. You had best run me through the belly[f];
'Twill be a valiant thrust.
Ism. I faint amongst ye.
Ant. Pray you, be not fearful; I have done, sweet lady;
My sword's already aw'd, and shall obey you:

---

[e] *from*] Weber silently printed " for ".

[f] *the belly*] So the first folio.—Omitted in the second folio; and by Sympson and the Editors of 1778.

I come not here to violate sweet beauty;
I bow to that.
    Ism. Brother, you see this gentleman,
This noble gentleman——
    Lis. Let him avoid, then,
And leave our walk.
    Ant. The lady may command, sir;
She bears an eye more dreadful than your weapon.
    Ism. What a sweet nature this man has!—Dear brother,
Put up your sword.
    Terzo. Let them put up, and walk, then.
    Ant. No more loud words: there's time enough before us:
For shame, put up! do honour to these beauties.
    Mart. Our way is this; we will not be denied it.
    Terzo. And ours is this; we will not be cross'd in it.
    Ant. Whate'er your way is, lady, 'tis a fair one;
And may it never meet with rude hands more,
Nor rough uncivil tongues!
    Ism. I thank you, sir,
Indeed, I thank you nobly.   [*Exeunt* ANTONIO *and* MARTINE.
                      A brave enemy!
Here's a sweet temper now! This is a man, brother;
This gentleman's anger is so nobly seated,
That it becomes him; yours proclaim ye monsters.
What if he be our[g] house-foe? we may brag on't;
We have ne'er a friend in all our house so honourable:
I had rather from an enemy, my brother,
Learn worthy distances and modest difference[h],
Than from a race of empty friends loud nothings.
I am hurt between ye.
    Amin. So am I, I fear too:
I am sure their swords were between my legs[i].—Dear cousin,
Why look you pale? where are you hurt?

---

  [g] *our*] Weber chose to print "your".

  [h] *modest difference*] "i. e. modesty in my difference with him." HEATH (*MS. Notes*). "A difference or quarrel modestly maintained." WEBER.—Altered by Sympson to "*modest* deference"; and so the Editors of 1778.

  [i] *I am sure their swords were between my legs*] So the first folio.—Omitted in the second folio; and by Sympson.

Ism. I know not;
But here methinks.
    Lis. Unlace her, gentle cousin.
    Ism. My heart, my heart! and yet I bless the hurter.
    Amin. Is it so dangerous?
    Ism. Nay, nay, I faint not.
    Amin. Here is no blood that I find; sure, 'tis inward.
    Ism. Yes, yes, 'tis inward; 'twas a subtle weapon;
The hurt not to be cur'd, I fear.
    Lis. The coach there!   [*To* Attendants *within.*
    Amin. May be a fright.
    Ism. Aminta, 'twas a sweet one;
And yet a cruel.
    Amin. Now I find the wound plain:
A wondrous handsome gentleman—
    Ism. Oh, no deeper!
Prithee, be silent, wench; it may be thy case[j].
    Amin. You must be search'd; the wound will rankle, cousin—
And of so sweet a nature——
    Ism. Dear Aminta,
Make it not sorer!
    Amin. And, on my life, admires you.
    Ism. Call the coach, cousin.
    Amin. The coach, the coach!
    Terzo. 'Tis ready.—Bring the coach there!
    [*To* Attendants *within.*
    Lis. Well, my brave enemies, we shall yet meet ye,
And our old hate shall testify——
    Terzo. It shall, cousin.   [*Exeunt.*

SCENE II.—*Toledo.—A street*[k].

Enter ANTONIO *and* MARTINE.

    Ant. Their swords! alas, I weigh 'em not, dear friend!
The indiscretion of the owners blunts 'em;

---

[j] *case*] So the second folio.—The first folio "cause."

[k] *A street*] Weber marked this scene "*A Room* in the House of Antonio"; but see the commencement of the next scene.

The fury of the house affrights not me,
It spends itself in words. Oh me, Martine!
There was a two-edg'd eye a lady carried,
A weapon that no valour can avoid,
Nor art, the hand of spirit, put aside.
Oh, friend, it broke out on me, like a bullet
Wrapt in a cloud of fire! that point, Martine,
Dazzled my sense, and was too subtle for me;
Shot like a comet in my face, and wounded,
To my eternal ruin, my heart's valour.
    Mart. Methinks she was no such piece.
    Ant. Blaspheme not, sir:
She is so far beyond weak commendation,
That Impudence will blush to think ill of her.
    Mart. I saw it not, and yet I had[1] both eyes open,
And I could judge. I know there is no beauty
Till our eyes give it 'em, and make 'em handsome:
What's red and white, unless we do allow 'em?
A green face else; and, methinks, such another——
    Ant. Peace, thou lewd[m] heretic! thou judge of beauties?
Thou hast an excellent sense for a sign-post, friend.
Didst[n] thou not see, (I'll swear thou art stone-blind[o] else,
As blind as Ignorance,) when she appear'd first,
Aurora breaking in the east, and through her face,
As if the Hours and Graces had strew'd roses,
A blush of wonder flying? when she was frighted
At our uncivil swords, didst thou not mark
How far beyond the purity of snow
The soft wind drives, whiteness of innocence,
Or any thing that bears celestial paleness,
She appear'd o' the sudden? Didst thou not[p] see her tears
When she entreated? oh, thou reprobate!
Didst thou not see those orient tears flow'd from her,

---

  [1] *saw - - - had*] Both the folios "see" - - "have". The modern editors print "see - - had".
  [m] *lewd*] i. e. wicked, vile.
  [n] *Didst*] Both the folios "Dost".
  [o] *stone-blind*] Both the folios "soon *blind*".
  [p] *not*] So the second folio.—Omitted in the first folio.

The little worlds of love? a set, Martine,
Of such sanctified beads, and a holy heart to love,
I could live ever a religious hermit.
 Mart. I do believe a little; and yet, methinks,
She was of the lowest stature.
 Ant. A rich diamond,
Set neat and deep. Nature's chief art, Martine,
Is to reserve her models curious,
Not cumbersome and great; and such a one,
For fear she should exceed upon her matter,
Has she fram'd this. Oh, 'tis a spark of beauty!
And where they appear so excellent in little,
They will but flame in great[q]; extension spoils 'em.
Martine, learn this; the narrower that our eyes
Keep way unto our object, still the sweeter
That comes unto us: great bodies are like countries,
Discovering still, toil and no pleasure finds 'em.
 Mart. A rare cosmographer for a small island!
Now I believe she is handsome.
 Ant. Believe heartily;
Let thy belief, though long a-coming, save thee.
 Mart. She was, certain, fair.
 Ant. But hark you, friend Martine;
Do not believe yourself too far before me,
For then you may wrong me, sir.
 Mart. Who bid you teach me?
Do you shew me meat, and stitch my lips, Antonio?
Is that fair play?
 Ant. Now, if thou shouldst abuse me—
And yet I know thee for an arrant wencher,
A most immoderate thing; thou canst not love long.
 Mart. A little serves my turn; I fly at all games:
But I believe[r].

---

 [q] *They will but flame in great*] " Seward [who proposed to read " *They will not flame in great* "] mistakes the meaning of the passage. The allusion, though rather obscurely expressed, is to the rays of light, which are infinitely more bright when collected in a small focus (a spark of beauty), than when dispersed; for then they only flame, but without brilliancy." MASON.

 [r] *But I believe*] The modern editors put a break after these words. But the sense is complete: see what precedes.

Ant. How if we never see her more?
She is our enemy.
Mart. Why are you jealous, then?
As far as I conceive, she hates our whole house.
Ant. Yet, good Martine——
Mart. Come, come; I have mercy on you:
You shall enjoy her in your dream, Antonio,
And I'll not hinder. Though, now I persuade myself——
Ant. Sit with persuasion down, and you deal honestly:
I will look better on her.

Enter AMINTA *with a letter.*

Mart. Stay; who's this, friend?
Ant. Is't not the other gentlewoman?
Mart. Yes. A letter!
She brings no challenge, sure? if she do, Antonio,
I hope she'll be a second too; I am for her.
Amin. A good hour, gentlemen!
Ant. You are welcome, lady:
'Tis like our late rude passage has pour'd on us
Some reprehension.
Amin. No, I bring no anger;
Though some deserv'd it.
Ant. Sure, we were* all to blame, lady;
But, for my part, in all humility,
And with no little shame, I ask your pardons:
Indeed, I wear no sword to fright sweet beauties.
Amin. You have it, and this letter; pray you, sir, view it,
　　　　　　　　　　　　[*Gives letter to* ANTONIO.
And my commission's done.
Mart. Have you none for me, lady?
Amin. Not at this time.
Mart. I am sorry for't; I can read too.
Amin. I am glad: but, sir, to keep you in your exercise,
You may chance meet with one ill-written.
Mart. Thank you:

---

* *were*] Weber chose to print "are".

So it be a woman's, I can pick the meaning;
For likely they have but one end.
>   *Amin.* You say true, sir. [*Exit.*
>   *Ant.* Martine, my wishes are come home, and loaden,

Loaden with brave return; most happy, happy!
I am a blessèd man! Where's the gentlewoman?
>   *Mart.* Gone, the spirit's gone. What news?
>   *Ant.* 'Tis from the lady;

From her we saw, from that same miracle:
I know her name now. Read but these three lines;
Read with devotion, friend, the lines are holy.
>   *Mart.* [*Reads*] *I dare not chide you in my letter, sir;*
> *'Twill be too gentle. If you please to look me* [t]
> *In the West-street, and find a fair stone window*
> *Carv'd with white Cupids, there I'll entertain you:*
> *Night and discretion guide you! Call me* ISMENIA.
>   *Ant.* Give it me again. Come, come; fly, fly! I am all fire.
>   *Mart.* There may be danger.
>   *Ant.* So there is to drink,

When men are thirsty; to eat hastily,
When we are hungry; so there is in sleep, friend,
Obstructions then may rise and smother us;
We may die laughing-chok'd; even at devotions,
An apoplexy, or a sudden palsy,
May strike us down.
>   *Mart.* May be, a train[u] to catch you.
>   *Ant.* Then I am caught, and let Love answer for it:

'Tis not my folly, but his infamy,
And if he be ador'd, and dare do vild[v] things.
>   *Mart.* Well, I will go.
>   *Ant.* She is a lady, sir,

A maid, I think; and, where that holy spell
Is flung about me, I ne'er fear a villany.
'Tis almost night; away, friend!

---

[t] *look me*] i. e. look out for me.

[u] *train*] See note, p. 90.

[v] *vild*] i. e. vile: see note, vol. i. 331.—Altered to "vile" by Sympson; and so his successors. (In this passage, which is wrongly pointed in all the eds., "*And if*" means simply—If.)

Mart. I am ready:
I think I know the house too.
　Ant. Then we are happy.　　　　　　　　　　*[Exeunt.*

SCENE III.—*Another street; before the house of* BELLIDES.

　ISMENIA *and* AMINTA *appear at a lower window.*

　Ism. Did you meet him?
　Amin. Yes.
　Ism. And did you give my letter?
　Amin. To what end went I?
　Ism. Are you sure it was he?
Was it that gentleman?
　Amin. Do you think I was blind?
I went to seek no carrier, nor no midwife.
　　Ism. What kind of man was he? thou may'st be deceiv'd,
　　　friend.
　　Amin. A man with a nose on's face; I think he had
　　　eyes too;
And hands, for, sure, he took it.
　　Ism. What an answer!
　　Amin. What questions are these to one that's hot and
　　　troubled!
Do you think me a babe? am I not able, cousin,
At my years and discretion, to deliver
A letter handsomely? is that such a hard thing?
Why, every wafer-woman[w] will undertake it;
A sempster's girl, or a tailor's wife, will not miss it:
A puritan hostess, cousin, would scorn these questions.
My legs are weary.
　　Ism. I'll make 'em well again.
　　Amin. Are they at supper?
　　Ism. Yes, and I am not well,
Nor desire no company. Look out; 'tis darkish.
　　Amin. I see nothing yet. Assure yourself, Ismenia,
If he be a man, he will not miss.

[w] *wafer-woman*] See note, vol. i. 32.

Ism. It may be he is modest,
And that may pull him back from seeing me;
Or has made some wild construction of my easiness:
I blush to think what I writ.
    Amin. What should you blush at?
Blush when you act your thoughts, not when you write 'em;
Blush soft between a pair of sheets, sweet cousin.
Though he be a curious-carried[x] gentleman, I cannot think
He's so unnatural to leave a woman,
A young, a noble, and a beauteous woman,
Leave her in her desires: men of this age
Are rather prone to come before they are sent for.
Hark! I hear something: up to the chamber, cousin!
You may spoil all else.

            Enter ANTONIO *and* MARTINE.
    Ism. Let me see. They are gentlemen;
It may be they.
    Amin. They are they. Get you up,
And like a load-star[y] draw him.
    Ism. I am shame-fac'd.
          [ISMENIA *and* AMINTA *withdraw from the window.*
    Ant. This is the street.
    Mart. I am looking for the house.
Close, close, pray you, close. Here.
    Ant. No; this is a merchant's;
I know the man well.
    Mart. And this a[z] 'pothecary's; I have lain here many times,
For a looseness in my hilts.
    Ant. Have you not pass'd it?
    Mart. No, sure;
There is no house of mark that we have scap'd yet.
    Ant. What place is this?
    Mart. Speak softer; may be spies.
If any, this; a goodly window too,

---

    [x] *curious-carried*] i. e. scrupulous in behaviour.
    [y] *load-star*] Both the folios "Land-*star*".
    [z] *this a*] Weber chose to print "*this* is *a*".

Carv'd fair[a] above; that I perceive. 'Tis dark;
But she has such a lustre——
   Ant. Yes, Martine;
So radiant she appears——
   Mart. Else we may miss, sir:
The night grows vengeance black; pray Heaven she shine
   clear!

IsMENIA *and* AMINTA *appear at an upper window, with a taper.*

Hark, hark! a window, and a candle too!
   Ant. Step close. 'Tis she: I see the cloud disperse;
And now the beauteous planet——
   Mart. Ha! 'tis indeed.—
Now, by the soul of love, a divine creature!   [*Aside.*
   Ism. Sir, sir!
   Ant. Most blessèd lady!
   Ism. Pray you, stand out.
   Amin. You need not fear; there's nobody now stirring.
   Mart. Beyond his commendation I am taken,
Infinite strangely taken.   [*Aside.*
   Amin. I love that gentleman;
Methinks he has a dainty nimble body:
I love him heartily.   [*Aside.*
   Ism. 'Tis the right gentleman;
But what to say to him—Sir——
   Amin. Speak.
   Ant. I wait still;
And will do till I grow another pillar,
To prop this house, so it please you.
   Ism. Speak softly;
And, pray you, speak truly too.
   Ant. I never lied, lady.
   Ism. And do not think me impudent to ask you—
I know you are an enemy, (speak low,)
But I would make you a friend.
   Ant. I am friend to beauty;
There is no handsomeness I dare be foe to.

[a] *fair*] Both the folios "far".

Ism. Are you married?
Ant. No.
Ism. Are you betroth'd?
Ant. No, neither.
Ism. Indeed, fair sir!
Ant. Indeed, fair sweet, I am not:
Most beauteous virgin, I am free as you are.
Ism. That may be, sir: then you are miserable,
For I am bound.
Ant. Happy the bonds that hold you!
Or do you put them on yourself for pleasure?
Sure, they be sweeter far than liberty;
There is no blessedness but in such bondage.
Give me that freedom, madam, I beseech you,
(Since you have question'd me so cunningly,)
To ask you whom you are bound to; he must be certain
More than human that bounds in such a beauty:
Happy that happy chain! such links are heavenly.
Ism. Pray you, do not mock me, sir.
Ant. Pray you, lady, tell me.
Ism. Will you believe? and will you keep it to you?
And not scorn what I speak?
Ant. I dare not, madam;
As oracle, what you say I dare swear to.
Ism. I'll set the candle by, for I shall blush now:
Fie, how it doubles in my mouth! it must out.—
'Tis you I am bound to.
Ant. Speak that word again;
I understand you not.
Ism. 'Tis you I am bound to.
Ant. Here is another gentleman.
Ism. 'Tis you, sir.
Amin. He may be lov'd too.
Mart. Not by thee; first curse me! [*Aside.*
Ism. And if I knew your name——
Ant. Antonio, madam.
Ism. Antonio, take this kiss; 'tis you I am bound to.
Ant. And, when I set you free, may Heaven forsake me!
Ismenia——

Ism. Yes, now I perceive you love me;
You have learn'd my name.
　Ant. Hear but some vows I make to you;
Hear but the protestations of a true love.
　Ism. No, no, not now; vows should be cheerful things,
Done in the clearest light, and noblest testimony:
No vow, dear sir! tie not my fair belief
To such strict terms: those men have broken credits,
Loose and dismember'd faiths, my dear Antonio,
That splinter 'em with vows.　Am I not too bold?
Correct me when you please.
　Ant. I had rather hear you;
For so sweet music never struck mine ears yet.
Will you believe now?
　Ism. Yes.
　Ant. I am yours.
　Amin[b]. Speak louder:
If you answer the priest so low, you will lose your wedding.
　Mart. Would I might speak! I would holla.　　[*Aside.*
　Ant. Take my heart;
And, if it be not firm and honest to you,
Heaven——
　Ism. Peace, no more! I'll keep your heart, and credit it;
Keep you your word.　When will you come again, friend?
For this time we have woo'd indifferently:
I would fain see you, when I dare be bolder.
　Ant. Why, any night.　Only, dear noble mistress,
Pardon three days: my uncle Julio
Has bound me to attend him upon promise,
Upon expectation too: we have rare sports there,
Rare country sports; I would you could but see 'em!
Dare you so honour me?
　Ism. I dare not be there;
You know I dare not; no, I must not, friend.
Where I may come with honourable freedom—
Alas, I am ill too! we in love——
　Ant. You flout me.

　　　[b] *Amin.*] Both the folios "Ism."; and so the modern editors.

Ism. Trust me, I do not; I speak truth; I am sickly,
And am in love; but you must be physician.
Ant. I'll make a plaster of my best affection.
Ism. Be gone: we have supp'd; I hear the people stir:
Take my best wishes. Give me no cause, Antonio,
To curse this happy night.
Ant. I'll lose my life first.
A thousand kisses!
Ism. Take ten thousand back again!
Mart. I am dumb with admiration [*Aside*].—Shall we go,
    sir?   [*Exeunt* ANTONIO *and* MARTINE.
Ism. Dost thou know his uncle?
Amin. No, but I can ask, cousin.
Ism. I'll tell thee more of that. Come, let's to bed both;
And give me handsome dreams, Love, I beseech thee!
Amin. H'as given you a handsome subject.
Ism. Pluck-to the windows.   [*Exeunt* [c] *above.*

ACT II.

SCENE I.—*The country. Before the mill of* FRANIO.

Enter BUSTOFA, *with a paper.*

Bust. [reads] *The thundering seas* [d], *whose watery fire
    washes the whiting-mops* [e],
The gentle whale, whose feet so fell flies o'er the mountain- [f]
    tops——

  [c] *Exeunt*] After this, the first folio has "*Six Chaires placed at the Arras*",— a direction addressed to the property-man, that he might have seats ready for Julio, Antonio, Martine, Gostanzo, Giraldo, and Philippo during the interlude in the following act.

  [d] *The thundering seas,* &c.] I may just notice that I have given this passage as two verses (instead of four), because it is so arranged when Bustofa afterwards speaks it in the character of Paris, and when Antonio exclaims "These are *long* lines."

  [e] *whiting-mops*] i. e. young whitings (as before, p. 135).

  [f] *mountain-*] Here both the folios "Mountains"; but twice afterwards "Mountain".

Fra. [*within*] Boy!
Bust. The thundering——
Fra. [*within*] Why, boy! Bustofa!
Bust. Here I am.—*The gentle whale*—

Enter FRANIO.

Fra. Oh, are you here, sir? where's your sister?
Bust. The gentle whale flies o'er the mountain-tops——
Fra. Where's your sister, man?
Bust. Washes the whiting-mops——
Fra. Thou liest; she has none to wash. Mops! the boy is half way out of his wits, sure. Sirrah, who am I?
Bust. The thundering seas——
Fra. Mad, stark mad!
Bust. Will you not give a man leave to con?
Fra. Yes, and 'fess too, ere I have done with you. Sirrah, am I your father?
Bust. The question is too hard for a child: ask me any thing that I have learned, and I'll answer you.
Fra. Is that a hard question,—Sirrah, am not I your father?
Bust. If I had my mother-wit, I could tell you.
Fra. Are you a thief?
Bust. So far forth as the son of a miller.
Fra. Will you be hanged?
Bust. Let it go by eldership.—*The gentle whale*——
Fra. Sirrah, lay by your foolish study there,
And beat your brains about your own affairs;
Or——
Bust. I thank you: you'd have me go under the sails, and beat my brains about your mill? a natural father you are!
Fra. I charge you go not to the sports to-day:
Last night I gave you leave; now I recant.
Bust. Is the wind turned since last night?
Fra. Marry, is it, sir: go no farther than my mill;
There's my command upon you.
Bust. I may go round about, then, as your mill does? I

SCENE I.] THE MAID IN THE MILL. 223

will see your mill gelded, and his stones fried in steaks, ere
I deceive the country so. Have I not my part to study?
how shall the sports go forward, if I be not there?
   Fra. They'll want their fool indeed, if thou be'st not there.
   Bust. Consider that, and go yourself.
   Fra. I have fears, sir, that I cannot utter:
You go not, nor your sister; there's my charge.
   Bust. The price of your golden thumb[f] cannot hold me.
                                    [*Cry of hounds within.*
   Fra. Ay, this was sport that I have tightly lov'd:
I could have kept company with the hounds——
   Bust. You are fit for no other company yet.
   Fra. Run with the hare, and been in the whore's tail,
i' faith.
   Bust. That was before I was born: I did ever mistrust I
was a bastard, because *lapis* is in the singular number
with me.
                Enter OTRANTE *and* GERASTO.
   Otr. Leave thou that game[g], Gerasto, and chase here;
Do thou but follow it with my desires,
Thou 'lt not return home empty.
   Ger. I am prepar'd,
My lord, with advantages[h]: and see,
Yonder's the subject I must work upon.
   Otr. Her brother? 'tis. Methinks it should be easy:
That gross compound cannot but diffuse
The soul in such a latitude of ease,
As to make dull her faculties and lazy:
What wit, above the least, can be in him,
That reason ties together?
   Ger. I have prov'd it, sir,

---

  [f] *golden thumb*] " In Chaucer's character of the Miller are the following lines ;
     'Wel coude he stelen corne, and tollen thries.
     And yet he had a *thomb of gold*, parde'. [*Cant. Tales*, v. 564.]
Dr. Morell and Mr. Tyrwhit both suppose that Chaucer alluded to the old proverb, 'Every honest miller has a *thumb of gold*; to which they reply in Somersetshire, 'None but a cuckold can see it.' To the same proverb our author evidently refers in Bustofa's speech. See Ray's *Proverbs*." REED.
  [g] *game*] So the second folio.—The first folio "gun".
  [h] *with advantages*] Sympson silently printed "*with* all *advantages* ".

And know the depth of it: I have the way
To make him follow me a hackney-pace,
With all that flesh about him; yes, and drag
His sister after him.   [*Cry of hounds within.*
            This baits the old one:
Rid you him, and leave me to the other.
    Otr. 'Tis well [*Exit* GERASTO].—Oh, Franio, the good
        day to you!
You were not wont to hear this music standing;
The beagle and the bugle you have lov'd,
In the first rank of huntsmen.
    Bust. The dogs cry out of[i] him now.
    Fra. Sirrah, leave your barking; I'll bite you else.
    Bust. Cur, cur?
    Fra. Slave, dost call me dog?
    Otr. Oh, fie, sir! he speaks Latin to you; he would know
why you'll bite him.
    Bust. Responde, cur?—You see his understanding, my lord.
    Fra. I shall have a time to curry you for this.—
But, my lord, to answer you: the days have been
I must have footed it before this hornpipe,
Though I had hazarded my mill a-fire,
And let the stones grind empty; but those dancings
Are done with me: I have good will to it still,
And that's the best I can do.
    Otr. Come, come, you shall be hors'd;
Your company deserves him; though you kill him,
Run him blind, I care not.
    Bust. He'll do't o' purpose, my lord, to bring him up to
the mill.
    Fra. Do not tempt me too far, my lord.
    Otr. There's a foot i' the stirrop; I'll not leave you now:
You shall see the game fall once again.
    Fra. Well, my lord, I'll make ready my legs for you, and
try 'em once a-horseback.—Sirrah, my charge; keep it.
                    [*Exit.*
    Bust. Yes, when you pare down your dish for conscience-

---

[i] *of*] i. e. (as Weber saw) on.—Sympson, at Seward's suggestion, printed
"for",—Mason approving!

sake, when your thumb's coined[j] into *bonæ et legalis*, when you are a true man, miller[k].

Otr. What's the matter, Bustofa?

Bust. My lord, if you have e'er a drunken jade that has the staggers, that will fall twice the height of our mill with him, set him o' the back on him; a galled jennet that will winch him out o' the saddle, and break one on's[l] necks or a shank of him (there was a fool going that way, but the ass had better luck); or one of your brave Barbaries, that would pass the Straits, and run into his own country with him: the first Moor he met would cut his throat for complexion's sake; there's as deadly feud between a Moor and a miller, as between black and white.

Otr. Fie, fie! this is unnatural, Bustofa,
Unless on some strong cause.

Bust. Be judge, my lord: I am studied in my part; the Julian feast is to-day, the country expects me; I speak all the dumb-shows; my sister chosen for a nymph—*The gentle whale, whose feet so fell*—Cry mercy! that was some of my part: but his charge is, to keep the mill, and disappoint the revels.

Otr. Indeed, there it speaks shrewdly for thee, the country expecting.

Bust. Ay, and for mine own grace too.

Otr. Yes, and being studied too, and the main speaker too.

Bust. The main! why, all my speech lies in the main and the dry ground together,—*The thundering seas, whose*, &c.

Otr. Nay, then, thou must go; thou'lt be much con-
      demn'd else:
But then, o' the other side, obedience.

Bust. Obedience! But speak your conscience now, my lord; am not I past asking blessing at these years? speak as you're a lord, if you had a miller to your father.

Otr. I must yield to you, Bustofa; your reasons are so

---

[j] *when your thumb's coined*, &c.] See note, p. 223.

[k] *when you are a true man, miller*] So Sympson rightly pointed the passage—"*a true man*" meaning—an honest man.—Both the folios have "*When you are a true* man-miller"; and so the Editors of 1778 and Weber!!

[l] *on's*] i. e. of his: so immediately before—"*on him*" for *of* him.

VOL. IX.   Q

strong, I cannot contradict. This I think, if you go, your sister ought to go along with you.

Bust. There I stumble now: she is not at age.

Otr. Why, she's fifteen, and upwards.

Bust. Thereabouts.

Otr. That's woman's ripe age; as full as thou art at one-and-twenty: she's manable, is she not?

Bust. I think not: poor heart, she was never tried, in my conscience. 'Tis a coy thing; she will not kiss you a clown, not if he would kiss her.

Otr. What, man?

Bust. Not if he would kiss her, I say.

Otr. Oh, 'twas cleanlier than I expected.—Well, sir, I'll leave you to your own; but my opinion is, You may take her along.—This is half way; The rest, Gerasto,—and I hunt my prey[m].   [*Aside.*

Bust. Away with the old miller, my lord! and the mill strikes sail[n] presently.   [*Exit* OTRANTE.

Enter PEDRO, *with* GERASTO *disguised as a blind Ballad-Singer.*

Ger. [*sings*]

> Come follow me, you country lasses,
> And you shall see such sport as passes[o]:
> You shall dance, and I will sing;
> Pedro, he shall rub the string;
> Each shall have a loose-bodied gown
> Of green, and laugh till you lie down.
> Come follow me, come follow, &c.

Enter FLORIMEL.

Bust. Oh, sweet Diego, the sweetest Diego! stay.—Sister Florimel——

Flor. What's that, brother?

---

[m]   *This is half way; The rest, Gerasto,—and I hunt my prey*] " The punctuation is Mason's, who explains the passage thus—' My business is half accomplished ; the rest I leave to Gerasto, with whose aid I shall hunt down the object of my pursuit.'" WEBER.

[n] *strikes sail*] " i. e. will cease to go." MASON.

[o] *passes*] i. e. surpasses.

Bust. Didst not hear Diego? hear him, and thou 'lt be ravished.

Flor. I have heard him sing, yet unravished, brother.

Bust. You had the better luck, sister. I was ravished by mine own consent. Come away; for the sports!

Flor. I have the fear of a father on me, brother.

Bust. Out! the thief is as safe as in his mill; he 's hunting with our great landlord, the Don Otrante.—Strike up, Diego!

Flor. But say he return before us, where 's our excuse?

Bust. Strike up, Diego!—Hast no strings to thy apron?

Flor. Well, the fault lie upon your head, brother.

Bust. My faults never mount so high, girl; they rise but to my middle at most.—Strike up, Diego!

Ger. Follow me by the ear; I 'll lead thee on, Bustofa, and pretty Florimel thy sister: oh, that I could see her!

Bust. Oh, Diego, there 's two pities upon thee! great pity thou art blind, and as great a pity thou canst not see.

Ger. [*sings*]

> You shall have crowns of roses, daisies,
> Buds where the honey-maker grazes [p];
> You shall taste the golden thighs,
> Such as in wax-chamber lies:
> What fruit [q] please you taste, freely pull,
> Till you have all your bellies full.
>   Come follow me, &c.

Bust. Oh, Diego! the Don was not so sweet when he perfumed the steeple [r].   [*Exeunt.*

SCENE II.—*A hall in the country-house of* JULIO.

Enter ANTONIO *and* MARTINE.

Mart. Why, how now, friend? thou art not lost again?

Ant. Not lost! why, all the world 's a wilderness; Some places peopled more by braver beasts

---

[p] *grazes*] Both the folios "gazes".

[q] *fruit*] The modern editors silently print "fruits".

[r] *Oh, Diego! the Don was not so sweet when he perfumed the steeple*] See note, vol. iii. 274, and p. 142 of the present vol.

Than others are; but faces, faces, man;
May a man be caught with faces?

Mart. Without wonder,
'Tis odds against him : may not a good face
Lead a man about by the nose? alas,
The nose is but a part against the whole!

Ant. But is it possible that two faces
Should be so twinn'd in form, complexion,
Figure, aspéct, that neither wen, nor mole,
The table of the brow, the eyes' lustre,
The lips' cherry, neither the blush nor smile,
Should give the one distinction from the other?
Does Nature work in moulds?

Mart. Altogether;
We are all one mould, one dust.

Ant. Thy reason's mouldy:
I speak from the form, thou the matter. Why,
Was it not ever one of Nature's glories,
Nay, her great piece of wonder, that amongst
So many millions millions of her works
She left the eye distinction, to cull out
The one from other; yet all one name, the face?

Mart. You must compare 'em by some other part
Of the body, if the face cannot do't.

Ant. Didst ask her name?

Mart. Yes, and who gave it her;
And what they promis'd more, besides a spoon,
And what apostle's picture[s]: she is christen'd too,
In token wherefore[t] she is call'd Isabella;

---

[s] *And what they promis'd more, besides a spoon,*

And what apostle's picture] Here Weber makes the following quotation from Steevens's note on Shakespeare's *Henry VIII.*, act v. sc. 2 (which I have slightly altered) : " Spoons, with the figure of an apostle terminating the handle of each (and hence called *apostle-spoons*), were formerly the usual gifts of sponsors at christenings. The better sort were of silver-gilt. Such persons as were at once opulent and generous gave the whole twelve ; those who were either more moderately rich or liberal escaped at the expence of the four evangelists ; or even sometimes contented themselves with presenting one spoon only, which exhibited the figure of any saint in honour of whom the child received its name."

[t] *wherefore*] Sympson silently printed " whereof " ; and so Weber.

The daughter of a country plough-swain by.
If this be not true, she lies.
　Ant. She cannot:
It would be seen a blister on her lip,
Should falsehood touch it, it is so tender.
Had her name held, 't had been Ismenia,
And not another of her name.
　Mart. Shall I speak?
　Ant. Yes,
If thou 'lt speak truth. Is she not wondrous like?
　Mart. As two garments of the same fashion,
Cut from the same piece; yet, if any excel,
This has the first; and in my judgment 'tis so.
　Ant. 'Tis my opinion.
　Mart. Were it the face
Where mine eye[s] should dwell, I would please both
With this, as soon as one with the other.
　Ant. And yet the other is the case of this[u]:
Had I not look'd upon Ismenia,
I ne'er had stay'd[v] beyond good-morrow's time
In view of this.
　Mart. Would I could leave him here!
'Twere a free passage to Ismenia.
I must now blow, as to put out the fire,
Yet kindle 't more [*Aside*].—You not consider, sir,
The great disparity is in their bloods,
Estates and fortunes: there is the rich beauty,
Which this poor homeliness is not endow'd with;
There 's difference enough.
　Ant. The least of all;
Equality is no rule in Love's grammar.

---

[u] *case of this*] Seward proposed to read "cause *of this;*" which Weber adopted; and Mason observes,—"I agree with Seward in reading 'cause' instead of 'case'; as Antonio says, that, had he not looked upon Ismenia before, he should not have dwelt upon the view of Isabella. So that his love for Ismenia was the cause of his attachment to Isabella." But, as "*this*" undoubtedly means—*this woman* (compare the preceding line, and the last line of the present speech), I cannot see how Seward's proposed reading, "*the* cause *of this,*" could have the meaning which he and Mason would make it bear. The poet (Rowley evidently) seems to use "*case*" here in the sense of—fellow.

[v] *stay'd*] Weber chose to print "stray'd".

That sole unhappiness is left to princes,
To marry blood: we are free disposers,
And have the power to equalize their bloods
Up to our own; we cannot keep it back:
'Tis a due debt from us.
   Mart. Ay, sir, had you
No father, nor uncle, nor such hinderers,
You might do with yourself at your pleasure;
But, as it is——
   Ant. As it is, 'tis nothing:
Their powers will come too late, to give me back
The yesterday I lost.
   Mart. Indeed, to say sooth,
Your opposition from the other part
Is of more force; there you run the hazard
Of every hour a life, had you supply;
You meet your dearest[w] enemy in love
With all his hate about him: 'twill be more hard
For your Ismenia to come home to you,
Than you to go to country Isabel.
   Ant. Tush! 'tis not fear removes me.
   Mart. No more! your uncle.

         Enter JULIO.

   Julio. Oh, the good hour upon you, gentlemen!
Welcome, nephew: speak it to your friend, sir;
It may be happier receiv'd from you,
In his acceptance.
   Ant. I made bold, uncle,
To do it before; and I think he believes it.
   Mart. 'Twas never doubted, sir.
   Julio. Here are sports, dons,
That you must look on with a loving eye,
And without censure, unless it be giving
My country neighbours' loves their yearly offerings,
That must not be refus'd, though 't be more pain
To the spectator than the painful actor;
It will abide no more test than the tinsel

---

   [w] *dearest*] i. e. direst, most hurtful (from the old English verb *dere* to hurt,—A. S. *derian*).

We clad our masques in for an hour's wearing,
Or the livery-lace sometimes on the cloaks of
A great don's followers: I speak no further
Than our own country, sir.
 Mart. For my part, sir,
The more absurd, 't shall be the better welcome.
 Julio. You'll find the guest you look for.—I heard, cousin,
You were at Toledo th' other day.
 Ant. Not late, sir.
 Julio. Oh fie! must I be plainer? you chang'd the point
With Terzo and Lisauro, two of the stock
Of our antagonists, the Bellides.
 Ant. A mere proffer, sir; the prevention
Was quick with us; we had done somewhat else.
This gentleman was engag'd in 't.
 Julio. I am the enemy
To his foe for it. That wildfire will crave
More than fair water to quench it, I suspect:
Whence it will come, I know not.
 Ant. I was about a gentle reconcilement;
But I do fear I shall go back again.
 Jul. Come, come; the sports are coming on us: nay,

   Enter GOSTANZO, GIRALDO, PHILIPPO, *and others.*

I have more guests to grace it.—Welcome, Don
Gostanzo, Giraldo, Philippo! Seat, seat, all! [*Music.*

    Enter a Boy *as* Cupid.

 Cupid. *Love is little, and therefore I present him;*
Love is a fire [x], *therefore you may lament him.*
 Mart. Alas, poor Love! who are they that can quench him?
 Julio. He's not without those members; fear him not.
 Cupid. *Love shoots, therefore I bear his bow about;*
And Love is blind, therefore my eyes are out.

---

 [x] *Love is a fire*] "A quibble is intended upon the word '*a fire*,'—*a-fire*, which is commonly used to express *on fire*. The presenter of Cupid is supposed to blunder; and, instead of saying that Love is '*a fire*', says that Love is '*a-fire*,' which rendered him an object of lamentation, and makes Martine ask, who are they that can quench him?" MASON. It does not appear that Cupid makes any blunder, though Martine chooses to understand him as if he had said "*a-fire*" instead of "*a fire.*"

Mart. I never heard Love give reason for what he did before.

Cupid. Let such as can see, see such as cannot. Behold, Our goddesses all three strive for the ball of gold! And here fair Paris comes, the hopeful youth of Troy, Queen Hecub's [x] *darling son, king Priam's only joy.*

Enter BUSTOFA *as* Paris.

Mart. Is this Paris? I should have taken him for Hector rather.

Bust. Paris at this time: pray you, hold your prating.

Ant. Paris can be angry.

Julio. Oh, at this time you must pardon him; he comes as a judge.

Mart. [Heaven's [y]] mercy on all that look [z] upon him, say I.

Bust. The thundering seas, whose watery fire washes the whiting-mops [a],
The gentle whale, whose feet so fell flies o'er the mountain-tops, No roars so fierce, no throats so deep, no howls can bring such fears, As Paris can, if garden from he call his dogs and bears [b].

Mart. Ay, those they were that I feared all this while.

Bust. Yes, Jack-an-apes——

Mart. I thank you, good Paris.

Bust. You may hold your peace, and stand further out o' the way, then: the lines will fall where they light.—

Yes, Jack-an-apes he hath to sport [c], *and faces make like mirth, Whilst bellowing bulls, the hornèd beasts, do toss from ground to earth: Blind bear there is, as Cupid blind*——

---

[x] *Hecub's*] Sympson silently printed "Hecuba's"; and so his successors.—In the notes on Shakespeare's *All's well that ends well*, act i. sc. 3 (where the Clown sings a fragment of a ballad containing the words "king Priam's joy"), this and the preceding line of our text are cited as from an "*old ballad*" !!

[y] [*Heaven's*] A break here in both the folios.

[z] *look*] Both the folios "looks".

[a] *whiting-mops*] See note, p. 221.

[b] *As Paris can, if garden from he call his dogs and bears*] "An allusion to Paris-garden on the Bankside, then celebrated for bear-baiting." WEBER.

[c] *to sport*] Both the folios "*to* sports".—" We should read '*to sport*', meaning that he had an ape to sport and make faces." MASON.

Ant. That bear would be whipped for losing of his eyes.
Bust. Be-whippèd man may see:
But we present no such content, but nymphs such as they be.
Ant. These are long lines.
Mart. Can you blame him, leading bulls and bears in 'em?

Enter a Shepherd [d], *with* ISMENIA *as* Juno, AMINTA *as* Pallas, FLORIMEL *as* Venus, *and three* Nymphs *attending.*

Bust. Go, Cupid blind, conduct the dumb; for ladies must
 not speak here:
Let shepherds sing with dancing feet, and cords of music break
 here. [*Song.*
Now, ladies, fight, with heels so light; by lot your luck must
 fall,
Where Paris please, to do you ease, and give the golden ball.
 [*Dance.*

Mart. If you played Paris now, Antonio, where would you bestow it?

Ant. I prithee, friend, take the full freedom of thought, but no words.

Mart. 'Protest there's a third, which by her habit should personate Venus, and, by consequence of the story, receive the honour's prize: and, were I a Paris, there it should be. Do you note her?

Ant. No; mine eye is so fixed, I cannot move it.

Cupid. The dance is ended; now to judgment, Paris.

Bust. Here, Juno, here!—But stay; I do espy
A pretty gleek [e] *coming from Pallas' eye:*
Here, Pallas, here!—Yet stay again; methinks
I see the eye of lovely Venus winks:
Oh, close them both! shut in those golden eyne;
And I will kiss those sweet blind cheeks of thine.
Juno is angry; yes, and Pallas frowns:
Would Paris now were gone from Ida's downs!

[d] *Enter a Shepherd*] Both the folios "*Enter Shepherd* singing": but he evidently does not sing till after the second line of the next speech. It would seem that we ought, either in this stage-direction to read "Shepherds," or in the second line of the next speech "shepherd."

[e] *gleek*] Equivalent here (I believe) to—ensnaring, captivating glance. Concerning this word, see Nares's *Gloss.* and Richardson's *Dict.*

They both are fair; but Venus has the mole,
The fairest hair, and sweetest dimple-hole:
To her, or her, or her, or her, or neither?
Can one man please three ladies all together?
No; take it, Venus; toss it at thy pleasure;
Thou art the lover's friend beyond his measure.
                                    [*Gives her the apple.*
  Julio. Paris has done what man can do, pleas'd one:
Who can do more?
  Mart. Stay; here's another person.

                Enter GERASTO *as* Mars.

  Ger. Come, lovely Venus; leave this lower orb,
And mount with Mars up to his glorious sphere.
  Bust. How now! what's he?
  Flor. I'm ignorant what to do, sir.
  Ger. Thy silver yoke of doves are in the team,
And thou shalt fly th[o]rough Apollo's beam:
I'll see thee seated in thy golden throne,
And hold with Mars a sweet conjunction.
                                    [*Exit with* FLORIMEL.
  Bust. Ha! what fellow's this has carried away my sister Venus? he never rehearsed his part with me before.
  Julio. What follows now, Prince Paris?
  Flo. [*within*] Help, help, help!
  Bust. Hue and cry! I think, sir, this is Venus' voice, mine own sister Florimel's.
  Mart. What, is there some tragic act behind?
  Bust. No, no, altogether comical; Mars and Venus are in the old conjunction, it seems.
  Mart. 'Tis very improper, then; for Venus never cries out when she conjoins with Mars.
  Bust. That's true indeed; they are out of their parts, sure: it may be 'tis the book-holder's[f] fault; I'll go see.
                                    [*Exit.*
  Julio. How like you our country revels, gentlemen?
  Gost., Gir., &c. Oh, they commend themselves, sir.
  Ant. Methinks now

              [f] *book-holder's*] i. e. prompter's.

Juno and Minerva should take revenge on Paris;
It cannot end without it.

Mart. I did expect,
Instead of Mars, the storm-gaoler Æolus;
And Juno proffering her Deiopeia[g]
As satisfaction to the blustering god,
To send his tossers forth.

Julio. It may so follow;
Let's not prejudicate the history.

Re-enter BUSTOFA.

Bust. Oh, oh, oh, oh!

Julio. So, here's a passion[h] towards.

Bust. Help, help, if you be gentlemen! my sister, my Venus! she's stolen away.

Julio. The story changes from our expectation.

Bust. Help! my father the miller will hang me else. God Mars is a bawdy villain: he said she should ride upon doves: she's horsed, she's horsed, whether she will or no.

Mart. Sure, I think he's serious.

Bust. She's horsed upon a double gelding, and a stone-horse in the breech of her: the poor wench cries "help," and I cry "help," and none of you will help.

Julio. Speak, is it the show? or dost thou bawl?

Bust. A pox on the ball! my sister bawls, and I bawl. Either bridle horse and follow, or give me a halter to hang myself: I cannot run so fast as a hog.

Julio. Why[i], follow me: I'll fill the country with pursuit, But I will find the thief. My house thus abus'd[j]?

[*Exit with* GOST., GIR., PHIL., *and others.*

Bust. 'Tis my house that's abused; the sister of my flesh and blood: oh, oh! [*Exit.*

First Nymph. 'Tis time we all shift for ourselves, if this be serious.

[g] *Juno proffering her Deiopeia,* &c.] See Virgil, *Æn.* 1. 72.

[h] *a passion*] "i. e. a pathetic speech. In *The Old Law*, by Massinger, Middleton, and Rowley, Lysander, after the mock-tragic speech of Gnotho, exclaims 'This *passion* has given some satisfaction yet.' [Massinger's *Works*, iv. 575, ed. 1813]." WEBER.

[i] *Why*] The first folio "Wie".—Omitted in the second folio. (At p. 259, "*Why,* 'tis reasonable," stands in the first folio, "Wie," &c.)

[j] *thus abus'd*] Qy. "*abus'd thus*"?

Sec. Nymph. However, I'll be gone.
Third Nymph. And I.   [*Exeunt three* Nymphs.
Ant. You need not fright your beauties, pretty souls,
With the least pale complexion of a fear.
Mart. Juno has better courage, and Minerva's more discreet.
Ism. Alas, my courage was so counterfeit,
It might have been struck from me with a feather!
Juno ne'er had so weak a presenter.
Amin. Sure, I was ne'er the wiser for Minerva,
That I find yet about me.   [ANTONIO *whispers* ISMENIA.
Ism. My dwelling, sir?
'Tis a poor yeoman's roof, scarce a league off,
That never sham'd me yet.
Ant. Your gentle pardon!
I vow my erring eyes had almost cast you
For one of the most mortal enemies
That our family has.
Ism. I am sorry, sir,
I am so like your foe: 'twere fit I hasted
From your offended sight.
Ant. Oh, mistake not!
It was my error, and I do confess it.
You'll not believe you're welcome; nor can I speak it;
But there's my friend can tell you; pray, hear him.
Mart. Shall I tell her, sir? I'm glad of the employment.
Ant. A kinswoman to that beauty?
Amin. Akin to her, sir;
But nothing to her beauty.
Ant. Do not wrong it;
It is not far behind her.
Amin. Her hinder parts
Are not far off, indeed, sir.
Mart. Let me but kiss you with his ardour now,
You shall feel how he loves you.
Ism. Oh, forbear!
'Tis not the fashion with us. But would you
Persuade me that he loves me?
Mart. I'll warrant you,
He dies in't; and that were witness enough on't.

Ism. Love me, sir! can you tell me for what reason?
Mart. Fie! will you ask me? that which you have about
   you.
Ism. I know nothing, sir.
Mart. Let him find it, then:
He constantly believes you have the thing
That he must love you for; much is apparent,
A sweet and lovely beauty.
Ism. So, sir; pray you,
Shew me one thing: did he ne'er love before?
I know you are his bosom-counsellor.
Nay, then, I see your answer is not ready;
I'll not believe you, if you study farther.
Mart. Shall I speak truth to you?
Ism. Or speak no more.
Mart. There was a smile thrown at him, from a lady,
Whose deserts might buy him treble, and lately
He receiv'd it; and I know where he lost it,—
In this face of yours: I know his heart's within you.
Ism. May I know her name?
Mart. In your ear you may,
With vow of silence.
Amin. He'll not give over, sir;
If he speak for you, he'll sure speed for you.
Ant. But that is not the answer to my question.
Amin. You are the first, in my virgin-conscience,
That ever spoke love to her: oh, my heart!
Ant. How do you?
Amin. Nothing, sir; but would I had
A better face! How well your pulse beats!
Ant. Healthfully;
Does it not?
Amin. It thumps prettily, methinks.
Ism. Alack, I hear it with much pity! how great
Is your fault, too, in wrong to the good lady!
Mart. You forget the difficult passage he has to her;
A hell of feud's between the families.
Ism. And that has often Love wrought by advantage
To peaceful reconcilement.

Mart. There impossible.

Ism. This way 'tis worser; it may seed again in her
Unto another generation;
For where, poor lady, is her satisfaction?

Mart. It comes in me: to be truth, I love her
(I'll go no farther for comparison)
As dear as he loves you.

Ism. How if she love not?

Mart. Tush, be that my pains! You know not what art
I have those ways.

Ism. Beshrow you! you have practis'd upon me:
Well, speed me here, and you with your Ismenia!

Mart. Go, the condition's drawn, ready dated;
There wants but your hand to 't.

Amin. Truly, you have taken
Great pains, sir.

Mart. A friendly part, no more, sweet beauty.

Amin. They are happy, sir, have such friends as you are:
But do you know you have done well in this?
How will his allies receive it? She, though I say 't,
Is of no better blood than I am.

Mart. There
I leave it; I am at farthest that way.

Ism. You shall extend your vows no larger now:
My heart calls you mine own, and that's enough.
Reason, I know, would have all yet conceal'd.
I shall not leave you unsaluted long,
Either by pen or person.

Ant. You may discourse
With me, when you think you 're alone; I shall
Be present with you.

Ism. Come, cousin, will you walk?

Amin. Alas, I was ready long since! In conscience,
You would with better will yet stay behind.

Ism. Oh, Love, I never thought thou 'dst been so blind!

[*Exeunt* ISMENIA *and* AMINTA.

Mart. You'll answer this, sir.

Ant. If e'er it be spoke on:
I purpose not to propound the question.

Re-enter JULIO.

Julio. 'Tis true the poor knave said: some ravisher,
Some of Lust's blood-hounds, have seiz'd upon her;
The girl is hurried, as the devil were with 'em,
And help'd their speed.
    Mart. It may be not so ill, sir.
A well-prepar'd lover may do as much
In hot blood as this, and perform it honestly.
    Julio. What! steal away a virgin 'gainst her will?
    Mart. It may be any man's case; despise nothing:
And that's a thief of a good quality,
Most commonly he brings his theft home again,
Though with a little shame.
    Julio. There's a charge by't
Faln upon me: Paris (the miller's son),
Her brother, dares not venture home again,
Till better tidings follow of his sister.
    Ant. You're the more beholding [j] to the mischance, sir:
Had I gone a-boot-haling [k], I should as soon
Have stoln him as his sister: marry, then,
To render him back in the same plight he is
May be costly; his flesh is not maintain'd with little.
    Julio. I think the poor knave will pine away; he cries
All-to-be-pitied yonder.
    Mart. Pray you, sir, let's go see him: I should laugh
To see him cry, sure.
    Julio. Well, you are merry, sir.—
Antonio, keep this charge (I have fears
Move me to lay it on you); pray, forbear
The ways of your enemies, the Bellides:
I have reason for my injunction, sir.   [*Exit.*

Re-enter AMINTA, *disguised as a* Page, *with a letter.*
    Ant. To me, sir? from whom?
    Amin. A friend, I dare vow, sir,
Though on the enemy's part; the lady Ismenia.

[j] *beholding*] i. e. beholden,—as frequently before.
[k] *a-boot-haling*] See note, vol. vii. 228.

Mart. Take heed; blush not too deep. Let me advise you
In your answer; it must be done heedfully.
 Ant. I should not see a masculine, in peace,
Out of that house.
 Amin. Alas, I am a child, sir!
Your hates cannot last till I wear a sword.
 Ant. Await me for your answer.
 Mart. He must see her,
To manifest his shame; 'tis my advantage:
While our blood's under us, we keep above;
But then we fall, when we do fall in love. [*Aside.*
[*Exeunt.*

ACT III.

SCENE I.—*A room in the country-house of* JULIO.

Enter JULIO *and* FRANIO.

 Fra. My lord, my lord, your house hath injur'd me,
Robb'd me of all the joys I had on earth.
 Julio. Where wert thou brought up, fellow?
 Fra. In a mill;
You may perceive it by my loud exclaims,
Which must rise higher yet.
 Julio. Obstreperous carl[1],
If thy throat's tempest could o'er-turn my house,
What satisfaction were it for thy child?
Turn thee the right way to thy journey's end:
Wilt have her where she is not?
 Fra. Here was she lost,
And here must I begin my footing after;
From whence, until I meet a power to punish,
I will not rest. You are not quick to grief;
Your hearing's a dead sense. Were your's the loss,
Had you a daughter stoln, perhaps be-whor'd,

---

[1] *carl*] "i. e. churl, clown." *Ed.* 1778.

(For to what other end should come the thief?)
You 'd play the miller then, be loud and high;
But, being not a sorrow of your own,
You have no help nor pity for another.
  Julio. Oh, thou hast op'd a sluice was long shut up,
And let a flood of grief in! a buried grief
Thy voice hath wak'd again, a grief as old
As likely 'tis thy child is: friend, I tell thee,
I did once lose a daughter.
  Fra. Did you, sir?
Beseech you, then, how did you bear her loss?
  Julio. With thy grief trebled.
  Fra. But was she stoln from you?
  Julio. Yes, by devouring thieves, from whom cannot
Ever return a satisfaction:
The wild beasts had her in her swathing-clothes.
  Fra. Oh, much good do 'em with her!
  Julio. Away, tough churl!
  Fra. Why, she was better eaten than my child,
Better by beasts than beastly men devour'd:
They took away a life, no honour, from her;
Those beasts might make a saint of her; but these
Will make my child a devil. But was she, sir,
Your only daughter?
  Julio. I ne'er had other, friend.

Enter GILLIAN.

  Gil. Where are you, man? your business lies not here.
Your daughter's in the pound; I have found where:
'Twill cost you dear, her freedom.
  Fra. I 'll break it down,
And free her without pay: horse-locks nor chains
Shall hold her from me.   [GILLIAN *whispers him.*
  Julio. I 'll take this relief:
I now have time to speak alone with grief.   [*Exit.*
  Fra. How! my landlord! he is lord of my lands,
But not my cattle: I 'll have her again, Gill.
  Gil. You are not mad upon the sudden now?
  Fra. No, Gill; I have been mad these five hours:

I'll sell my mill, and buy a Roaring [Meg^j];
I'll batter down his house, and make a stews on't.
 Gil. Will you gather up your wits a little,
And hear me? The king's near by, in progress^k;
Here I have got our supplication drawn,
And there's the way to help us.
 Fra. Give it me, Gill:
I will not fear to give it to the king.
To his own hands, God bless him, will I give it;
And he shall set the law upon their shoulders,
And hang 'em all that had a hand in it.
 Gil. Where's your son?
 Fra. He shall be hang'd in flotches^l:
The dogs shall eat him in Lent; there's cats' meat
And dogs' meat enough about him.
 Gil. Sure, the poor girl is the count's whore by this time.
 Fra. If she be the count's whore, the whore's count shall
Pay for it; he shall pay for a new maidenhead.
 Gil. You are so violous!—This I'm resolv'd;
If she be a whore once, I'll renounce her.
You know, if every man had his right, she is
None of our child, but a mere foundling
(And I can guess the owner for a need too);
We have but foster'd her.

^j *a Roaring* [*Meg*] The word "*Meg*" has dropt out of both the folios. Sympson did not perceive that any thing was wanting: the Editors of 1778 and Weber got no further than marking the omission by a break.—Concerning the celebrated piece of ordnance called *Roaring Meg*, various passages, besides the following, might be adduced from our early writers;

"With thondryng noyes was shot of *roeryng Meg*,
 And throw the thickst she thompt orethawrt the waies," &c.
  Churchyard's *Siege of Edenbrough Castell*, fol. 94—*Chippes*, ed. 1575.

"O Cupid, grant that my blushing prove not a linstock, and give fire too suddenly to the *Roaring Meg* of my desires!" Middleton's *Blurt, Master Constable*, act ii. sc. 2, *Works*, i. 263, ed. Dyce.

"Ever since guns came up; the first was your *roaring Meg*." Middleton and Rowley's *Fair Quarrel*, act ii. sc. 2—Ibid. iii. 485.

"Or the rough rumbling *roaring Meg* of Barwicke".
 To the honour of O Toole, p. 19,—Taylor's *Workes*, ed. 1630.

"The great long Dutchman, and *roaring Marget* a Barwicke".
  The Odcombian Banquet, &c., 1611, sig. P.

^k *in progress*] i.e. travelling in state to visit different parts of his dominions.
^l *flotches*] i.e. flitches. So the first folio.—The second folio "flitches;" and so the modern editors.

Fra. Gill, no more of that!
I'll cut your tongue out, if you tell those tales.
[*A flourish within.*
Hark, hark! these toters[m] tell us the king's coming.
Get you gone; I'll see if I can find him. [*Exeunt.*

SCENE II.—*An apartment in the royal residence*[n].

Enter LISAURO, TERZO, PEDRO, *and* MONCADO.

Lis. Does the king remove to-day?

Terzo. So say[o] the harbingers,
And keeps his way on to Valentia;
There ends the progress.

Pedro. He hunts this morning, gentlemen,
And dines i' the fields: the court is all in readiness.

Lis. Pedro, did you send for this tailor? or you, Moncado?
This light French demi-lance that follows us?

Pedro. No, I assure ye on my word, I am guiltless;
I owe him too much to be inward[p] with him.

Monc. I am not quit, I am sure: there is a reckoning
Of some four scarlet cloaks and two lac'd suits
Hangs on the file still, like a fearful comet,
Makes me keep off.

Lis. I am in too, gentlemen,
I thank his faith, for a matter of three hundred.

Terzo. And I for two. What a devil makes he this way?
I do not love to see my sins before me.

Pedro. 'Tis the vacation, and these things break out
To see the court, and glory in their debtors.

Terzo. What do you call him? for I never love
To remember their names that I owe money to;
'Tis not genteel: I shun 'em like the plague ever.

Lis. His name's Vertigo, (hold your heads, and wonder!)
A Frenchman, and a founder of new fashions:
The revolutions of all shapes and habits
Run madding through his brains.

[m] *toters*]—Or *tooters*,—i.e. persons sounding horns,—trumpeters.

[n] *An apartment in the royal residence.*] The king is now "in progress:" see the preceding page.

[o] *say*] Both the folios "saies".

[p] *inward*] "i.e. intimate". WEBER.

Monc. He is very brave.

Lis. The shreds of what he steals from us, believe it,
Makes him a mighty man. He comes:—have at you!

Enter VERTIGO.

Vert. Save ye together, my sweet gentlemen!
I have been looking——

Terzo. Not for money, sir?
You know the hard time.

Vert. Pardon me, sweet signior;
Good faith, the least thought in my heart: your love, gentle-
    men,
Your love's enough for me. Money! hang money!
Let me preserve your love.

Lis. Yes, marry, shall you;
And we our credit. You would see the court?

Monc. He shall see every place.

Vert. Shall I, i' faith, gentlemen?

Pedro. The cellar, and the buttery, and the kitchen,
The pastry, and the pantry.

Terzo. Ay, and taste too
Of every office, and be free of all too;
That he may say, when he comes home in glory—

Vert. And I will say, i' faith, and say it openly,
And say it home too. Shall I see the king also?

Lis. Shalt see him every day; shalt see the ladies
In their French clothes; shalt ride a-hunting with 'em [p];
Shalt have a mistress too.—We must fool handsomely
To keep him in belief we honour him;
He may call on us else.

Pedro. A pox upon him!
Let him call at home in 's own house for salt butter.

Vert. And, when the king puts on a new suit—

Terzo. Thou shalt see it first,
And dissect his doublets, that thou mayst be perfect.

---

[p] *'em*] Both the folios "him"; and so the Editors of 1778 and Weber. Sympson printed "them".—The misprint of "him" for "'em" or "them" is of very frequent occurrence: for examples of it, see my *Remarks on Mr. Collier's and Mr. Knight's editions of Shakespeare*, p. 64.

Vert. The wardrobe I would fain view, gentlemen,
Fain come to see the wardrobe.
　Lis. Thou shalt see it,
And see the secret of it, dive into it;
Sleep in the wardrobe, and have revelations
Of fashions five year hence.
　Vert. Ye honour me,
Ye infinitely honour me.
　Terzo. Any thing i' the court, sir,
Or within the compass of a courtier——
　Vert. My wife shall give ye thanks.
　Terzo. You shall see any thing;
The privat'st place, the stool, and where 'tis emptied.
　Vert. Ye make me blush, ye pour your bounties, gentlemen,
In such abundance.
　Lis. I will shew thee presently
The order that the king keeps when he comes
To open view, that thou mayst tell thy neighbours
Over a shoulder of mutton, thou hast seen something;
Nay, thou shalt present the king for this time——
　Vert. Nay, I pray, sir,——
　Lis. That thou mayst know what state there does belong
　　to it.
Stand there, I say; and put on a sad[q] countenance,
Mingled with height; be cover'd and reserv'd;
Move like the sun, by soft degrees, and glorious.—
Into your order, gentlemen, uncover'd!
The king appears.—We'll sport with you a while, sir;
I am sure you are merry with us all the year long, tailor.—
　　　　　　　　　　　　　　　　　　　　　　[*Aside.*
Move softer still; keep in that fencing leg, monsieur;
Turn to no side.
　　　　　　Enter FRANIO *out of breath.*
　Terzo. What's this that appears to him?
　Lis. H 'as a petition, and he looks most lamentably:
Mistake him, and we are made.

---

[q] *sad*] i. e. serious, grave.

Fra. This is the king, sure,
The glorious king; I know him by his gay clothes. [*Aside.*
　Lis. Now bear yourself, that you may say hereafter——
　Fra. I have recover'd breath; I'll speak unto him pre-
　　sently.— [*Aside.*
May it please your gracious majesty to consider
A poor man's case! [*Kneels.*
　Vert. What's your will, sir?
　Lis. You must accept, and read it.
　Terzo. The tailor will run mad, upon my life, for 't.
　Pedro. How he mumps and bridles! he will ne'er cut
　　clothes again.
　Vert. And what's your grief?
　Monc. He speaks i' the nose like his goose.
　Fra. I pray you, read there; I am abus'd and frump'd, sir,
By a great man, that may do ill by authority:
Poor honest men are hang'd for doing less, sir.
My child is stoln, the Count Otrante stole her:
A pretty child she is, although I say it,
A handsome mother[r]: he means to make a whore of her,
A silken whore; his knaves have filch'd her from me;
He keeps lewd knaves, that do him beastly offices.
I kneel for justice: shall I have it, sir?

　　　　　Enter PHILIPPO *and* Lords.

　Phil. What pageant's this?
　Lis. The king!—
Tailor, stand off: here ends your apparition.—
Miller, turn round, and there address your paper;
There, there's the king, indeed.
　Fra. May it please your majesty——
　Phil. Why didst thou kneel to that fellow?
　Fra. In good faith, sir,

---

[r] *mother*] i. e. a young girl, maid. " A *Modher*, or *Modder*, *Moththler*, a girl, or young wench; used all over the eastern parts of England, v. g. Es. Suff. Norf. Cambr. From the ancient Danish word *Moer*." Ray's *South and East Country Words*, p. 81, ed. 1768 (where Spelman is cited for the derivation). It is written also *mawther*, or *mauther*. See Gifford's Ben Jonson's *Works*, iv. 153, Moor's *Suffolk Words*, and Forby's *Vocab. of East Anglia*.

I thought he had been a king, he was so gallant:
There's none here wears such gold.
  Phil. So foolishly?
You have golden business, sure. Because I am homely
Clad, in no glittering suit, I am not look'd on.
Ye fools, that wear gay clothes, love to be gap'd at,
What are you better when your end calls on you?
Will gold preserve ye from the grave? or jewels?
Get golden minds, and fling away your trappings;
Unto your bodies minister warm raiments,
Wholesome and good; glitter within, and spare not:
Let my court have rich souls; their suits I weigh not.—
And what are you that took such state upon you?
Are you a prince?
  Lis. The prince of tailors, sir:
We owe some money to him, an't like your majesty.
  Phil. If it like him, would ye ow'd more! be modester:—
And you less saucy, sir; and leave this place;
Your pressing-iron will make no perfect courtier:
Go stitch at home, and cozen your poor neighbours:
Shew such another pride, I'll have you whipt for 't!
And get worse clothes; these but proclaim your felony.—
And what's your paper?
  Fra. I beseech you read it.
  Phil. What's here? the Count Otrante task'd for a base
    villany!
For stealing of a maid!
  First Lord. The Count Otrante!
Is not the fellow mad, sir?
  Fra. No, no, my lord;
I am in my wits: I am a labouring man,
And we have seldom leisure to run mad:
We have other business to employ our heads in;
We have little wit to lose too. If we complain,
And if a heavy lord lie on our shoulders,
Worse than a sack of meal, and oppress our poverties,
We are mad straight, and whoop'd[s], and tied in fetters,

---

[s] *whoop'd*] Spelt in both the folios "*whop'd*"—"i. e. insulted with shouts." MASON,—who yet was inclined to read "whipp'd," which Sympson gave at the suggestion of a friend.

Able to make a horse mad, as you use us.
You are mad for nothing, and no man dare proclaim it;
In you a wildness is a noble trick,
And cherish'd in ye, and all men must love it;
Oppressions of all sorts sit like new clothes,
Neatly and handsomely, upon your lordships:
And, if we kick, when[t] your honours spur us,
We are knaves and jades, and ready for the justice.
I am a true miller.

Phil. Then thou art a wonder[u].

Sec. Lord. I know the man reputed for a good man,
An honest and substantial fellow.

Phil. He speaks sense,
And to the point: greatness begets much rudeness.—
How dare you, sirrah, 'gainst so main a person,
A man of so much noble note and honour,
Put up this base complaint? must every peasant
Upon a saucy will affront great lords?
All fellows, miller?

Fra. I have my reward, sir:
I was told, one greatness would protect another,
As beams support their fellows; now I find it.
If 't please your grace to have me hang'd, I am ready;
'Tis but a miller and a thief despatch'd:
Though I steal bread, I steal no flesh to tempt me.
I have a wife; an't please him to have her too,
With all my heart; 'twill make my charge the less, sir;
She 'll hold him play a while. I have a boy too;
He 's able to instruct his honour's hogs,
Or rub his horse' heels: when it please his lordship,
He may make him his slave too, or his bawd;
The boy is well bred, can exhort his sister.
For me, the prison, or the pillory,
To lose my goods, and have mine ears cropt off,
Whipt like a top, and have a paper stuck before me,—
For abominable honesty to his own daughter;
I can endure, sir; the miller has a stout heart,
Tough as his toll-pin.

[t] *kick, when*] Sympson silently printed "*kick* but *when*".
[u] *a wonder*] In being *true*, i. e. honest.

Phil. I suspect this shrewdly:
Is it his daughter that the people call
The miller's fair maid?
Sec. Lord. It should seem so, sir.
Phil. Be sure you be i' the right, sirrah.
Fra. If I be i' the wrong, sir,
Be sure you hang me; I will ask no courtesy.
Your grace may have a daughter, (think of that, sir,)
She may be fair, and she may be abus'd too,
(A king is not exempted from these cases,)
Stoln from your loving care——
Phil. I do much pity him.
Fra. But Heaven forbid she[u] should be in that venture
That mine is in at this hour! I 'll assure your grace,
The lord wants a water-mill, and means to grind with her:
Would I had his stones to set! I would fit him for it.
Phil. Follow me, miller, and let me talk with you farther:—
And keep this private all, upon your loyalties!
To-morrow morning, though I am now beyond him,
And the less look'd for, I 'll break my fast with the good
    count.
No more; away! all to our sports; be silent.
             [*Exeunt* PHILIPPO, Lords, *and* FRANIO.
Vert. What grace shall I have now?
Lis. Choose thine own grace,
And go to dinner when thou wilt, Vertigo;
We must needs follow the king.
Terzo. You heard the sentence.
Monc. If you stay here, I'll send thee a shoulder of venison.
Go home, go home; or, if thou wilt disguise,
I 'll help thee to a place to feed the dogs.
Pedro. Or thou shalt be special tailor to the king's monkey;
'Tis a fine place. We cannot stay.
Vert. No money,
Nor no grace, gentlemen?
Terzo. 'Tis too early, tailor;
The king has not broke his fast yet.

---

[u] *forbid she*] Weber chose to print "*forbid* that *she*".

Vert. I shall look for ye
The next term, gentlemen.
　Pedro. Thou shalt not miss us:
Prithee, provide some clothes: and, dost thou hear, Vertigo?
Commend me to thy wife: I want some shirts too.
　Vert. I have chambers for ye all.
　Lis. They are too musty;
When they are clear, we'll come.
　　　　　　　　　　[*Exeunt all except* VERTIGO.
　Vert. I must be patient
And provident; I shall never get home else.　　[*Exit.*

SCENE III.—*A room in the country-house of* OTRANTE.

Enter OTRANTE *and* FLORIMEL.

　Otr. Prithee, be wiser, wench; thou canst not scape me:
Let me with love and gentleness enjoy that,
That may be still preserv'd with love, and long'd for.
If violence lay rough hold, I shall hate thee;
And, after I have enjoy'd thy maidenhead,
Thou wilt appear so stale and ugly to me,
I shall despise thee, cast thee off.
　Flor. I pray you, sir,
Begin it now, and open your doors to me.
I do confess I am ugly; let me go, sir;
A gipsy-girl; why would your lordship touch me?
Fie, 'tis not noble! I am homely bred,
Coarse, and unfit for you; why do you flatter me?
There be young ladies many, that will love you,
That will dote on you; you are a handsome gentleman:
What will they say when once they know your quality?
"A lord a miller! take your toll-dish with you;
You that can deal with gurgeons[v] and coarse flour,

---

　[v] *gurgeons*] Written also *grudgeons*; see Richardson's Dict. " *Gurgeons*, pollard (between fine flour and bran). Also used in Glamorganshire." *Gloss. of Herefordshire Prov. Words*, 1839. " *Gurgeons*, pollard, coarse flour." Akerman's *Wiltshire Gloss.*—Both the folios " Gudgins " ; and so Sympson ("gudgeons"), though he proposed the true reading in a note.

'Tis pity you should taste what manchet[w] means."
Is this fit, sir, for your repute and honour?
   Otr. I'll love thee still.
   Flor. You cannot; there's no sympathy
Between our births, our breeding, arts, conditions;
And where these are at difference, there's no liking.
This hour, it may be, I seem handsome to you,
And you are taken with variety
More than with beauty; to-morrow, when you have enjoy'd me,
Your heat and lust assuag'd, and come to examine,
Out of a cold and penitent condition,
What you have done, whom you have shar'd your love with,
Made partner of your bed, how it will vex you,
How you will curse the devil that betray'd you!
And what shall become of me then?
   Otr. Wilt thou hear me?
   Flor. As hasty as you were then to enjoy me,
As precious as this beauty shew'd unto you,
You'll kick me out of doors, you will whore[x], and ban me;
And, if I prove with child with your fair issue,
Give me a pension of five pound a-year
To breed your heir withal, and so good[y] speed me!
   Otr. I'll keep thee like a woman.
   Flor. I'll keep myself, sir,
Keep myself honest, sir; there's the brave keeping.
If you will marry me——
   Otr. Alas, poor Florimel!
   Flor. I do confess I am too coarse and base, sir,
To be your wife; and it is fit you scorn me;
Yet such as I have crown'd the lives of great ones:
To be your whore I am sure I am too worthy,
(For, by my troth, sir, I am truly honest,)
And that's an honour equal to your greatness.
   Otr. I'll give thee what thou wilt.
   Flor. Tempt me no more, then:
Give me that peace, and then you give abundance.

---

   [w] *manchet*] i.e. small loaf or roll of the finest white bread.
   [x] *whore*] i.e. call me whore.
   [y] *good*] Weber silently printed "God".

I know you do but try me; you are noble;
All these are but to try my modesty :
If you should find me easy, and once coming,
I see your eyes already, how they would fright me ;
I see your honest heart, how it would swell,
And burst itself into a grief against me ;
Your tongue in noble anger, now, even now, sir,
Ready to rip my loose thoughts to the bottom,
And lay my shame unto myself wide open.
You are a noble lord ; you pity poor maids;
The people are mistaken in your courses ;
You, like a father, try 'em to the uttermost ;
As they do gold, you purge the dross from them,
And make them shine.

   Otr. This cunning cannot help you :
I love you to enjoy you ; I have stoln you
To enjoy you now, not to be fool'd with circumstance.
Yield willingly, or else——

   Flor. What ?

   Otr. I will force you :
I will not be delay'd : a poor base wench,
That I in courtesy make offer to,
Argue with me ?

   Flor. Do not; you will lose your labour :
Do not, my lord; it will become you poorly.
Your courtesy may do much on my nature,
For I am kind as you are, and as tender.
If you compel, I have my strengths to fly to,
My honest thoughts, and those are guards about me :
I can cry too, and noise enough I dare make,
And I have curses that will call down thunder ;
For all I am a poor wench, Heaven will hear me.
My body you may force, but my will never :
And be sure I do not live, if you do force me,
Or have no tongue to tell your beastly story ;
For, if I have, and if there be a justice——

   Otr. Pray you, go in here : I'll calm myself for this time,
And be your friend again.

   Flor. I am commanded.   [*Exit.*

Otr. You cannot scape me yet; I must enjoy you:
I'll lie with thy wit, though I miss thy honesty.
Is this a wench for a boor's hungry bosom?
A morsel for a peasant's base embraces?
And must I starve, and the meat in my mouth?
I'll none of that.

Enter GERASTO.

Ger. How now, my lord? how speed[z] you?
Have you done the deed?

Otr. No, pox upon 't, she is honest.

Ger. Honest! what's that? you take her bare denial:
Was there ever wench brought up in a mill, and honest?
That were a wonder worth a chronicle:
Is your belief so large? What did she say to you?

Otr. She said her honesty was all her dowry;
And preach'd unto me, how unfit, and homely,
Nay, how dishonourable, it would seem in me
To act my will; popt me i' the mouth with modesty—

Ger. What an impudent quean was that! that's their
trick ever.

Otr. And then discours'd to me very learnedly,
What fame and loud opinion would tell of me.
A wife she touch'd at——

Ger. Out upon her, varlet!
Was she so bold? these home-spun things are devils:
They'll tell you a thousand lies, if you'll believe 'em,
And stand upon their honours like great ladies;
They'll speak unhappily too good words to cozen you,
And outwardly seem saints; they'll cry downright also,
But 'tis for anger that you do not crush 'em.
Did she not talk of being with child?

Otr. She touch'd at it.

Ger. The trick of an arrant whore, to milk your lordship:
And then a pension nam'd?

Otr. No, no, she scorn'd it:
I offer'd any thing; but she refus'd all,
Refus'd it with a confident hate.

---

[z] *speed*] So the second folio.— The first folio "sped"; and so the modern editors.

Ger. You thought so.
You should have taken her then, turn'd her, and tew'd her
I' the strength of all her resolution, flatter'd her,
And shak'd her stubborn will; she would have thank'd you,
She would have lov'd you infinitely: they must seem modest,
It is their parts: if you had play'd your part, sir,
And handled her as men do unmann'd hawks [a],
Cast her [b], and mail'd her up in good clean linen [c],
And there have coy'd [d] her, you had caught her heart-strings.
These tough virginities, they blow like white thorns,
In storms and tempests.
   Otr. She is beyond all this;
As cold and harden'd as the virgin crystal.
   Ger. Oh, force her, force her, sir! she longs to be ravish'd;
Some have no pleasure but in violence;
To be torn in pieces is their paradise:
'Tis ordinary in our country, sir, to ravish all;
They will not give a penny for their sport,
Unless they be put to it, and terribly;
And then they swear they 'll hang the man comes near 'em,
And swear it on his lips too.
   Otr. No, no forcing;
I have another course, and I will follow it.
I command you, and do you command your fellows,
That when you see her next, disgrace and scorn her:
I 'll seem to put her out o' the doors o' the sudden,
And leave her to conjecture, then seize on her.
Away! be ready straight.
   Ger. We shall not fail, sir.   [*Exit.*
   Otr. Florimel!
Re-enter FLORIMEL.
   Flor. My lord?
   Otr. I am sure you have now consider'd,

   [a] *unmann'd hawks*] i. e. hawks not yet tamed, not made familiar with man.

   [b] *Cast her*] "To *cast a hawk*, is to take her in your hands before the pinions of her wings, and to hold her from bating or striving, when you administer any thing unto her." Latham's *Faulconry* (*Explan. of Words of Art*), 1658.

   [c] *mail'd her up in good clean linen*] "'*Mail'd*'," says Mason, "refers to the hood used to reclaim hawks",—wrongly. See the quotation from R. Holme, vol. i. 302.

   [d] *coy'd*] i. e. stroked, caressed.

And like a wise wench weigh'd a friend's displeasure,
Repented your proud thoughts, and cast your scorn off.
   Flor. My lord, I am not proud; I was never beautiful,
Nor scorn I any thing that's just and honest.
   Otr. Come, to be short, can you love yet? You told me
Kindness would far compel you: I am kind to you,
And mean to exceed that way.
   Flor. I told you too, sir,
As far as it agreed with modesty,
With honour, and with honesty, I would yield to you.
Good my lord, take some other theme; for love,
Alas, I never knew yet what it meant,
And on the sudden, sir, to run through volumes
Of his most mystic art, 'tis most impossible;
Nay, to begin with lust, which is an heresy,
A foul one too; to learn that in my childhood—
Oh, good my lord!
   Otr. You will not out of this song?
Your modesty, and honesty? is that all?
I will not force you.
   Flor. You are too noble, sir.
   Otr. Nor play the childish fool, and marry you:
I am yet not mad.
   Flor. If you did, men would imagine——
   Otr. Nor will I woo you at that infinite price,
It may be, you expect.
   Flor. I expect your pardon,
And a discharge, my lord; that's all I look for.
   Otr. No, nor fall sick for love.
   Flor. 'Tis a healthful year, sir.
   Otr. Look you; I'll turn you out o' doors, and scorn you.
   Flor. Thank you, my lord.
   Otr. A proud slight peat [e] I found you,
A fool, it may be too——
   Flor. An honest woman,
Good my lord, think me.
   Otr. And a base I leave you:
So, fare you well.

   [e] *peat*] "i. e. pet." WEBER.

Flor. Blessing attend your lordship! [*Exit* OTRANTE.
This is hot love, that vanisheth like vapours:
His ague's off, his burning fits are well quench'd,
I thank Heaven for't.—His men! they will not force me?

Re-enter GERASTO *with* Servants.

Ger. What dost thou stay for? dost thou not know the way,
Thou base unprovident whore?
Flor. Good words, pray ye, gentlemen.
First Serv. Has my lord smok'd you over, good-wife miller?
Is your mill broken, that you stand so useless?
Sec. Serv. An impudent quean! upon my life, she is unwholesome:
Some base discarded thing my lord has found her;
He would not have turn'd her off o' the sudden else.
Ger. Now against every sack, my honest sweetheart,
With every Smig[e] and Smug——
Flor. I must be patient.
Ger. And every greasy guest, and sweaty rascal,
For his royal hire[f] between his fingers, gentlewoman!
First Serv. I fear thou hast given my lord the [pox][g], thou damn'd thing!
Sec. Serv. I have seen her in the stews.
Ger. The knave her father
Was bawd to her there, and kept a tippling-house.——
You must even to it again; a modest function!
Flor. If ye had honesty, ye would not use me
Thus basely, wretchedly, though your lord bid ye;
But He that knows——
Ger. Away, thou carted impudence,
You meat for every man! A little meal
Flung in your face makes you appear so proud.
Flor. This is inhuman. Let these tears persuade you,
If ye be men, to use a poor girl better:
I wrong not you, I am sure; I call you gentlemen.

---

[e] *Smig*] So the second folio.—The first folio " Sim ".

[f] *his royal hire*] " Alluding to a denomination of coin called a *royal*." MASON. See note, vol. iii. 9.

[g] [*pox*] A break here in both the folios.

Re-enter OTRANTE.

Otr. What business is here? Away!
[*Exeunt* GERASTO *and* Servants.
Are not you gone yet?

Flor. My lord, this is not well, although you hate me
(For what I know not), to let your people wrong me,
Wrong me maliciously, and call me——

Otr. Peace!
And mark me what we say, advisedly,
Mark as you love that that you call your credit.
Yield now, or you are undone; your good name's perish'd;
Not all the world can buoy [h] your reputation;
'Tis sunk for ever else: these people's tongues will poison you;
Though you be white as innocence, they'll taint you;
They will speak terrible and hideous things;
And people in this age are prone to credit;
They'll let fall nothing that may brand a woman:
Consider this, and then be wise, and tremble!
Yield yet, and yet I'll save you.

Flor. How?

Otr. I'll shew you.
Their mouths I'll seal up; they shall speak no more
But what is honourable and honest of you,
And saint-like they shall worship you: they are mine,
And what I charge 'em, Florimel——

Flor. I am ruin'd!
Heaven will regard me yet: they are barbarous wretches.—
[*Aside.*
Let me not fall, my lord!

Otr. You shall not, Florimel:
Mark how I'll work your peace, and how I honour you.—
Who waits there? come all in.

Re-enter GERASTO *and* Servants.

Ger. Your pleasure, sir?

Otr. Who dare say this sweet beauty is not heavenly?

---

[h] *buoy*] Sympson's correction.—Both the folios "huy".

This virgin, the most pure, the most untainted,
The holiest thing?
　Ger. We know it, my dear lord:
We are her slaves; and that proud impudence
That dares disparage her, this sword, my lord——
　First Serv. They are rascals, base, the sons of common women,
That wrong this virtue, or dare own a thought
But fair and honourable of her: when we slight her,
Hang us, or cut's in pieces; let's tug i' the galleys!
　Sec. Serv. Brand us for villains!
　Flor. Why, sure, I dream: these are all saints.
　Otr. Go, and live all her slaves.
　Ger. We are proud to do it.
　　　　　　　　　　[Exeunt GERASTO *and* Servants.
　Otr. What think you now? am not I able, Florimel,
Yet to preserve you?
　Flor. I am bound to your lordship;
You are all honour: and, good my lord, but grant me,
Until to-morrow, leave to weigh my fortunes,
I'll give you a free answer, perhaps a pleasing;
Indeed, I'll do the best I can to satisfy you.
　Otr. Take your good time: this kiss: till then, farewell, sweet.　　　　　　　　　　*[Exeunt severally.*

ACT IV.

SCENE I.—*The neighbourhood of Toledo. A grove*[e].

Enter ANTONIO, MARTINE, *and* BUSTOFA.

　Mart. By all means discharge your follower.
　Ant. If we can get him off.—Sirrah, Bustofa,
Thou must needs run back.
　Bust. But I must not, unless you send a bier, or a lictor at my back: I do not use to run from my friends.
　Ant. Well, go will serve turn; I have forgot—

---

[e] *A grove*] So Weber marked this scene; and, however objectionable his choice of place may seem, I know not what other is to be preferred.

Bust. What, sir?

Ant. See, if I can think on't now!

Bust. I know what 'tis now.

Ant. A pistolet of that!

Bust. Done! You have forgot a device to send me away: you are going a-smocking perhaps?

Mart. His own! due, due, i'faith, Antonio;
The pistolet's his own.

Ant. I confess it:
There 'tis [*Gives pistolet*]. Now, if you could afford out of it
A reasonable excuse to mine uncle——

Bust. Yes, I can; but an excuse will not serve your turn: it must be a lie, a full lie; 'twill do no good else. If you'll go to the price of that——

Ant. Is a lie dearer than an excuse?

Bust. Oh, treble! this is the price of an excuse; but a lie is two more. Look, how many foils go to a fair fall, so many excuses to a full lie; and less cannot serve your turn, let any tailor i' the town make it.

Mart. Why, 'tis reasonable; give him his price.——

[ANTONIO *gives* BUSTOFA *two pistolets.*
Let it be large enough now.

Bust. I'll warrant you; cover him all over.

Ant. I would have proof of one now.

Bust. What! stale[i] my invention beforehand? you shall pardon me for that. Well, I'll commend you to your uncle, and tell him you'll be at home at supper with him.

Ant. By no means; I cannot come to-night, man.

Bust. I know that too: you do not know a lie when you see it.

Mart. Remember, it must stretch for all night.

---

[i] *stale*] See note, p. 14. So Sympson.—Both the folios " scale "; and so the Editors of 1778. (The same misprint occurs in the old copies of Shakespeare's *Coriolanus*, act i. sc. 1,—

" I will venture
To *scale* 't a little more ",—

and has been carefully retained in the three latest editions of the great dramatist, though Theobald had long ago corrected the passage, and though Gifford in a most decisive note had proved that the true reading is " *stale* ".)

Bust. I shall want stuff: I doubt 'twill come to the other pistolet.

Ant. Well, lay out; you shall be no loser, sir.

Bust. It must be faced, you know; there will be a yard of dissimulation at least, city-measure, and cut upon an untroth or two; lined with fables^j, that must needs be, cold weather's coming; if it had a galloon of hypocrisy, 'twould do well; and hooked together with a couple of conceits, that's necessity. Well, I'll bring in my bill: I'll warrant you as fair a lie by that time I have done with it, as any gentleman i' the town can swear to, if he would betray his lord and master. [*Exit.*

Ant. So, so; this necessary trouble's over.

Mart. I would you had bought an excuse of him
Before he went! you'll want one for Ismenia.

Ant. Tush, there needs none, there's no suspicion yet;
And I'll be arm'd, before the next encounter,
In a fast tie with my fair Isabel.

Re-enter BUSTOFA.

Mart. Yes,
You'll find your errand is before you now.

Bust. Oh, gentlemen, look to yourselves! ye are men of another world else: your enemies are upon you; the old house of the Bellides will fall upon your heads: Signior Lisauro——

Ant. Lisauro!

Bust. And Don what call you him? he's a gentleman, yet he has but a yeoman's name: Don Tarso, Tarso, and a dozen at their heels——

Ant. Lisauro, Terzo, nor a dozen more,
Shall fright me from my ground, nor shun my path,
Let 'em come on in their^k ablest fury.

Mart. 'Tis worthily resolv'd. I'll stand by you, sir:
This way! I am thy true friend.

^j *fables*] " Mr. Theobald," says Sympson, " dislikes the reading of '*fables*' here, and proposes to correct ' sables,' as being the better lining." How could Theobald fail to perceive that " fables " (which the sense positively requires) is used by Bustofa with a playful allusion to the word of similar sound—sables ?

^k *in their*] Sympson silently printed " *in* all *their* ".

Bust. I'll be gone, sir, that one may live to tell what's become of you.—Put up[1], put up: will you never learn to know a lie from an Æsop's fables? There's a taste for you now!   [*Exit.*

Enter ISMENIA *and* AMINTA.

Mart. Look, sir, what time of day is it?
Ant. I know not;
My eyes go false, I dare not trust 'em now.
I prithee, tell me, Martine, if thou canst,
Is that Ismenia or Isabella?
  Mart. This is the lady; forget not Isabella.
  Ant. If this face may be borrow'd and lent out,
If it can shift shoulders, and take other tires,
So, 'tis mine where'er I find it.
  Ism. Be sudden:
I cannot hold out long.   [*Exit* AMINTA.
  Mart. Believe't, she frowns.
  Ant. Let it come, she cannot frown me off on 't.
How prettily it wooes me to come nearer!—
How do you, lady, since yesterday's pains?
Were you not weary? of my faith——
  Ism. I think you were.
  Ant. What, lady?
  Ism. Weary of your faith; 'tis a burden
That men faint under, though they bear little of it.
  Mart. So; this is to the purpose.   [*Aside.*
  Ant. You came home
In a fair hour, I hope.
  Ism. From whence, sir?

Re-enter AMINTA.

  Amin. Sir, there's a gentlewoman without desires
To speak with you.
  Ant. They were pretty homely toys; but your presence
Made them illustrious.
  Ism. My cousin speaks to you.
  Amin. A gentlewoman, sir; Isabella
She names herself.

---

[1] *Put up*] i. e. sheathe your swords.

Mart. So, so; it hits finely now. [*Aside.*
Ant. Name yourself how you please, speak what you please,
I'll hear you cheerfully.
Ism. You are not well.—
Request her in: she may have more acquaintance
With his passions, and better cure for 'em.
Amin. She's nice[m] in that, madam: poor soul, it seems
She's fearful of your displeasure.
Ism. I'll quit her
From that presently, and bring her in myself. [*Exit.*
Mart. How carelessly do you behave yourself,
When you should call all your best faculties
To counsel in you! how will you answer
The breach you made with fair Ismenia?
Have you forgot the retrograde vow you took
With her, that now is come in evidence?
You'll die upon your shame; you need no more
Enemies of the house, but the lady now:
You shall have your despatch.

Re-enter ISMENIA *dressed as* Juno.

Ant. Give me that face,
And I am satisfied, upon whose shoulders
Soe'er it grows. Juno, deliver us
Out of this amazement! beseech you, goddess,
Tell us of our friends; how does Ismenia?
And how does Isabella? both in good health,
I hope, as you yourself are.
Ism. I am at farthest
In my counterfeit [*Aside*].—My Antonio,
I have matter against you may need pardon,
As I must crave of you.
Ant. Observe you, sir,
What evidence is come against me: what think you
The hydra-headed jury will say to't?
Mart. 'Tis I am fool'd:
My hopes are pour'd into the bottomless tubs;

[m] *nice*] i. e. scrupulous.

'Tis labour for the house of Bellides[n]:
I must not seem so yet [*Aside*].—But, in sooth, lady,
Did you imagine your changeable face
Hid you from me? by this hand, I knew you!

Ant. I went by the face; and by these eyes I might
Have been deceiv'd.

Ism. You might indeed, Antonio;
For this gentleman did vow to Isabella,
That he it was that lov'd Ismenia,
And not Antonio.

Mart. Good: and was not that
A manifest confession that I knew you?
I else had been unjust unto my friend.
'Twas well remember'd: there I found you out;
And speak your conscience now.

Ant. But did he so protest?

Ism. Yes, I vow to you, had Antonio
Wedded Isabella, Ismenia
Had not been lost; there had been her lover.

Ant. Why, much good do you, friend! take her to you;
I crave but one; here have I my wish full:
I am glad we shall be so near neighbours.

Mart. Take both, sir; Juno to boot, three parts in one;
St. Hilary bless you[o]!—Now, opportunity,
Beware to meet with falsehood! if thou canst,
Shun it. My friend's faith's turning from him. [*Aside.*

Ism. Might I not justly accuse Antonio

---

[n] *My hopes are pour'd into the bottomless tubs;*
'Tis labour for the house of Bellides] "In this passage, Martine alludes not only to the family of his adversaries, but to the ancient story of the Bellides [Belides], the fifty daughters of Danaus, the son of Belus, who all, except Hypermnestra, murdered their husbands on their wedding-night; for which crime, as the poets feign, they were condemned in Tartarus to draw water eternally in sieves [to fill with water a vessel full of holes]." MASON.

[o] *St. Hilary bless you*] "Here I think Martine's speech should end, and Antonio speak the remainder:
My friend's faith's turning from him,
plainly appears to be Antonio's upbraidings to Martine." SEWARD. "[The whole of] this speech belongs to Martine. - - These last words mean, that he was about to lose the fidelity he owed his friend." MASON (who first gave the proper punctuation).

For a love-wanderer? You know no other
But me for another, and confess troth now?
   Ant. Here was my guide; where'er I find this face
I am a lover. Marry, I must not miss
This freckle then (I have the number of 'em),
Nor this dimple; not a silk from this brow;
I carry the full idea ever with me.
If nature can so punctually parallel,
I may be cozen'd.
   Ism. Well, all this is even:
But now, to perfect all, our love must now
Come to our enemies' hands, where neither part
Will ever give consent to it.
   Ant. Most certain:
For which reason it must not be put to 'em.
Have we not prevention in our own hands?
Shall I walk by the tree, desire the fruit,
Yet be so nice to pull[p], till I ask leave
Of the churlish gardener, that will deny me?
   Ism. Oh, Antonio!
   Ant. 'Tis manners to fall to
When grace is said.
   Ism. That holy act's to come.
   Mart. You may ope an oyster or two before grace.
   Ant. Are there not double vows as valuable
And as well spoke as any friar utters?
Heaven has heard all.
   Ism. Yes; but stays the blessing,
Till all dues be done: Heaven is not serv'd by halves.
We shall have ne'er a father's blessing here:
Let us not lose the better from above.
   Ant. You take up weapons of unequal force;
It shews you cowardly. Hark in your ear.
   Amin. Have I lost all employment? would this proffer
Had been made to me, though I had paid it with
A reasonable penance!   [*Aside.*
   Mart. Have I pass'd

---

[p] *so nice to pull*] "i. e. so scrupulous of pulling". Mason.

All thy fore-lock, Time ? I'll stretch a long arm
But I'll catch hold again, (do but look back
Over thy shoulder,) and have a pull at thee.   [*Aside.*

Ism. I hear you, sir; nor can I hear too much
While you speak well: you know th' accustom'd place
Of our night-parley; if you can ascend,
The window shall receive you; you may find there
A corrupted churchman to bid you welcome.

Ant. I would meet no other man.

Ism. Aminta, you hear this.

Amin. With joy, madam, because it pleases you:
It may be mine own case another time.
Now you go the right way, ask the banes[q] out;
Put it past father or friends to forbid it,
And then you're sure.—Sir, your Hymen-taper
I'll light up for you; the window shall shew you
The way to Sestos.

Ant. I will venture drowning.

Mart. The simile holds not: 'tis hanging rather.
You must ascend your castle by a ladder;
To the foot I'll bring you.

Ant. Leave me to climb it.

Mart. If I do turn you off?

Ant. Till night, farewell; then better.

Ism. Best it should be[r];
But peevish hatred keeps back that degree[s].

   [*Exeunt* ISMENIA *and* AMINTA.

Mart. I never look'd so smooth as now I purpose:
And then, beware ! Knave is at worst of knave
When he smiles best and the most seems to save.   [*Aside.*
   [*Exeunt.*

---

   q *banes*] See note, vol. v. 444. The Editors of 1778 gave "bans"; Weber "banns".

   r *Till night, farewell; then better.*

Ism. *Best it should be*] In this passage, as Mason saw, the words "*better*" and "*best*" refer to the preceding "*fare*" in "*farewell*": but, surely, the alteration of "*farewell*" to "fare well", which Mason proposed and Weber adopted, is altogether improper.

   s *degree*] The Editors of 1778 silently printed "decree"; and so Weber !

SCENE II.—*A room in the country-house of* JULIO.

Enter JULIO.

Julio. My mind's unquiet: while Antonio
My nephew's abroad, my heart is not at home;
Only my fears stay with me; bad company!
But I cannot shift 'em off. This hatred
Betwixt the house of Bellides and us
Is not fair war; 'tis civil, but uncivil.
We are near neighbours; were of love as near,
Till a cross misconstruction ('twas no more,
In conscience) put us so far asunder:
I would 'twere reconcil'd! it has lasted
Too many sun-sets. If grace might moderate,
Man should not lose so many days of peace,
To satisfy the anger of one minute.
I could repent it heartily. I sent
The knave to attend my Antonio too,
Yet he returns no comfort to me neither.

Enter BUSTOFA.

Bust. No, I must not——
Julio. Ha! he's come.
Bust. I must not; 'twill break his heart to hear it.
Julio. How! there's bad tidings: I must obscure and hear it:
He will not tell me for breaking of my heart;
'Tis half-split already. [*Aside, and then retires.*
Bust. I have spied him. Now to knock down a don with a lie, a silly harmless lie: 'twill be valiantly done, and nobly perhaps.
Julio. I cannot hear him now.
Bust. Oh, the bloody days that we live in! the envious, malicious, deadly days that we draw breath in!
Julio. Now I hear too loud.
Bust. The children that never shall be born may rue it; for men, that are slain now, might have lived to have got children that might have cursed their fathers.

Julio. Oh, my posterity is ruined!
Bust. Oh, sweet Antonio!
Julio. Oh, dear Antonio!
Bust. Yet it was nobly done of both parts: when he and Lisauro met——
Julio. Oh, death has parted 'em!
Bust. "Welcome, my mortal foe," says one: "Welcome, my deadly enemy," says th' other. Off go their doublets, they in their shirts, and their swords stark naked; here lies Antonio, here lies Lisauro; he comes upon him with an *imbroccata*, that he puts by with a *punta reversa;* Lisauro recoils me two paces and some six inches back, takes his career, and then, oh——
Julio. Oh!
Bust. Runs Antonio quite thorough—
Julio. Oh, villain!
Bust. Quite thorough between the arm and the body; so yet [t] he had no hurt at that bout.
Julio. Goodness be praised!
Bust. But then, at next encounter, he fetches me up Lisauro; Lisauro makes out a lunge at him, which he thinking to be a *passado*, Antonio's foot slipping, down, oh, down——
Julio. Oh, now thou art lost!
Bust. Oh, but the quality of the thing! both gentlemen, both Spanish Christians; yet one man to shed—
Julio. Say his enemy's blood.
Bust. His hair, may come by divers casualties, though he never go into the field with his foe; but a man to lose nine ounces and two drams of blood at one wound, thirteen and a scruple at another, and to live till he die in cold blood—yet the surgeon, that cured him, said, if *pia mater* had not been perished, he had been a lives man till this day.
Julio. There he concludes he is gone.
Bust. But all this is nothing: now I come to the point——
Julio. Ay, the point, that's deadly; the ancient blow
Over the buckler ne'er went half so deep.

---

[t] *yet*] Silently altered to "that" by the Editors of 1778; and so Weber.

Bust. Yet pity bids me keep in my charity; for me to pull an old man's ears from his head with telling of a tale—oh, foul tale! no; be silent, tale. Furthermore, there is the charge of burial; every one will cry " blacks, blacks," [u] that had but the least finger dipt in his blood, though ten degrees removed when 'twas done. Moreover, the surgeon (that made an end of him) will be paid; sugar-plums and sweet-breads; yet, I say, the man may recover again, and die in his bed.

Julio. What motley stuff is this? [*coming forward*] Sirrah, speak truth,
What hath befallen my dear Antonio?
Restrain your pity in concealing it;
Tell me the danger full; take off your care
Of my receiving it; kill me that way,
I'll forgive my death: what thou keep'st back from truth
Thou shalt speak in pain; do not look to find
A limb in his right place, a bone unbroke,
Nor so much flesh unbroil'd of all that mountain,
As a worm might sup on: despatch, or be despatch'd.

Bust. Alas, sir, I know nothing, but that Antonio is a man of God's making to this hour: 'tis not two since I left him so.

Julio. Where didst thou leave him?

Bust. In the same clothes he had on when he went from you.

Julio. Does he live?

Bust. I saw him drink.

Julio. Is he not wounded?

Bust. He may have a cut i' the leg by this time; for Don Martine and he were at whole slashes.

Julio. Met he not with Lisauro?

Bust. I do not know her.

Julio. Her! Lisauro is a man, as he is.

Bust. I saw ne'er a man like him.

Julio. Didst thou not discourse
A fight betwixt Antonio and Lisauro?

[u] *blacks*] " i. e. mourning clothes." WEBER.

Bust. Ay, to myself; I hope a man may give himself the lie, if it please him.

Julio. Didst thou lie, then?

Bust. As sure as you live now.

Julio. I live the happier by it. When will he return?

Bust. That he sent me to tell you; within these ten days at farthest.

Julio. Ten days! he's not wont to be absent two.

Bust. Nor I think he will not: he said he would be at home to-morrow; but I love to speak within my compass.

Julio. You shall speak within mine, sir, now.—Within there!

Enter Servants.

Take this fellow into custody; Keep him safe, I charge you.

Bust. Safe! do you hear? take notice what plight you find me in; if there want but a collop or a steak o' me, look to 't.

Julio. If my nephew return not in his health to-morrow, Thou goest to the rack.

Bust. Let me go to the manger first; I had rather eat oats than hay. [*Exit with* Servants.

Enter BELLIDES *with a letter.*

Bel. By your leave, sir.

Julio. For aught I know yet, you are welcome, sir.

Bel. [*Giving letter*] Read that, and tell me so; or, if thy spectacles
Be not easy, keep thy nose unsaddled, and ope
Thine ears: I can speak thee the contents; I made 'em.
'Tis a challenge, a fair one, I'll maintain 't:
I scorn to hire my second to deliver 't,
I bring 't myself. Dost know me, Julio?

Julio. Bellides!

Bel. Yes; is not thine hair on end now?

Julio. Somewhat amaz'd at thy rash hardiness:
How durst thou come so near thine enemy?

Bel. Durst!
I dare come nearer : thou art a fool, Julio.
   Julio. Take it home to thee, with a knave to boot.
   Bel. Knave to thy teeth again! and all that's quit.
Give me not a fool more than I give thee,
Or, if thou dost, look to hear on't again.
   Julio. What an encounter's this!
   Bel. A noble one :
My hand is to my words ; thou hast it there :
There I do challenge thee, if thou dar'st, be
Good friends with me; or I'll proclaim thee coward.
   Julio. Be friends with thee!
   Bel. I'll shew thee reasons for't :
A pair of old coxcombs, (now we go together,)
Such as should stand examples of discretion,
The rules of grammar to unwilling youth
To take out lessons by ; we, that should check
And quench the raging fire in others' bloods,
We strike the battle to destruction ?
Read 'em the black art ? and make 'em believe
It is divinity ? Heathens, are we not ?
Speak thy conscience ; how hast thou slept this month,
Since this fiend haunted us?
   Julio. Sure, some good angel
Was with us both last night. Speak thou truth now ;
Was it not last night's motion ?
   Bel. Dost not think
I would not lay hold of it at first proffer,
Should I ne'er sleep again ?
   Julio. Take not all from me ;
I'll tell the doctrine of my vision :—
" Say that Antonio, best of thy blood,
Or any one the least allied to thee,
Should be the prey unto Lisauro's sword,
Or any of the house of Bellides "——
   Bel. Mine was the just inversion. On, on!
   Julio. " How would thine eyes have emptied thee in sorrow,
And left the conduit ^v of nature dry !

---

   ^v *conduit*] So the second folio.—The first folio " condiment ".

Thy hands have turn'd rebellious to the balls,
And broke the glasses! with thine own curses
Have torn thy soul, left thee a statue
To propagate thy next posterity!"
 Bel. "Yes, and thou causer!" so it said to me;
"They fight but your mischiefs; the young men were friends,
As is the life and blood coagulate
And curded in one body; but this is yours,
An inheritance that you have gather'd for 'em,
A legacy of blood, to kill each other
Throughout your generations." Was't not so?
 Julio. Word for word.
 Bel. Nay, I can go farther yet.
 Julio. 'Tis far enough: let us atone [w] it here,
And in a reconcilèd circle fold
Our friendship new again.
 Bel. The sign's in Gemini;
An auspicious house; 't has join'd both ours again.
 Julio. You cannot proclaim me coward now, Don Bellides.
 Bel. No; thou'rt a valiant fellow; so am I:
I'll fight with thee at this hug, to the last leg
I have to stand on, or breath or life left.
 Julio. This is the salt unto humanity,
And keeps it sweet.
 Bel. Love! oh, life stinks without it!—
I can tell you news.
 Julio. Good has long been wanting.
 Bel. I do suspect, and I have some proof on't
(So far as a love-epistle comes to),
That Antonio your nephew and my daughter
Ismenia are very good friends before us.
 Julio. That were a double wall about our houses,
Which I could wish were builded.
 Bel. I had it from
Antonio's intimate, Don Martine;
And yet, methought, it was no friendly part
To shew it me.
 Julio. Perhaps 'twas his consent:

<small>[w] *atone*] i. e. reconcile.</small>

Lovers have policies as well as statesmen;
They look not always at the mark they aim at.

Bel. We'll take up cudgels, and have one bout with 'em:
They shall know nothing of this union;
And, till they find themselves most desperate,
Succour shall never see 'em.

Julio. I'll take your part, sir.

Bel. It grows late; there's a happy day past us.

Julio. The example, I hope, to all behind it.   [*Exeunt.*

SCENE III.—*Toledo. A street. Before the house of* BELLIDES.

AMINTA *appears at the window with a taper.*

Amin. Stand fair, light of love! which epithet and place
Adds to thee honour; to me it would be shame [x]:
We must be weight in love, no grain too light.
Thou art the land-mark; but, if Love be blind
(As many that can see have so reported),
What benefit canst thou be to his darkness?
Love is a jewel (some say) inestimable,
But, hung at the ear, deprives our own sight [z],
And so it shines to others, not ourselves.
I speak my skill; I have only heard on 't,
But I could wish a nearer document.

---

[x] *to me it would be shame*] Because "*light-of-love*" meant—a light woman, a wanton: see note, vol. vii. 227.—Theobald, not understanding the passage, proposed to read in the preceding line, "*Stand fair,* light love!"

[z] *But, hung at the ear, deprives our own sight*] Sympson proposed to read,

"*But, hung at the ear,* is depriv'd *our own sight:*"

and Heath (*MS. Notes*) conjectured,

"*But, hung at the ear, deprives* it *our own sight*".

No alteration is required, the old text being doubtless genuine. Here "*deprives*" means simply—takes away; as in Shakespeare's *Hamlet,* act i. sc. 4,

"Which might *deprive* your sovereignty of reason";

(where, assuredly, "*sovereignty*" is not, as Gifford supposed, a title of respect). The general meaning of the present passage is rightly explained by the Editors of 1778; "We think the poets designed to compare love to a jewel, whose lustre is seen by the rest of the world, and not by the *wearer.*"

Alas, the ignorant desire to know!
Some say, Love's but a toy, and with a but——
Now, methinks, I should love it ne'er the worse;
A toy is harmless sure, and may be play'd with;
It seldom goes without his adjunct, *pretty*,
" A pretty toy," we say; 'tis metre [a] to *joy* too.
Well, here may be a mad night yet, for all this:
Here's a priest ready, and a lady ready;
A chamber ready, and a bed ready;
'Tis then but making unready [b], and that's soon done.
My lady is my cousin; I myself;
Which is nearest, then? My desires are mine;
Say they be hers too, is't a hanging matter?
It may be ventur'd in a worser cause:
I must go question with my conscience.
I have the word: sentinel, do thou stand;
Thou shalt not need to call, I 'll be at hand.　　[*Exit above.*

Enter ANTONIO *and* MARTINE.

　Ant. Are we not dogg'd behind us, think'st thou, friend?
　Mart. I heard not one bark, sir.
　Ant. There are that bite
And bark not, man; methought I spied two fellows,
That through two streets together walk'd aloof,
And wore their eyes suspiciously upon us.
　Mart. Your jealousy, nothing else; or such perhaps
As are afraid as much of us; who knows
But about the like business? but, for your fear's sake,
I 'll advise and entreat one courtesy.
　Ant. What is that, friend?
　Mart. I will not be denied, sir;
Change your upper garments with me.
　Ant. It needs not.
　Mart. I think so too; but I will have it so,
If you dare trust me with the better, sir.
　Ant. Nay, then——

　　　　　[a] *metre*] "i. e. rhyme." WEBER.
　　　　　[b] *making unready*] "i. e. undressing." MASON.

VOL. IX.　　　　　T

Mart. If there should be danger towards,
There will be the main mark, I am sure.
Ant. Here thou tak'st from me——
Mart. Tush! the general
Must be safe, however the battle goes. [*They change cloaks.*
See you the beacon yonder?
Ant. Yes; we are near shore.
Mart. Come, land, land! you must clamber by the cliff;
Here are no stairs to rise by.

    As ANTONIO *is climbing up to the window, enter two* Gentlemen, *with weapons drawn, who set upon* MARTINE.

Ant. Ay! are you there?
    [ANTONIO *comes down to the rescue of* MARTINE: *the* Gentlemen *are driven off by* ANTONIO *and* MARTINE; *and exit* ANTONIO *pursuing them.* MARTINE *ascends to the window, where* AMINTA *re-appears.*
Amin. Antonio?
Mart. Yes. Ismenia?
Amin. Thine own.
Mart. Quench the light; thine eyes are guides illustrious.
Amin. 'Tis necessary.   [*Exeunt above.*

           Re-enter ANTONIO.

Ant. [c] Your legs have sav'd your lives, whoe'er you are.—
Friend! Martine! where art thou? not hurt, I hope.—
Sure, I was farthest in the pursuit of 'em:
My pleasures are forgotten through my fears.
The light's extinct: it was discreetly done;
They could not but have notice of the broil,
And, fearing that might call up company,
Have carefully prevented, and clos'd up:
I do commend the heed. Oh, but my friend!
I fear his hurt.—Friend! friend! it cannot be
So mortal, that I should lose thee quite, friend:
A groan! any thing that may discover thee!
Thou art not sunk so far, but I might hear thee:
I'll lay mine ear as low as thou canst fall.

    [c] *Ant.*] Both the folios " Mar."

Friend! Don Martine! I must answer for thee
('Twas in my cause thou fell'st), if thou be'st down.—
Such dangers stand betwixt us and our joys,
That, should we forethink ere we undertake,
We'd sit at home, and save. What a night's here!
Purpos'd for so much joy, and now dispos'd
To so much wretchedness! I shall not rest in 't:
If I had all my pleasures there within,
I should not entertain 'em with a smile.
Good night to you! mine will be black and sad:
A friend cannot, a woman may be had [d]. [*Exit.*

ACT V.

SCENE I.—*A room in the house of* BELLIDES.

Enter ISMENIA *and* AMINTA.

Ism. Oh, thou false——
Amin. Do your daring'st: he's mine own,
Soul and body mine, church and chamber mine,
Totally mine.
Ism. Dar'st thou face thy falsehood?
Amin. Shall I not give a welcome to my wishes,
Come home so sweetly? Farewell your company,
Till you be calmer, woman! [*Exit.*
Ism. Oh, what a heap
Of misery has one night brought with it!

Enter ANTONIO.

Ant. Where is he? Do you turn your shame from me?
You're a blind adulteress; you know you are.
Ism. How's that, Antonio?

---

[d] *had*] So Sympson silently.—Both the folios "bad"; and so the Editors of 1778.

Ant. Till I have vengeance,
Your sin's not pardonable: I will have him,
If hell hide him not! you've had your last of him.   [*Exit.*
 Ism. What did he speak? I understood him not:
He call'd me a foul name; it was not mine;
He took me for another, sure.

Enter BELLIDES.

Bel. Ha! are you there?
Where's your sweetheart? I have found you, traitor
To my house! wilt league with mine enemy?
You'll shed his blood, you'll say: ha! will you so?
And fight with your heels upwards? No, minion;
I have a husband for you (since you're so rank),
And such a husband as thou shalt like him,
Whether thou wilt or no,—Antonio!
 Ism. It thunders with the storm now.
 Bel. And to-night
I will have it despatch'd; I'll make it sure, I:
By to-morrow this time thy maidenhead
Shall not be worth a chequin [e], if it were
Knock'd at an out-cry [f]. Go; I'll ha' you before me:
Shough, shough! up to your coop, pea-hen!
 Ism. Then I'll try my wings.   [*Exit.*
 Bel. Ay! are you good at that? stop, stop, thief! stop
   there!   [*Exit.*

SCENE II.—*A room in the country-house of* OTRANTE.

Enter OTRANTE *and* FLORIMEL.

Flor. [*sings*]
> Now, having leisure, and a happy wind,
> Thou mayst at pleasure cause the stones to grind;
> Sails spread, and grist here ready to be ground,
> Fie, stand not idly, but let the mill go round!

Otr. Why dost thou sing and dance thus? why so merry?

---

[e] *chequin*] i. e. the Italian coin so called.—Both the folios "chicken"; and so Sympson and the Editors of 1778!   [f] *out-cry*] "i. e. auction." MASON.

Why dost thou look so wantonly upon me,
And kiss my hands?
 Flor. If I were high enough,
I would kiss your lips too.
 Otr. Do; this is some kindness;
This tastes of willingness; nay, you may kiss still.
But why o' the sudden now does the fit take you,
Unoffer'd or uncompell'd? why these sweet courtesies?
Even now you would have blush'd to death to kiss thus:
Prithee, let me be prepar'd to meet thy kindness;
I shall be unfurnish'd else to hold thee play, wench:
Stay now a little, and delay your blessings;
If this be love, methinks it is too violent:
If you repent you of your strictness to me,
It is so sudden, it wants circumstance.
 Flor. Fie, how dull!   [*Sings.*

> How long shall I pine for love?
> How long shall I sue in vain?
> How long, like the turtle-dove,
> Shall I heavily thus complain?
> Shall the sails of my love stand still?
> Shall the grist[g] of my hopes be unground?
>   Oh fie, oh fie, oh fie!
> Let the mill, let the mill go round!

 Otr. Prithee, be calm a little:
Thou mak'st me wonder; thou that wert so strange[h],
And read such pious rules to my behaviour
But yesternight, thou that wert made of modesty,
Shouldst in a few short minutes turn thus desperate!
 Flor. You are too cold.
 Otr. I do confess I freeze now;
I am another thing all over me:
It is my part to woo, not to be courted.
Unfold this riddle; 'tis to me a wonder,
That now o' th' instant, ere I can expect,
Ere I can turn my thoughts, and think upon
A separation of your honest carriage

---

  [g] *grist*] Both the folios "grists".
  [h] *strange*] i. e. coy.

From the desires of youth, thus wantonly,
Thus beyond expectation——

Flor. I will tell you,
And tell you seriously, why I appear thus,
To hold you no more ignorant and blinded :
I have no modesty ; I am truly wanton ;
I am that you look for, sir : now, come up roundly !
If my strict face and counterfeited staidness [i]
Could have won on you, I had caught you that way,
And you should ne'er have come to have known who hurt you.
Prithee, sweet count, be more familiar with me.
However we are open in our natures,
And apt to more desires than you dare meet with,
Yet we affect to lay the gloss of good on 't.
I saw you touch'd not at the bait of chastity,
And that it grew distasteful to your palate
To appear so holy ; therefore I take my true shape :
Is your bed ready, sir ? you shall quickly find me. [*Sings.*

> On the bed I 'll throw thee, throw thee down ;
>   Down being laid,
>   Shall we be afraid
> To try the rites that belong to love ?
> No, no ; there I 'll woo thee with a crown ;
>   Crown our desires,
>   Kindle the fires ;
> When love requires, we should wanton prove ;
> We 'll kiss, we 'll sport, we 'll laugh, we 'll play :
> If thou com'st short, for thee I 'll stay ;
> If thou unskilful art, the ground [j]
> I 'll kindly teach : we 'll have the mill go round.

Otr. Are you no maid ?
Flor. Alas, my lord, no, certain !
I am sorry you are so innocent to think so.
Is this an age for silly maids to thrive in ?

[i] *staidness*] So the first folio ("*staiednesse*") ; but, the dot over the *i* being somewhat blurred and looking like an *l*, Weber asserted that it gave "staledness".—The second folio "statelyness" ; and so Sympson and Weber.

[j] *If thou unskilful art, the ground,* &c.] So the first folio.—The second folio has "*If thou unskilful art* on *the ground*", &c. ; and so (with a comma after "*art*") the Editors of 1778 and Weber !!

It is so long too since I lost it, sir,
That I have no belief I ever was one :
What should you do with maidenheads? you hate 'em;
They are peevish pettish things, that hold no game up,
No pleasure neither; they are sport for surgeons;
I 'll warrant you, I 'll fit you beyond maidenhead :
A fair and easy way men travel right in,
And with delight, discourse, and twenty pleasures,
They enjoy their journey; madmen creep through hedges.

   Otr. I am metamorphos'd! [*Aside.*]—Why do you appear,
I conjure you, beyond belief thus wanton?
   Flor. Because I would give you pleasure beyond belief.
                                                      [*Sings.*

> Think me still
> In my father's mill,
> Where I have oft been found-a,
> Thrown on my back
> On a well-fill'd sack,
> While the mill has still gone round-a :
> Prithee, sirrah, try thy skill;
> And again let the mill go round-a!

   Otr. Then you have traded?
   Flor. Traded! how should I know else how to live, sir,
And how to satisfy such lords as you are,
Our best guests and our richest?
   Otr. How I shake now!—   [*Aside.*
You take no base men?
   Flor. Any that will offer;
All manner of men, and all religions, sir,
We touch at in our time; all states and ages;
We exempt none.   [*Sings.*

> The young one, the old one,
> The fearful, the bold one,
>   The lame one, though ne'er so unsound,
> The Jew or the Turk,
> Have leave for to work,
>   The whilst that the mill goes round.

   Otr. You are a common thing, then?
   Flor. No matter, since you have your private pleasure,
And have it by an artist excellent;
Whether I am thus or thus, your men can tell you.

Otr. My men! defend me! how I freeze together,
And am on ice! Do I bite at such an orange,
After my men? I am preferr'd! [*Aside.*
Flor. Why stay you?
Why do we talk, my lord, and lose our time?
Pleasure was made for lips, and sweet embraces;
Let lawyers use their tongues.—Pardon me, Modesty!
This desperate way must help, or I am miserable. [*Aside.*
Otr. She turns, and wipes her face; she weeps for certain:
Some new way now: she cannot be thus beastly;
She is too excellent fair to be thus impudent:
She knows the elements of common looseness,
The art of lewdness[k]—that, that, that—

Enter a Servant.

How now, sir?
Serv. The king, an't please your lordship, is alighted
Close at the gate.
Otr. The king!
Serv. And calls for you, sir;
Means to breakfast here too.
Flor. Then I am happy. [*Aside.*
Otr. Stolen so suddenly?—Go, lock her up;
Lock her up where the courtiers may not see her;
Lock her up closely, sirrah, in my closet.
Serv. I will, my lord. What, does she yield yet?
Otr. Peace!
She is either a damn'd devil, or an angel.—
No noise, upon your life, dame, but all silence!

[Servant *locks up* FLORIMEL *in the closet, and then exit.*

Enter PHILIPPO, Lords, LISAURO, TERZO, *and* VERTIGO.

Your majesty heaps too much honour on me,
With such delight to view each several corner
Of a rude pile; there's no proportion in't, sir.

---

[k] *The art of lewdness*] Seward proposed to read " Not *the art* (or *act*) *of lewdness*"; and Heath (*MS. Notes*) would give the passage thus,—
" She *know* the elements of common looseness!
The art of lewdness! that, that, that --"
supposing that Otrante, had he not been interrupted, would have said " that *is impossible.*"

Phil. Methinks 'tis handsome, and the rooms along
Are neat and well contriv'd; the gallery
Stands pleasantly and sweet. What rooms are these?
　Otr. They are sluttish ones.
　Phil. Nay, I must see.
　Otr. Pray you, do, sir:
They are lodging-chambers over a homely garden.
　Phil. Fit still, and handsome; very well.—And those?
　Otr. Those lead to the other side o' th' house, an't like
　　　you.
　Phil. Let me see those.
　Otr. You may; the doors are open.—
What should this view mean? I am half suspicious.
　　　　　　　　　　　　　　　　　　　　　[*Aside.*
　Phil. This little room?
　Otr. 'Tis mean; a place for trash, sir,
For rubbish of the house.
　Phil. I would see this too:
I will see all.
　Otr. I beseech your majesty,—
The savour of it, and the coarse appearance——
　Phil. 'Tis not so bad; you would not offend your house
　　　with it:
Come, let me see.
　Otr. Faith, sir——
　Phil. I'faith, I will see.
　Otr. My groom has the key, sir; and 'tis ten to one——
　Phil. But I will see it.—Force the lock, my lords;
There be smiths enough to mend it.—I perceive
You keep some rare things here, you would not shew, sir.
　　　　　　　[*They burst open the door of the closet.*
　Terzo. Here's a fair maid, indeed!
　Phil. By my faith, is she;
A handsome girl!—Come forward; do not fear, wench.—

　　　　　　　　Re-enter FLORIMEL.

Ay, marry, here's a treasure worth concealing.—
Call in the miller.　　　　　　　　　[*Exit a* Lord.
　Otr. Then I am discover'd!—　　　　　　[*Aside.*

I['ll] confess all before the miller comes, sir:
T'was but intention; from all act I am clear yet.

Re-enter Lord *with* FRANIO.

Phil. Is this your daughter?
Fra. Yes, an't please your highness,
This is the shape of her: for her substance, sir,
Whether she be now honourable or dishonourable,
Whether she be a white rose or a canker[1], is the question.
I thank my lord, he made bold with my filly.—
If she be for your pace, you had best preserve her, sir;
She is tender-mouth'd; let her be broken handsomely.
Phil. Maid, were you stoln?
Flor. I went not willingly,
An't please your grace; I was never bred so boldly.
Phil. How has he us'd you?
Flor. Yet, sir, very nobly.
Phil. Be sure you tell truth.—And be sure, my lord,
You have not wrong'd her; if you have, I tell you,
You have lost me, and yourself too.—Speak again, wench.
Flor. He has not wrong'd me, sir; I am yet a maid;
By all that's white and innocent, I am, sir!
Only I suffer'd under strong temptations,
The heat of youth; but Heaven deliver'd me.—
My lord, I am no whore, for all I feign'd it,
And feign'd it cunningly, and made you loathe me:
'Twas time to out-do you; I had been robb'd else,
I had been miserable: but I forgive you.
Phil. What recompense for this?
Otr. A great one, sir;
First a repentance, and a hearty one.—
Forgive me, sweet!
Flor. I do, my lord.
Otr. I thank you:
The next, take this, and these; all I have, Florimel!

[*Offers jewels.*

Flor. No, good my lord; these often corrupt maidens;

---

canker] i. e. wild rose, or dog-rose.

I dare not touch at these; they are lime for virgins:
But, if you'll give me——
　Otr. Any thing in my power,
Or in my purchase.
　Flor. Take heed, noble sir;
You'll make me a bold asker.
　Otr. Ask me freely.
　Flor. Ask you! I do ask you, and I deserve you;
I have kept you from a crying sin would damn you
To men and time; I have preserv'd your credit,
That would have died to all posterity:
Curses of maids shall never now afflict you,
Nor parents' bitter tears make your name barren:
If he deserves well that redeems his country,
And as a patriot be remember'd nobly,
Nay, set the highest; may not I be worthy
To be your friend, that have preserv'd your honour?
　Otr. You are, and thus I take you; thus I seal you
Mine own, and only mine.
　Phil. Count, she deserves you.—
And let it be my happiness to give you.—
　　　　　　　　　　　　[*Gives her to* OTRANTE.
I have given a virtuous maid now, I dare say it;
'Tis more than blood. I'll pay her portion, sir;
And 't shall be worthy you.
　Fra. I'll sell my mill;
I'll pay some too; I'll pay the fiddlers,
And we'll have all i' the country at this wedding.
Pray, let me give her too.—Here, my lord, take her,
Take her with all my heart, and kiss her freely:
Would I could give you all this hand has stoln too,
In portion with her! 'twould make her a little whiter.
The wind blows fair now: get me a young miller.
　Vert. She must have new clothes.
　Terzo. Yes.
　Vert. Yes, marry, must she.—
If 't please you, madam, let me see the state of your body;
I'll fit you instantly.
　Phil. Art not thou gone yet?

Vert. An't please your grace, a gown, a handsome gown now,
An orient gown——
   Phil. Nay, take thy pleasure of her.
   Vert. Of cloth of tissue—I can fit you, madam;—
My lords, stand out o' the light;—a curious body,—
The neatest body in Spain this day,—with embroider'd flowers;
A clinquant[m] petticoat of some rich stuff,
To catch the eye: I have a thousand fashions.
Oh, sleeve, oh, sleeve! I'll study all night, madam,
To magnify your sleeve.
   Otr. Do, superstitious tailor[n],
When you have more time.
   Flor. Make me no more than woman, and I am thine.
   Otr. Sir, happily my wardrobe, with your help,
May fit her instantly: will you try her?
   Vert. If I fit her not, your wardrobe cannot:
But, if the fashion be not there, you mar her.
           [*Exeunt* OTRANTE, FLORIMEL, *and* VERTIGO.

      Enter Constable *and* Officers, *bringing in* ANTONIO.
   Ant. Is my offence so great, ere I be convict,
To be torn with rascals? If it be law,
Let 'em be wild horses rather than these.
   Phil. What's that?
   Con. This is a man suspected of murder, if it please your grace.
   Phil. It pleases me not, friend. But who suspects him?
   Con. We that are your highness' extraordinary officers, we that have taken our oaths to maintain you in peace.
   Phil. 'Twill be a great charge to you.
   Con. 'Tis a great charge, indeed; but then we call our

---

[m] *clinquant*] " i. e. glittering, shining [French, *clinquant*, tinsel]." WEBER.

[n] *superstitious tailor*] The epithet " *superstitious* " is used here with a quibble. Compare;

      "There's rabbi Abimelech a learnèd cobbler,
      Rabbi Lazarus a *superstitchious* tailor."

Middleton and Rowley's *World tost at tennis*,—Middleton's *Works*, v. 170, ed. Dyce.

neighbours to help us. This gentleman and another were fallen out (yet that's more than I am able to say, for I heard no words between 'em, but what their weapons spoke, clash and clatter); which we seeing, came with our bills of government[o], and first knocked down their weapons, and then the men.

Phil. And this you did to keep the peace?

Con. Yes, an't like your grace, we knocked 'em down, to keep the peace. This we laid hold on, the other we set in the stocks: that I could do by mine own power, without your majesty.

Phil. How so, sir?

Con. I am a shoemaker by my trade.

Enter AMINTA.

Amin. Oh, my husband!
Why stands my husband as a man endanger'd?
Restore him me, as you are merciful!
I'll answer for him.

Ant. What woman's this? what husband?—
Hold thy bawling: I know thee for no wife.

Amin. You married me last night.

Ant. Thou liest! I neither was
In church nor house last night, nor saw I thee.
A thing that was my friend, I scorn to name now,
Was with Ismenia, like a thief, and there
He violated a sacred trust: this thou mayst know, Aminta.

Amin. Are not you he?

Ant. No; nor a friend of his:
Would I had killèd him! I hope I have.

Amin. That was my husband, royal sir, that man,
That excellent man!

Ant. That villain, that thief!

Enter BELLIDES.

Bel. Have I caught you, sir? well overtaken!—
This is mine enemy.—Pardon, my sovereign!

Phil. Good charity, to crave pardon for your enemy!

---

[o] *bills of government*] Another quibble on the word "*bills*": see p. 160.

Bel. Mine own pardon, sir, for my joy's rudeness.
In what place better could I meet my foe,
And both of us so well provided too?
He with some black blood-thirsty crime upon him,
That (ere the horse-leech burst) will suck him dry;
I with a second accusation,
Enough to break his neck, if need should be;
And then to have even Justice' self to right us;
How should I make my joys a little civil,
They might not keep this noise?
　Ant. Here is some hope:
Should the axe be dull, the halter is preparing.
　Phil. What's your accusation, sir? We have heard the
　　former.

Enter JULIO.

　Bel. Mine, my lord? a strong one.
　Julio. A false one, sir,
At least malicious; an evidence
Of hatred and despite: he would accuse
My poor kinsman of that he never dream'd of,
Nor, waking, saw,—the stealing of his daughter;
She whom, I know, he would not look upon.—
Speak, Antonio, didst thou ever see her?
　Ant. Yes, sir; I have seen her.
　Bel. Ah, ha, friend Julio!
　Julio. He might; but how? with an unheedful eye,
An accidental view, as men see multitudes,
That the next day dare not precisely say
They saw that face or that, amongst 'em all.—
Didst thou so look on her?
　Bel. Guilty, guilty!
His looks hang themselves.
　Phil. Your patience, gentlemen:
I pray you tell me if I be in error;
I may speak often when I should but hear:
This is some show you would present us with,
And I do interrupt it: pray you, speak,
(It seems no more) is't any thing but a show?
　Bel. My lord, this gentlewoman can shew you all;

So could my daughter too, if she were here:
By this time they are both immodest enough.
She is fled me, and I accuse this thief for't:
Don Martine, his own friend, 's my testimony;
A practis'd night-work!

Phil. That Martine's the other
In your custody; he was forgotten:
Fetch him hither.

Con. We'll bring the stocks and all else, an't please your grace. [*Exit with* Officers.

Amin. That man's my husband certain, instead of this:
Both would have deceiv'd, and both beguil'd^p. [*Aside.*

Enter BUSTOFA *with a sack, and* ISMENIA *disguised as a country girl*^q.

Bust. So ho, miller, miller! look out, miller!—Is there ne'er a miller amongst you here, gentlemen?

Terzo. Yes, sir, here is a miller amongst gentlemen,
A gentleman miller.

Bust. I should not be far off, then; there^r went but a pair of shears and a bodkin between us.—Will you to work, miller? here's a maid has a sackful of news for you: shall your stones walk? will you grind, miller?

Phil. This your son, Franio?

Fra. My ungracious, my disobedient,
My unnatural, my rebel son, my lord.

Bust. Fie! your hopper runs over, miller.

Fra. This villain (of my own flesh and blood) was accessary
To the stealing of my daughter.

Bust. Oh, mountain, shalt thou call a molehill a scab upon the face of the earth? though a man be a thief, shall a miller call him so? Oh, egregious!

---

^p *Both would have deceiv'd, and both beguil'd*] "*Both*" means, of course, herself and Martine. Seward proposed to read "—*and both are beguil'd*" (which would be no improvement to the metre at least): the Editors of 1778 remark that "the old reading bears the same sense."

^q *as a country girl*] Weber gave "*habited as Juno*": but see Bustofa's second speech in this page, and the last speech of the next page.

^r *there*] Weber chose to print "here".

Julio. Remember, sirrah, who you speak before.

Bust. I speak before a miller, a thief in grain; for he steals corn: he that steals a wench, is a true man to him.

Phil. Can you prove that, you may help another cause
That was in pleading.

Bust. I'll prove it strongly. He that steals corn, steals the bread of the commonwealth; he that steals a wench, steals but the flesh.

Phil. And how is the bread-stealing more criminal than the flesh?

Bust. He that steals bread, steals that which is lawful every day; he that steals flesh, steals nothing from the fasting day: *ergo*, to steal the bread is the arranter theft.

Phil. This is to some purpose.

Bust. Again, he that steals flesh, steals for his own belly-ful; he that steals bread, robs the guts of others: *ergo*, the arranter thief the bread-stealer. Again, he that steals flesh, steals once, and gives over; yes, and often pays for it; the other steals every day, without satisfaction. To conclude, bread-stealing is the more capital crime; for what he steals, he puts it in at the head; he that steals flesh (as the Dutch author says) puts it in at the foot (the lower member).—Will you go as you are now, miller?

Phil. How has this satisfied you, Don Bellides?

Bel. Nothing, my lord; my cause is serious:
I claim a daughter from that loving thief there.

Ant. I would I had her for you, sir!

Bel. Ah, ha, Julio!

Julio. How said you, Antonio? wish you, you had his
    daughter?

Ant. With my soul[r] I wish her; and my body
Shall perish, but I will enjoy my soul's wish.
I would have slain my friend for his deceit,
But I do find his own deceit hath paid him.

Julio. Will you vex my soul forth? no other choice
But where my hate is rooted?—Come hither, girl:
Whose pretty maid art thou?

---

[r] *With my soul*] Sympson silently printed " *With* all *my soul.*"

Ism. The child of a poor man, sir.

Julio. The better for it. With my sovereign's leave, I'll wed thee to this man, will he, nill he.

Phil. Pardon me, sir, I'll be no love-enforcer; I use no power of mine unto those ends.

Julio. Wilt thou have him?

Ism. Not unless he love me.

Ant. I do love thee: farewell all other beauties! I settle here.—You are Ismenia?   [*Aside to* ISMENIA.

Ism. The same I was; better nor worse, Antonio.

Ant. I shall have your consent here, I am sure, sir.

Bel. With all my heart, sir; nay, if you accept it, I'll do this kindness to mine enemy, And give her as a father.

Ant. She'll thank you as a daughter;— Will you not, Ismenia?

Bel. How! Ismenia!

Ism. Your daughter, sir.

Bel. Possible?[s]—Away, you feeble-witted things! You thought you had caught the old ones: you wade, you wade In shallow fords; we can swim, we: look here! We made the match; we are all friends, good friends: Thin, thin! why, the fool knew all this, this fool.

Bust. Keep that to yourself, sir; what I knew I knew: this sack is a witness.—Miller, this is not for your thumbing: here's gold lace[t]; you may see her in her[u] holiday clothes if you will: I was her wardrobe-man.

Re-enter Constable *and* Officers, *bringing in* MARTINE[v].

Ant. You beguil'd me well, sir.

Mart. Did you speak to me, sir?

Ant. It might seem to you, Martine; your conscience Has quick ears.

[s] *Possible?*] So the first folio.—The second folio "Is't *possible?*"; and so the modern editors.

[t] *Miller, this is not for your thumbing: here's gold lace*] See note, p. 223.

[u] *her*] Weber chose to print "the".

[v] *Martine*] Here the old eds. mark also the entrance of "*Aminta*": but see p. 285.

Mart. My sight was a little dim i' the dark, indeed;
So was my feeling cozen'd; yet I'm content:
I am the better understander now;
I know my wife wants nothing of a woman:
There you're my junior.
    Ant. You are not hurt?
    Mart. Not shrewdly hurt; I have good flesh to heal, you
        see;
Good round flesh. These cherries will be worth chopping,
Crack stones and all: I should not give much to boot
To ride in your new, and you in my old ones now.
    Ant. You mistake the weapon: are you not hurt?
    Mart. A little scratch; but I shall claw it off well enough.

            Enter GILLIAN.

    Gil. I can no longer own what is not mine,
With a free conscience [*Aside*].—My liege, your pardon!
    Phil. For what?—Who knows this woman?
    Fra. I best, my lord;
I have been acquainted with her these forty summers,
And as many winters, were it spring again:
She's like the gout; I can get no cure for her.
    Phil. Oh, your wife, Franio?
    Fra. 'Tis "oh, my wife" indeed, my lord;
A painful stitch to my side; would it were pick'd out!
    Phil. Well, sir, your silence.
    Bust. Will you be older and older every day than other? the longer [v] you live the older still? must his majesty command your silence, ere you'll hold your tongue?
    Phil. Your reprehension runs into the same fault:
Pray, sir, will you be silent?
    Bust. I have told him of this before now, my liege; but age will have his course, and his weaknesses——
    Phil. Good sir, your forbearance.
    Bust. And his frailties, and his follies, as I may say, that cannot hold his tongue ere he be bidden——
    Phil. Why, sirrah——
    Bust. But I believe your majesty will not be long troubled

---

    [v] *longer*] Weber chose to print "older"!

with him: I hope that woman has something to confess will hang 'em both.

Phil. Sirrah, you'll pull your destiny upon you,
If you cease not the sooner.

Bust. Nay, I have done, my liege: yet it grieves me that I should call that man father, that should be so shameless, that, being commanded to hold his tongue——

Phil. To the porter's lodge[w] with him!

Bust. I thank your grace; I have a friend there.

Phil. Speak, woman:
If any interruption meet thee more,
It shall be punish'd sharply.

Gil. Good my liege, (I dare not,)
Ask you the question why that old man weeps.

Phil. Who? Count Julio? I observ'd it not.—
You hear the question, sir; will you give the cause?

Julio. Oh, my lord, it hardly will get passage
(It is a sorrow of that greatness grown),
'Less it dissolve in tears, and come by parcels!

Gil. I'll help you, sir, in the delivery,
And bring you forth a joy. You lost a daughter.

Julio. 'Twas that recounted thought brought forth these sorrows.

Gil. She's found again. Know you this mantle, sir?

Julio. Ha! [*Shewing mantle.*

Gil. Nay, leave your wonder; I'll explain it to you.
This did enwrap your child, whom ever since
I have call'd mine, when [her][x] nurse Amaranta,
In a remove from Mora to Corduba,
Was seiz'd on by a fierce and hungry bear;
She was the ravin's prey[y], as Heaven so would:

---

[w] *the porter's lodge*] Where formerly servants and dependants of the great used to receive corporal punishment.

[x] [*her*] I have inserted this word at the suggestion of Heath (*MS. Notes*).

[y] *the ravin's prey*] "i. e. the ravenous creature's prey; not the 'raven's', as the modern editors read." WEBER,—who is inaccurate in stating that the modern editors give "raven's" (which, after all, is the more correct form: in *Valentinian* we have had, and according to both the folios,—

"Why do we like to feed the greedy *raven* [i. e. ravenousness]
Of these blown men," &c.   vol. v. 306.)

He, with his booty fill'd, forsook the babe:
All this was in my sight; and so long I saw,
Until the cruel creature left my sight;
At which advantage I adventur'd me
To rescue the sweet lamb: I did it, sir;
And ever since I have kept back your joy,
And made it mine. But age hath wearied me,
And bids me back restore unto the owner
What I unjustly kept these fourteen years.
   Julio. Oh, thou hast ta'en so many years from me,
And made me young as was her birth-day to me!—
Oh, good my liege, give my joys a pardon!
I must go pour a blessing on my child,
Which here would be too rude and troublesome.   [*Exit.*
   Phil. Franio, you knew this before?
   Bust. Oh, oh! *Item* for you, miller!
   Fra. I did, my liege; I must confess I did:
And I confess I ne'er would have confess'd,
Had not that woman's tongue begun to me.
We poor ones love, and would have comforts, sir,
As well as great. This is no strange fault, sir;
There's many men keep other men's children,
As though they were their own.
   Bust. It may stretch farther yet: I beseech you, my liege, let this woman be a little farther examined; let the wards[z] of her conscience be searched: I would know how she came by me; I am a lost child, if I be theirs: though I have been brought up in a mill, yet I had ever a mind, methought, to be a greater man.
   Phil. She will resolve[a] you, sure.
   Gil. Ay, ay, boy; thou art mine own flesh and blood,
Born of mine own body.
   Bust. 'Tis very unlikely that such a body should bear me: there's no trust in these millers. Woman, tell the truth: my father shall forgive thee, whatsoever he was, were he knight, squire, or captain; less he should not be.

---

[z] *wards*] The correction of the Editors of 1778 (which was anticipated by Heath, *MS. Notes*).—Both the folios " words ".—Sympson printed " wounds ".

[a] *resolve*] i. e. inform, satisfy.

Gil. Thou art mine own child, boy.
Bust. And was the miller my father?
Gil. Wouldst thou make thy mother a whore, knave?
Bust. Ay, if she make me a bastard.—The rack must make her confess, my lord; I shall never come to know who I am else. I have a worshipful mind in me, sure; methinks I do scorn poor folks.

Re-enter OTRANTE, FLORIMEL, JULIO, *and* VERTIGO.

Phil. Here comes the brightest glory of the day;
Love yok'd with love, the best equality,
Without the level of estate or person.
Julio. You both shall be rewarded bountifully;
We'll be a-kin too; brother and sister shall
Be chang'd with us ever.
Bust. Thank you, uncle: my sister is my cousin yet, at the last cast.—Farewell, sister-foster! if I had known the civil law would have allowed it, thou hadst had another manner of husband than thou hast; but much good do thee! I'll dance at thy wedding, kiss the bride, and so—
Julio. Why, how now, sirrah?
Bust. 'Tis lawful now, she's none of my sister.   [*Sings.*

>   It was a miller and a lord,
>   That had a scabbard and a sword,
>   He put it up, in the country word;
>   The miller and his daughter.
>
>   She has a face, and she can sing;
>   She has a grace, and she can spring;
>   She has a place with another thing,
>   Tradoodle.

Fra. A knavish brother of yours, my lord.
Bust. Would I were acquainted with your tailor, noble brother!
Otr. You may; there he is; mine, newly entertain'd.
Vert. If you have any work for me, I can fit you, sir; I fitted the lady.
Bust. My sister, tailor? what fits her will hardly fit me.
Vert. Who fits her may fit you, sir; the tailor can do both.

Bust. You have a true yard, tailor?

Vert. Ne'er a whit too long, I warrant you.

Bust. [*sings*]

> Then, tailor, march with me away:
> I scorn these robes, I must be gay;
> My noble brother he shall pay
> Tom Tailor.

[*Exeunt* BUSTOFA *and* VERTIGO.

Phil. Your recover'd friendships are sound, gentlemen?

Bel. At heart, at heart, my lord: the worm shall not
Beyond many ages find a breach to enter at.

Phil. These lovers' unities I will not doubt of.
How happy have you made our progress, then,
To be the witness of such fair accords!
Come, now we'll eat with you, my lord Otrante:
'Tis a charge sav'd; you must not grudge your guest;
'Tis both my welcome, and your wedding-feast.

[*Exeunt.*

In the prefatory matter to this play I omitted to notice,—that portions of it furnished a droll entitled *The Surprise*, which may be found in Kirkman's collection, *The Wits, or Sport upon Sport, Part First*, 1672, p. 167 (see vol. i. 200 of the present work).

A

WIFE FOR A MONTH.

A Wife for a Moneth.

In the folios, 1647, 1679.
The second folio adds "*A Tragi-comedy.*"

THIS tragi-comedy, the unassisted work of Fletcher, was licensed by Sir Henry Herbert May 27, 1624, and acted by the King's Servants: see Malone's *Shakespeare* (by Boswell), iii. 226. We also learn that it was performed "by the K. players, at St. James, the 9 Febru. [1636-7]." *Ibid.* p. 239.

"The Character and Story of Alphonso," says Langbaine, "and his Brother Frederick's Carriage to him, much resembles the History of Sancho the Eighth, King of Leon. I leave the Reader to the perusal of his Story in Mariana and Louis de Mayerne Turquet." *Acc. of Engl. Dram. Poets*, p. 216. "Our poet," observes Weber, "had certainly *The Maid's Tragedy* in his mind when he wrote the latter acts of this play. The scene in the bed-chamber, together with Valerio's abstinence from his wife, will bring to the memory of any attentive reader similar scenes in that tragedy, differently conducted however," &c.

A Wife for a Month was one of those dramas in which Betterton distinguished himself at the commencement of his career: see p. 205. In Langbaine's days, however, the play had ceased to be represented, for he mentions it as "well worth reviving."

PROLOGUE.

You are welcome, gentlemen; and would our feast
Were so well season'd, to please every guest!
Ingenuous appetites, I hope we shall,
And their examples may prevail in all
Our noble friends. Who writ this, bid me say [a],
He had rather dress, upon a triumph-day,
My lord-mayor's feast, and make him sauces too,
Sauce for each several mouth; nay, further go,
He had rather build up those invincible pies,
And castle-custards [b], that affright all eyes,
Nay, eat 'em all and their artillery,
Than dress for such a curious company
One single dish: yet he has pleas'd ye too,
And you have confess'd he knew well what to do.
Be hungry as you were wont to be, and bring
Sharp stomachs to the stories he shall sing,
And he dare yet, he says, prepare a table
Shall make you say, well drest, and he well able.

[a] *may prevail in all Our noble friends. Who writ this, bid me say,* &c.] The first folio thus,—
"may prevaile in all
(Our noble friends) who writ this, bid me say," &c.
The second folio has,—
" may prevail in all.
Our noble *friend*, who writ this, bid me say," &c.
and so the modern editors. But would the prologue-speaker call the poet " our noble friend"? Surely not.

[b] *castle-custards*] As before: see note, vol. vii. 49.

DRAMATIS PERSONÆ.

ALPHONSO, eldest son of the late king of Naples.
FREDERICK[c], his younger brother, the reigning king.
SORANO, a lord, chief counsellor to FREDERICK.
VALERIO, a young lord[d].
CAMILLO, }
CLEANTHES, } court-lords.
MENALLO, }
RUGIO, a lord, } friends to ALPHONSO
MARCO, a friar, }
PODRAMO, servant to SORANO.
TONY, FREDERICK'S fool.

CASTRUCCIO, captain of the castle.
Lawyer.
Physician.
Captain.
Cutpurse.
Friars.
Citizens, Guard, Attendants.

MARIA[e], wife to FREDERICK.
EVANTHE, sister to SORANO.
CASSANDRA, her waiting-woman.
Citizens' Wives.
Ladies.

PERSONS IN THE MASQUE.

Cupid.
The Graces.
Fancy.
Desire.
Delight.
Hope.
Fear.

Distrust.
Jealousy.
Care.
Ire.
Poverty.
Despair.

SCENE,—*Naples.*

The principal actors were—

Joseph Taylor.   Robert Benfield.
Richard Robinson.   John Underwood.
Nicholas Toolie.   George Birch.

Fol. 1679.

---

[c] *Frederick, &c.*] In the second folio (which alone gives the *Dram. Pers.*) Frederick is called "usurper" : but compare act i. sc. 2 ;
"he [Alphonso] was his eldest,
And noblest too, had not fair Nature stopt in him,
For which cause *this was chosen to inherit,*
Frederick the younger."

[d] *a young lord*] See act iii. sc. 3, "Cheer up, my noble *lord,*" &c., and act iv. sc. 2, "Call hither *Lord Valerio.*"

[e] *Maria*] "The queen has been nameless hitherto ; but in the first folio, '*Mar.*' is prefixed to her speeches in the first act, and I have ventured to name her *Maria* upon this testimony throughout the play." WEBER.

A

WIFE FOR A MONTH.

ACT I.

SCENE I.—*An apartment in the Palace.*

Enter FREDERICK, SORANO, VALERIO, CAMILLO, CLEANTHES, MENALLO, *and* Attendants.

Sor. Will your grace speak?
Fred. Let me alone, Sorano:
Although my thoughts seem sad, they are welcome to me.
 Sor. You know I am private as your secret wishes,
Ready to fling my soul upon your service,
Ere your command be on 't[a].
 Fred. Bid those depart.
 Sor. You must retire, my lords.
 Cam. What new design
Is hammering in his head now?
 Cle. Let's pray heartily
None of our heads meet with it: my wife's old,
That's all my comfort.
 Men. Mine's ugly, that I am sure on,
And I think honest too; 'twould make me start else.
 Cam. Mine's troubled in the country with a fever,
And some few infirmities else.   He looks again;

---

[a] *your command be on 't*] Weber chose to print " you *command* me *on 't* " !!

Come, let's retire: certain, 'tis some she-business,
This new lord is employ'd[b].
              [*Exeunt* CAMILLO, CLEANTHES, *and* MENALLO.
  Val. I'll not be far off,
Because I doubt the cause.   [*Aside, and then retires.*
  Fred. Are they all gone?
  Sor. All but your faithful servant.
  Fred. I would tell thee,
But 'tis a thing thou canst not like.
  Sor. Pray you, speak it:
Is it my head? I have it ready for you, sir:
Is't any action in my power? my wit?
I care not of what nature, nor what follows.
  Fred. I am in love.
  Sor. That's the least thing of a thousand,
The easiest to achieve.
  Fred. But with whom, Sorano?
  Sor. With whom you please; you must not be denied, sir.
  Fred. Say, it be with one of thy kinswomen?
  Sor. Say, with all;
I shall more love your grace, I shall more honour you;
And would I had enough to serve your pleasure!
  Fred. Why, 'tis thy sister, then, the fair Evanthe;
I'll be plain with thee.
  Sor. I'll be as plain with you, sir;
She brought not her perfections to the world,
To lock them in a case, or hang 'em by her;
The use is all she breeds 'em for; she is yours, sir.
  Fred. Dost thou mean seriously?
  Sor. I mean my sister;
And, if I had a dozen more, they were all yours.
Some aunts I have, they have been handsome women;
My mother's dead, indeed; and some few cousins,
That are now shooting up, we shall see shortly.

[b]   *certain, 'tis some she-business,*
This new lord is employ'd] "Mr. Sympson, without authority or notice, reads,
            " *This new lord's employ'd* in ";
which proves he did not understand the poet. Camillo, a *good* man, is intended
to say, 'Certainly 'tis some illicit amour, AS this [*bad*] lord is employed.'" J.
N., *ed.* 1778.

Fred. No; 'tis Evanthe.

Sor. I have sent my man unto her,
Upon some business to come presently
Hither[c]; she shall come: your grace dare speak unto her?
Large golden promises, and sweet language, sir,
You know what they work; she is a complete courtier:
Besides, I'll set in.

Fred. She waits upon my queen:
What jealousy and anger may arise,
Incensing her——

Sor. You have a good sweet lady,
A woman of so even and still a temper,
She knows not anger: say, she were a Fury,
I had thought you had been absolute, the great king,
The fountain of all honours, place[d], and pleasures,
Your will and your commands unbounded also:
Go, get a pair of beads[e], and learn to pray, sir.

Enter Servant.

Serv. My lord, your servant stays.

Sor. Bid him come hither,
And bring the lady with him.   [*Exit* Servant.

Fred. I will woo her;
And either lose myself, or win her favour.

Sor. She is coming in.

Fred. Thy eyes shoot through the door;
They are so piercing, that the beams they dart
Give new light to the room.

Enter PODRAMO *and* EVANTHE.

Evan. Whither dost thou go?
This is the king's side, and his private lodgings:
What business have I here?

Pod. My lord sent for you.

---

[c] *Hither*] Means, of course, (as Weber explained it,)—to the palace. Sympson, choosing to understand it as meaning—"into Frederick's apartments", altered the punctuation unnecessarily; and so the Editors of 1778.

[d] *place*] Sympson's proposed correction, which was adopted by his successors.—The folios "playes" and "plays".

[e] *a pair of beads*] i.e. a set of beads (so, formerly, a *pair* of cards meant—a pack of cards.

Evan. His lodgings are below; you are mistaken;
We left them at the stair-foot.
  Pod. Good sweet madam——
  Evan. I am no counsellor, nor important[e] suitor,
Nor have no private business through these chambers,
To seek him this way. O' my life, thou art drunk;
Or worse than drunk, hir'd to convey me hither
To some base end! Now I look on thee better,
Thou hast a bawdy face, and I abhor thee,
A beastly bawdy face! I'll go no further.
  Sor. Nay, shrink not back; indeed you shall, good sister.
Why do you blush? the good king will not hurt you;
He honours you, and loves you.
  Evan. Is this the business?
  Sor. Yes, and the best you ever will arrive at,
If you be wise.
  Evan. My father was no bawd, sir,
Nor of that worshipful stock, as I remember.
  Sor. You are a fool.
  Evan. You are that I shame to tell you.
  Fred. Gentle Evanthe——
  Evan. The gracious queen, sir,
Is well and merry, Heaven be thank'd for it;
And, as I think, she waits you in the garden.
  Fred. Let her wait there; I talk not of her garden;
I talk of thee, sweet flower.
  Evan. Your grace is pleasant,
To mistake a nettle for a rose.
  Fred. No rose,
Nor lily, nor no glorious hyacinth,
Are of that sweetness, whiteness, tenderness,
Softness, and satisfying blessedness,
As my Evanthe.
  Evan. Your grace speaks very feelingly:
I would not be a handsome wench in your way, sir,
For a new gown.
  Fred. Thou art all handsomeness:

---

[e] *important*] "i. e. importunate." MASON.

Nature will be asham'd to frame another,
Now thou art made; thou hast robb'd her of her cunning[f]:
Each several part about thee is a beauty.
   Sor. Do you hear this, sister?
   Evan. Yes, unworthy brother:
But all this will not do.
   Fred. But love, Evanthe,
Thou shalt have more than words; wealth, ease, and honours,
My tender wench.
   Evan. Be tender of my credit,
And I shall love you, sir, and I shall honour you.
   Fred. I love thee to enjoy thee, my Evanthe,
To give thee the content of love.
   Evan. Hold, hold, sir;
You are too fleet: I have some business this way,
Your grace can ne'er content.
   Sor. You stubborn toy!
   Evan. Good my lord Bawd, I thank you.
   Fred. Thou shalt not go. Believe me, sweet Evanthe,
So high I will advance thee for this favour,
So rich and potent I will raise thy fortune,
And thy friends mighty——
   Evan. Good your grace, be patient;
I shall make the worst honourable wench that ever was,
Shame your discretion and your choice.
   Fred. Thou shalt not.
   Evan. Shall I be rich, do you say, and glorious,
And shine above the rest, and scorn all beauties,
And mighty in command?
   Fred. Thou shalt be any thing.
   Evan. Let me be honest too, and then I'll thank you:
Have you not such a title to bestow too?
If I prove otherwise, I would know but this, sir;
Can all the power you have, or all the riches,
But tie men's tongues up from discoursing of me,
Their eyes from gazing at my glorious folly,
Time that shall come, from wondering at my impudence,

---

[f] *cunning*] i. e. skill.

And they that read my wanton life, from curses?
Can you do this? have you this magic in you?
This is not in your power, though you be a prince, sir,
No more than evil is in holy angels,
Nor I, I hope[g].   Get wantonness confirm'd
By act of parliament an honesty,
And so receiv'd by all, I'll hearken to you.
Heaven guide your grace!   [*Going.*

   Fred. Evanthe, stay a little:
I'll no more wantonness; I'll marry thee.
   Evan. What shall the queen do?
   Fred. I'll be divorc'd from her.
   Evan. Can you tell why? what has she done against you?
Has she contriv'd a treason 'gainst your person?
Abus'd your bed? does disobedience urge you?
   Fred. That's all one; 'tis my will.
   Evan. 'Tis a most wicked one,
A most absurd one, and will shew a monster.
I had rather be a whore, and with less sin,
To your present lust, than queen to your injustice.
Yours is no love, Faith and Religion fly it,
Nor has no taste of fair affection in it:
Some hellish flame abuses your fair body,
And hellish Furies blow it,—look behind you!
Divorce you from a woman of her beauty,
Of her integrity, her piety!
Her love to you, to all that honours you,
Her chaste and virtuous love, are these fit causes?
What will you do to me, when I have cloy'd you?
You may find time out in eternity,
Deceit and violence in heavenly justice,
Life in the grave, and death among the blessèd,
Ere stain or brack[h] in her sweet reputation.
   Sor. You have fool'd enough; be wise now, and a woman:
You have shew'd a modesty sufficient,
If not too much, for court.

---

   [g] *Nor I, I hope*] "i. e. nor am I, I hope, in your power." MASON.

   [h] *brack*] i. e. breach, break.

Evan. You have shew'd an impudence
A more experienc'd bawd would blush and shake at.—
You will make my kindred mighty?—
  Fred. Prithee, hear me.
  Evan. I do, sir, and I count it a great offer.
  Fred. Any of thine.
  Evan. 'Tis like enough you may clap honour on them;
But how 'twill sit, and how men will adore it,
Is still the question. I'll tell you what they'll say, sir,
What the report will be, and 'twill be true too
(And it must needs be comfort to your master[i]),
"These are the issues of her impudence."
I'll tell your grace, so dear I hold the queen,
So dear that honour that she nurs'd me up in,
I would first take to me, for my lust, a Moor,
One of your galley-slaves, that cold and hunger,
Decrepit misery, had made a mock-man,
Than be your queen.
  Fred. You are bravely resolute.
  Evan. I had rather be a leper, and be shunn'd,
And die by pieces, rot into my grave,
Leaving no memory behind to know me,
Than be a high whore to eternity.
  Fred. You have another gamester[j], I perceive by you;
You durst not slight me else.
  Sor. I'll find him out;
Though he lie next thy heart hid, I'll discover him;
And you, proud peat[k], I'll make you curse your insolence.
  Val. Tongue of an angel, and the truth of Heaven!
How am I blest!   [*Aside, and then exit.*
  Sor. Podramo, go in haste   [*Aside to him.*
To my sister's gentlewoman (you know her well),
And bid her send her mistress presently
The lesser cabinet she keeps her letters in,

---

[i] *master*] "Seward reads 'minister', instead of '*master*'; but unnecessarily. Evanthe means to call Sorano Frederick's master, or instructor in his schemes of iniquity." Mason.

[j] *gamester*] i. e. dissolute gallant : see note, vol. vi. 222.

[k] *peat*] "i. e. pet [as before, p. 255]." Weber.

And such-like toys, and bring it to me instantly.
Away!
   Pod. I am gone.   [*Exit.*
   Sor. The queen!
   Fred. Let's quit the place; she may grow jealous.
                        [*Exeunt* FREDERICK *and* SORANO.

               Enter MARIA, *and two* Ladies.
   Mar. So suddenly departed! what's the reason?
Does my approach displease his grace? are my eyes
So hateful to him? or my conversation
Infected, that he flies me?—Fair Evanthe!
Are you there? then I see his shame.
   Evan. 'Tis true, madam,
'T has pleas'd his goodness to be pleasant with me.
   Mar. 'Tis strange to find thy modesty in this place:
Does the king offer fair? does thy face take him?
Ne'er blush, Evanthe, 'tis a very sweet one:
Does he rain gold, and precious promises,
Into thy lap? will he advance thy fortunes?
Shalt thou be mighty, wench?
   Evan. Never mock, madam;
'Tis rather on your part to be lamented,
At least reveng'd. I can be mighty, lady,
And glorious too, glorious and great as you are.
   Mar. He will marry thee?
   Evan. Who would not be a queen, madam?
   Mar. 'Tis true, Evanthe; 'tis a brave ambition,
A golden dream, that may delude a good mind.
What shall become of me?
   Evan. You must learn to pray;
Your age and honour will become a nunnery.
   Mar. Wilt thou remember me?   [*Weeps.*
   Evan. She weeps.—Sweet lady,   [*Kneels.*
Upon my knees I ask your sacred pardon
For my rude boldness; and know, my sweet mistress,
If e'er there were ambition in Evanthe,
It was and is to do you faithful duties.
'Tis true I have been tempted by the king,

And with no few and potent charms, to wrong you,
To violate the chaste joys of your bed;
And, those not taking hold, to usurp your state:
But she, that has been bred up under you,
And daily fed upon your virtuous precepts,
Still growing strong by example of your goodness,
Having no errant motion from obedience,
Flies from these vanities as mere illusions,
And, arm'd with honesty, defies all promises:
In token of this truth, I lay my life down
Under your sacred foot, to do you service.
   Mar. [*raising her*] Rise, my true friend, thou virtuous bud
      of beauty!
Thou virgins' honour, sweetly blow and flourish!
And that rude nipping wind that seeks to blast thee,
Or taint thy root, be curs'd to all posterity!
To my protection from this hour I take you;
Yes, and the king shall know——
   Evan. Give his heat way, madam,
And 'twill go out again; he may forget all.   [*Exeunt.*

SCENE II.—*Another apartment in the same.*

Enter CAMILLO, CLEANTHES, *and* MENALLO.

   Cam. What have we to do with the times? we cannot
      cure 'em.
Let 'em go on: when they are swoln with surfeits,
They'll burst and stink; then all the world shall smell 'em.
   Cle. A man may live a bawd, and be an honest man.
   Men. Yes, and a wise man too; 'tis a virtuous calling.
   Cam. To his own wife especially, or to his sister;
The nearer to his own blood, still the honester:
There want such honest men; would we had more of 'em!
   Men. To be a villain is no such rude matter.
   Cam. No, if he be a neat one, and a perfect:
Art makes all excellent. What is it, gentlemen,

In a good cause to kill a dozen coxcombs[1],
That blunt rude fellows call good patriots?
Nothing, nor ne'er look'd after.
   Men. 'Tis e'en as much,
As easy too, as honest, and as clear,
To ravish matrons, and deflower coy wenches:
But here they are so willing, 'tis a compliment.
   Cle. To pull down churches with pretension
To build 'em fairer, may be done with honour;
And all this time believe no God.
   Cam. I think so;
'Tis faith enough if they name him in their angers,
Or on their rotten tombs engrave an angel.
Well, brave Alphonso, how happy had we been,
If thou hadst reign'd!
   Men. Would I had his disease,
Tied, like a leprosy, to my posterity,
So he were right again!
   Cle. What is his malady?
   Cam. Nothing but sad and silent melancholy,
Laden with griefs and thoughts, no man knows why neither.
The good Brandino, father to the princes[m],
Us'd all the art and industry that might be,
To free Alphonso from this dull calamity,
And seat him in his rule; he was his eldest,
And noblest too, had not fair Nature stopt in him,
For which cause this was chosen to inherit,
Frederick the younger.
   Cle. Does he use his brother
With that respect and honour that befits him?
   Cam. He is kept privately, as they pretend,
To give more ease and comfort to his sickness;
But he has honest servants, the grave Rugio
And friar Marco, that wait upon his person,
And in a monastery he lives.
   Men. 'Tis full of sadness,
To see him when he comes to his father's tomb

---

[1] *coxcombs*] i. e. fools: see note, vol. iii. 123.
[m] *princes*] The folios "Princesse" and "Princess".

(As once a day that is his pilgrimage),
Whilst in devotion the quire sings an anthem,
How piously he kneels, and, like a virgin
That some cross fate had cozen'd of her love,
Weeps till the stubborn marble sweats with pity,
And to his groans the whole quire bears a chorus.

    Enter FREDERICK, SORANO *with a cabinet, and* PODRAMO.
  Cam. So do I too.—The king, with his contrivers!
This is no place for us.
          [*Exeunt* CAMILLO, CLEANTHES, *and* MENALLO.
  Fred. This is a jewel;
Lay it aside. What paper's that?
  Pod. A letter;
But 'tis a woman's, sir, I know by the hand
And the false orthography; they write old Saxon.
  Fred. May be her ghostly mother's that instructs her.
  Sor. No, 'tis a cousin's, and came up with a great cake.
  Fred. What's that?
  Sor. A pair of gloves the duchess gave her;
For so the outside says.
  Fred. That other paper?
  Sor. A charm for the tooth-ache; here's nothing but saints
      and crosses.
  Fred. Look in that box; methinks that should hold secrets.
  Pod. 'Tis paint, and curls of hair; she begins to exercise.
A glass of water too: I would fain taste it,
But I am wickedly afraid 'twill silence me;
Never a conduit-pipe to convey this water?
  Sor. These are all rings, death's-heads, and such mementos,
Her grandmother and worm-eaten aunts left to her,
To tell her what her beauty must arrive at.
  Fred. That, that?
  Pod. They are written songs, sir, to provoke young ladies.
Lord, here's a prayer-book! how these agree!
Here's a strange union!
  Sor. Ever by a surfeit
You have a julep set, to cool the patient.
  Fred. Those, those?

Sor. They are verses; *To the blest Evanthe.*
Fred. Those may discover. Read them out, Sorano.
Sor. [*reads*]
TO THE BLEST EVANTHE.

Let those complain that feel Love's cruelty,
  And in sad legends write their woes ;
With roses gently h'as corrected me,
  My war is without rage or blows :
    My mistress' eyes shine fair on my desires,
    And hope springs up inflam'd with her new fires.

No more an exile will I dwell,
  With folded arms, and sighs all day,
Reckoning the torments of my hell,
  And flinging my sweet joys away :
    I am call'd home again to quiet peace ;
    My mistress smiles, and all my sorrows cease.

Yet, what is living in her eye,
  Or being blest with her sweet tongue,
If these no other joys imply ?
  A golden gyve, a pleasing wrong :
    To be your own but one poor month, I'd give
    My youth, my fortune, and then leave to live.

Fred. This is my rival; that I knew the hand now!
Sor. I know it, I have seen it; 'tis Valerio's,
That hopeful gentleman's that was brought up
With you, and by your charge nourish'd and fed,
At the same table, with the same allowance.
Fred. And all this courtesy to ruin me?
Cross my desires? h'ad better have fed humblier,
And stood at greater distance from my fury ;—
Go for him quickly, find him instantly,
Whilst my impatient heart swells high with choler ;—
Better have lov'd Despair, and safer kiss'd her.
                    [*Exeunt* SORANO *and* PODRAMO.

Enter EVANTHE *and* CASSANDRA.
Evan. Thou old weak fool! dost thou know to what end,

To what betraying end, he got this casket?
Durst thou deliver him, without my ring,
Or a command from mine own mouth, that cabinet
That holds my heart? you unconsiderate ass,
You brainless idiot!
  Cas. I saw you go with him,
At the first word commit your person to him,
And make no scruple: he is your brother's gentleman,
And, for any thing I know, an honest man;
And might not I upon the same security
Deliver him a box?
  Evan. A bottle-head!
  Fred. You shall have cause to chafe, as I will handle it.
[*Aside.*
  Evan. I had rather thou hadst deliver'd me to pirates,
Betray'd me to uncurable diseases,
Hung up my picture in a market-place[n],
And sold me to vild[o] bawds!
  Cas. As I take it, madam,
Your maidenhead lies not in that cabinet;
You have a closer, and you keep the key too:
Why are you vex'd thus?
  Evan. I could curse thee wickedly,
And wish thee more deform'd than age can make thee!
Perpetual hunger, and no teeth to satisfy it[p],
Wait on thee still, nor sleep be found to ease it!

[n] *Hung up my picture in a market-place*] " This seems to allude to a custom which formerly was frequent at Naples, of hanging up the pictures of the most celebrated courtezans in the public parts of the town, to serve as directions where they lived. See Mrs. Behn's play of *The Rover, or the Banished Cavaliers*, where the scene is laid in the same place." REED.—" The same allusion occurs in *Pericles, Prince of Tyre* [act iv. sc. 3]," &c. WEBER.

[o] *vild*] i. e. vile: see note, vol. i. 331.—The folios "wilde" and "wild"; and so Sympson, though he proposed to read " *vild*": his successors printed "vile".—We have had already in these plays instances of " *vild* " being mistaken for "wild" by the old printers: see notes, vol. i. 368, vol. ii. 93, vol. iii. 50, 521, vol. vi. 362. So too in the Sec. Part of Marlowe's *Tamburlaine*, act v. sc. 1, where the 8vo gives rightly " *Vild* tyrant! barbarous bloody Tamburlaine!" the 4to has " Wild".

[p] *no teeth to satisfy it*] " Sympson proposes to read ' *no* meat *to satisfy it*,' instead of ' *teeth* '; but the latter is the better expression. The want of teeth is more tantalising than the want of meat." MASON.

Those hands that gave the casket, may the palsy
For ever make unuseful, even to feed thee!
Long winters, that thy bones may turn to isicles
No hell can thaw again, inhabit by thee!
Is thy care like thy body, all one crookedness?
How scurvily thou criest now, like a drunkard!
I'll have as pure tears from a dirty spout.
Do, swear thou didst this ignorantly, swear it,
Swear and be damn'd, thou half-witch!
  Cas. These are fine words:
Well, madam, madam——
  Evan. 'Tis not well, thou mummy!
'Tis impudently, basely done, thou dirty——
  Fred. Has your young sanctity done railing, madam,
Against your innocent squire? Do you see this sonnet,
This loving script? do you know from whence it came too?
  Evan. I do, and dare avouch it pure and honest.
  Fred. You have private visitants, my noble lady,
That in sweet numbers court your goodly virtues,
And to the height of adoration.
  Evan. Well, sir,
There's neither heresy nor treason in it.
  Fred. A prince may beg at the door, whilst these feast
       with you;
A favour or a grace from such as I am,
Coarse common things——

             Enter VALERIO *with* PODRAMO.

                You are welcome. Pray, come near, sir:
Do you know this paper?
  Val. I am betray'd [*Aside*].—I do, sir;
'Tis mine, my hand and heart.—If I die for her,
I am thy martyr, Love, and time shall honour me. [*Aside.*
  Cas. You saucy sir, that came in my lady's name
For her gilt cabinet, you cheating sir too,
You scurvy usher, with as scurvy legs
And a worse face, thou poor base hanging-holder[q],

---

[q] *thou poor base hanging-holder*] Compare *The Wild-Goose-Chase*, act iii. sc. 1:
  "One that is throughly pac'd, a clean-made gentleman,
  Can *hold a hanging* up with approbation," &c.
                                vol. viii. 166.

How durst thou come to me with a lie in thy mouth,
An impudent lie——
   Pod. Holla, good Gill! you hobble.
   Cas. A stinking lie, more stinking than the teller,
To play the pilfering knave? There have been rascals
Brought up to fetch and carry, like your worship,
That have been hang'd for less; whipt there are daily;
And, if the law will do me right——
   Pod. What then, old maggot?
   Cas. Thy mother was carted younger:—I'll have thy hide,
Thy mangy hide, embroider'd with a dog-whip,
As it is now with potent pox, and thicker.
   Fred. Peace, good antiquity! I'll have your bones else
Ground into gunpowder to shoot at cats with ;
One word more, and I'll blanch thee like an almond:
There's no such cure for the she-falling sickness
As the powder of a dried bawd's skin. Be silent!—
You are very prodigal of your service here, sir;
Of your life more, it seems.
   Val. I repent neither,
Because your grace shall understand it comes
From the best part of love, my pure affection;
And, kindled with chaste flame, I will not fly from it.
If it be error to desire to marry,
And marry her that sanctity would dote on,
I have done amiss; if it be a treason
To graft my soul to virtue, and to grow there,
To love the tree that bears such happiness
(Conceive me, sir; this fruit was ne'er forbidden),
Nay, to desire to taste too, I am traitor.
Had you but plants enough of this blest tree, sir,
Set round about your court, to beautify it,
Deaths twice so many, to dismay the approachers,
The ground would scarce yield graves to noble lovers.
   Fred. 'Tis well maintain'd. You wish and pray to Fortune,
Here in your sonnet, (and she has heard your prayers,)
So much you dote upon your own undoing,
But one month to enjoy her as your wife,
Though at the expiring of that time you die for't.

Val. I could wish many, many ages, sir;
To grow as old as Time in her embraces,
If Heaven would grant it, and you smile upon it;
But, if my choice were two hours, and then perish,
I would not pull my heart back.
    Fred. You have your wish:
To-morrow I will see you nobly married;
Your month take out in all content and pleasure;
The first day of the following month you die for 't.
Kneel not: not all your prayers can divert me.—
Now mark your sentence; mark it, scornful lady!
If, when Valerio's dead, within twelve hours
(For that 's your latest time) you find not out
Another husband, on the same condition
To marry you again, you die yourself too.
    Evan. Now you are merciful, I thank your grace.
    Fred. If, when you are married, you but seek to scape
Out of the kingdom, you, or she, or both,
Or to infect men's minds with hot commotions,
You die both instantly.—Will you love me now, lady?
My tale will now be heard; but now I scorn you.
              [*Exeunt all except* VALERIO *and* EVANTHE.
    Evan. Is our fair love, our honest, our entire,
Come to this hazard?
    Val. 'Tis a noble one,
And I am much in love with malice for it;
Envy could not have studied me a way,
Nor Fortune pointed out a path to honour,
Straighter and nobler, if she had her eyes.
When I have once enjoy'd my sweet Evanthe,
And blest my youth with her most dear embraces,
I have done my journey here, my day is out;
All that the world has else is foolery,
Labour, and loss of time: what should I live for?
Think but man's life a month, and we are happy.
I would not have my joys grow old for any thing:
A Paradise, as thou art, my Evanthe,
Is only made to wonder at a little,
Enough for human eyes, and then to wander from.

Come, do not weep, sweet; you dishonour me;
Your tears and griefs but question my ability,
Whether I dare die. Do you love entirely?
Evan. You know I do.
Val. Then grudge not my felicity.
Evan. I'll to the queen.
Val. Do any thing that's honest;
But, if you sue to him, in death I hate you.
                              [*Exeunt severally.*

ACT II.

SCENE I.—*A street.*

Enter CAMILLO, CLEANTHES, *and* MENALLO.
Cam. Was there ever heard of such a marriage?
Men. Marriage and hanging go by destiny;
'Tis the old proverb; now they come together.
Cle. But a month married, then to lose his life for't?
I would have a long month sure, that pays the soldiers[r].

---

[r] *I would have a long month sure, that pays the soldiers*] Here Weber cites *The Witch of Edmonton,* by Rowley, Dekker, and Ford, act iii. sc. 1;
"*Cuddy.* Yes, I was ten days together there the last Shrove-tide.
Sec. Clown. How could that be, when there are but seven days in the week?
Cuddy. Prithee, peace! I reckon *stila nova* as a traveller: thou understandest as a fresh-water farmer, that never saw a week beyond sea. Ask any soldier that ever received his pay but in the Low-Countries, and he'll tell thee there are *eight days in the week there*, hard by."
And our author's *Fair Maid of the Inn,* act iv. sc. 2;
"*Ped.* I have another business too, because I mean to leave Italy, and bury myself in those nether parts of the *Low-Countries.*
For. What's that, sir?
Ped. Marry, I would fain make *nine days to the week,* for the more ample benefit of *the captain.*"
On the first of these passages, Gifford quotes Butler's *Hudibras,* P. ii. C. i. 513;
" The soldier does it every day,
Eight to the week, for sixpence pay."

Cam. Or get all the almanacks burnt (that were a rare trick),
And have no month remember'd.

Enter TONY, *with an urinal.*

How now, Tony? Whose water are you casting?

Tony. A sick gentleman's,
Is very sick, much troubled with the stone;
He should not live above a month, by his urine:
About St. David's Day it will go hard with him;
He will then be troubled with a pain in his neck too.

Men. A pestilent fool!—When wilt thou marry, Tony?

Tony. When I mean to be hang'd; and 'tis the surer contract.

Cle. What think you of this marriage of Valerio's?

Tony. They have given him a hot custard,
And mean to burn his mouth with it. Had I known
He had been given to die honourably,
I would have help'd him to a wench, a rare one,
Should have kill'd him in three weeks, and sav'd the sentence.

Cam. There be them would have spar'd ten days of that too.

Tony. It may be so; you have women of all virtues:
There be some guns that I could bring him to,
Some mortar-pieces that are plac'd i' the suburbs[s],
Would tear him into quarters in two hours;
There be also of the race of the old cockatrices,
That would despatch him with once looking on him.

Men. What month wouldst thou choose, Tony,
If thou hadst the like fortune?

Tony. I would choose
A mull'd-sack month, to comfort my belly; for sure
My back would ache for't; and, at the month's end,
I would be most dismally drunk, and scorn the gallows.

Men. I would choose March, for I would come in like a lion.

---

[s] *suburbs*] "The outskirts of towns were anciently the peculiar and privileged residence of strumpets." WEBER.

Tony. But you'd go out like a lamb, when you went to hanging.

Cam. I would take April, take the sweet o' th' year,
And kiss my wench upon the tender flowrets,
Tumble on every green, and, as the birds sung,
Embrace, and melt away my soul in pleasure.

Tony. You would go a-Maying gaily to the gallows.

Cle. Prithee, tell us some news.

Tony. I'll tell ye all I know:
You may be honest, and poor fools, as I am,
And blow your fingers' ends.

Cam. That's no news, fool.

Tony. You may be knaves, then, when you please, stark knaves,
And build fair houses; but your heirs shall have none of 'em.

Men. These are undoubted.

Tony. Truth is not worth the hearing.
I'll tell you news, then: there was a drunken sailor,
That got a mermaid with child as she went a-milking,
And now she sues him in the bawdy-court for it;
The infant monster is brought up in Fish-street.

Cam. Ay, this is something.

Tony. I'll tell you more: there was a fish taken,
A monstrous fish, with a sword by his side, a long sword,
A pike in 's neck, and a gun in 's nose, a huge gun,
And letters of mart[t] in 's mouth from the Duke of Florence.

Cle. This is a monstrous lie.

Tony. I do confess it:
Do you think I would tell you truths, that dare not hear 'em?
You are honest things we courtiers scorn to converse with.

[*Exit.*

Cam. A plaguy fool! But let's consider, gentlemen,
Why the queen strives not to oppose this sentence:
The kingdom's honour suffers in this cruelty.

Men. No doubt the queen, though she be virtuous,
Winks at the marriage; for by that only means
The king's flame lessens to the youthful lady,

---

[t] *letters of mart*] See note, p. 16.

If not goes out: within this month, I doubt not,
She hopes to rock asleep his anger also.
Shall we go see the preparation?
'Tis time, for strangers come to view the wonder.
   Cam. Come, let's away. Send my friends happier weddings!
                                                      [*Exeunt.*

SCENE II.—*An apartment in the Palace.*

Enter MARIA *and* EVANTHE.

   Mar. You shall be merry; come, I'll have it so:
Can there be any nature so unnoble,
Or anger so inhuman, to pursue this?
   Evan. I fear there is.
   Mar. Your fears are poor and foolish.
Though he be hasty, and his anger death,
His will, like torrents, not to be resisted,
Yet law and justice go along to guide him;
And what law or what justice can he find
To justify his will? what act or statute,
By human or divine establishment,
Left to direct us, that makes marriage death?
Honest fair wedlock? 'Twas given for increase,
For preservation of mankind, I take it;
He must be more than man, then, that dare break it.
Come, dress you handsomely (you shall have my jewels),
And put a face on that contemns base Fortune;
'Twill make him more insult to see you fearful:
Outlook[u] his anger.
   Evan. Oh, my Valerio!
Be witness, my pure mind, 'tis thee I grieve for!
   Mar. But shew it not. I would so crucify him
With an innocent neglect of what he can do,
A brave strong pious scorn, that I would shake him.
Put all the wanton Cupids in thine eyes,

---

    [u] *Outlook*] "i. e. face down." WEBER.

And all the graces on that Nature gave thee;
Make up thy beauty to that height of excellence
(I'll help thee, and forgive thee), as if Venus
Were now again to catch the God of War
In his most rugged anger. When thou hast him
(As 'tis impossible he should resist thee),
And kneeling at thy conquering feet for mercy,
Then shew thy virtue, then again despise him,
And all his power; then, with a look of honour
Mingled with noble chastity, strike him dead.

Evan. Good madam, dress me;
You arm me bravely.

Mar. Make him know his cruelty
Begins with him first; he must suffer for it;
And that thy sentence is so welcome to thee,
And to thy noble lord, you long to meet it.
Stamp such a deep impression of thy beauty
Into his soul, and of thy worthiness,
That when Valerio and Evanthe sleep
In one rich earth, hung round about with blessings,
He may run mad, and curse his act. Be lusty;
I'll teach thee how to die too, if thou fear'st it.

Evan. I thank your grace: you have prepar'd me strongly;
And my weak mind——

Mar. Death is unwelcome never,
Unless it be to tortur'd minds and sick souls,
That make their own hells; it is such a benefit
When it comes crown'd with honour, shews so sweet too!
Though they paint it ugly, that's but to restrain us,
For every living thing would love it else,
Fly boldly to their peace ere Nature call'd 'em:
The rest we have from labour and from trouble
Is some incitement; every thing alike,
The poor slave that lies private [v] has his liberty
As amply as his master in that tomb,

---

[v] *private*] "Means obscure, or undistinguished; as we say, a private man, a private soldier." MASON.

The earth as light upon him [v], and the flowers
That grow about him smell as sweet, and flourish;
But, when we love [w] with honour to our ends,
When Memory and Virtue [x] are our mourners,
What pleasures there! they are infinite, Evanthe.
Only, my virtuous wench, we want our senses,
That benefit we are barr'd; 'twould make us proud else,
And lazy [y] to look up to happier life,
The blessings of the people would so swell us.

 Evan. Good madam, dress me; you have drest my soul:
The merriest bride I'll be, for all this misery,
The proudest to some eyes too.

 Mar. 'Twill do better;
Come, shrink no more.

 Evan. I am too confident.   [*Exeunt.*

SCENE III.—*Another apartment in the same.*

Enter FREDERICK *and* SORANO.

 Sor. You are too remiss, and wanton in your angers;
You mould things handsomely, and then neglect 'em:

---

[v]   *in that tomb,*
The earth as light upon him, &c.] Seward, because "no particular tomb had been specified", would read,
     " *in* the *tomb*
  The earth's *as light upon him,*" &c.
and Mason thought him right in reading "the *tomb*".—According to Heath (*MS. Notes*), "'*that*' is by way of emphasis, the tomb which attracts the eyes of spectators",—a strange interpretation to proceed from one who had just before explained "*private*"—"without a monument."—Weber sagaciously observes, in defence of "*that*", that "the queen may be supposed to point to a tomb from the window"!!—Surely, "*that tomb*" means nothing more than— the tomb the idea of which is implied in what has been previously said concerning death, &c.   [w] *love*] Qy. "live"?

[x] *Virtue*] So the second folio.—The first folio " vertues "; and so the modern editors (" virtues ").

[y] *lazy*] "The last editors [of 1778] wish to read 'crazy', and say they have no doubt that '*lazy*' is a corruption. But '*lazy*' is clearly the right reading, and signifies indolent or careless. The queen means to say, that if we enjoyed our senses in the grave, we should be so proud and delighted with the praises and blessings of the people, that we should not be anxious for a state of more perfect happiness." MASON.

A powerful prince should be constant to his power still,
And hold up what he builds; then people fear him.
When he lets loose his hand, it shews a weakness,
And men examine or contemn his greatness:
A scorn of this high kind should have call'd up
A revenge equal, not a pity in you.
   Fred. She is thy sister.
   Sor. An she were my mother,
Whilst I conceive 'tis you she has wrong'd [z], I hate her,
And shake her nearness off. I study, sir,
To satisfy your angers that are just,
Before your pleasures.
   Fred. I have done that already,
I fear, has pull'd too many curses on me.
   Sor. Curses or envies, on Valerio's head
(Would you take my counsel, sir) they should all light,
And with the weight not only crack his scull,
But his fair credit. The exquisite vexation
I have devis'd (so please you give way in 't,
And let it work) shall more afflict his soul,
And trench upon that honour that he brags of,
Than fear of death in all the frights he carries.
If you sit down here, they will both abuse you,
Laugh at your poor relenting power, and scorn you.
What satisfaction can their deaths bring to you,
That are prepar'd and proud to die, and willingly,
And at their ends will thank you for that honour?
How are you nearer the desire you aim at?
Or, if it be revenge your anger covets,
How can their single deaths give you content, sir?
Petty revenges end in blood, slight angers;
A prince's rage should find out new diseases
Death were a pleasure to [a], to pay proud fools with.

---

   [z] *conceive 'tis you she has wrong'd*] So the second folio.—The first folio "*conceive she has you wrong'd*".

   [a] *to*] Both the folios have "*too*"; and so Sympson and the Editors of 1778. —Mason (who first corrected the slight error of the press, and gave the right punctuation) observes that the meaning is "that a prince's rage should suggest new torments, compared with which death itself would be a pleasure."

Fred. What should I do?

Sor. Add but your power unto me,
Make me but strong by your protection,
And you shall see what joy and what delight,
What infinite pleasure this poor month shall yield him.
I'll make him wish he were dead on's marriage-day,
Or bed-rid with old age; I'll make him curse,
And cry and curse, give me but power.

Fred. You have it:
Here, take my ring; I am content he pay for't.
[*Gives ring.*

Sor. It shall be now revenge, as I will handle it;
He shall live after this to beg his life too:
Twenty to one, by this thread, as I'll weave it,
Evanthe shall be yours.

Fred. Take all authority,
And be most happy!

Sor. Good sir, no more pity! [*Exeunt severally.*

SCENE IV.—*Before the door of the Hall of the Palace.*

Enter TONY, *three* Citizens, *and three* Wives.

First Wife. Good Master Tony, put me in.

Tony. Where do you dwell?

First Wife. Forsooth, at the sign of the Great Shoulder of Mutton.

Tony. A hungry man would hunt your house out instantly:
Keep the dogs from your door. Is this lettice-ruff[a] your husband?
A fine sharp sallad to your sign.

Sec. Wife. Will you put me in too?

Third Wife. And me, good Master Tony?

Tony. Put ye all in!
You had best come twenty more; you think 'tis easy,
A trick of legerdemain, to put ye all in:

---

[a] *lettice-ruff*] Or *lattice-ruff*,—i. e. a ruff with reticulated work.

'Twould pose a fellow that had twice my body,
Though it were all made into chines and fillets.
 Sec. Wife. Put's in to the wedding, sir; we would fain see
  that.
 First Wife. And the brave masque too.
 Tony. You two are pretty women.—
Are you their husbands?
 Sec. Cit. Yes, for want of better.
 Tony. I think so too; you would not be so mad else
To turn 'em loose to a company of young courtiers,
That swarm like bees in May, when they see young wenches.—
You must not squeak.
 Third Wife. No, sir; we are better tutor'd.
 Tony. Nor, if a young lord offer you the courtesy[b]——
 Sec. Wife. We know what 'tis, sir.
 Tony. Nor you must not grumble,
If you be thrust up hard; we thrust most furiously.
 First Wife. We know the worst.
 Tony. Get you two in, then, quietly,
     [*Suffers First and Second Wife to pass in.*
And shift for yourselves.—We must have no old women,
They are out of use, unless they have petitions;
Besides, they cough so loud, they drown the music.—
You would go in too? but there is no place for ye;
I am sorry for 't; go, and forget your wives;
Or pray they may be able to suffer patiently:
You may have heirs may prove wise aldermen:
Go, or I 'll call the guard.
 Third Cit. We will get in;
We 'll venture broken pates else.
 Tony. 'Tis impossible,
You are too securely arm'd.
      [*Exeunt* Citizens *and third* Wife.

---

[b] *Nor, if a young lord offer you the courtesy*——] " This scene ridicules the crowding of citizens to the court-masques, in the reigns of James and Charles I., where it appears the citizens' wives who possessed any share of beauty were admitted, while their unfortunate husbands were contemptuously rejected," &c. WEBER. See note, vol. ii. 479.

      How they flock hither,
And with what joy the women run by heaps
To see this marriage! they tickle to think of it;
They hope for every month a husband too.
Still how they run, and how the wittols [c] follow 'em!
The weak things that are worn between the legs,
That brushing, dressing, nor new naps can mend,
How they post to see their own confusion!
This is a merry world.

     Enter FREDERICK.

 Fred. Look to the door, sirrah;
Thou art a fool, and mayst do mischief lawfully.
 Tony. Give me your hand: you are my brother fool;
You may both make the law, and mar it presently.
Do you love a wench?
 Fred. Who does not, fool?
 Tony. Not I,
Unless you will give me a longer lease to marry her.
 Fred. What are all these that come? what business have
   they?
 Tony. Some come to gape,—those are my fellow-fools;
Some to get home their wives,—those be their own fools;
Some to rejoice with thee,—those be the time's fools;
And some, I fear, to curse thee,—those are poor fools,
A set, people call them honest [d].

    CASSANDRA *passes over the stage.*

      Look, look, king, look!
A weather-beaten lady new-careen'd!
 Fred. An old one.

---

 [c] *wittols*] "i.e. patient cuckolds conscious of their wives' infidelity." WEBER.
 [d]   *those are poor fools,*
A set, people call them honest] The folios have no comma after "set".—Seward proposed to read "Yet *people call them honest*", and Sympson "And yet *people*", &c.—The Editors of 1778 supposed that "*A set people*" might perhaps signify—formal, precise people.—Heath (*MS. Notes*) conjectured "*A set of people*", &c.—Mason first gave the right punctuation, comparing what Sorano says (act v. sc. 3),—
    "They are such
  The foolish people call their country's honours," &c.

Tony. The glasses of her eyes are new-rubb'd over,
And the worm-eaten records in her face
Are daub'd up neatly;
She lays her breasts out too, like two[e] poach'd eggs
That had the yelks[f] suck'd out. They get new heads also,
New teeth, new tongues, (for the old are all worn out,)
And, as 'tis hop'd, new tails.

Fred. For what?

Tony. For old courtiers;
The young ones are too stirring for their travels.

Fred. Go, leave your knavery, and help to keep the door
 well;
I will have no such press.

Tony. Lay thy hand o' thy heart, king.

Fred. I'll have you whipp'd.

Tony. The fool and thou are[g] parted. [*Exit.*

Fred. Sorano, work, and free me from this spell:
'Twixt love and scorn there's nothing felt but hell. [*Exit.*

SCENE V.—*An apartment in the same.*

VALERIO *discovered,* Servants *assisting to dress him;* CAMILLO,
 CLEANTHES, *and* MENALLO.

Val. Tie on my scarf; you are so long about me!—
Good my lords, help:—give me my other cloak;
That hat and feather.—Lord, what a tailor's this,
To make me up thus strait! one sigh would burst me;
I have not room to breathe.—Come, button, button,
Button, apace.

Cam. I am glad to see you merry, sir.

Val. 'Twould make you merry, had you such a wife,
And such an age to enjoy her in.

Men. An age, sir!

Val. A month's an age to him that is contented;

---

[e] *two*] Both the folios " to ".

[f] *yelks*] i. e. yolks.—The modern editors print " yolks ".

[g] *are*] So the first folio.—The second folio "art"; and so the modern editors.

What should I seek for more?—Give me my sword.—
Ha, my good lords! that every one of you now
Had but a lady of that youth and beauty
To bless yourselves this night with! would ye not?
Pray ye, speak uprightly.
   Cle. We confess you happy,
And we could well wish such another banquet;
But, on that price, my lord——
   Val. 'Twere nothing, else;
No man can ever come to aim at Heaven,
But by the knowledge of a hell.—These shoes are heavy,
And, if I should be call'd to dance, they'll clog me;
Get me some pumps.—I'll tell you, brave Camillo,
And you, dear friends; the king has honour'd me,
Out of his gracious favour, has much honour'd me,
To limit me my time; for who would live long?
Who would be old? 'tis such a weariness,
Such a disease, that hangs like lead upon us.
As it increases, so vexations,
Griefs of the mind, pains of the feeble body,
Rheums, coughs, catarrhs; we are but our living coffins:
Beside, the fair soul's old too, it grows covetous;
Which shews all honour is departed from us,
And we are earth again.
   Cle. You make fair use, sir.
   Val. I would not live to learn to lie, Cleanthes,
For all the world; old men are prone to that too.—
Thou that hast been a soldier, Menallo,
A noble soldier, and defied all danger,
Adopted thy brave arm the heir to victory,
Wouldst thou live so long till thy strength forsook thee?
Till thou grew'st only a long tedious story
Of what thou hadst been? till thy sword hung[g] by,
And lazy spiders fill'd the hilt with cobwebs?
   Men. No, sure, I would not.
   Val. 'Tis not fit you should:
To die a young man is to be an angel;

---

   [g] *hung*] Both the folios "hang"; and so the modern editors.

Our great good parts put wings unto our souls[h].—
Pray you, tell me, is't a handsome masque we have?
   Cam. We understand so.
   Val. And the young gentlemen dance?
   Cle. They do, sir; and some dance well.
   Val. They must, before the ladies.
We'll have a rouse[i] before we go to bed, friends,
A lusty one; 'twill make my blood dance too.
   Cam. Ten[j], if you please.
   Val. And we'll be wondrous merry.   [*Music within.*
They stay, sure: come; I hear the music; forward!
You shall have all gloves presently.
   Men. We attend, sir;   [*Exit* VALERIO.
But first we must look to the doors; the king has charg'd
   us.   [*Exeunt.*

SCENE VI.—*The Hall of the Palace. A curtain in the back-ground.*

   Enter two Servants.   [*Knocking within.*
   First Serv. What a noise do you keep there!—Call my
      fellows o' the guard.—
You must cease now until the king be enter'd;
He is gone to the temple now.
   Sec. Serv. Look to that back door,
And keep it fast; they swarm like bees about it.

   Enter CAMILLO, CLEANTHES, MENALLO; TONY *following, who remains at the door.*

   Cam. Keep back those citizens; and let their wives in,
Their handsome wives.

---

[h] *Our great good parts put wings unto our souls*] Is followed in both the old eds. by
    "We'll have a rouse before we go to bed, friends,"
a line which they repeat presently. The intermediate lines, we may presume, had been crossed out in the prompter's book.

[i] *rouse*] i. e. bumper,—drinking-bout: see Gifford's note on Massinger's Works, i. 240, ed. 1813.

[j] *Ten*] i. e., as Mason saw, ten *rouses*.—The Editors of 1778 supposed that a quibble was intended here, referring "*Ten*" to the preceding word "*too*"—*two*.

Tony. They have crowded me to verjuice;
I sweat like a butter-box.
First Serv. Stand further off there!
Men. Take the women aside, and talk with 'em in private;
Give 'em that they came for.
Tony. The whole court cannot do it;
Besides, the next masque, if we use 'em so,
They 'll come by millions to expect our largess.
We have broke a hundred heads.
Cle. Are they so tender?
Tony. But 'twas behind; before they have all murrions [j].
Cam. Let in those ladies; make 'em room, for shame there!
Tony. They are no ladies; there's one bald before 'em;
A gentlewoman bald! they are curtail'd queans in hir'd clothes [k]:
They come out of Spain, I think; they are very sultry.
Men. Keep 'em in breath for an ambassador:
Methinks, my nose shakes at their memories.
What bouncing's that?   [*Knocking within.*
First Cit. [*within*] I am one of the music, sir.
Sec. Cit. [*within*] I have sweet-meats for the banquet.
Cam. Let 'em in.
Tony. They lie, my lord: they come to seek their wives;
Two broken citizens.
Cam. Break 'em more; they are but brusled [l] yet.—
Bold rascals! offer to disturb your wives?
Cle. Lock the doors fast. The music, hark! the king comes.   [*Music within.*

[j] *murrions*] "Properly *morions*,—helmets, casques." WEBER. Tony means,—before, they are all well defended by their horns.

[k] *A gentlewoman bald! they are curtail'd queans in hir'd clothes*] "The baldness alluded to was the consequence of the venereal disease. They are probably called '*curtail'd queans*', in allusion to the short mantles [waistcoats] anciently worn by prostitutes." WEBER. See note, vol. i. 39.

[l] *brusled*] "Mason proposes to read 'bruised'; but the old text is right. *Brusle* occurs with the same signification in these plays as *brustle*, which Skinner explains to *crackle*, to make a small noise." WEBER.—And see the various Provincial Glossaries: but, surely, the context shews that, in the present passage, "*brusled*" must mean—slightly broken.

Enter FREDERICK, MARIA, VALERIO, EVANTHE, SORANO,
Ladies, *and* Attendants.

A Masque.
The curtain is drawn. Cupid, with his eyes bound, descends in a chariot, the Graces *sitting by him.*

Cupid. *Unbind me, my delight; this night is mine.*
[The Graces unbind his eyes.
Now let me look upon what stars here shine,
Let me behold the beauties, then clap high
My colour'd wings, proud of my deity.
I am satisfied: bind me again, and fast;
My angry bow will make too great a waste
Of beauty else. Now call my masquers in,
Call with a song, and let the sports begin;
Call all my servants, the effects of love,
And to a measure let them nobly move.

SONG BY THE GRACES.
Come, you servants of proud Love,
 Come away!
Fairly, nobly, gently move:
Too long, too long you make us stay.
Fancy, Desire, Delight, Hope, Fear,
Distrust, and Jealousy, be you too here;
Consuming Care, and raging Ire,
And Poverty in poor attire,
March fairly in, and last Despair.
Now full music strike the air.

Enter the Masquers, *Fancy, Desire, Delight, Hope, Fear, Distrust, Jealousy, Care, Ire, Poverty, Despair: they dance; after which Cupid speaks.*

Cupid. *Away! I have done; the day begins to light.—*
[*Exeunt* Masquers.
Lovers, you know your fate; good night, good night!
[Cupid *and the* Graces *ascend in the chariot.*

Fred. Come, to the banquet: when that's ended, sir,
I'll see you a-bed, and so, good night. Be merry;
You have a sweet bed-fellow.

Val. I thank your grace,
And ever shall be bound unto your nobleness.

Fred. I pray I may deserve your thanks. Set forward!
[*Exeunt.*

ACT III.

SCENE I.—*A Cathedral. A tomb in the back-ground.*

Enter divers Friars [m] *leading in* ALPHONSO; RUGIO, *and* MARCO.

Marco. The night grows on: lead softly to the tomb,
And sing not till I bid ye; let the music
Play gently as he passes.
 Rug. Oh, fair picture,
That wert the living hope of all our honours!
How are we banish'd from the joy we dream'd of!—
Will he ne'er speak more?
 Marco. 'Tis full three months, Lord Rugio,
Since any articulate sound came from his tongue.
Set him down gently.   [ALPHONSO *is set in a chair.*
 Rug. What should the reason be, sir?
 Marco. As 'tis in nature with those loving husbands
That sympathise their wives' pains and their throes
When they are breeding (and 'tis usual too;
We have it by experience), so in him, sir,
In this most noble spirit that now suffers;
For, when his honour'd father, good Brandino,
Fell sick, he felt the griefs, and labour'd with them;
His fits and his disease he still inherited,
Grew the same thing, and, had not Nature check'd him,
Strength and ability, he had died that hour too.
 Rug. Emblem of noble love!
 Marco. That very minute
His father's breath forsook him, that same instant,
(A rare example of his piety
And love paternal) the organ of his tongue
Was never heard to sound again: so near death

---

[m] *Friars*] Here both the folios "Monks": but see act iv. sc. 4, act v. sc. 1.

He seeks to wait upon his worthy father,
But that we force his meat, he were one body.
  Rug. He points to the tomb.
  Marco. That is the place he honours;
A house, I fear, he will not be long out of.
He will to the tomb: good my lord, lend your hand.
                    [ALPHONSO *is led to the tomb.*
Now sing the funeral song, and let him kneel,
For then he is pleas'd.   [*A song.*
  Rug. Heaven, lend thy powerful hand,
And ease this prince!
  Marco. He will pass back again.   [*Exeunt.*

SCENE II.—*An apartment in the Palace.*

Enter VALERIO.

  Val. They drink abundantly; I am hot with wine too,
Lustily warm. I'll steal now to my happiness;
'Tis midnight, and the silent hour invites me:
But she is up still, and attends the queen.
Thou dew of wine and sleep, hang on their eye-lids,
Steep their dull senses in the healths they drink,
That I may quickly find my lov'd Evanthe!
The king is merry too, and drank unto me;
Sign of fair peace. Oh, this night's blessedness!
If I had forty heads, I would give all for it.
Is not the end of our ambitions,
Of all our human studies, and our travels,
Of our desires, the obtaining of our wishes?
Certain, it is; and there man makes his centre.
I have obtain'd Evanthe, I have married her:
Can any fortune keep me from enjoying her?

Enter SORANO.

I have my wish; what's left me to accuse now?—
I am friends with all the world, but thy base malice:
Go, glory in thy mischiefs, thou proud man,

And cry it to the world, thou hast ruin'd virtue:
How I contemn thee and thy petty malice!
And with what scorn I look down on thy practice [n]!

Sor. You'll sing me a new song anon, Valerio,
And wish these hot words——

Val. I despise thee, fellow!
Thy threats or flatteries, all I fling behind me.
I have my end, I have thy noble sister,
A name too worthy of [o] thy blood: I have married her,
And will enjoy her too.

Sor. 'Tis very likely.

Val. And that short month I have to bless me with her
I'll make an age: I'll reckon each embrace
A year of pleasure, and each night a jubilee,
Every quick kiss a spring; and, when I mean
To lose myself in all delightfulness,
Twenty sweet summers I will tie together:
In spite of thee and thy malignant master,
I will die old in love, though young in pleasure.

Sor. But that I hate thee deadly, I could pity thee;
Thou art the poorest miserable thing
This day on earth; I'll tell thee why, Valerio:
All thou esteem'st, and build'st upon for happiness,
For joy, for pleasure, for delight, is past thee,
And, like a wanton dream, already vanish'd.

Val. Is my love false?

Sor. No, she is constant to thee;
Constant to all thy misery she shall be,
And curse thee too.

Val. Is my strong body weaken'd,
Charm'd, or abus'd with subtle drink? speak, villain!

Sor. Neither; I dare speak, thou art still as lusty
As when thou lov'd'st her first, as strong and hopeful.
The month thou hast given thee is a month of misery,
And where thou think'st each hour shall yield a pleasure,
Look for a killing pain, for thou shalt find it:
Before thou diest, each minute shall prepare it,

---

[n] *practice*] See note, p. 6.

[o] *of*] "We should probably read 'for'." MASON.

And ring so many knells to sad afflictions;
The king has given thee a long month to die in,
And miserably die.
   Val. Undo thy riddle;
I am prepar'd, whatever fate shall follow.
   Sor. Dost thou see this ring?
   Val. I know it too.
   Sor. Then mark me:
By virtue of this ring, this I pronounce to thee;
'Tis the king's will.
   Val. Let me know it suddenly.
   Sor. If thou dost offer to touch Evanthe's body,
Beyond a kiss, though thou art married to her,
And lawfully, as thou think'st, mayst enjoy her,
That minute she shall die.
   Val. Oh, devil!
   Sor. If thou discover this command unto her,
Or to a friend that shall importune thee,
And why thou abstain'st, and from whose will, ye all perish,
Upon the self-same forfeit. Are you fitted, sir?
Now, if you love her, you may preserve her life still;
If not, you know the worst. How falls your month out?
   Val. This tyranny could never be invented
But in the school of hell, earth is too innocent:
Not to enjoy her when she is my wife!
When she is willing too!
   Sor. She is most willing,
And will run mad to miss; but, if you hit her,
Be sure you hit her home, and kill her with it
(There are such women that will die with pleasure),
The axe will follow else, that will not fail
To fetch her maidenhead, and despatch her quickly;
Then shall the world know you are the cause of murder,
And, as 'tis requisite, your life shall pay for't.
   Val. Thou dost but jest; thou canst not be so monstrous
As thou proclaim'st thyself; thou art her brother,
And there must be a feeling heart within thee
Of her afflictions: wert thou a stranger to us,
And bred amongst wild rocks, thy nature wild too,

Affection in thee, as thy breeding, cold,
And unrelenting as the rocks that nourish'd thee,
Yet thou must shake to tell me this; they tremble
When the rude sea threatens divorce amongst 'em,
They that are senseless things shake at a tempest;
Thou art a man——

    Sor. Be thou too, then; 'twill try thee;
And patience now will best become thy nobleness.

    Val. Invent some other torment to afflict me,
All, if thou please, put all afflictions on me,
Study thy brains out for 'em; so this be none,
I care not of what nature, nor what cruelty,
Nor of what length.

    Sor. This is enough to vex you.

    Val. The tale of Tantalus is now prov'd true,
And from me shall be register'd authentic:
To have my joys within my arms, and lawful,
Mine own delights, yet dare not touch! Even as
Thou hat'st me, brother, let no young man know this,
As thou shalt hope for peace when thou most need'st it,
Peace in thy soul! Desire the king to kill me,
Make me a traitor, any thing, I'll yield to it,
And give thee cause, so I may die immediately;
Lock me in prison where no sun may see me,
In walls so thick no hope may e'er come at me,
Keep me from meat, and drink, and sleep, I'll bless thee;
Give me some damnèd potion to deliver me,
That I may never know myself again, forget
My country, kindred, name, and fortune; last,
That my chaste love may never appear before me;
This were some comfort.

    Sor. All I have I have brought you,
And much good may it do you[p], my dear brother!
See you observe it well; you will find about you
Many eyes set, that shall o'erlook your actions:
If you transgress, you know—and so, I leave you.   [*Exit.*

---

[p] *much good may it do you*] So the second folio.—The first folio "*much may it do ye* with it".

A WIFE FOR A MONTH.

Val. Heaven be not angry, and I have some hope yet[q];
[*Kneels.*
Look on my harmless youth! Angels of pity,
To whom I kneel, be merciful unto me,
And from my bleeding heart wipe off my sorrows!
The power, the pride, the malice, and injustice
Of cruel men are bent against mine innocence:
You that control the mighty wills of princes,
And bow their stubborn aims, look on my weakness,
And, when you please, and how, allay my miseries! [*Exit.*

[q] *Val. Heaven be not angry, and I have some hope yet,* &c.] In the first folio thus;
"*Val.* Heaven be not angry, and I have some hope yet,
And when you please, and how allay my miseries.

Enter Frederick.
To whom I kneele be mercifull unto me,
Looke on my harmelesse youth Angels of pitty,
And from my bleeding heart wipe off my sorrowes,
The power, the pride, the malice and injustice
Of cruell men are bent against mine innocence.
You that controwle the mighty wills of Princes,
And bow their stubborne *armrs,* look on my weaknesse,
And when you please, and how, allay my miseries. *Exit.*
Fred. Hast thou been with him?
Sor. Yes, and given him that Sir," &c.

The second folio has only;
"*Val.* Heaven be not angry, and I have some hope yet. [*Exit.*
Enter Frederick, and Sorano.
Fred. Hast thou been with him?
Sor. Yes, and given him that Sir," &c.

Sympson, except that he printed "my *innocence*" and "*stubborn* Armes," gave, in his text, the passage according to the first folio; but he repeated it in a note, where he altered the punctuation, struck out the second line and the stage-direction "*Enter Frederick*", and changed "armes" to "*arms*".—The Editors of 1778 adopted his corrections, and also transposed the second and third lines.—Mason, observing that "'*stubborn*' is an epithet more applicable to the mind than the body," proposed to read "aims" instead of "arms".—Weber omitted the second line, and the stage-direction, remarking that their insertion "may be accounted for by supposing that the intermediate lines were crossed out in the prompter's book, and afterwards restored according to the general practice professed by the editors of the first folio, without attending to the repetition of the line, and without transferring the stage-direction." He rejected the transposition made by the Editors of 1778 (which, I think, is absolutely necessary), as well as Mason's correction "aims" (which is undoubtedly the true reading; see my *Remarks on Mr. Collier's and Mr. Knight's editions of Shakespeare,* p. 152-3).

SCENE III.—*Ante-room to a bed-chamber in the same.*

Enter FREDERICK *and* SORANO.

Fred. Hast thou been with him?

Sor. Yes, and given him that, sir,
Will make him curse his birth; I told you which way.
Did you but see him, sir, but look upon him,
With what a troubled and dejected nature
He walks now in a mist, with what a silence,
As if he were the shroud he wrapt himself in,
And no more of Valerio but his shadow,
He seeks obscurity to hide his thoughts in,
You would wonder and admire, for all you know it.
His jollity is down, vail'd [r] to the ground, sir,
And his high hopes of full delights and pleasures
Are turn'd tormentors to him, strong diseases.

Fred. But is there hope of her?

Sor. It must fall necessary
She must dislike him, quarrel with his person
(For women once deluded are next devils),
And, in the height of that opinion, sir,
You shall put on again, and she must meet you.

Fred. I am glad of this.

Sor. I'll tell you all the circumstance
Within this hour. But, sure, I heard your grace,
To-day as I attended, make some stops,
Some broken speeches, and some sighs between;
And then your brother's name I heard distinctly,
And some sad wishes after.

Fred. You are i' the right, sir;
I would he were as sad as I could wish him,
Sad as the earth!

Sor. Would you have it so?

Fred. Thou hear'st me.
Though he be sick, with small hope of recovery,
That hope still lives, and men's eyes live upon it,

---

[r] *vail'd*] i. e. lowered.

And in their eyes their wishes: my Sorano,
Were he but cold once in the tomb he dotes on
(As 'tis the fittest place for melancholy),
My court should be another Paradise,
And flow with all delights.
   Sor. Go to your pleasures;
Let me alone with this: hope shall not trouble you,
Nor he, three days.
   Fred. I shall be bound unto thee.
   Sor. I'll do it neatly too; no doubt shall catch me.
   Fred. Be gone. They are going to bed; I'll bid good
      night to 'em.
   Sor. And mark the man: you'll scarce know 'tis Valerio.
                                                [Exit.

       Enter VALERIO, CAMILLO, CLEANTHES, *and* MENALLO.
   Cam. Cheer up, my noble lord; the minute's come,
You shall enjoy the abstract of all sweetness.
We did you wrong; you need no wine to warm you,
Desire shoots through your eyes like sudden wildfires.
   Val. Beshrew me, lords, the wine has made me dull;
I am I know not what.
   Fred. Good pleasure to you!
Good night and long too! as you find your appetite,
You may fall to.
   Val. I do beseech your grace,   [*Aside to* FREDERICK.
For which of all my loves and services
Have I deserv'd this?
   Fred. I am not bound to answer you.
   Val. Nor I bound to obey in unjust actions.
   Fred. Do as you please; you know the penalty,
And, as I have a soul, it shall be executed!
Nay, look not pale; I am not us'd to fear, sir:
If you respect your lady—Good night to you!   *[Exit.*
   Val. But for respect to her, and to my duty,
That reverent duty that I owe my sovereign,
Which anger has no power to snatch me from,
The good night should be thine, good night for ever!—
                                                 [Aside.

The king is wanton, lords; he would needs know of me
How many nick-chases I would make to-night.
  Men. My lord, no doubt you'll prove a perfect gamester.
  Val. Faith, no; I am unacquainted with the pleasure;
Bungle a set I may.—How my heart trembles,
And beats my breast as it would break his way out!—
                                                [*Aside.*
Good night, my noble friends.
  Cle. Nay, we must see you
Toward your bed, my lord.
  Val. Good faith, it needs not;
'Tis late, and I shall trouble you.
  Cam. No, no;
Till the bride come, sir——
  Val. I beseech you, leave me;
You will make me bashful else, I am so foolish;
Besides, I have some few devotions, lords,
And he that can pray with such a book in 's arms——
  Cam. We 'll leave you, then; and a sweet night wait upon
    you!
  Men. And a sweet issue of this sweet night crown you!
  Cle. All nights and days be such till you grow old, sir!
  Val. I thank ye:
              [*Exeunt* CAMILLO, CLEANTHES, *and* MENALLO.
              'tis a curse sufficient for me,
A labour'd one too, though you mean a blessing.—
What shall I do? I am like a wretched debtor,
That has a sum to tender on the forfeit
Of all he is worth, yet dare not offer it.
Other men see the sun, yet I must wink at it,
And, though I know 'tis perfect day, deny it.
My veins are all on fire, and burn like Ætna,
Youth and desire beat 'larums to my blood,
And add fresh fuel to my warm affections.
I must enjoy her; yet, when I consider,
When I collect myself, and weigh her danger,
The tyrant's will, and his power taught to murder,
My tender care controls my blood within me,
And, like a cold fit of a peevish ague,

[SCENE III.] A WIFE FOR A MONTH.

Creeps to my soul, and flings an ice upon me,
That locks all powers of youth up : but prevention^r—
Oh, what a blessedness 'twere to be old now,
To be unable, bed-rid with diseases,
Or halt on crutches to meet holy Hymen;
What a rare benefit! But I am curs'd:
That that speaks other men most freely happy,
And makes all eyes hang on their expectations,
Must prove the bane of me, youth and ability.
She comes to bed; how shall I entertain her?

Enter MARIA, EVANTHE, *Ladies, and* TONY.

Tony. Nay, I come after too; take the fool with ye,
For lightly[s] he is ever one at weddings.

Mar. Evanthe, make you unready[t], your lord stays for you;
And, prithee, be merry.

Tony. Be very merry, chicken;
Thy lord will pipe to thee anon, and make thee dance too.

First Lady. Will he so, goodman Ass?

Tony. Yes, goody filly:
An you had such a pipe, that pip'd so sweetly,
You would dance to death; you have learnt your cinque-a-pace[u].

Evan. Your grace desires that that is too free in me;
I am merry at the heart.

Tony. Thou wilt be anon;
The young smug boy will give thee a sweet cordial.

Evan. I am so taken up in all my thoughts,

---

^r *That locks all powers of youth up: but prevention*——] So the second folio.—The first folio has no point after "*up*", and places a semicolon at the end of the line.—Mason says, "If we read,

'That locks all powers of youth up *by* prevention',

the sentence will be sense and complete." But, as Weber observes, Mason's alteration is "very tame".

^s *lightly*] "i. e. commonly." MASON.

^t *make you unready*] "i. e. undress yourself." MASON.

^u *cinque-a-pace*] Properly *cinque-pace*. See note, vol. vii. 156. (The same quibble *cinque—sink* occurs in Shakespeare's *Much ado about Nothing*, act ii. sc. 1.)

So possess'd, madam, with the lawful sweets
I shall this night partake of with my lord,
So far transported (pardon my immodesty)——
   Val. Alas, poor wench, how shall I recompense thee!
                                                                  [*Aside.*
   Evan. That though they must be short, and snatch'd away too
Ere they grow ripe, yet I shall far prefer 'em
Before a tedious pleasure with repentance.
   Val. Oh, how my heart aches!   [*Aside.*
   Evan. Take off my jewels, ladies,
And let my ruff loose: I shall bid good night to ye;
My lord stays here.
   Mar. My wench, I thank thee heartily,
For learning how to use thy few hours handsomely;
They will be years, I hope. Off with your gown now.—
Lay down the bed there.
   Tony. Shall I get into it,
And warm it for thee? a fool's fire is a fine thing:
And I'll so buss thee!
   Mar. I'll have you whipp'd, you rascal!
   Tony. That will provoke me more.—I'll talk with thy husband:
He's a wise man, I hope.
   Evan. Good night, dear madam.—
Ladies, no further service; I am well.—
I do beseech your grace to give us this leave;
My lord and I to one another freely,
And privately, may do all other ceremonies;
Woman[u] and page we'll be to one another,
And trouble you no farther.
   Tony. Art thou a wise man?
   Val. I cannot tell thee, Tony; ask my neighbours.
   Tony. If thou be'st so, go lie with me to-night
(The old fool will lie quieter than the young one,
And give thee more sleep); thou wilt look to-morrow else
Worse than the prodigal fool the ballad speaks of,
That was squeez'd through a horn.

---

      [u] *Woman*] Both the folios " Women."

Val. I shall take thy counsel.

Mar. Why, then, good night, good night, my best Evanthe,
My worthy maid! and, as that name shall vanish,
A worthy wife, a long and happy!—Follow, sirrah.

Evan. That shall be my care. Goodness rest with your
grace!

Mar. Be lusty, lord, and take your lady to you;
And that power that shall part ye be unhappy!

Val. Sweet rest unto you!—to ye all, sweet ladies!—
Tony, good night.

Tony. Shall not the fool stay with thee?

Mar. Come away, sirrah. [*Exeunt* MARIA *and* Ladies.

Tony. How the fool is sought for!

> Sweet malt is made of easy fire;
> A hasty horse will quickly tire;
> A sudden leaper sticks i' the mire;
> Phlebotomy, and the word "lie nigher,"
> Take heed of, friend, I thee require.
> This from an almanack I stole;
> And learn this lesson from a fool.

Good night, my bird.

Evan. Good night, wise Master Tony. [*Exit* TONY.
Will you to bed, my lord? come, let me help you.

Val. To bed, Evanthe! art thou sleepy?

Evan. No;
I shall be worse, if you look sad upon me.
Pray you, let's to bed.

Val. I am not well, my love.

Evan. I'll make you well; there's no such physic for you
As your warm mistress' arms.

Val. Art thou so cunning[v]?

Evan. I speak not by experience (pray you, mistake not);
But, if you love me——

Val. I do love so dearly,
So much above the base bent of desire,
I know not how to answer thee.

Evan. To bed, then;

---

[v] *cunning*] i. e. skilful.

There I shall better credit you. Fie, my lord!
Will you put a maid to 't, to teach you what to do?
An innocent maid? are you so cold a lover?
In truth, you make me blush: 'tis midnight too,
And 'tis no stoln love, but authoris'd openly,
No sin we covet. Pray, let me undress you;
You shall help me. Prithee, sweet Valerio,
Be not so sad; the king will be more merciful.

   Val. May not I love thy mind?

   Evan. And I yours too;
'Tis a most noble one, adorn'd with virtue;
But, if we love not one another really,
And put our bodies and our minds together,
And so make up the concord of affection,
Our love will prove but a blind superstition.
This is no school to argue in, my lord,
Nor have we time to talk away allow'd us:
Pray, let 's despatch. If any one should come
And find us at this distance, what would they think?
Come, kiss me, and to bed.

   Val. That I dare do,
And kiss again.

   Evan. Spare not; they are your own, sir.

   Val. But to enjoy thee is to be luxurious,
Too sensual in my love, and too ambitious.—
Oh, how I burn! [*Aside.*]—To pluck thee from the stalk
Where now thou grow'st a sweet bud and a beauteous,
And bear'st the prime and honour of the garden,
Is but to violate thy spring, and spoil thee.

   Evan. To let me blow, and fall alone, would anger you.

   Val. Let 's sit together thus, and, as we sit,
Feed on the sweets of one another's souls.
The happiness of love is contemplation,
The blessedness of love is pure affection,
Where no allay of actual dull desire,
Of pleasure that partakes with wantonness,
Of human fire that burns out as it kindles,
And leaves the body but a poor repentance,
Can ever mix: let 's fix on that, Evanthe;

That's everlasting, the other^w casual;
Eternity breeds one, the other Fortune,
Blind as herself, and full of all afflictions:
Shall we love virtuously?
   Evan. I ever lov'd so.
   Val. And only think our love? the rarest pleasure
(And that we most desire, let it be human),
If once enjoy'd, grows stale, and cloys our appetites:
I would not lessen in my love for any thing,
Nor find thee but the same in my short journey,
For my love's safety^x.
   Evan. Now I see I am old, sir,
Old and ill-favour'd too, poor and despis'd,
And am not worth your noble fellowship,
Your fellowship in love; you would not else
Thus cunningly seek to betray a maid,
A maid that honours you thus piously,
Strive to abuse the pious love she brings you.
Farewell, my lord; since you have a better mistress,
(For it must seem so, or you are no man,)
A younger, happier, I shall give her room,
So much I love you still.
   Val. Stay, my Evanthe:
Heaven bear me witness, thou art all I love,
All I desire! and now, have pity on me!—
I never lied before; forgive me, Justice!
Youth and Affection, stop your ears unto me!   [*Aside.*
   Evan. Why do you weep? If I have spoke too harshly,
And unbeseeming, my belovèd lord,
My care and duty, pardon me.
   Val. Oh, hear me,
Hear me, Evanthe!—I am all on torture,

---

^w *the other*] Both the folios "*the* tother" (see notes, vol ii. 45, vol. vii. 453), which I have not retained, because in the next line they have "*the other*".

^x *Nor find thee but the same in my short journey,*
   For my love's safety] "Valerio would not suffer the least abatement of her affection, if he might save——what by it? his love? his *life*, to be sure, he designed to say, and the true reading is, '*For my* life's *safety.*'" SYMPSON.—"Very good sense may be made out of the text: 'He would not lessen in his love for any thing, and therefore wishes to find her still the same, that his love may not lessen.' In his 'short journey' his *life's safety* is quite out of the question." *Ed.* 1778.

And this lie tears my conscience as I vent it!— [*Aside*.
I am no man.
 Evan. How, sir!
 Val. No man for pleasure;
No woman's man.
 Evan. Goodness forbid, my lord!
Sure, you abuse yourself.
 Val. 'Tis true, Evanthe;
I shame to say you will find it. [*Weeps*.
 Evan. He weeps bitterly:
'Tis my hard fortune; bless all young maids from it!—
[*Aside*.
Is there no help, my lord, in art will comfort you?
 Val. I hope there is.
 Evan. How long have you been destitute?
 Val. Since I was young.
 Evan. 'Tis hard to die for nothing.— [*Aside*.
Now you shall know, 'tis not the pleasure, sir,
(For I am compell'd to love you spiritually,)
That women aim at, I affect you for;
'Tis for your worth: and kiss me; be at peace;
Because I ever lov'd you, I still honour you,
And with all duty to my husband follow you.
Will you to bed now? you are asham'd, it seems.
Pygmalion pray'd, and his cold stone took life:
You do not know with what zeal I shall ask, sir,
And what rare miracle that may work upon you.
Still blush? prescribe your law.
 Val. I prithee, pardon me:
To bed, and I'll sit by thee, and mourn with thee,
Mourn both our fortunes, our unhappy ones:
Do not despise me; make me not more wretched!
I pray to Heaven, when I am gone, Evanthe,
(As my poor date is but a span of time now,)
To recompense thy noble patience,
Thy love and virtue, with a fruitful husband,
Honest and honourable!
 Evan. Come, you have made me weep now.
All fond desire die here! and welcome chastity,
Honour and chastity! Do what you please, sir. [*Exeunt*.

ACT IV.

SCENE I.—*An apartment in the Monastery.*

Enter, on one side, RUGIO *and* MARCO; *on the other,* SORANO *with a little glass phial.*

Rug. What ails this piece of mischief to look sad?
He seems to weep too.
 Marco. Something is a-hatching,
And of some bloody nature too, Lord Rugio,
This crocodile mourns thus cunningly.
 Sor. Hail, holy father!
And good day to the good Lord Rugio!
How fares the sad prince, I beseech you, sir?
 Rug. 'Tis like you know; you need not ask that question:
You have your eyes and watches on his miseries
As near as ours; I would they were as tender!
 Marco. Can you do him good? As the king and you appointed him,
So he is still; as you desir'd I think too,
For every day he is worse: Heaven pardon all!
Put off your sorrow; you may laugh now, lord;
He cannot last long to disturb your master:
You have done worthy service to his brother,
And he most memorable love.
 Sor. You do not know, sir,
With what remorse I ask, nor with what weariness
I groan and bow under this load of honour;
And how my soul sighs for the beastly services
I have done his pleasures, these be witness with me!
And from your piety believe me, father,
I would as willingly unclothe myself
Of title (that becomes me not, I know;
Good men and great names best agree together),
Cast off the glorious favours, and the trappings
Of sound and honour, wealth and promises,
His wanton pleasures have flung on my weakness,

And choose to serve my country's cause and virtue's,
Poorly and honestly, and redeem my ruins,
As I would hope remission of my mischiefs.

Rug. Old and experienc'd men, my lord Sorano,
Are not so quickly caught with gilt hypocrisy.
You pull your claws in now, and fawn upon us,
As lions do to entice poor foolish beasts;
And beasts we should be too, if we believ'd you:
Go, exercise your art——

Sor. For Heaven-sake, scorn me not,
Nor add more hell to my afflicted soul
Than I feel here! as you are honourable,
As you are charitable, look gently on me!
I will no more to court, be no more devil:
I know I must be hated even of him
That was my love now; and the more he loves me
For his foul ends, when they shall once appear to him,
Muster before his conscience, and accuse him,
The fouler and the more falls his displeasure:
Princes are fading things, so are their favours.

Marco. He weeps again[x];
His heart is touch'd, sure, with remorse.

Sor. See this,
And give me fair attention: good my lord,
And worthy father, see; within this phial,
The remedy and cure of all my honour,
And of the sad prince, lies.

Rug. What new trick's this?

Sor. 'Tis true, I have done offices abundantly
Ill and prodigious to the prince Alphonso;
And, whilst I was a knave, I sought his death too.

Rug. You are too late convicted to be good yet.

Sor. But, father, when I felt this part afflict me,
This inward part, and call'd me to an audit
Of my misdeeds and mischiefs——

Marco. Well; go on, sir.

Sor. Oh, then, then, then! what was my glory then, father?

---

[x] *He weeps again*] Qy. are these words a stage-direction? (Sorano had previously wept, when he said, " these [i. e. my tears] be witness with me!" p. 347). The measure is complete without them.

The favour of the king, what did that ease me?
What was it to be bow'd to by all creatures?
Worshipp'd, and courted? what did this avail me?
I was a wretch, a poor lost wretch!
  Marco. Still better.
  Sor. Till, in the midst of all my grief, I found
Repentance; and a learned man to give the means to it;
A Jew, an honest and a rare physician:
Of him I had this jewel; 'tis a jewel,
And, at the price of all my wealth, I bought it.
If the king knew it, I must lose my head;
And willingly, most willingly, I would suffer.
A child may take it, 'tis so sweet in working.
  Marco. To whom would you apply it to^y?
  Sor. To the sick prince;
It will in half a day dissolve his melancholy.
  Rug. I do believe; and give him sleep for ever.
What impudence is this, and what base malice,
To make us instruments of thy abuses!
Are we set here to poison him?
  Sor. Mistake not;
Yet I must needs say, 'tis a noble care,
And worthy virtuous servants. If you will see
A flourishing estate again in Naples,
And great Alphonso reign, that's truly good,
And like himself able to make all excellent,
Give him this drink; and this good health unto him! [*Drinks.*
I am not so desperate yet to kill myself.
Never look on me as a guilty man,
Nor on the water as a speedy poison:
I am not mad, nor laid out all my treasure,
My conscience and my credit, to abuse ye.
How nimbly and how cheerfully it works now
Upon my heart and head! sure, I am a new man:
There is no sadness that I feel within me,
But, as it meets it, like a lazy vapour

---

  ^y *to*] So the first folio ("*too*").—Omitted in the second folio; and by Sympson and the Editors of 1778.—Repetitions of this kind are frequent in our early writers: see notes, vol. vi. 389, 524.

How it flies off! Here, give it him with speed:
You are more guilty than I ever was,
And worthier of the name of evil subjects,
If but an hour you hold this from his health.

Rug. 'Tis some rare virtuous thing, sure; he is a good man;
It must be so: come, let's apply it presently;
And may it sweetly work!

Sor. Pray, let me hear on't;
And carry it close, my lords.

Marco. Yes, good Sorano.

      [*Exeunt* RUGIO *and* MARCO *with the phial.*

Sor. Do, my good fools, my honest pious coxcombs,
My wary fools too! have I caught your wisdoms?
You never dream'd I knew an antidote,
Nor how to take it to secure mine own life;
I am an ass! Go, give him the fine cordial,
And, when you have done, go dig his grave, good friar.
Some two hours hence we shall have such a bawling,
And roaring up and down for *aqua-vitæ*,
Such rubbing, and such 'nointing, and such cooling!
I have sent him that will make a bonfire in's belly:
If he recover it, there is no heat in hell, sure.   [*Exit.*

  SCENE II.—*An apartment in the Palace.*

   Enter FREDERICK *and* PODRAMO.

Fred. Podramo!

Pod. Sir?

Fred. Call hither Lord Valerio;
And let none trouble us.

Pod. It shall be done, sir.   [*Exit.*

Fred. I know he wants no additions to his tortures,
He has enough for human blood to carry[z];

---

[z] *He has enough for human blood to carry*] After this line, both the folios have,—
   "Yet I must vex him further";
and so the modern editors, though those of 1778 observed that it "seems to be an interpolation; and was perhaps occasioned by the players' omitting the two next lines."

So many, that I wonder his hot youth
And high-bred spirit breaks not into fury;
I must yet torture him a little further,
And make myself sport with his miseries;
My anger is too poor else. Here he comes.

Enter VALERIO.

Now, my young-married lord, how do you feel yourself?
You have the happiness you ever aim'd at,
The joy and pleasure.
　Val. Would you had the like, sir!
　Fred. You tumble in delights with your sweet lady,
And draw the minutes out in dear embraces;
You live a right lord's life.
　Val. Would you had tried it,
That you might know the virtue but to suffer!
Your anger, though it be unjust and insolent,
Sits handsomer upon you than your scorn;
To do a wilful ill, and glory in it,
Is to do it double, double to be damn'd too.
　Fred. Hast thou not found a loving and free prince?
High in his favours too? that has conferr'd
Such hearts-ease, and such heaps of comfort on thee,
All thou couldst ask?
　Val. You are too grown a tyrant
Upon so suffering and so still a subject:
You have put upon me such a punishment,
That, if your youth were honest, it would blush at;
But you are a shame to nature, as to virtue.
Pull not my rage upon you: 'tis so just,
It will give way to no respect. My life,
My innocent life, (I dare maintain it, sir,)
Like a wanton prodigal you have flung away;
Had I a thousand more, I would allow 'em,
And be as careless of 'em as your will is:
But, to deny those rights the law has given me,
The holy law, and make her life the penance,
Is such a studied and unheard-of malice,
No heart that is not hir'd from hell dare think of;

To do it then too, when my hopes were high,
High as my blood, all my desires upon me,
My free affections ready to embrace her,
And she mine own! Do you smile at this? is 't done well?
Is there not Heaven above you that sees all? [*Exit.*

Enter CASSANDRA.

Fred. Come hither, Time. How does your noble mistress?
Cas. As a gentlewoman may do in her case that 's newly married, sir;
Sickly sometimes, and fond, an't like your majesty[a].
Fred. She is breeding, then?
Cas. She wants much of her colour,
And has her qualms as ladies use to have, sir,
And her disgusts.
Fred. And keeps her chamber?
Cas. Yes, sir.
Fred. And eats good broths and jellies?
Cas. I am sure she sighs, sir,
And weeps, good lady!
Fred. Alas, good lady, for it!
She should have one could comfort her, Cassandra,
Could turn those tears to joys, a lusty comforter.
Cas. A comfortable man does well at all hours,
For he brings comfortable things.
Fred. Come hither;
And hold your fan between, you have eaten onions.—
Her breath stinks like a fox, her teeth are contagious;
These old women are all elder-pipes [*Aside*].—Do you mark me? [*Gives a purse.*
Cas. Yes, sir; but does your grace think I am fit,
That am both old and virtuous?
Fred. Therefore the fitter, the older still the better;
I know thou art as holy as an old cope,
Yet, upon necessary use——
Cas. 'Tis true, sir.

[a] *and fond, an't like your majesty*] Sympson's proposed correction (and compare p. 378. l. 16).—Both the folios "*and fond* on't, *like your Majesty*"; and so the modern editors. Here "*fond*" means—foolish.

Fred. Her feeling sense is fierce still: speak unto her,
(You are familiar,) speak, I say, unto her,
Speak to the purpose; tell her this, and this. [*Whispers.*
 Cas. Alas, she is honest, sir, she is very honest!
And would you have my gravity——
 Fred. Ay, ay;
Your gravity will become the cause the better.
I'll look thee out a knight shall make thee a lady too,
A lusty knight, and one that shall be rul'd by thee;
And add to these, I'll make 'em good c. No mincing,
Nor ducking out of nicety d, good lady,
But do it home. We'll all be friends too, tell her,
And such a joy——
 Cas. That's it that stirs me up, sir;
I would not for the world attempt her chastity,
But that they may live lovingly hereafter.
 Fred. For that I urge it too.
 Cas. A little evil
May well be suffer'd for a general good, sir.
I'll take my leave of your majesty.
 Fred. Go fortunately;
Be speedy too. [*Exit* CASSANDRA.
                Here comes Valerio:
If his affliction e have allay'd his spirit,
My work has end.
           Re-enter VALERIO.
                Come hither, Lord Valerio;
How do you now?
 Val. Your majesty may guess,
Not so well, nor so fortunate as you are,
That can tie up men's honest wills and actions f.

  c *And add to these, I'll make 'em good*] "i. e. and, though you should add to these further conditions, I'll fulfil them." MASON.
  d *nicety*] i. e. scrupulousness, preciseness.
  e *affliction*] The Editors of 1778 silently printed "afflictions"; and so Weber.
  f *That can tie up men's honest wills and actions*] "In the first folio, some lines which occur before, (p. 351,) are repeated here; from—
     'You have the happiness,' &c. to the line,
      'Sits handsomer upon you than your scorn.'" WEBER.
In consequence, probably, of the scene having been shortened in the representation.

Fred. You clearly see now, brave Valerio,
What 'tis to be the rival to a prince,
To interpose against a raging lion:
I know you have suffer'd, infinitely suffer'd,
And with a kind of pity I behold it;
And, if you dare be worthy of my mercy,
I can yet heal you (yield up your Evanthe),
Take off my sentence also.
 Val. I fall thus low, sir;   [*Kneels.*
My poor sad heart under your feet I lay,
And all the service of my life.
 Fred. Do this, then,
For without this 'twill be impossible:
Part with her for a while.
 Val. You have parted us;
What should I do with that I cannot use, sir?
 Fred. 'Tis well consider'd: let me have the lady,
And thou shalt see how nobly I'll befriend thee,
How all this difference——
 Val. Will she come, do you think, sir?
 Fred. She must be wrought (I know she is too modest),
And gently wrought, and cunningly.
 Val. 'Tis fit, sir.
 Fred. And secretly it must be done.
 Val. As thought.
 Fred. I'll warrant you, her honour shall be fair still;
No soil nor stain shall appear on that, Valerio.
You see a thousand that bear sober faces,
And shew off as inimitable modesties;
You would be sworn too that they were pure matrons,
And most chaste maids; and yet, to augment their fortunes,
And get them noble friends——
 Val. They are content, sir,
In private to bestow their beauties on 'em.
 Fred. They are so, and they are wise; they know no want
  for 't,
For no eye sees they want their honesties.
 Val. If it might be carried thus—
 Fred. It shall be, sir.

Val. I'll see you dead first! [*Aside*].—With this caution,
Why, sure, I think it might be done.
Fred. Yes, easily.
Val. For what time would your grace desire her body?
Fred. A month or two. It shall be carried still
As if she kept[g] with you, and were a stranger,
Rather a hater, of the grace I offer;
And then I will return her, with such honour—
Val. 'Tis very like [*Aside*].—I dote much on your honour.
Fred. And load her with such favour too, Valerio—
Val. She never shall claw off [*Aside*].—I humbly thank you.
Fred. I'll make ye both the happiest, and the richest,
And the mightiest too——
Val. But who shall work her, sir?
For, on my conscience, she is very honest,
And will be hard to cut as a rough diamond.
Fred. Why, you must work her; any thing from your tongue,
Set off with golden and persuasive language,
Urging your dangers too——
Val. But all this time
Have you the conscience, sir, to leave me nothing,
Nothing to play withal?
Fred. There be a thousand;
Take where thou wilt.
Val. May I make bold with your queen?
She is useless to your grace, as it appears, sir,
And but a loyal wife, that may be lost too:
I have a mind to her, and then 'tis equal.
Fred. How, sir!
Val. 'Tis so, sir. Thou most glorious impudence,
Have I not wrongs enow to suffer under,
But thou must pick me out to make a monster?
A hated wonder to the world? Do you start
At my entrenching on your private liberty,
And would you force a highway through mine honour,

---

[g] *kept*] "i. e. dwelt." WEBER.

And make me pave it too? But that thy queen
Is of that excellence in honesty,
And guarded with divinity about her,
No loose thought can come near, nor flame unhallow'd,
I would so right myself!
　Fred. Why, take her to you;
I am not vex'd at this; thou shalt enjoy her:
I'll be thy friend, if that may win thy courtesy.
　Val. I will not be your bawd, though, for your royalty.
Was I brought up and nourish'd in the court,
With thy most royal brother and thyself,
Upon thy father's charge, thy happy father's,
And suck'd the sweetness of all human arts,
Learn'd arms and honour, to become a rascal?
Was this the expectation of my youth,
My growth of honour? Do you speak this truly,
Or do you try me, sir? for I believe not,
At least I would not, and methinks 'tis impossible
There should be such a devil in a king's shape,
Such a malignant fiend.
　Fred. I thank you, sir!
To-morrow is your last day, and look to it!
Get from my sight, away!
　Val. You are——Oh,
My heart's too high and full to think upon you!
　　　　　　　　　　　　　　　　[*Exeunt severally.*

SCENE III.—*Another apartment in the same.*

Enter EVANTHE *and* CASSANDRA.

　Evan. You think it fit, then, mortified Cassandra,
That I should be a whore?
　Cas. Why a whore, madam?
If every woman that upon necessity
Did a good turn (for there's the main point, mark it)
Were term'd a whore, who would be honest, madam?
Your lord's life, and your own, are now in hazard;

Two precious lives may be redeem'd with nothing,
Little or nothing; say, an hour's or day's sport,
Or such a toy; the end to it is [not]^h wantonness,
That we call lust, that maidens lose their fame for,
But a compell'd necessity of honour,
Fair as the day, and clear as innocence;
Upon my life and conscience, a direct way——
　Evan. To be a rascal.
　Cas. 'Tis a kind of rape too;
That keeps you clear; for, where your will's compell'd,
Though you yield up your body, you are safe still.
　Evan. Thou art grown a learnèd bawd; I ever look'd
Thy great sufficiency would break out.
　Cas. You may,
You that are young and fair, scorn us old creatures;
But you must know my years ere you be wise, lady,
And my experience too. Say the king lov'd you?
Say it were nothing else?
　Evan. Ay, marry, wench,
Now thou com'st to me.
　Cas. Do you think princes' favours are such slight things,
To fling away when you please? There be young ladies,
Both fair and honourable, that would leap to reach 'em,
And leap aloft too.
　Evan. Such are light enough;
I am no vaulter, wench. But canst thou tell me,
Though he be a king, whether he be sound or no?
I would not give my youth up to infection.
　Cas. As sound as honour ought to be, I think, lady.
Go to! be wise; I do not bid you try him;
But, if he love you well, and you neglect him,
Your lord's life hanging on the hazard of it——
If you be so wilful proud——
　Evan. Thou speak'st to the point still;
But when I have lien^i with him, what am I then, gentlewoman?
　Cas. What are you! why, the same you are now, a woman,

---

^h [*not*] Inserted by Sympson.

^i *lien*] So the first folio ("*lyen*").—Here the second folio "lain" (and so the modern editors); but afterwards (p. 368 l. 25) it has "*lyen*."

A virtuous woman, and a noble woman;
Touching at what is noble, you become so.
Had Lucrece e'er been thought of, but for Tarquin?
She was before a simple unknown woman;
When she was ravish'd, she was a reverent saint:
And do you think she yielded not a little,
And had a kind of will to have been re-ravish'd?
Believe it, yes. There are a thousand stories
Of wondrous loyal women, that have slipp'd,
But it has been on the ice of tender honour,
That kept 'em cool still to the world. I think you are blest,
That have such an occasion in your hands to beget
A chronicle, a faithful one.
 Evan. It must needs be much honour.
 Cas. As you may make it, infinite, and safe too;
And, when 'tis done, your lord and you may live
So quietly, and peaceably together,
And be what you please!
 Evan. But, suppose this, wench,
The king should so delight me with his company,
I should forget my lord, and no more look on him?
 Cas. That's the main hazard; for I tell you truly,
I have heard report speak he's an infinite pleasure,
Almost above belief: there be some ladies,
And modest to the world too, wondrous modest,
That have had the blessedness to try his body,
That I have heard proclaim him a new Hercules.
 Evan. So strongly able?
 Cas. There will be the danger;
You being but a young and tender lady,
Although your mind be good, yet your weak body,
At first encounter too, to meet with one
Of his unconquer'd strength——
 Evan. Peace, thou rude bawd,
Thou studied old corruptness! tie thy tongue up,
Your hir'd base tongue! Is this your timely counsel?
Dost thou seek to make me dote on wickedness,
Because 'tis ten times worse than thou deliver'st it?
To be a whore, because he has sufficiency

To make a hundred? Oh, thou impudence!
Have I reliev'd thy age to mine own ruin,
And worn thee in my bosom, to betray me?
Can years and impotence win nothing on thee
That's good and honest, but thou must go on still?
And, where thy blood wants heat to sin thyself,
Force thy decrepit will to make me wicked?
   Cas. I did but tell you——
   Evan. What the damned'st woman,
The cunning'st and the skilful'st bawd, comes short of:
If thou hadst liv'd ten ages to be damn'd in,
And exercis'd this art the devil taught thee,
Thou couldst not have express'd it more exactly.
   Cas. I did not bid you sin.
   Evan. Thou wooed'st me to it;
Thou, that art fit for prayer and the grave,
Thy body earth already and corruption,
Thou taught'st the way. Go, follow your fine function:
There are houses of delight, that want good matrons,
Such grave instructors; get thee thither, monster,
And read variety of sins to wantons;
And, when they roar with pains, learn to make plasters.
   Cas. This we have for our good wills.
   Evan. If e'er I see thee more,
Or any thing that's like thee, to affright me,
By this fair light, I'll spoil thy bawdry!
I'll leave thee neither eyes nor nose to grace thee!
When thou want'st bread, and common pity towards thee,
And art a-starving in a ditch, think of me;
Then die, and let the wandering bawds lament thee:
Be gone; I charge thee, leave me!

Enter FREDERICK.

   Cas. You'll repent this.   [*Exit.*
   Fred. She's angry, and t'other crying too; my suit's cold:
I'll make your heart ache, stubborn wench, for this!—
                                                  [*Aside.*
Turn not so angry from me; I will speak to you.

Are you grown proud with your delight, good lady?
So pamper'd with your sport, you scorn to know me?
 Evan. I scorn you not; I would you scorn'd not me, sir,
And forc'd me to be weary of my duty!
I know your grace; would I had never seen you!
 Fred. Because I love you, because I dote upon you,
Because I am a man that seek to please you?
 Evan. I have man enough already to content me,
As much, as noble, and as worthy of me,
As all the world can yield.
 Fred. That's but your modesty:
You have no man—nay, never look upon me,
I know it, lady—no man to content you;
No man that can, or, at the least, that dare,
Which is a poorer man, and nearer nothing.
 Evan. Be nobler, sir, inform'd.
 Fred. I'll tell thee, wench,
The poor condition of this poorer fellow,
And make thee blush for shame at thine own error:
He never tender'd yet a husband's duty
To thy warm longing bed.
 Evan. How should he know that?   [*Aside.*
 Fred. I am sure he did not, for I charg'd him no,
Upon his life I charg'd him, but to try him.
Could any brave or noble spirit stop here?
Was life to be preferr'd before affection?
Lawful and long'd-for too?
 Evan. Did you command him?
 Fred. I did, in policy, to try his spirit.
 Evan. And could he be so dead-cold to observe it?
Brought I no beauty nor no love along with me?
 Fred. Why, that is it that makes me scorn to name him.
I should have lov'd him, if he had ventur'd for 't;
Nay, doted on his bravery.
 Evan. Only charg'd,
And with that spell sit down! Dare men fight bravely
For poor slight things, for drink, or ostentation,
And there endanger both their lives and fortunes,
And for their lawful loves fly off with fear?

Fred. 'Tis true;
And with a cunning base fear too to abuse thee,
Made thee believe, poor innocent Evanthe,
Wretched young girl, it was his impotency:
Was it not so? deny it.
    Evan. Oh, my anger!
At my years, to be cozen'd with a young man!
    Fred. A strong man too: certain, he lov'd you dearly!
    Evan. To have my shame and love mingled together,
And both flung on me like a weight to sink me!
I would have died a thousand times!
    Fred. So would any,
Any that had the spirit of a man:
I would have been kill'd in your arms.
    Evan. I would he had been,
And buried in mine arms! that had been noble:
And what a monument would I have made him!
Upon this breast he should have slept in peace,
Honour and everlasting Love his mourners;
And I still weeping, till old Time had turn'd me,
And pitying powers above, into pure crystal.
    Fred. Hadst thou lov'd me, and had my way been stuck
With deaths, as thick as frosty nights with stars,
I would have ventur'd.
    Evan. Sure, there is some trick in't:
Valerio ne'er was coward.   [*Aside.*
    Fred. Worse than this too,
Tamer, and seasoning of a baser nature,
He set your woman on you to betray you,
Your bawdy woman, or your sin-solicitor
(I pray, but think what this man may deserve now);
I know he did, and did it to please me too.
    Evan. Good sir, afflict me not too fast: I feel
I am a woman, and a wrong'd one too,
And sensible I am of my abuses.
Sir, you have lov'd me——
    Fred. And I love thee still,
Pity thy wrongs, and dote upon thy person.
    Evan. To set my woman on me! 'twas too base, sir.

Fred. Abominable vild[h].
Evan. But I shall fit him.
Fred. All reason and all law allows it to you;
And you are a fool, a tame fool, if you spare him.
Evan. You may speak now, and happily prevail too;
And I beseech your grace be angry with me.
Fred. I am at heart.—She staggers in her faith,
And will fall off, I hope; I'll ply her still.— [*Aside.*
Thou abus'd innocence, I suffer with thee!
If I should give him life, he would still betray thee;
That fool that fears to die for such a beauty,
Would for the same fear sell thee unto misery:
I do not say[i] he would have been bawd himself too.
Evan. Follow'd thus far? nay, then I smell the malice;
It tastes too hot of practis'd wickedness:
There can be no such man, I am sure no gentleman.
Shall my anger make me whore, and not my pleasure?
My sudden unconsiderate rage abuse me?
Come home again, my frighted faith, my virtue,
Home to my heart again! [*Aside.*]—He be a bawd too?
Fred. I will not say he offer'd, fair Evanthe.
Evan. Nor do not dare: 'twill be an impudence,
And not an honour, for a prince to lie.
Fie, sir, a person of your rank to trifle!
I know you do lie.
Fred. How!
Evan. Lie shamefully;
And I could wish myself a man but one day,
To tell you openly, you lie too basely.
Fred. Take heed, wild fool!
Evan. Take thou heed, thou tame devil!

[h] *vild*] i. e. vile: see note, vol. i. 331.—The modern editors print "vile."

[i] *I do not say,* &c.] "From Evanthe's answer, it seems probable the poet wrote, '*I* DARE *say*,' &c." *Ed.* 1778,—Mason approving of the alteration.—"Surely, had the editors read a little further, they would have struck out this useless note. Frederick says again,

'I will *not* say he offer'd, fair Evanthe.'

He evidently goes gradually and artfully to work, afraid of Evanthe's suspicions being roused by an accusation too downright, and seems insidiously to retract his first assertions, to gain her confidence more strongly." WEBER.

Thou all Pandora's box, in a king's figure!
Thou hast almost whor'd my weak belief already,
And, like an engineer, blown up mine honour:
But I shall countermine, and catch your mischief;
This little fort you seek I shall man nobly,
And strongly too, with chaste obedience
To my dear lord, with virtuous thoughts that scorn you.
Victorious Thamyris[j] ne'er won more honour
In cutting off the royal head of Cyrus
Than I shall do in conquering thee. Farewell;
And, if thou canst be wise, learn to be good too;
'Twill give thee nobler lights than both thine eyes do.
My poor lord and myself are bound to suffer;
And, when I see him faint under your sentence,
I'll tell you more; it may be, then I'll yield too.

Fred. Fool, unexampled shall[k] my anger follow thee!

[*Exeunt severally.*

SCENE IV.—*An apartment in the Monastery.*

Enter RUGIO *and* MARCO.

Rug. Curse on our sights[1]! our fond credulities!
A thousand curses on the slave that cheated us,
The damnèd slave!

Marco. We have e'en sham'd our service,

---

[j] *Thamyris*] So the first folio (" *Tameris* ").—The second folio " Thomyris ". —The name of this Scythian queen is variously written by ancient authors.

[k] *Fool, unexampled shall,* &c.] The modern editors point, " *Fool unexampled, shall,*" &c.: but the epithet " *unexampled* " belongs to " *anger* " (which Heath did not perceive, when, in his *MS. Notes,* he proposed altering "*shall*" to "*still*").

[1] *Curse on our sights*] Both the folios " Curst ", &c.—" Sympson says, that every body sees that this must be wrong [and proposes to read " Curse on our *light,* our fond credulities!" which was adopted by the Editors of 1778]; but I see clearly that it is right. They curse their sights, because it was their eyes deceived them. They gave no credit to Sorano until they saw him drink the poison; and, accordingly, Rugio afterwards says,

'——That we should be such blockheads,
As to be taken with his drinking first,
And never think what antidotes are made for!' " MASON.

Brought our best care[1] and loyalties to nothing:
'Tis the most fearful poison, the most potent——
Heaven give him patience! Oh, it works most strongly,
And tears him——Lord!
   Rug. That we should be so stupid
To trust the arrant'st villain that e'er flatter'd,
The bloodiest too! to believe a few soft words from him,
And give way to his prepar'd tears!
   Alph. [*within*] Oh, oh, oh!
   Rug. Hark, friar Marco,
Hark, the poor prince! That we should be such blockheads,
As to be taken with his drinking first,
And never think what antidotes are made for!
Two wooden sculls we have, and we deserve to be hang'd for't:
For certainly it will be laid to our charge;
As certain, too, it will despatch him speedily.
Which way to turn, or what to——
   Marco. Let us pray:
Heaven's hand is strong.
   Rug. The poison's strong, you would say.
Would any thing—He comes; let 's give him comfort.

      ALPHONSO *is brought in, on a couch, by two* Friars.

   Alph. Give me more air, air, more air! Blow, blow[m]!
Open, thou eastern gate, and blow upon me!
Distil thy cold dews, oh, thou icy moon!
And, rivers, run through my afflicted spirit!
I am all fire, fire, fire! the raging Dog-star
Reigns in my blood! Oh, which way shall I turn me?
Ætna, and all his flames, burn in my head!
Fling me into the ocean, or I perish!
Dig, dig, dig, till[n] the springs fly up,
The cold, cold springs, that I may leap into 'em,
And bathe my scorch'd limbs in their purling pleasures!
Or shoot me up into the higher region,

---

[1] *care*] Qy. "*cares*"? compare p. 373 l. 11.

[m] *Blow, blow*] Sympson silently printed "*Blow, blow,* blow."

[n] *till*] Sympson silently printed "until" (but, to make the line perfectly metrical, he ought to have added another "*dig*").

Where treasures of delicious snow are nourish'd,
And banquets of sweet hail!
   Rug. Hold him fast, friar:
Oh, how he burns!
   Alph. What, will ye sacrifice me?
Upon the altar lay my willing body,
And pile your wood up, fling your holy incense;
And, as I turn me, you shall see all flame,
Consuming flame. Stand off me, or you are ashes!
   Rug. and Marco. Most miserable wretches!
   Alph. Bring hither Charity,
And let me hug her, friar: they say she's cold,
Infinite cold; devotion cannot warm her.
Draw me a river of false lovers' tears
Clean through my breast; they are dull, cold, and forgetful,
And will give ease. Let virgins sigh upon me,
Forsaken souls; their° sighs are precious;
Let them all sigh. Oh, hell, hell, hell! oh, horror!
   Marco. To bed, good sir.
   Alph. My bed will burn about me:
Like Phaeton, in all-consuming flashes
I am enclos'd! Let me fly, let me fly, give room!
Betwixt the cold bear and the raging lionᵖ
Lies my safe way. Oh, for a cake of ice now,
To clap unto my heart to comfort me!
Decrepit Winter, hang upon my shoulders,

° *their*] Both the folios "the".

ᵖ *Betwixt the cold bear and the raging lion*, &c.] Seward, in his Preface, citing this passage, gives,—

    "'Twixt *the cold* bears, far from *the raging lion*," &c.

which he defends at great length in a note: and his alteration was adopted by the Editors of 1778!! "The old reading, notwithstanding Seward's learned argument, I believe to be the true one. The allusion is to the story of Phaeton, and particularly to this line—

    In medio tutissimus ibis.

The word '*safe*' proves this allusion." MASON. "This Mr. Seward is a blockhead of the provoking species. In his itch for correction, he forgot the words —'lies my safe way!' The Bear is the extreme pole, and thither he would travel over the space contained between it and 'the raging lion'." Coleridge's *Remains*, ii. 314.

And let me wear thy frozen icicles
Like jewels round about my head, to cool me!
My eyes burn out, and sink into their sockets,
And my infected brain like brimstone boils!
I live in hell, and several Furies vex me!
Oh, carry me where no sun ever shew'd yet
A face of comfort, where the earth is crystal
Never to be dissolv'd! where nought inhabits
But night and cold, and nipping frosts, and winds
That cut the stubborn rocks and make them shiver!
Set me there, friends!
   Rug. Hold fast; he must to bed, friar.
What scalding sweats he has!
   Marco. He'll scald in hell for't,
That was the cause.
   Alph. Drink, drink, a world of drink!
Fill all the cups, and all the antique vessels,
And borrow pots; let me have drink enough!
Bring all the worthy drunkards of the time,
The experienc'd drunkards, let me have them all,
And let them drink their worst, I'll make them idiots!
I'll lie upon my back, and swallow vessels,
Have rivers made of cooling wine run through me,
Not stay for this man's health, or this great prince's,
But take an ocean, and begin to all!
Oh, oh!
   Marco. He cools a little; now away with him,
And to his warm bed presently.
   Alph. No drink?
No wind? no cooling air?
   Rug. You shall have any thing.—
His hot fit lessens; Heaven, put in a hand now,
And save his life!—There's drink, sir, in your chamber,
And all cool things.
   Alph. Away, away; let's fly to 'em!
                        [*Exeunt, carrying* ALPHONSO.

SCENE V.—*An apartment in the Palace.*

Enter VALERIO *and* EVANTHE.

Evan. To say you were impotent! I am asham'd on 't:
To make yourself no man! to a fresh maid too,
A longing maid! upon her wedding-night also,
To give her such a dor q!
  Val. I prithee, pardon me.
  Evan. Had you been drunk, 't had been excusable;
Or, like a gentleman, under the surgeon's hands,
And so not able, there had been some colour;
But wretchedly to take a weakness to you,
A fearful weakness, to abuse your body,
And let a lie work like a spell upon you,
A lie to save your life——
  Val. Will you give me leave, sweet?
  Evan. You have taken too much leave, and too base leave
    too,
To wrong your love. Hast thou a noble spirit?
And canst thou look up to the people's loves,
That call thee worthy, and not blush, Valerio?
Canst thou behold me that thou hast betray'd thus,
And no shame touch thee?
  Val. Shame attend the sinful!
I know my innocence.
  Evan. Ne'er think to face it; that's a double weakness,
And shews thee falser still. The king himself,
Though he be wicked, and our enemy,
But juster than thou r, in pity of my injuries,
Told me the truth.
  Val. What did he tell, Evanthe?
  Evan. That, but to gain thy life a fortnight longer,
Thy lov'd poor life, thou gav'st up all my duties.

---

q *dor*] See note, vol. vii. 48.

r *juster than thou*] The first folio "*juster then* thine".—The second folio "*juster than thou* art"; and so the modern editors.

Val. I swear 'tis false! my life and death are equal;
I have weigh'd 'em both, and find 'em but one fortune.
But kings are men, and live as men, and die too,
Have the affections men have, and their falsehoods;
Indeed, they have more power to make 'em good.
The king's to blame: it was to save thy life, wench,
Thy innocent life, that I forbore thy bed,
For, if I had touch'd thee, thou hadst died; he swore it.

Evan. And was not I as worthy to die nobly,
To make a story for the time that follows,
As he that married me? What weakness, sir,
Or disability, do you see in me,
Either in mind or body, to defraud me
Of such an opportunity? Do you think I married you
Only for pleasure, or content in lust?
To lull you in mine arms, and kiss you hourly?
Was this my end? I might have been a queen, sir,
If that had caught me, and have known all delicates:
There's few that would have shunn'd so fair an offer.
Oh, thou unfaithful fearful man, thou hast kill'd me!
In saving me this way, thou hast destroy'd me,
Robb'd me of that thy love can never give more!
To be unable, to save *me!* Oh, misery!
Had I been my Valerio, thou Evanthe,
I would have lien with thee under a gallows,
Though the hangman had been my Hymen, and the Furies,
With iron whips and forks, ready to torture me:
I would have hugg'd thee too, though hell had gap'd at me.
Save *my* life! that expected to die bravely,
That would have woo'd it too! Would I had married
An eunuch, that had truly no ability,
Than such a fearful liar! Thou hast done me
A scurvy courtesy, that has undone me.

Val. I'll do no more; since you are so nobly fashion'd,
Made up so strongly, I'll take my share with you;
Nay, dear, I'll learn of you.

Evan. He weeps too, tenderly;
My anger's gone [*Aside*].—Good my lord, pardon me;
And, if I have offended, be more angry:

It was a woman's flash, a sudden valour,
That could not lie conceal'd.
 Val. I honour you;
By all the rites of holy marriage,
And pleasures of chaste love, I wonder at you!
You appear the vision of a heaven unto me,
Stuck all with stars of honour shining clearly,
And all the motions of your mind celestial:
Man is a lump of earth; the best man spiritless,
To such a woman; all our lives and actions
But counterfeits in arras[8], to this virtue.
Chide me again; you have so brave an anger,
And flows so nobly from you, thus deliver'd,
That I could suffer like a child to hear you,
Nay, make myself guilty of some faults to honour you.
 Evan. I'll chide no more; you have robb'd me of my
  courage,
And with a cunning patience check'd my impudence.
Once more, forgiveness!   [*She kneels.*
 Val. Will this serve, Evanthe? [*Raises and kisses her.*
And this, my love? Heaven's mercy be upon us!
But did he tell no more?
 Evan. Only this trifle;
You set my woman on me, to betray me:
'Tis true, she did her best; a bad old woman!
It stirr'd me, sir.
 Val. I cannot blame thee, jewel.
 Evan. And, methought, when your name was sounded
  that way——
 Val. He that will spare no fame will spare no name, sweet.
Though, as I am a man, I am full of weakness,
And may slip happily into some ignorance,
Yet at my years to be a bawd, and cozen
Mine own hopes with my doctrine——
 Evan. I believe not,
Nor never shall. Our time is out to-morrow.
 Val. Let's be to-night, then, full of fruitfulness;

---

   [8] *counterfeits in arras*] i. e. pictures in tapestry.

Now we are both of one mind, let's be happy:
I am no more a wanting man, Evanthe;
Thy warm embraces shall dissolve that impotence,
And my cold lie shall vanish with thy kisses.
You hours of night, be long as when Alcmena
Lay by the lusty side of Jupiter;
Keep back the day, and hide his golden beams
Where the chaste watchful Morning may not find 'em!
Old doting Tithon, hold Aurora fast,
And, though she blush the day-break from her cheeks,
Conceal her still! Thou heavy Wain, stand firm,
And stop the quicker revolutions!
Or, if the day must come to spoil our happiness,
Thou envious sun, peep not upon our pleasure;
Thou, that all lovers curse, be far off from us!

 Evan. Then let's to bed; and this night, in all joys
And chaste delights——

   Enter CASTRUCCIO, *with a Guard.*

 Cast. Stay: I must part ye both;
It is the king's command, who bids me tell you,
To-morrow is your last hour.

 Val. I obey, sir:
In heaven we shall meet, captain, where King Frederick
Dare not appear to part us.

 Cast. Mistake me not;
Though I am rough in doing of my office,
You shall find, sir, you have a friend to honour you.

 Val. I thank you, sir.

 Evan. Pray, captain, tell the king,
They that are sad on earth in heaven shall sing. [*Exeunt.*

ACT V.

SCENE I.—*An apartment in the Monastery.*

Enter MARCO *and* RUGIO.

Rug. Have you writ to the captain of the castle?
Marco. Yes, and charg'd him,
Upon his soul's health, that he be not cruel;
Told him Valerio's worth among the people,
And how it must be punish'd in posterity,
Though he scape now.
Rug. But will not he, friar Marco,
Betray this to the king?
Marco. Though he be stubborn,
And of a rugged nature, yet he is honest,
And honours much Valerio.
Rug. How does Alphonso?
For now, methinks, my heart is light again,
And pale fear fled.
Marco. He is as well as I am;
The rogue, against his will, has sav'd his life:
A desperate poison has re-cur'd the prince.
Rug. To me 'tis most miraculous.
Marco. To me too,
Till I consider why it should do so;
And now I have found it a most excellent physic:
It wrought upon the dull, cold, misty parts
That clogg'd his soul, (which was another poison,
A desperate too,) and found such matter there,
And such abundance also to resist it,
And wear away the dangerous heat it brought with it,
The pure blood and the spirits scap'd untainted.
Rug. 'Twas Heaven's high hand, none of Sorano's pity.
Marco. Most certain 'twas; had the malicious villain
Given him a cooling poison, he had paid him.
Rug. The captain of the castle!

Enter CASTRUCCIO.

Marco. Oh, you are welcome.
How does your prisoner?
    Cast. He must go for dead;
But, when I do a deed of so much villany,
I'll have my skin pull'd o'er mine ears, my lord:
Though I am the king's, I am none of his abuses.
How does your royal charge? that I might see once!
    Marco. I pray, see now; you are a trusty gentleman.

Enter ALPHONSO *and* Friars.

    Alph. Good fathers, I thank Heaven, I feel no sickness——
    Cast. He speaks again!
    Alph. Nothing that bars the free use of my spirit:
Methinks the air is sweet to me, and company
A thing I covet now.—Castruccio!
    Cast. Sir?—
He speaks and knows! For Heaven-sake, break my pate, lord,
That I may be sure I sleep not!
    Alph. Thou wert honest,
Ever among the rank of good men counted.
I have been absent long out of the world;
A dream I have liv'd: how does it look, Castruccio?
What wonders are abroad?
    Cast. I fling off duty
To your dead brother (for he is dead in goodness),
And to the living hope of brave Alphonso,
The noble heir of nature and of honour,
I fasten my allegiance.
    Marco. Softly, captain;
We dare not trust the air with this blest secret.—
Good sir, be close again: Heaven has restor'd you,
And by miraculous means, to your fair health,
And made the instrument your enemies' malice,
Which does prognosticate your noble fortune;
Let not our careless joy lose you again, sir,
Help to deliver you to a further danger:
I pray you, pass in, and rest a while forgotten;

For, if your brother come to know you are well again,
And ready to inherit, as your right,
Before we have strength enough to assure your life,
What will become of you? and what shall we
Deserve, in all opinions that are honest,
For our loss of judgment, care, and loyalty?

Rug. Dear sir, pass in. Heaven has begun the work,
And blest us all; let our endeavours follow,
To preserve this blessing to our timely uses [8],
And bring it to the noble end we aim at:
Let our cares work now, and our eyes pick out
An hour to shew you safely to your subjects,
A secure hour.

Alph. I am counsell'd: ye are faithful.

Cast. Which hour shall not be long, as we shall handle it.
Once more, the tender of my duty.

Alph. Thank you.

Cast. Keep you the monastery.

Rug. Strong enough, I'll warrant you.

[*Exeunt, on one side,* ALPH., MARCO, RUG., *and* Friars; *on the other,* CASTRUCCIO.

SCENE II.—*The court of the Palace.*

Enter TONY *and* PODRAMO.

Pod. Who are all these that crowd about the court, fool? Those strange new faces?

Tony. They are suitors, coxcomb,
Dainty fine suitors to the widow-lady.
Thou hadst best make one of 'em; thou wilt be hang'd as
    handsomely
At the month's end, and with as much joy follow'd
(An't were to-morrow), as many mourning bawds for thee,
And holy nuns, whose vestal fire ne'er vanishes,
In sackcloth smocks, as if thou wert heir apparent
To all the impious suburbs and the sink-holes.

Pod. Out, you base rogue!

---

[8] *uses*] Weber chose to print "issues".

Tony. Why dost abuse thyself?
Thou art to blame; I take thee for a gentleman.
But why does not thy lord and master marry her?
Pod. Why, she is his sister.
Tony. 'Tis the better, fool;
He may make bold with his own flesh and blood,
For, o' my conscience, there's none else will trust him:
Then he may pleasure the king at a dead pinch too,
Without a Mephistophilus[t], such as thou art,
And engross the royal disease like a true subject.
Pod. Thou wilt be whipp'd.
Tony. I am sure thou wilt be hang'd;
I have lost a ducat else, which I would be loath
To venture without certainty. They appear.
   [*Lawyer, Physician, Captain,* and Cutpurse *pass over the stage.*
Pod. Why, these are rascals.
Tony. They were meant to be so:
Does thy master deserve better kindred?
Pod. There's an old lawyer,
Trimm'd up like a galley-foist[u]; what would he do with her?
Tony. As usurers do with their gold; he would look on her,
And read her over once a-day, like a hard report,
Feed his dull eye, and keep his fingers itching:
For any thing else, she may appeal to a parliament;
Sub-pœnas and *posteas*[v] have spoil'd his codpiece.
There's a physician too, older than he,
A[w] Galen *gallinaceus,* but he has lost his spurs;
He would be nibbling too.
Pod. I mark'd the man,
If he be a man.

---

[t] *Mephistophilus*] "A familiar spirit attending upon Doctor Faustus." SYMPSON. Marlowe's *Faustus* had rendered this name familiar to all.

[u] *a galley-foist*] "i. e. a vessel [properly a long barge with oars] dressed out and decorated, The city-barge, which was used upon the Lord-Mayor's day, when he was sworn into his office at Westminster, used to be called the *galley-foist.*" REED. Perhaps I need hardly add that here the allusion is not to the Lord Mayor's barge, which is always spoken of as "THE galley-foist": see vol. ii 221.

[v] *posteas*] Both the folios " *Post* Kaes ".

[w] *A*] Mason's correction.—Both the folios " And ".

Tony. H'as much ado to be so;
Cerecloths and syrups glew him close together,
He would fall a-pieces else: mending of she-patients,
And then trying whether they be right or no
In his own person (there's the honest care on 't),
Has mollified the man. If he do marry her,
And come but to warm him well at Cupid's bonfire,
He will bulge so subtilly and suddenly,
You may snatch him up by parcels, like a sea-wreck.
Will your worship go, and look upon the rest, sir,
And hear what they can say for themselves?
   Pod. I'll follow thee.   [*Exeunt.*

SCENE III.—*The Hall in the Palace.*

Enter CAMILLO, MENALLO, CLEANTHES, *and* CASTRUCCIO.

Cam. You tell us wonders.
Cast. But I tell you truths;
They are both well.
Men. Why are not we in arms, then?
And all the island given to know [x]——
Cast. Discreetly
And privately it must be done; 'twill miss else,
And prove our ruins. Most of the noble citizens
Know it by me, and stay the hour to attend it.
Prepare your hearts and friends, let theirs be right too,
And keep about the king, to avoid suspicion.
When you shall hear the castle-bell, take courage,
And stand like men. Away! the king is coming.
            [*Exeunt all except* CASTRUCCIO.

Enter FREDERICK *and* SORANO.

Fred. Now, captain, what have you done with your
    prisoner?
Cast. He is dead, sir, and his body flung i' the sea,
To feed the fishes; 'twas your will, I take it;

---

[x] *And all the island given to know*] "As the scene is throughout at *Naples*, this expression, if not a corruption, is a flagrant oversight." SYMPSON.

I did it from a strong commission,
And stood not to capitulate.
  Fred. 'Tis well done,
And I shall love you for your faith. What anger
Or sorrow did he utter at his end?
  Cast. Faith, little, sir, that I gave any ear to:
He would have spoke, but I had no commission
To argue with him, so I flung him off.
His lady would have seen; but I lock'd her up,
For fear her woman's tears should hinder us.
  Fred. 'Twas trusty still.—I wonder, my Sorano,
We hear not from the monastery: I believe
They gave it not, or else it wrought not fully.
  Cast. Did you name the monastery?
  Fred. Yes, I did, captain.
  Cast. I saw the friar this morning, and Lord Rugio,
Bitterly weeping, and wringing of their hands;
And all the holy men hung down their heads.
  Sor. 'Tis done, I'll warrant you.
  Cast. I ask'd the reason.
  Fred. What answer hadst thou?
  Cast. This in few words, sir,—
Your brother's dead; this morning he deceas'd.
I was your servant, and I wept not, sir;
I knew 'twas for your good.
  Fred. It shall be for thine too,
Captain; indeed it shall.—Oh, my Sorano,
Now we shall live!
  Sor. Ay, now there's none to trouble you.
  Fred. Captain, bring out the woman; and give way
To any suitor that shall come to marry her,
Of what degree soever.
  Cast. It shall be done, sir.   [*Exit* CASTRUCCIO.
  Fred. Oh, let me have a lusty banquet after it!
I will be high and merry.
  Sor. There be some lords
That I could counsel you to fling from court, sir;
They pry into our actions. They are such
The foolish people call their country's honours,

Honest brave things, and style them with such titles,
As if they were the patterns of the kingdom;
Which makes them proud, and prone to look into us,
And talk at random of our actions.
They should be yours, lovers of your commands ʸ,
And followers of your will, bridles and curbs
To the hard-headed commons that malign us.

  Re-enter CAMILLO, MENALLO, CLEANTHES, *and* TONY.

They come here to do honour to my sister,
To laugh at your severity, and fright us :
If they had power, what would these men do!
Do you hear, sir, how privily they whisper?
 Fred. I shall silence 'em,
And to their shames, within this week, Sorano ;
In the mean time, have patience.
 Sor. How they leer ᶻ,
And look upon me as I were a monster!
And talk and jeer!—How I shall pull your plumes, lords,
How I shall humble ye within these two days!
Your great names, nor your country, cannot save ye. [*Aside.*

  Re-enter CASTRUCCIO *with* EVANTHE.
 Fred. Let in the suitors.   [*Exit* CASTRUCCIO.
     Yet submit, I'll pardon you :
You are half-undone already ; do not wind
My anger to that height, it may consume you,
And utterly destroy thee, fair Evanthe :
Yet I have mercy.
 Evan. Use it to your bawds ;
To me use cruelty, it best becomes you,
And shews more kingly : I contemn your mercy !
It is a cozening and a bawdy mercy.
Can any thing be hop'd for, to relieve me?
Or is it fit I thank you for a pity,
When you have kill'd my lord?

 ʸ *They should be yours, lovers of your commands*] The first folio " *They should be* your *lovers of your commands*".—The second folio " *They should be lovers of your commands*".—Sympson printed silently " *They should be lovers*, sir, *of your commands*"; and so his successors.

 ᶻ *leer*] The correction of the Editors of 1778.—The folios "jeere" and "joer"; and so Sympson.

Enter Lawyer, Physician, Captain, *and* Cutpurse.

Fred. Who will have her?
Evan. My tears are gone,
My tears of love to[z] my dear Valerio;
But I have fill'd mine eyes again with anger;
Oh, were it but so powerful to consume you!
My tongue with curses I have arm'd against you
(With maiden curses, that Heaven crowns with horrors),
My heart set round with hate against thy tyranny.
Oh, would my hands could hold the fire of heaven,
Wrapt in the thunder that the gods revenge with,
That, like stern Justice, I might fling it on thee!
Thou art a king of monsters, not of men,
And shortly thou wilt turn this land to devils.
  Fred. I'll make you one first, and a wretched devil.—
Come, who will have her?
  Law. I, an't like your majesty. I am a lawyer;
I can make her a jointure of any man's land in Naples;—
And she shall keep it too; I have a trick for it.
  Tony. Canst thou make her a jointure of thine honesty,
Or thy ability, thou lewd abridgment?
Those are nonsuited and flung o'er the bar.
  Phy. An't please your majesty to give me leave,
I dare accept her; and though old I seem, lady,
Like Æson, by my art I can renew
Youth and ability.
  Tony. In a powdering-tub
Stew thyself tender again, like a cock-chicken;
The broth may be good, but the flesh is not fit for dogs, sure.
  Capt. Lady, take me, and I'll maintain thine honour:
I am a poor captain, as poor people call me,
Very poor people; for my soldiers, they
Are quarter'd in the outsides of the city,
Men of ability to make good a highway;
We have but two grand enemies that oppose us,
The Don Gout and the gallows.
  Tony. I believe you;

---

[z] *to*] The modern editors silently print "unto".

And both these you will bind her for a jointure.—
Now, Signior Firk [a] !

Cut. Madam, take me, and be wise :
I am rich and nimble, and those are rare in one man ;
Every man's pocket is my treasury,
And no man wears a suit but fits me neatly.
Clothes you shall have, and wear the purest linen,—
I have a tribute out of every shop, lady ;
Meat you shall eat,—I have my caters [b] out too,—
The best and lustiest ; and drink good wine, good lady,
Good quickening wine, wine that will make you caper;
And, at the worst——

Tony. It is but capering short, sir.
You seldom stay for agues or for surfeits ;
A shaking fit of a whip sometimes o'ertakes you.
Marry, you die most commonly of chokings ;
Obstructions of the halter are your ends ever :
Pray, leave your horn and your knife [c] for her to live on.

Evan. Poor wretched people, why do you wrong yourselves ?
Though I fear'd death, I should fear you ten times more ;
You are every one a new death, and an odious :
The earth will purify corrupted bodies ;
You'll make us worse, and stink eternally.
Go home, go home, and get good nurses for you ;
Dream not of wives.

Fred. You shall have one of 'em,
If they dare venture for you.

Evan. They are dead already,
Crawling diseases that must creep into
The next grave they find open : are these fit husbands
For her you have lov'd, sir ? though you hate me now,

---

[a] *Firk*] Equivalent here to Filch,—Cutpurse. But see note, vol. iv. 216.

[b] *caters*] "i. e. caterers." WEBER. As frequently before, vol. i. 122, &c.— The Editors of 1778 printed " cat'rers ".

[c] *your horn and your knife*] Pick-pockets were said to place a case, or thimble, of horn on their thumbs, to support the edge of the knife in the act of cutting purses : see Gifford's ed. of Jonson's *Works*, iv. 413, and my ed. of Middleton's *Works*, ii. 536.

And hate me mortally, as I hate you,
Your nobleness (in that you have done otherwise,
And nam'd Evanthe once as your poor mistress)
Might offer worthier choice.
　Fred. Speak, who dare take her
For one month, and then die?
　Phy. Die, sir!
　Fred. Ay, die, sir;
That's the condition.
　Phy. One month is too little
For me to repent in for my former pleasure,
[And] to go still on [d], unless I were sure she would kill me,
And kill me delicately before my day.
Make it up a year; for by that time I must die,
My body will hold out no longer.
　Fred. No, sir;
It must be but a month.
　Law. Then farewell, madam!
This is like to be a great year of dissention
Among good people, and I dare not lose it;
There will be money got.
　Capt. Bless your good ladyship!
There's nothing in the grave but bones and ashes:
In taverns there's good wine, and excellent wenches,
And surgeons while we live.
　Cut. Adieu, sweet lady!
Lay me, when I am dead, near a rich alderman,
I cannot pick his purse: no, I'll no dying;
Though I steal linen, I'll not steal my shrowd yet.
　Law., Phy., Capt., Cut. Send you a happy match! [*Exeunt.*
　Tony. And you all halters!
You have deserv'd 'em richly.—These do all villanies,
And mischiefs of all sorts, yet those they fear not:
To flinch where a fair wench is at the stake!
　Evan. Come, your sentence! let me die. You see, sir,
None of your valiant men dare venture on me;

---

[d] [*And*] *to go still on*, &c.] So Weber,—an insertion recommended also by Heath (*MS. Notes*).—Mason says that we must either suppose the sentence to be imperfect, or read " And *go still on* ".

A month's a dangerous thing. Will you, then, be willing^c
To die at the time prefix'd? that I must know too,
And know it beyond doubt.
    Fred. What if I did, wench?
    Evan. On that condition, if I had it certain,
I would be your any thing, and you should enjoy me:
However in my nature I abhor you,
Yet, as I live, I would be obedient to you:
But, when your time came, how I should rejoice!
How then I should bestir myself to thank you!
To see your throat cut, how my heart would leap, sir!
I would die with you; but first I would so torture you,
And cow you in your end, so despise you,
For a weak and wretched coward you must end, sure!
Still make you fear and shake, despis'd, still laugh at you!
    Fred. Away with her! let her die instantly!

    Enter VALERIO *disguised.*

    Cam. Stay; there's another, and a gentleman;
His habit shews no less. May be, his business
Is for this lady's love.
    Fred. Say why you come, sir,
And what you are.
    Val. I am descended nobly,
A prince by birth, and by my trade a soldier,
A prince's fellow; Abydos brought me forth;
My parents, Duke Agenor and fair Ægla;
My business hither, to renew my love
With a young noble spirit, call'd Valerio:
Our first acquaintance was at sea, in fight

---

    ^c *A month's a dangerous thing. Will you, then, be willing,* &c.] Both the folios have here (what they presently repeat),—
    "*A moneth's a dangerous thing.*
        Enter Valerio disguis'd.
    Fred. Away with her, let her dye instantly.
    Evan. Will you then be willing" &c.
The intermediate lines between " A month's a dangerous thing " and " Away with her! let her die instantly!" having most probably (as Weber remarks) "been crossed out in the prompter's copy, and restored in the first folio, without sufficient attention to accuracy."

Against a Turkish man-of-war, a stout one,
Where lion-like I saw him shew his valour,
And, as he had been made of complete virtue,
Spirit and fire, no dregs of dull earth in him——
   Evan. Thou art a brave gentleman, and bravely speak'st
     him.
   Val. The vessel dancing under him for joy,
And the rough whistling winds becalm'd to view him,
I saw the child of honour, for he was young,
Deal such an alms amongst the spiteful pagans,
(His towering sword flew like an eager falcon,)
And round about his reach invade the Turks;
He had entrench'd himself in his dead quarries[f];
The silver crescents on the tops they carried
Shrank in their heads to see his rage so bloody,
And from his fury suffer'd sad eclipses;
The game of death was never play'd more nobly;
The meagre thief grew wanton in his mischiefs,
And his shrunk hollow eyes smil'd on his ruins.
   Evan. Heaven keep this gentleman from being a suitor,
For I shall ne'er deny him, he's so noble!   [*Aside.*
   Val. But what can last long? Strength and spirit wasted,
And fresh supplies flew on upon this gentleman,
Breathless and weary with oppression,
And almost kill'd with killing. 'Twas my chance,
In a tall[g] ship I had, to view the fight;
I set into him, entertain'd the Turk,
And for an hour gave him so hot a breakfast,
He clapp'd all linen up he had to save him,
And like a lover's thought he fled our fury:
There first I saw the man I lov'd, Valerio;
There was acquainted, there my soul grew to him,
And his to me; we were the twins of friendship.
   Evan. Fortune protect this man, or I shall ruin him!
                                                                [*Aside.*
   Val. I made this voyage to behold my friend,
To warm my love anew at his affection;

            [f] *quarries*] See note, p. 115.
            [g] *tall*] i. e. stout.

But, since I landed, I have heard his fate:
My father's had not been to me more cruel.
I have lamented too, and yet I keep
The treasure of a few tears for you, lady;
For, by description, you were his Evanthe.
 Evan. Can he weep that's a stranger to my story,
And I stand still and look on? Sir, I thank you:
If noble spirits after their departure
Can know, and wish, certain his soul gives thanks too.
There are your tears again; and, when yours fail, sir,
Pray you, call to me, I have some store to lend you.
Your name?
 Val. Urbino.
 Evan. That I may remember,
That little time I have to live, your friendships,
My tongue shall study both.
 Fred. Do you come hither
Only to tell this story, Prince Urbino?
 Val. My business now is, sir, to woo this lady.
 Evan. Blessing defend you! do you know the danger?
 Val. Yes, and I fear it not; danger's my playfellow;
Since I was man, 't has been my best companion.—
I know your doom; 'tis for a month you give her,
And then his life you take that marries her.
 Fred. 'Tis true; nor can your being born a prince,
If you accept the offer, free you from it.
 Val. I not desire it; I have cast[h] the worst,
And even that worst to me is many blessings.
I lov'd my friend, not measur'd out by time,
Nor hir'd by circumstance of place and honour;
But for his wealthy self and worth I lov'd him,
His mind and noble mould he ever mov'd in;
And woo his friend because she was worthy of him,
The only relic that he left behind, sir,
To give his ashes honour.—Lady, take me,
And in me keep Valerio's love alive still.
When I am gone, take those that shall succeed me:

[h] *cast*] i. e. considered.

Heaven must want light, before you want a husband,
To raise up heirs of love and noble memory
To your unfortunate——
   Evan. Am I still hated?
Hast thou no end, oh, fate, of my affliction?
Was I ordain'd to be a common murderess?
And of the best men too? Good sir——
   Val. Peace, sweet!
Look on my hand.   [*Aside to her.*
   Evan. I do accept the gentleman.—
I faint with joy!   [*Aside.*
   Fred. I stop it: none shall have her.
Convey this stranger hence.
   Val. [*throwing off his disguise*] I am no stranger. Hark
       to the bell that rings!   [*Bell rings within.*
Hark, hark, proud Frederick, that was king of mischief!
Hark, thou abhorr'd man! dost thou hear thy sentence?
Does not this bell ring in thine ears thy ruin?
   Fred. What bell is this?
   Cam. The castle-bell. Stand sure, sir,
And move not; if you do, you perish.
   Men. It rings your knell!——Alphonso! King Alphonso!
   All. Alphonso! King Alphonso!
   Fred. I am betray'd!—
Lock fast the palace.
   Cam. We have all the keys, sir,
And no door here shall shut without our licence.
   Cle. Do you shake now, Lord Sorano? no new trick?
Nor speedy poison to prevent this business?
No bawdy meditation now to fly to?
   Fred. Treason, treason, treason!
   Cam. Yes, we hear you,
And we have found the traitor in your shape, sir;
We'll keep him fast too.   [*They seize* FREDERICK.

     Enter ALPHONSO, RUGIO, MARCO, CASTRUCCIO, *and* MARIA,
                             with Guard.

   Fred. Recover'd! then I am gone;
The sun of all my pomp is set and vanish'd.

Alph. Have you not forgot this face of mine, King
 Frederick?
Brother, I am come to see you, and have brought
A banquet, to be merry with your grace:
I pray, sit down, I do beseech your majesty,
And eat, eat freely, sir. Why do you start?
Have you no stomach to the meat I bring you?
Dare you not taste? have you no antidotes?
You need not fear; Sorano's a good apothecary.
Methinks you look not well;—some fresh wine for him,
Some of the same he sent me by Sorano!—
I thank you for't, it sav'd my life, I am bound to you;
But how 'twill work on you——I hope your lordship
Will pledge him too; methinks you look but scurvily,
And would be put into a better colour;
But I have a candied toad for your good lordship.
 Sor. Would I had any thing that would despatch me,
So it were down, and I out of this fear once! [*Aside.*
 Fred. Sir, thus low, as my duty now compels me,
 [*He and* MARIA *kneel.*
I do confess my unbounded sins, my errors,
And feel within my soul the smarts already.
Hide not the noble nature of a brother,
The pity of a friend, from my afflictions;
Let me a while lament my misery,
And cast the load off of my wantonness,
Before I find your fury; then strike home
(I do deserve the deepest blow of Justice);
And then how willingly, oh, death, I'll meet thee!
 Alph. Rise, madam; those sweet tears are potent
 speakers:—
And, brother, live; but in the monastery
Where I liv'd, with the self-same silence too:
I'll teach you to be good against your will, brother:
Your tongue has done much harm; that must be dumb
 now;
The daily pilgrimage to my father's tomb
(Tears, sighs, and groans, you shall wear out your days with,
And true ones too) you shall perform, dear brother;

VOL. IX. C C

Your diet shall be slender to enforce these;
Too light a penance, sir.
   Fred. I do confess it.
   Alph. Sorano, you shall——
   Sor. How he studies for it!
Hanging's the least part of my penance, certain.   [*Aside.*
                                                 [EVANTHE *kneels.*
   Alph. What lady's that that kneels?
   Cast. The chaste Evanthe.
   Alph. Sweet, your petition?
   Evan. 'Tis for this bad man, sir,
Abominable bad, but yet my brother.
   Alph. The bad man shall attend as bad a master,
And both shall be confin'd within the monastery:
His rank flesh shall be pull'd with daily fasting;
But once a-week he shall smell meat, he will surfeit else;
And his immodest mind compell'd to prayer;
On the bare boards he shall lie, to remember
The wantonness he did commit in beds;
And drink fair water; that will ne'er inflame him:
He sav'd my life, though he purpos'd to destroy me,
For which I'll save his, though I make it miserable.—
Madam, at court I shall desire your company;   [*To* MARIA.
You are wise and virtuous; when you please to visit
My brother Frederick, you shall have our licence.—
My dear best friend Valerio!
   Val. Save Alphonso!
   All. Long live Alphonso, king of us and Naples!
   Alph. Is this the lady that the wonder goes on?
Honour'd sweet maid!—Here, take her, my Valerio;
The king now gives her, she is thine own without fear.—
Brother, have you so much provision that is good,
Not season'd by Sorano and his cooks,
That we may venture on with honest safety,
We and our friends?
   Fred. All that I have is yours, sir.
   Alph. Come, then; let's in, and end this nuptial;
Then to our coronation with all speed.—
My virtuous maid, this day I'll be your bride-man,

And see you bedded to your own desires too.—
Beshrew me, lords, who is not merry hates me!
Only Sorano shall not bear my cup.
Come, now forget old pains and injuries,
As I must do, and drown all in fair healths:
That kingdom's blessèd, where the king begins
His true love first, for there all loves are twins. [*Exeunt.*

EPILOGUE.

WE have your favours, gentlemen, and you
Have our endeavours (dear friends, grudge not now).
There's none of you, but when you please can sell
Many a lame horse, and many a fair tale tell;
Can put off many a maid unto a friend,
That was not so since the action at Mile-end[1]:
Ours is a virgin yet, and they that love
Untainted flesh, we hope our friends will prove.

[1] *the action at Mile-end*] " At Mile-end the train-bands were frequently exercised, and of course mock-fights were exhibited there. The action here referred to is perhaps the same with the one alluded to in *Monsieur Thomas* (vol. vii. 365) and *The Knight of the Burning Pestle* (vol. ii. 156)." WEBER.

RULE A WIFE AND HAVE A WIFE.

Rvle a Wife and have a Wife. A Comœdy. Acted by his Majesties Servants. Written by John Fletcher Gent. Oxford, Printed by Leonard Lichfield Printer to the University Anno 1640, 4to.

In the folio 1679.

This comedy, wholly from the pen of Fletcher, was licensed Oct. 19, 1624, by Sir Henry Herbert, among whose memoranda we also find the following notices concerning it;

"Upon All-hollows night, 1624, the king beinge at Roiston, no play.

"The night after, my Lord Chamberlin had *Rule a Wife and Have a Wife* for the ladys, by the kings company.

"Upon St. Steevens night, the prince only being there, *Rule a Wife and Have a Wife*, by the kings company. Att Whitehall."

Malone's *Shakespeare* (by Boswell), iii. 226, 228.

The under-plot of Perez and Estifania is derived from the eleventh of Cervantes' *Novelas Exemplares*, entitled *El Casamiento Engañoso*: Weber's analysis of that tale is now (with very considerable alterations) subjoined.

"The alferez[a] Campuzano one morning issued from the Hospital of the Resurrection in Valladolid. His yellow countenance, and the thinness of his legs, shewed that he had been long under the care of the surgeon. He was met by his friend the licentiate Peralta, who, astonished at his appearance, and wondering that he had not joined the army in Flanders, expressed a wish to be informed how he had been reduced to such a condition. Campuzano said that he owed it to a woman whom he had married; and related the following adventures.—Being one day in company with the captain Pedro de Herrera, two women entered the room, one of whom, taking the captain aside, requested him to carry letters to a relation in Flanders. The alferez addressed himself to the other lady, whose face was partly concealed by a veil, which he in vain urged her to withdraw; and his curiosity was the more inflamed by her displaying a very white hand adorned with sparkling rings. He was, at that time, in splendid attire, and had a great chain about his neck (which Peralta recollected to have seen him wear); and he thought it impossible that any woman could resist his good looks and magnificent dress. The lady, however, was deaf to all his entreaties to remove the veil: but at last she directed him to send a servant after her to note her

---

[a] *alferez*] i. e. ensign.

place of abode, and then to visit her himself, promising that she would receive him courteously, and that their acquaintance, if they happened to like each other, should terminate in a closer intimacy. He readily obeyed her; and, on going to her house next day, he found that she was about thirty, of considerable though not superlative beauty. After several visits, the fair one, whose name was Donna Estefania de Caicedo, consented to share her large possessions with him. They were accordingly married in the presence of two friends of Campuzano, and a youth whom Estefania stated to be her cousin. The goods of the husband, consisting of his great chain and other articles, were transferred to the dwelling of the lady, to whom he also paid a sum of 400 reals, for the expences of the house. After some days had passed in every kind of luxury, one morning, before the pair had risen, they heard a loud knocking, and a servant girl informed them that Donna Clementa Bueso, accompanied by Don Lope Melendez de Almendarez, was at the door. Estefania had scarcely time to desire her husband not to be disturbed by any thing that should occur, and to maintain an obstinate silence, when her mistress entered, who was not a little surprised to find her bed occupied. The poor gulled Alferez, having put on his clothes, was led into another room by Estefania, who assured him that the whole was a mere deception, to make Don Lope believe that the house belonged to Donna Clementa, in order to induce him to espouse her; and that, after their marriage, every circumstance would be discovered, and the mansion restored to herself, the rightful owner. The couple then retired to a mean house in the neighbourhood, whither the trunk of the alferez was carried, and where, for six days, he continually reproached his wife with the absurd promise she had made to her friend. One morning, in the absence of Estefania, the hostess questioned him concerning his frequent quarrels with his spouse; and having heard the tale of the marriage, and the subsequent adventures, she (after some hesitation) told him that Donna Clementa was the real owner of the mansion, and that Estefania had no possessions except the clothes upon her back; adding, that she could only excuse her when she reflected what an excellent husband had been obtained by the trick. At this intelligence, Campuzano was on the point of desperation. He immediately took his sword, and went in search of his wife, but was unable to find her; and a visit to the mansion of Donna Clementa only confirmed the relation of the hostess. On returning to his lodgings, he found that Estefania had been there, and that, hearing of the disclosure made to him by the hostess, and of his rage in consequence, she had opened the trunk, rifled it, and left the house.—Here the licentiate interrupted the narrative of his friend, and expatiated upon the loss he had sustained, particularly that of the large golden chain, which he supposed to be worth two hundred ducats. But Campuzano said that the chain and his other trinkets were no more than excellent counterfeits, and that the value of all he possessed did not exceed ten or twelve escudoes.—He discovered that the pretended cousin, who had acted as witness at the marriage, was the lover of his spouse, whom he immediately abandoned to her fate. A disease, which he owed to his unfortunate marriage, soon attacked him in all its virulence; and, as he had no means of procuring the proper remedies elsewhere, he had been obliged to enter the hospital."—" The rest of the tale," adds Weber, " is merely an introduction to the twelfth and most admirable of Cervantes's novels, —a conversation Campuzano is supposed to have overheard between Berganza and Cipion, two of the hospital dogs."

Till the theatres were closed by authority, this comedy was doubtless popular. A droll taken from it, and called *An Equall Match*, which was acted during the suppression of play-houses, is extant in Kirkman's collection, *The Wits, or Sport upon Sport, Part First*, 1672, p. 45 (see vol. i. 200 of the present work). On the revival of dramatic entertainments, it again became a favourite; and with some alterations (made when Garrick brought out the play[b] at Drury-lane Theatre in 1759) it still continues to be occasionally performed.

[b] "Though the alteration [of *Rule a Wife and Have a Wife*] has been actually printed with his [Garrick's] name annexed, yet we can no longer ascribe it to him, having seen an express and positive disavowal of it under his hand, in a letter dated Aug. 19, 1776." *Biog. Dram.* ed. 1812.

PROLOGUE.

PLEASURE attend ye! and about ye sit
The springs of mirth, fancy, delight, and wit,
To stir you up! Do not your looks let fall,
Nor to remembrance our late errors call,
Because this day we're Spaniards all again[a],
The story of our play, and our scene Spain:
The errors, too, do not for this cause hate;
Now we present their wit, and not their state.
Nor, ladies, be not angry, if you see
A young fresh beauty, wanton, and too free,
Seek to abuse her husband; still 'tis Spain;
No such gross errors in your kingdom reign;
You're vestals all[b]; and, though we blow the fire,
We seldom make it flame up to desire.

[a] *Nor to remembrance our late errors call, Because this day we're Spaniards all again*, &c.] The allusion here is doubtless to Middleton's *Game at Chess*, which had been produced at the Globe very shortly before the 12th August, 1624. In that remarkable drama Middleton ventured to bring upon the stage both the English and the Spanish court (a great portion of the satire being aimed at Gondomar). As might be expected, the play proved highly attractive; and it had been already performed "for nine days together", when, in consequence of a complaint made by the Spanish ambassador to King James, it was suppressed, and the author and actors were cited before the Privy Council. We find, however, that eventually no punishment was inflicted either on Middleton or on the actors, except that the latter were for a time interdicted from performing that or any other play; and the lenity shown towards them is probably to be attributed to the circumstance that *A Game at Chess* had been produced under the authority of the Master of the Revels. See Middleton's *Works*, vol. iv. ed. Dyce, and the Account of the author prefixed to vol. i. of that collection.

[b] *You're vestals all*, &c.] So Seward, at Sympson's suggestion; and so his successors.—Both the old eds. "W'are".—Among Heath's *MS. Notes* I find the following defence of the old reading. "The same persons who blow the fire and make it flame are most certainly the *Vestals*, who had anciently no other

Take no example neither to begin,
For some by precedent delight to sin;
Nor blame the poet if he slip^c aside
Sometimes lasciviously, if not too wide;
But hold your fans close, and then smile at ease:
A cruel scene did never lady please.
Nor, gentlemen, pray, be not you displeas'd,
Though we present some men fool'd, some diseas'd,
Some drunk, some mad: we mean not you, you're free;
We tax no farther than our comedy;
You are our friends; sit noble, then, and see.

employment than to tend and take care of the sacred fire. The sense is, We players pretty nearly resemble the ancient Vestals; we keep the fire of love alive, and gently blow it, for such is for the most part the tendency of the pieces we represent; but we seldom make it flame up as high as desire; our action has very rarely so dangerous an effect as that upon the audience." In spite of these ingenious remarks, I agree with Seward that the context requires "You're." To suppose that the poet would make "these harlotry players" call themselves "*vestals*" is surely ridiculous.

^c *slip*] Weber chose to print " slipt ".

DRAMATIS PERSONÆ.

DUKE of Medina.
JUAN DE CASTRO, a colonel.
SANCHIO,
ALONZO,   } Captains.
MICHAEL PEREZ,[c]
LEON, brother to ALTEA.
CACAFOGO, a usurer.
LORENZO, Coachman, Boy, and other Servants.

MARGARITA, a rich heiress.
ALTEA,
ESTEFANIA,   } her attendants.
Other Ladies,
CLARA.
Three old Ladies.
Old woman.
Two Maids.

SCENE,—*Seville*[d], *and a Country-house near it.*

---

[c] *Michael Perez*] Is called in the modern editions " *the Copper Captain* ". The old eds. do not give the *Dram. Pers.*

[d] *Seville*] See the last scene of the first act, p. 409.

RULE A WIFE AND HAVE A WIFE.

ACT I.

SCENE I.—*Seville. A room in a lodging-house.*

Enter JUAN *and* PEREZ.

Perez. Are your companies full, colonel?
Juan. No, not yet, sir;
Nor will not be this month yet, as I reckon.
How rises your command?
Perez. We pick up still,
And, as our moneys hold out, we have men come:
About that time I think we shall be full too.
Many young gallants go.
Juan. And unexperienc'd:
The wars are dainty dreams to young hot spirits;
Time and experience will allay those visions.
We have strange things to fill our numbers [a]:
There's one Don Leon, a strange [b] goodly fellow,
Recommended to me from some noble friends,
For my alferez [c]: had you but seen his person,
And what a giant's promise it protesteth!
Perez. I have heard of him, and that he hath serv'd before too.
Juan. But no harm done, nor never meant, Don Michael,

---

[a] *numbers*] Seward silently printed "*numbers* up".
[b] *strange*] "i. e. uncommonly." MASON.—Theobald proposed to read "strong", which was adopted by the Editors of 1778.
[c] *alferez*] "i. e. ensign. *Spanish*." WEBER.

That came to my ears yet. Ask him a question,
He blushes like a girl, and answers little,
To the point less; he wears a sword, a good one,
And good clothes too; he is whole-skinn'd, has no hurt yet;
Good promising hopes; I never yet heard certainly
Of any gentleman that saw him angry.

Perez. Preserve him; he'll conclude a peace, if need be.
Many as strong [c] as he will go along with us,
That swear as valiantly as heart can wish,
Their mouths charg'd with six oaths at once, and whole ones,
That make the drunken Dutch creep into mole-hills.

Juan. 'Tis true, such we must look for. But, Michael Perez,
When heard you of Donna Margarita, the great heiress?

Perez. I hear every hour of her, though I never saw her;
She is the main discourse. Noble Don Juan de Castro,
How happy were that man could catch this wench up,
And live at ease! she is fair, and young, and wealthy,
Infinite wealthy, and as gracious too
In all her entertainments, as men report.

Juan. But she is proud, sir; that I know for certain;
And that comes seldom without wantonness:
He that shall marry her must have a rare hand.

Perez. Would I were married! I would find that wisdom,
With a light rein to rule my wife: if ever woman
Of the most subtlest [d] mould went beyond me,
I would give the boys leave to hoot me out o' the parish.

Enter Servant.

Serv. Sir, there be two gentlewomen attend to speak with you.

Juan. Wait on 'em in.

Perez. Are they two handsome women?

Serv. They seem so, very handsome; but they are veil'd, sir.

[c] *strong*] "Used here ironically." ED. 1778.—Theobald proposed to read "strange".—Seward printed "stout".

[d] *subtlest*] "So the quarto reads, according to the phraseology of the age. The modern editors read, with the folio 1679, 'subtile'." WEBER.

Perez. Thou putt'st sugar in my mouth; how it melts
  with me!
I love a sweet young wench.
  Juan. Wait on them in, I say.   [*Exit* Servant.
  Perez. Don Juan!
  Juan. How you itch, Michael! how you burnish!
Will not this soldier's heat out of your bones yet?
Do your eyes glow now?
  Perez. There be two.
  Juan. Say honest;
What shame have you, then^e!
  Perez. I would fain see that:
I have been in the Indies twice, and have seen strange things;
But, two honest women!——one I read of once.
  Juan. Prithee, be modest.
  Perez. I'll be any thing.

  Re-enter Servant, *with* CLARA *and* ESTEFANIA *veiled.*

  Juan. You are welcome, ladies.
  Perez. Both hooded! I like 'em well though.
They come not for advice in law, sure, hither:
May be they would learn to raise the pike; I am for 'em.
They are very modest; 'tis a fine preludium.   [*Aside.*
  Juan. With me, or with this gentleman, would you speak,
     lady?
  Clara. With you, sir, as I guess; Juan de Castro.
                                                    [*Unveils.*
  Perez. Her curtain opens; she is a pretty gentlewoman.
                                                    [*Aside.*
  Juan. I am the man, and shall be bound to fortune,
I may do any service to your beauties.
  Clara. Captain, I hear you are marching down to Flanders,
To serve the Catholic king.
  Juan. I am, sweet lady.
  Clara. I have a kinsman, and a noble friend,
Employ'd in those wars; may be, sir, you know him;

---

^e *What shame have you, then!*] "The meaning, as the last editors [of 1778] explain it, is probably 'how will you be *disgraced*, if you offer gallantry where it will not be accepted!'" WEBER. Theobald proposed to read "*What share*", &c.

Don Campuzano[f], captain of carbines,
To whom I would request your nobleness
To give this poor remembrance.   [*Gives a letter.*
  Juan. I shall do it;
I know the gentleman, a most worthy captain.
  Clara. Something in private.
  Juan. Step aside; I'll serve thee. [*Exeunt* JUAN *and* CLARA.
  Perez. Prithee, let me see thy face.
  Estef. Sir, you must pardon me:
Women of our sort, that maintain fair memories[g],
And keep suspect off from their chastities,
Had need wear thicker veils.
  Perez. I am no blaster of a lady's beauty,
Nor bold intruder on her special favours;
I know how tender reputation is,
And with what guards it ought to be preserv'd, lady:
You may to me.
  Estef. You must excuse me, signior;
I come not here to sell myself.
  Perez. As I am a gentleman!
By the honour of a soldier!
  Estef. I believe you;
I pray you, be civil; I believe you would see me,
And, when you have seen me, I believe you will like me;
But in a strange place, to a stranger too,
As if I came on purpose to betray you!
Indeed, I will not.
  Perez. I shall love you dearly;
And 'tis a sin to fling away affection:
I have no mistress, no desire to honour
Any but you.—Will not this oyster open?—   [*Aside.*
I know not, you have struck me with your modesty—
She will draw, sure [*Aside.*]—so deep, and taken from me
All the desire I might bestow on others——
Quickly, before they come!
  Estef. Indeed, I dare not:
But, since I see you are so desirous, sir,

---

  [f] *Campuzano*] "In the novel of Cervantes this is the name of the person who answers to the Michael Perez of the play." WEBER. See p. 391.
  [g] *memories*] i. e. reputations.

To view a poor face that can merit nothing
But your repentance——
　Perez. It must needs be excellent.
　Estef. And with what honesty you ask it of me;
When I am gone let your man follow me,
And view what house I enter; thither come;
For there I dare be bold to appear open,
And, as I like your virtuous carriage then,
I shall be able to give welcome to you.

　　　　　　Re-enter JUAN *and* CLARA.
She hath done her business; I must take my leave, sir.
　Perez. I'll kiss your fair white hand, and thank you, lady:
My man shall wait, and I shall be your servant.—
Sirrah, come near; hark.　　　　　[*Whispers* Servant.
　Serv. I shall do it faithfully.　　　　　[*Exit.*
　Juan. You will command me no more services?
　Clara. To be careful of your noble health, dear sir,
That I may ever honour you.
　Juan. I thank you,
And kiss your hands.—Wait on the ladies down there!
　　　[*To* Servants *within.*—*Exeunt* CLARA *and* ESTEFANIA.
　Perez. You had the honour to see the face that came to you.
　Juan. And 'twas a fair one: what was yours, Don Michael?
　Perez. Mine was i' th' eclipse, and had a cloud drawn
　　　over it;
But I believe well, and I hope, 'tis handsome:
She had a hand would stir a holy hermit.
　Juan. You know none of 'em?
　Perez. No.
　Juan. Then I do, captain;
But I'll say nothing till I see the proof on 't.—
Sit close, Don Perez, or your worship's caught:
I fear a fly[h].　　　　　　　　　　　[*Aside.*

[h] *I fear a fly*] " Seward is right in supposing that this is an allusion to fishing [with flies]; which is confirmed by the preceding line, and by a passage in the 2d act [4th scene], where Estefania says,

　　　'He is mine own, I have him:
　　　I told thee what would tickle him like a trout;
　　　And as I cast it, so I caught him daintily', &c. " MASON.

Perez. Were those she brought love-letters?

Juan. A packet to a kinsman now in Flanders. Yours was very modest, methought.

Perez. Some young unmanag'd thing;
But I may live to see——

Juan. 'Tis worth experience.

Let's walk abroad, and view our companies. [*Exeunt.*

SCENE II.—*A street.*

Enter SANCHIO *and* ALONZO.

Sanc. What, are you for the wars, Alonzo?

Alon. It may be ay,
It may be no; e'en as the humour takes me.
If I find peace amongst the female creatures,
And easy entertainment, I'll stay at home;
I am not so far oblig'd yet to long marches
And mouldy biscuits, to run mad for honour.
When you are all gone, I have my choice before me.

Sanc. Of which hospital thou wilt sweat in. Wilt thou never leave whoring?

Alon. There is less danger in't than gunning, Sanchio:
Though we be shot sometimes, the shot's not mortal;
Besides, it breaks no limbs.

Sanc. But it disables 'em:
Dost thou see how thou pullest thy legs after thee,
As they hung by points[h]?

Alon. Better to pull 'em thus, than walk on wooden ones;
Serve bravely for a billet to support me.

Sanc. Fie, fie! 'tis base.

Alon. Dost thou count it base to suffer?
Suffer abundantly? 'tis the crown of honour.
You think it nothing to lie twenty days
Under a surgeon's hands, that has no mercy.

Sanc. As thou hast done, I am sure. But I perceive now

[h] *points*] See note, vol. ii. 197.

Why you desire to stay; the orient heiress,
The Margarita, sir[i]!
Alon. I would I had her!
Sanc. They say she will marry.
Alon. Yes, I think she will.
Sanc. And marry suddenly, as report goes, too:
She fears her youth will not hold out, Alonzo.
Alon. I would I had the sheathing on 't!
Sanc. They say too
She has a greedy eye, that must be fed
With more than one man's meat.
Alon. Would she were mine!
I would cater for her well enough. But, Sanchio,
There be too many great men that adore her;
Princes, and princes' fellows, that claim privilege.
Sanc. Yet those stand off i' the way of marriage:
To be tied to a man's pleasure is a second labour[j].
Alon. She has bought a brave house here in town.
Sanc. I have heard so.
Alon. If she convert it now to pious uses,
And bid poor gentlemen welcome!
Sanc. When comes she to it?
Alon. Within these two days; she is in the country yet,
And keeps the noblest house!
Sanc. Then there's some hope of her.
Wilt thou go my way?
Alon. No, no, I must leave you,
And repair to an old gentlewoman that
Has credit with her, that can speak a good word.
Sanc. Send thee good fortune! but make thy body sound
  first.
Alon. I am a soldier, and too sound a body
Becomes me not. Farewell, Sanchio. [*Exeunt severally.*

---

[i] *the orient heiress,*
The Margarita, sir] " He calls her *orient* in allusion to her name,—*Margarita* being the Spanish (Latin, and Italian) for a pearl: the same allusion occurs in act iii. sc. 3". WEBER (the note altered).

[j] *To be tied to a man's pleasure is a second labour*] " To obtain a man's pleasure, is the first labour; to be tied to it, a second. This appears to be Sanchio's meaning." MASON.

SCENE III.—*Another street; before the house of* MARGARITA.

Enter Servant[k].

Serv. 'Tis this or that house, or I have lost my aim;
They are both fair buildings. She walk'd plaguy fast;
And hereabouts I lost her.

Enter ESTEFANIA.

Stay; that's she,
'Tis very she. She makes me a low court'sy.
Let me note the place; the street I well remember.
[*Exit* ESTEFANIA *into the house of* MARGARITA.
She is in again. Certain some noble lady:
How happy should I be if she love my master!
A wondrous goodly house; here are brave lodgings,
And I shall sleep now like an emperor,
And eat abundantly: I thank my fortune.
I'll back with speed, and bring him happy tidings. [*Exit.*

SCENE IV.—*The Country.*—*Before the house of*
MARGARITA.

Enter three old Ladies.

First Lady. What should it mean, that in such haste we are sent for?

Sec. Lady. Belike the Lady Margaret has some business
She would break to us in private.

Third Lady. It should seem so.
'Tis a good lady, and a wise young lady.

Sec. Lady. And virtuous enough too, I warrant you,
For a young woman of her years: 'tis pity
To load her tender age with too much virtue.

---

[k] *Servant*] The old eds. add "*of Michael Perez*", a piece of information quite unnecessary for those who have read the first scene of the play.

Third Lady. 'Tis more sometimes than we can well away with¹.

Enter ALTEA.

Altea. Good morrow, ladies.
All. Morrow, my good madam.
First Lady. How does the sweet young beauty, Lady Margaret?
Sec. Lady. Has she slept well after her walk last night?
First Lady. Are her dreams gentle to her mind?
Altea. All's well;
She's very well: she sent for you thus suddenly,
To give her counsel in a business
That much concerns her.
Sec. Lady. She does well and wisely,
To ask the counsel of the ancient'st, madam;
Our years have run through many things she knows not.
Altea. She would fain marry.
First Lady. 'Tis a proper calling,
And well beseems her years. Who would she yoke with?
Altea. That's left to argue on. I pray, come in,
And break your fast; drink a good cup or two,
To strengthen your understandings; then she'll tell ye.
Sec. Lady. And good wine breeds good counsel; we'll yield to you. [*Exeunt.*

SCENE V.—*Seville.—A street.*

Enter JUAN *and* LEON.

Juan. Have you seen any service?
Leon. Yes.
Juan. Where?
Leon. Every where.
Juan. What office bore you?
Leon. None; I was not worthy.
Juan. What captains know you?

---

¹ *away with*] i. e. endure (" 'I cannot *away* with,'" Richardson observes, " is—I cannot *move* with ; in unison with." *Dict.* in v. *Away*).

Leon. None; they were above me.

Juan. Were you never hurt?

Leon. Not that I well remember;
But once I stole a hen, and then they beat me.
Pray, ask me no long questions; I have an ill memory.

Juan. This is an ass [*Aside*].—Did you never draw your sword yet?

Leon. Not to do any harm, I thank Heaven for 't.

Juan. Nor ne'er ta'en prisoner?

Leon. No, I ran away,
For I had ne'er no money to redeem me.

Juan. Can you endure a drum?

Leon. It makes my head ache.

Juan. Are you not valiant when you are drunk?

Leon. I think not;
But I am loving, sir.

Juan. What a lump is this man!—— [*Aside.*
Was your father wise?

Leon. Too wise for me, I 'm sure,
For he gave all he had to my younger brother.

Juan. That was no foolish part, I 'll bear you witness.
Canst thou lie with a woman?

Leon. I think I could make shift, sir;
But I am bashful.

Juan. In the night?

Leon. I know not;
Darkness indeed may do some good upon me.

Juan. Why art thou sent to me to be my officer,
Ay, and commended too, when thou dar'st not fight?

Leon. There be more officers of my opinion,
Or I am cozen'd, sir; men that talk more too.

Juan. How wilt thou scape a bullet?

Leon. Why, by chance:
They aim at honourable men; alas, I am none, sir!

Juan. This fellow has some doubts in 's talk, that strike me;
He cannot be all fool.— [*Aside.*

Enter ALONZO.

Welcome, Alonzo!

Alon. What have you got there? Temperance into your company? The spirit of peace? we shall have wars by th' ounce, then.

Enter CACAFOGO.

Oh, here's another pumpion[m]; let him loose for luck-sake; The cramm'd son of a starv'd usurer, Cacafogo: Both their brains butter'd cannot make two spoonfuls.

Cac. My father's dead; I am a man of war too, Moneys, demesnes; I have ships at sea too, captains.

Juan. Take heed o' th' Hollanders; your ships may leak else.

Cac. I scorn the Hollanders; they are my drunkards.

Alon. Put up your gold, sir; I'll borrow it else.

Cac. I am satisfied, you shall not.— Come out; I know thee; meet mine anger instantly!

Leon. I never wrong'd you.

Cac. Thou hast wrong'd mine honour; Thou look'dst upon my mistress thrice lasciviously; I'll make it good.

Juan. Do not heat yourself; you will surfeit.

Cac. Thou wann'st my money, too, with a pair of base bones, In whom there was no truth; for which I beat thee, I beat thee much: now I will hurt thee dangerously; This shall provoke thee. [*Strikes* LEON.

Alon. You struck too low by a foot, sir.

Juan. You must get a ladder when you would beat this fellow.

Leon. I cannot choose but kick again; pray, pardon me. [*Kicks* CACAFOGO.

Cac. Hadst thou not ask'd my pardon, I had kill'd thee. I leave thee as a thing despis'd.—*Beso las manos*[n] *á vuestra señoria.* [*Exit.*

---

[m] *pumpion*] i. e. pumpkin.

[n] *Beso las manos*, &c.] Both the old eds. "*assoles manus a vostra siniare a Maistre*": for what "*a Maistre*" is intended, a very acute Spaniard, to whom I submitted the passage, was unable to conjecture.

Alon. You have scap'd by miracle; there is not, in all
 Spain,
A spirit of more fury than this fire-drake[o].
  Leon. I see he is hasty; and I would give him leave
To beat me soundly, if he would take my bond.
  Juan. What shall I do with this fellow?
  Alon. Turn him off:
He will infect the camp with cowardice,
If he go with thee.
  Juan. About some week hence, sir,
If I can hit upon no abler officer,
You shall hear from me.
  Leon. I desire no better.
             [*Exeunt, on one side,* JUAN *and* ALONZO; *on
              the other,* LEON.

SCENE VI.—*Seville.*—*An apartment in the house of*
               MARGARITA.

Enter ESTEFANIA *and* PEREZ.

  Perez. You have made me now too bountiful amends, lady,
For your strict carriage when you saw me first.
These beauties were not meant to be conceal'd;
It was a wrong to hide so sweet an object;
I could now chide you, but it shall be thus: [*Kisses her.*
No other anger ever touch your sweetness!
  Estef. You appear to me so honest and so civil,
Without a blush, sir, I dare bid you welcome.
  Perez. Now let me ask your name.
  Estef. 'Tis Estefania;
The heir of this poor place.
  Perez. Poor, do you call it?
There's nothing that I cast mine eyes upon,
But shews both rich and admirable; all the rooms
Are hung as if a princess were to dwell here;

[o] *fire-drake*] See note, p. 88.

The gardens, orchards, every thing so curious!
Is all that plate your own too?
  Estef. 'Tis but little,
Only for present use; I have more and richer,
When need shall call, or friends compel me use it.
The suits you see of all the upper chambers
Are those that commonly adorn the house:
I think I have, besides, as fair as Seville,
Or any town^p in Spain, can parallel.
  Perez. Now, if she be not married, I have some hopes.—
                                                    [*Aside.*
Are you a maid?
  Estef. You make me blush to answer;
I ever was accounted so to this hour,
And that's the reason that I live retir'd, sir.
  Perez. Then would I counsel you to marry presently,—
If I can get her, I am made for ever,—   [*Aside.*
For every year you lose, you lose a beauty;
A husband now, an honest careful husband,
Were such a comfort! Will you walk above stairs?
  Estef. This place will fit our talk; 'tis fitter far, sir;
Above there are day-beds^q, and such temptations
I dare not trust, sir.
  Perez. She is excellent wise withal too.   [*Aside.*
  Estef. You nam'd a husband; I am not so strict, sir,
Nor tied unto a virgin's solitariness,
But if an honest, and a noble one,
Rich, and a soldier (for so I have vow'd he shall be),
Were offer'd me, I think I should accept him;
But, above all, he must love.
  Perez. He were base else.—

---

  ^p   *as fair as Seville,*
Or any town, &c.] The 4to has,—
                  " *as faire as* civill,
        Or any towne ", &c.
The second folio (the editor of which did not perceive that "civill" was a corruption of the city's name) reads,—
                  " *as fair, as civil,*
        As *any town* ", &c.
  ^q *day-beds*] i. e. a sort of couches or sofas.

There's comfort minister'd in the word soldier:
How sweetly should I live! [*Aside.*

Estef. I am not so ignorant,
But that I know well how to be commanded,
And how again to make myself obey'd, sir:
I waste but little, I have gather'd much;
My rial not the less worth, when 'tis spent,
If spent by my direction: to please my husband,
I hold it as indifferent in my duty,
To be his maid i' the kitchen, or his cook,
As in the hall to know myself the mistress.

Perez. Sweet, rich, and provident! now fortune stick to
me!— [*Aside.*
I am a soldier, and a bachelor, lady;
And such a wife as you I could love infinitely:
They that use many words, some are deceitful;
I long to be a husband, and a good one;
For 'tis most certain I shall make a precedent
For all that follow me to love their ladies.
I am young, you see, able I would have you think too;
If 't please you know, try me before you take me.
'Tis true, I shall not meet in[r] equal wealth with you;
But jewels, chains, such as the war has given me,
A thousand ducats I dare presume on[s]
In ready gold, (now as your care may handle it)
As rich clothes too as any he bears arms, lady.

Estef. You are a true gentleman, and fair, I see by you;
And such a man I had rather take——

Perez. Pray, do so:
I'll have a priest o' the sudden.

Estef. And as suddenly
You will repent too.

Perez. I'll be hang'd or drown'd first,
By this, and this, and this kiss! [*Kisses her.*

[r] *in*] Weber chose to print "an".
[s] *A thousand ducats I dare presume on*] Seward silently printed, for the metre,—
"A thousand ducats *too* I dare presume on".
His successors regulated this passage very improperly.

Estef. You are a flatterer;
But I must say there was something, when I saw you first,
In that most noble face that stirr'd my fancy.
　Perez. I'll stir it better ere you sleep, sweet lady.
I'll send for all my trunks, and give up all to you,
Into your own dispose, before I bed you;
And then, sweet wench——
　Estef. You have the art to cozen me.　　　[*Exeunt.*

ACT II.

SCENE I.—*The Country.—An apartment in the house of* MARGARITA.

Enter MARGARITA, *two old* Ladies[t], *and* ALTEA.
　Marg. Sit down, and give me your opinions seriously.
　First Lady. You say you have a mind to marry, lady?
　Marg. 'Tis true, I have, for to preserve my credit;
Yet not so much for that as for my state[u], ladies;
Conceive me right, there lies the main o' the question:
Credit I can redeem, money will imp it[v];
But when my money's gone, when the law shall seize that,
And for incontinency strip me of all——
　First Lady. Do you find your body so malicious that way?
　Marg. I find it as all bodies are that are young and lusty,
Lazy, and high-fed; I desire my pleasure,
And pleasure I must have.
　Sec. Lady. 'Tis fit you should have;
Your years require it, and 'tis necessary,

---

　[t] *two old Ladies*] Both the 4to and the second folio "*two Ladies*": but they are evidently two of the three ancient dames who have previously appeared in act i. sc. 4.
　[u] *state*] i. e. estate.
　[v] *imp it*] i. e. repair it. A term in falconry, which has frequently occurred before,—vol. i. 191, vol. viii. 8, &c.

As necessary as meat to a young lady;
Sleep cannot nourish more.
   First Lady. But might not all this be, and keep you single?
You take away variety in marriage,
The abundance of the pleasure you are barr'd then :
Is 't not abundance that you aim at?
   Marg. Yes;
Why was I made a woman?
   Sec. Lady. And every day a new?
   Marg. Why fair and young, but to use it?
   First Lady. You are still i' the right; why would[w] you marry, then?
   Altea[x]. Because a husband stops all doubts in this point,
And clears all passages.
   Sec. Lady. What husband mean you?
   Altea. A husband of an easy faith, a fool,
Made by her wealth, and moulded to her pleasure;
One, though he see himself become a monster,
Shall hold the door, and entertain the maker.
   Sec. Lady. You grant there may be such a man?
   First Lady. Yes, marry;
But how to bring 'em to this rare perfection?
   Sec. Lady. They must be chosen so; things of no honour,
Nor outward honesty.
   Marg. No, 'tis no matter;
I care not what they are, so they be lusty.
   Sec. Lady. Methinks now, a rich lawyer; some such fellow,
That carries credit and a face of awe,
But lies with nothing but his clients' business.
   Marg. No, there's no trusting them; they are too subtle;
The law has moulded 'em of natural mischief.
   First Lady. Then some grave governor,
Some man of honour, yet an easy man.

---

  [w] *would*] Silently altered to "should" by the Editors of 1778 ; and so Weber.

  [x] *Altea*] In the 4to, throughout this scene, and occasionally afterwards, the prefix to Altea's speeches is "4", i. e., as Weber saw, the fourth woman,—Margarita and the two old Ladies being the other three : Seward and the Editors of 1778 misunderstood it.

Marg. If he have honour, I am undone; I'll none such:
I'll have a lusty man; honour will cloy me.
　Altea. 'Tis fit you should, lady;
And to that end, with search, and wit, and labour,
I have found one out, a right one and a perfect;
He is made as strong as brass, is of brave years too,
And doughty of complexion.
　Marg. Is he a gentleman?
　Altea. Yes, and a soldier; as gentle as you would wish
　　　him;
A good fellow, wears good clothes.
　Marg. Those I'll allow him;
They are for my credit. Does he understand
But little?
　Altea. Very little.
　Marg. 'Tis the better.
Have not the wars bred him up to anger?
　Altea. No;
He will not quarrel with a dog that bites him;
Let him be drunk or sober, he's one silence.
　Marg. H'as no capacity what honour is?
For that's the soldier's god.
　Altea. Honour's a thing too subtle for his wisdom;
If honour lie in eating, he is right honourable.
　Marg. Is he so goodly a man, do you say?
　Altea. As you shall see, lady;
But, to all this, he's but a trunk.
　Marg. I would have him so;
I shall add branches to him to adorn him.
Go, find me out this man, and let me see him;
If he be that motion[y] that you tell me of,
And make no more noise, I shall entertain him:
Let him be here.
　Altea. He shall attend your ladyship.　　　[*Exeunt.*

<small>[y] *motion*] "i. e. puppet." REED.</small>

SCENE II.—*Seville.—A street.*

Enter JUAN, ALONZO, *and* PEREZ.

Juan. Why, thou art not married indeed?
Perez. No, no; pray, think so:
Alas, I am a fellow of no reckoning,
Not worth a lady's eye!
Alon. Wouldst thou steal a fortune,
And make none of all thy friends acquainted with it,
Nor bid us to thy wedding?
Perez. No, indeed;
There was no wisdom in't, to bid an artist,
An old seducer, to a female banquet:
I can cut up my pie without your instructions.
Juan. Was it the wench i' the veil?
Perez. Basta[z]; 'twas she;
The prettiest rogue that e'er you look'd upon,
The loving'st thief!
Juan. And is she rich withal too?
Perez. A mine, a mine; there is no end of wealth, colonel:
I am an ass, a bashful fool! Prithee, colonel,
How do thy companies fill now?
Juan. You are merry, sir;
You intend a safer war at home, belike now?
Perez. I do not think I shall fight much this year, colonel;
I find myself given to my ease a little:
I care not if I sell my foolish company;
They are things of hazard.
Alon. How it angers me,
This fellow at first sight should win a lady,
A rich young wench; and I, that have consum'd
My time and art in searching out their subtleties,
Like a fool'd alchemist, blow up my hopes still!— [*Aside.*
When shall we come to thy house and be freely merry?

---

[z] *Basta*] i. e. enough (as frequently before, vol. iii. 526, &c.) The word is both Italian and Spanish; here, of course, the latter. (In vol. vii. 248, vol. viii. 46, 474, where the speakers are Spaniards, I have, by an oversight, merely explained the word with a reference to earlier notes, in which it is mentioned as being Italian.)—Both the old eds. " Basto ".

Perez. When I have manag'd her a little more:
I have a house to entertain an army.
    Alon. If thy wife be fair, thou wilt have few less come to
        thee.
    Perez. But where they 'll get entertainment is the point,
        signior;
I beat no drum.
    Alon. You need none but her tabor.
    Perez[a]. May be I 'll march, after a month or two,
To get me a fresh stomach. I find, colonel,
A wantonness in wealth, methinks I agree not with;
'Tis such a trouble to be married too,
And have a thousand things of great importance,
Jewels, and plate[b], and fooleries, molest me;
To have a man's brains whimsied with his wealth!
Before, I walk'd contentedly.

                Enter Servant.
    Serv. My mistress, sir, is sick, because you are absent;
She mourns, and will not eat.
    Perez. Alas, my jewel!—
Come, I 'll go with thee.—Gentlemen, your fair leaves:
You see I am tied a little to my yoke;
Pray, pardon me: would ye had both such loving wives!
    Juan. I thank you   [*Exeunt* PEREZ *and* Serv.
For your old boots!—Never be blank, Alonzo,
Because this fellow has outstript thy fortune:
Tell me ten days hence what he is, and how
The gracious state of matrimony stands with him.
Come, let's to dinner. When Margarita comes,
We 'll visit, both; it may be then your fortune.   [*Exeunt.*

    [a] *Perez*] Omitted in both the old eds.
    [b] *plate*] Both the old eds. "plates"; and so the modern editors. "Mr. Mason,"says Weber, "proposes to read '*plate*,' but the text ['plates'] is correct according to the phraseology of the age": and Nares in his *Gloss.*, as erroneously, cites the present passage with the reading "plates", under "*Plate.* A piece of silver money". Compare act i. sc. 6, "Is all that *plate* your own?"; act iii. sc. 1, "And new *plate* bought, new jewels, to give lustre"; act iii. sc. 4, "No *plate*", &c.; act iii. sc. 5, "The hangings and the *plate* too?"; act iv. sc. 1, "No *plate*", &c.; and act iv. sc. 3, "my *plate*, and jewels", "the hangings, *plate*, and jewels", "I shall take view o' the *plate* anon."

SCENE III.—*The Country.*—*An apartment in the house of* MARGARITA.

Enter MARGARITA, *two old Ladies*[c], *and* ALTEA.

Marg. Is he come?
Altea. Yes, madam; h'as been here this half hour.
I have question'd him of all that you can ask him,
And find him as fit as you had made the man:
He will make the goodliest shadow for iniquity!
Marg. Have ye search'd him, ladies?
Ladies. He's a man at all points,
A likely man.
Marg. Call him in, Altea.

ALTEA *brings in* LEON.

A man of a good presence [d]!—Pray you, come this way—
Of a lusty body!—Is his mind so tame?
Altea. Pray you, question him; and, if you find him not
Fit for your purpose, shake him off; there's no harm done.
Marg. Can you love a young lady?—How he blushes!
Altea. Leave twirling of your hat, and hold your head up,
And speak to the lady.
Leon. Yes, I think I can;
I must be taught; I know not what it means, madam.
Marg. You shall be taught. And can you, when she pleases,
Go ride abroad, and stay a week or two?
You shall have men and horses to attend you,
And money in your purse.
Leon. Yes, I love riding;
And, when I am from home, I am so merry!
Marg. Be as merry as you will. Can you as handsomely,
When you are sent for back, come with obedience,
And do your duty to the lady loves you?
Leon. Yes, sure, I shall.

---

[c] *two old Ladies*] The 4to "the *Ladies*", the sec. folio "*Ladies*": but see note, p. 411. There are only two; for in the 4to the prefix to Altea's speeches throughout this scene is "4": see note, p. 412.

[d] *presence*] i. e. demeanour.

Marg. And when you see her friends here,
Or noble kinsmen, can you entertain
Their servants in the cellar, and be busied,
And hold your peace, whate'er you see or hear of?
   Leon. 'Twere fit I were hang'd else.
   Marg. Let me try your kisses.—
How the fool shakes!—I will not eat you, sir.— [*Kisses him.*
Beshrew my heart, he kisses wondrous manly!—
Can you do any thing else?
   Leon. Indeed, I know not;
But, if your ladyship will please to instruct me,
Sure I shall learn.
   Marg. You shall, then, be instructed.
If I should be this lady that affects you,
Nay, say I marry you——
   Altea. Hark to the lady.
   Marg. What money have you?
   Leon. None, madam, nor friends.
I would do any thing to serve your ladyship.
   Marg. You must not look to be my master, sir,
Nor talk i' th' house as though you wore the breeches;
No, nor command in any thing.
   Leon. I will not;
Alas, I am not able! I have no wit, madam.
   Marg. Nor do not labour to arrive at any;
'Twill spoil your head. I take you upon charity,
And like a servant you must be unto me:
As I behold your duty, I shall love you,
And, as you observe me, I may chance lie with you.
Can you mark these?
   Leon. Yes, indeed, forsooth.
   Marg. There is one thing
That if I take you in, I put you from me,
Utterly from me; you must not be saucy,
No, nor at any time familiar with me;
Scarce know me when I call you not.
   Leon. I will not:
Alas, I never knew myself sufficiently!
   Marg. Nor must not now.

Leon. I'll be a dog to please you.

Marg. Indeed, you must fetch and carry as I appoint you.

Leon. I were to blame else.

Marg. Kiss me again.—A strong fellow!
There is a vigour in his lips.—If you see me
Kiss any other, twenty in an hour, sir,
You must not start, nor be offended.

Leon. No,
If you kiss a thousand I shall be contented;
It will the better teach me how to please you.

Altea. I told you, madam.

Marg. 'Tis the man I wish'd for.—
The less you speak——

Leon. I'll never speak again, madam,
But when you charge me; then I'll speak softly too.

Marg. Get me a priest; I'll wed him instantly.—
But, when you are married, sir, you must wait upon me,
And see you observe my laws.

Leon. Else you shall hang me.

Marg. I'll give you better clothes when you deserve 'em.—
Come in, and serve for witnesses.

Altea and Ladies. We shall, madam.

Marg. And then away to the city presently;
I'll to my new house and new company.

[*Exit with* Ladies.

Leon. A thousand crowns are thine, an[d] I am a made man.

Altea. Do not break out too soon.

Leon. I know my time, wench. [*Exeunt.*

---

[d] *an*] The 4to "&"; the sec. folio "and" (the old spelling of "*an*"), which is given by the Editors of 1778 and Weber, who put a semicolon before it. Sympson silently omitted it. |Leon means, of course,—A thousand crowns shall be yours for having assisted me, if I make my fortune by this trick.

SCENE IV.—*Seville.—A hall in the house of*
MARGARITA.

Enter CLARA *and* ESTEFANIA.

Clara. What, have you caught him?
Estef. Yes.
Clara. And do you find him
A man of those hopes that you aim'd at?
Estef. Yes, too;
And the most kind man, and the ablest also
To give a wife content: he is sound as old wine,
And, to his soundness, rises on the palate;
And there's the man! I find him rich too, Clara.
Clara. Hast thou married him?
Estef. What, dost thou think I fish without a bait, wench?
I bob for fools: he is mine own, I have him:
I told thee what would tickle him like a trout;
And as I cast it, so I caught him daintily,
And all he has I have stow'd at my devotion.
Clara. Does thy lady know this? she is coming now to
 town,
Now to live here in this house.
Estef. Let her come;
She shall be welcome, I am prepar'd for her;
She is mad, sure, if she be angry at my fortune,
For what I have made bold.
Clara. Dost thou not love him?
Estef. Yes, entirely well,
As long as there he stays, and looks no farther
Into my ends; but, when he doubts, I hate him,
And that wise hate will teach me how to cozen him.
[A lady-tamer he, and reads men warnings] e
How to decline f their wives, and curb their manners,

---

e [*A lady-tamer he, and reads men warnings*] Added by Seward,—something being evidently wanting here.

f *decline*] "i. e. lower, or subdue." MASON.

To put a stern and strong rein to their natures;
And holds he is an ass not worth acquaintance,
That cannot mould a devil to obedience.
I owe him a good turn for these opinions,
And, as I find his temper, I may pay him.
Oh, here he is; now you shall see a kind man.

Enter PEREZ.

Perez. My Estefania! shall we to dinner, lamb?
I know thou stay'st for me.
   Estef. I cannot eat else.
   Perez. I never enter, but methinks a paradise
Appears about me.
   Estef. You are welcome to it, sir.
   Perez. I think I have the sweetest seat in Spain, wench;
Methinks the richest too. We'll eat i' the garden,
In one o' th' arbours, (there 'tis cool and pleasant,)
And have our wine cool'd in the running fountain.—
Who's that?
   Estef. A friend of mine, sir.
   Perez. Of what breeding?
   Estef. A gentlewoman, sir.
   Perez. What business has she?
Is she a learned woman i' the mathematics?
Can she tell fortunes?
   Estef. More than I know, sir.
   Perez. Or has she e'er a letter from a kinswoman,
That must be deliver'd in my absence, wife?
Or comes she from the doctor to salute you,
And learn your health? She looks not like a confessor.
   Estef. What need all this? why are you troubled, sir?
What do you suspect? she cannot cuckold you;
She is a woman, sir, a very woman.
   Perez. Your very woman may do very well, sir[g],
Toward the matter; for, though she cannot perform it
In her own person, she may do it by proxy:
Your rarest jugglers work still by conspiracy.

---

[g] *sir*] Though Perez is here echoing his wife, yet the word *sir* (as various passages in these plays have already shown) was frequently employed in addressing females.

Estef. Cry you mercy, husband! you are jealous, then,
And happily suspect me?
Perez. No, indeed, wife.
Estef. Methinks you should not till you have more cause,
And clearer too. I am sure you have heard say, husband,
A woman forc'd will free herself through iron;
A happy, calm, and good wife, discontented,
May be taught tricks.
Perez. No, no; I do but jest with you.
Estef. To-morrow, friend, I'll see you.
Clara. I shall leave you
Till then, and pray all may go sweetly with you.
[*Exit. Knocking within.*
Estef. Why, where's this girl? Who's at the door?
Perez. Who knocks there?
Is't for the king you come, you knock so boisterously?
Look to the door.
Enter Maid.
Maid. [*Aside to* ESTEF.] My lady, as I live, mistress! my lady's come!
She's at the door; I peep'd through, and I[h] saw her,
And a stately company of ladies with her. [*Exit.*
Estef. This was a week too soon; but I must meet with her,
And set a new wheel going, and a subtle one,
Must blind this mighty Mars, or I am ruin'd. [*Aside.*
Perez. What are they at door?
Estef. Such, my Michael,
As you may bless the day they enter'd here;
Such for our good.
Perez. 'Tis well.
Estef. Nay, 'twill be better,
If you will let me but dispose the business,
And be a stranger to it, and not disturb me:
What have I now to do but to advance your fortune?
Perez. Do; I dare trust thee. I am asham'd I was[i] angry;
I find thee a wise young wife.

[h] *I*] Silently omitted by Weber.

[i] *was*] So Seward silently.—Both the old eds. "am;" and so the Editors of 1778 and Weber: but it is evidently a mistake occasioned by the occurrence of the word just before.

Estef. I'll wise your worship
Before I leave you [*Aside*].—Pray you, walk by, and say
    nothing,
Only salute them, and leave the rest to me, sir:
I was born to make you a man.   [*Exit*[j].

   Perez. The rogue speaks heartily;
Her good-will colours in her cheeks; I am born to love her.
I must be gentler to these tender natures;
A soldier's rude harsh words befit not ladies,
Nor must we talk to them as we talk to our officers.
I'll give her way, for 'tis for me she works now;
I am husband, heir, and all she has.

      Enter MARGARITA, LEON, ALTEA, ESTEFANIA, *and* Ladies.

                                         Who are these?
What flaunting things? A woman of rare presence[k]!
Excellent fair! This is too big for a bawdy-house,
Too open-seated too.   [*Aside.*

   Estef. My husband, lady.
   Marg. You have gain'd a proper man.
   Perez. Whate'er I am, I am your servant, lady. [*Kisses her.*
   Estef. [*Aside to* PEREZ] Sir, be rul'd now, and I shall make
      you rich:
This is my cousin; that gentleman dotes on her,
Even to death; see, how he observes[l] her!
   Perez. She is a goodly woman.
   Estef. She is a mirror;
But she is poor; she were for a prince's side else.
This house she has brought him to, as to her own,
And presuming upon me and upon my courtesy,—
Conceive me short,—he knows not but she is wealthy;
Or, if he did know otherwise, 'twere all one,
He is so far gone.
   Perez. Forward. She has a rare face.

---

  [j] *Exit*] I may just observe that this stage-direction is wanting in the old eds., which, however, mark presently the entrance of Estefania with Margarita, &c.

  [k] *presence*] See note, p. 416.

  [l] *observes*] i. e. treats with obsequious attention.

Estef. This we must carry with discretion, husband,
And yield unto her for four days.
Perez. Yield our house up,
Our goods, and wealth!
Estef. All this is but in seeming,
To milk the lover on. Do you see this writing?
[*Shews a paper.*
Two hundred pound a-year, when they are married,
Has she seal'd to for our good. The time's unfit now;
I'll shew it you to-morrow.
Perez. All the house?
Estef. All, all; and we'll remove too, to confirm him:
They'll into the country suddenly again
After they are match'd, and then she'll open to him.
Perez. The whole possession, wife? Look what you do.
A part o' th' house——
Estef. No, no, they shall have all,
And take their pleasure too; 'tis for our 'vantage.
Why, what's four days? had you a sister, sir,
A niece or mistress, that requir'd this courtesy,
And should I make a scruple to do you good?
Perez. If easily it would come back——
Estef. I swear, sir,
As easily as it came on. Is it not pity
To let such a gentlewoman for a little help[m]?
You give away no house.
Perez. Clear but that question.
Estef. I'll put the writings into your hand.
Perez. Well, then.
Estef. And you shall keep them safe.
Perez. I am satisfied.
Would I had the wench so too!
Estef. When she has married him,
So infinite his love is link'd unto her,
You, I, or any one that helps at this pinch,
May have Heaven knows what.

---

[m] *To let such a gentlewoman for a little help*] " i. e. to obstruct or hinder the advancement of such a lady, for want of some little assistance." *Ed.* 1778.

Perez. I'll remove the goods straight,
And take some poor house by; 'tis but for four days.
  Estef. I have a poor old friend; there we'll be.
  Perez. 'Tis well, then.
  Estef. Go handsome off, and leave the house clear.
  Perez. Well.
  Estef. That little stuff we'll use shall follow after,
And a boy to guide you. Peace, and we are made both.
                                    [*Exit* PEREZ.
  Marg. Come, let's go in. Are all the rooms kept sweet, wench?
  Estef. They are sweet and neat.
  Marg. Why, where's your husband?
  Estef. Gone, madam.
When you come to your own, he must give place, lady.
  Marg. Well, send you joy! You would not let me know't;
Yet I shall not forget you.
  Estef. Thank your ladyship!   [*Exeunt.*

ACT III.

SCENE I.—*Seville.*—*A hall in the house of* MARGARITA.

Enter MARGARITA, ALTEA, *and* Boy.

Altea. Are you at ease now? is your heart at rest,
Now you have got a shadow, an umbrella,
To keep the scorching world's opinion
From your fair credit?
  Marg. I am at peace, Altea:
If he continue but the same he shews,
And be a master of that ignorance
He outwardly professes, I am happy:
The pleasure I shall live in, and the freedom,
Without the squint-eye of the law upon me,
Or prating liberty of tongues that envy!
  Altea. You are a made woman.

Marg. But, if he should prove now
A crafty and dissembling kind of husband,
One read in knavery, and brought up in the art
Of villany conceal'd?
   Altea. My life, an innocent [m].
   Marg. That's it I aim at,
That's it I hope too; then I am sure I rule him;
For innocents are like obedient children
Brought up under a hard mother-in-law, a cruel,
Who, being not us'd to breakfasts and collations,
When they have coarse bread offer'd 'em, are thankful,
And take it for a favour too. Are the rooms
Made ready to entertain my friends? I long to dance now,
And to be wanton. Let me have a song. [*Song by the Boy* [n].
Is the great couch up the Duke of Medina sent?
   Altea. 'Tis up and ready.
   Marg. And day-beds [o] in all chambers?
   Altea. In all, lady;
Your house is nothing now but various pleasures;
The gallants begin to gaze too.
   Marg. Let 'em gaze on;
I was brought up a courtier, high and happy,
And company is my delight, and courtship,
And handsome servants [p] at my will. Where's my good husband?
Where does he wait?
   Altea. He knows his distance, madam;
I warrant you, he is busy in the cellar
Amongst his fellow-servants, or asleep,
Till your command awake him.
   Marg. 'Tis well, Altea;
It should be so; my ward I must preserve him [q].

[m] *an innocent*] "i. e. a natural fool, an idiot." WEBER.

[n] *Song by the Boy*] The old have no stage-direction here; nor do the modern editors add any. But nothing can be plainer than that the Boy is introduced in this scene merely for the purpose of singing a song.

[o] *day-beds*] See note, p. 409.

[p] *servants*] "i. e. lovers." WEBER. See note, vol. i. 213.

[q] *my ward I must preserve him*] See note, vol. iv. 96.

Enter LEON *and* Servant.

Who sent for him? how dare he come uncall'd for?
His bonnet on too!
  Altea. Sure, he sees you not.
  Marg. How scornfully he looks!
  Leon. Are all the chambers
Deck'd and adorn'd thus for my lady's pleasure?
New hangings every hour for entertainment,
And new plate bought, new jewels, to give lustre?
  Serv. They are, and yet there must be more and richer;
It is her will.
  Leon. Hum—is it so? 'tis excellent.
It is her will too, to have feasts and banquets,
Revels and masques?
  Serv. She ever lov'd 'em dearly,
And we shall have the bravest house kept now, sir!
I must not call you master (she has warn'd me),
Nor must not put my hat off to you.
  Leon. 'Tis no fashion;
What though I be her husband, I am your fellow.
I may cut first [r]?
  Serv. That's as you shall deserve, sir.
  Leon. And, when I lie with her——
  Serv. May be I'll light you;
On the same point you may do me that service. [*Exit.*

Enter a Lady.

  Lady. Madam, the Duke Medina, with some captains,
Will come to dinner, and have sent rare wine,
And their best services.
  Marg. They shall be welcome.
See all be ready in the noblest fashion,
The house perfum'd. [*Exit Lady.*] Now I shall take my
    pleasure,
And not my neighbour Justice maunder [s] at me.—

---

[r] *I may cut first*] "i. e. I may be allowed to carve first at the servants' table."
WEBER.

[s] *maunder*] i. e. mutter, grumble (properly applied to beggars who mutter or whine out supplications for charity: see a passage in vol. i. 181, and p. 30 of the present vol.).

Go, get your best clothes on; but, till I call you,
Be sure you be not seen: dine with the gentlewomen,
And behave yourself cleanly, sir; 'tis for my credit.

Enter a Second Lady.

Sec. Lady. Madam, the Lady Julia——
Leon. That's a bawd,
A three-pil'd bawd ᵗ, bawd-major to the army. [*Aside.*
Sec. Lady. Has brought her coach to wait upon your ladyship,
And to be inform'd if you will take the air this morning.
Leon. The neat air of her nunnery. [*Aside.*
Marg. Tell her, no;
I' th' afternoon I'll call on her.
Sec. Lady. I will, madam. [*Exit.*
Marg. Why are not you gone to prepare yourself?
May be you shall be sewer to the first course,—
A portly presence!—Altea, he looks lean;
'Tis a wash ᵘ knave, he will not keep his flesh well.
Altea. A willing, madam, one that needs no spurring.
Leon. Faith, madam, in my little understanding,
You had better entertain your honest neighbours,
Your friends about you, that may speak well of you,
And give a worthy mention of your bounty.
Marg. How now! what's this?
Leon. 'Tis only to persuade you:
Courtiers are but tickle things to deal withal,
A kind of marchpane men ᵛ, that will not last, madam;
An egg and pepper goes farther than their potions,
And in a well-built body a poor parsnip
Will play his prize ʷ above their strong potabiles.
Marg. The fellow's mad!
Leon. He that shall counsel ladies
That have both liquorish and ambitious eyes,
Is either mad or drunk, let him speak gospel.

ᵗ *A three-pil'd bawd*] Equivalent to—a bawd of the most perfect skill in her vocation. See note, vol. i. 296.

ᵘ *wash*] i. e. washy: as before, vol. v. 63.

ᵛ *marchpane men*] See note, vol. iv. 186.

ʷ *play his prize*] See note, vol. vi. 529.

Altea. He breaks out modestly. [*Aside.*
Leon. Pray you, be not angry;
My indiscretion has made bold to tell you
What you'll find true.
Marg. Thou dar'st not talk?
Leon. Not much, madam:
You have a tie upon your servant's tongue;
He dares not be so bold as reason bids him:
'Twere fit there were a stronger on your temper.
Ne'er look so stern upon me; I am your husband:
But what are husbands? read the New World's wonders,
And you will scarce find such deformities,
Such husbands as this monstrous world produces ˣ;
They are shadows to conceal your venial virtues,
Sails to your mills, that grind with all occasions,
Balls that lie by you, to wash out your stains,
And bills nail'd up with horns ʸ before your stories,
To rent out lust ᶻ.
Marg. Do you hear him talk?
Leon. I have done, madam:
An ox once spoke, as learnèd men deliver;
Shortly I shall be such; then I'll speak wonders:
Till when, I tie myself to my obedience. [*Exit.*
Marg. First, I'll untie myself! Did you mark the gentleman,
How boldly and how saucily he talk'd,
And how unlike the lump I took him for,
The piece of ignorant dough? he stood up to me,
And mated ᵃ my commands! This was your providence,

ˣ   *read the New World's wonders,*
And you will scarce find such deformities,
Such husbands as this monstrous world produces] Both the old eds. thus;
        " read the new worlds wonders,
            Such husbands as this monstrous world produces,
            And you will scarce find such deformities,"—
and so the modern editors. Mason saw that the last two lines should be transposed.
ʸ *horns*] The 4to " horne ". The second folio " horn ".
ᶻ *lust*] Both the old eds. " last."
ᵃ *mated*] " i. e. opposed [as my match, or equal]." *Ed.* 1778.

Your wisdom, to elect this gentleman,
Your excellent forecast in the man, your knowledge!
What think you now?

Altea. I think him an ass still:
This boldness some of your people have blown into him,
This wisdom too, with strong wine; 'tis a tyrant,
And a philosopher also, and finds out reasons.

Marg. I'll have my cellar lock'd, no school kept there,
Nor no discovery: I'll turn my drunkards,
Such as are understanding in their draughts,
And dispute learnedly the *whys* and *wherefores*,
To grass immediately: I'll keep all fools,
Sober or drunk, still fools, that shall know nothing,
Nothing belongs to mankind, but obedience;
And such a hand I'll keep over this husband!

Altea. He will fall again; my life, he cries by this time:
Keep him from drink; he has a high constitution.

Re-enter LEON.

Leon. Shall I wear my new suit, madam?

Marg. No, your old clothes;
And get you into the country presently,
And see my hawks well train'd: you shall have victuals,
Such as are fit for saucy palates, sir,
And lodgings with the hinds; it is too good too.

Altea. Good madam, be not so rough with repentance [b]:
You see now he's come round again.

Marg. I see not
What I expect to see.

Leon. You shall see, madam,
If it shall please your ladyship.

Altea. He's humbled;
Forgive, good lady.

Marg. Well, go get you handsome,
And let me hear no more.

Leon. Have you yet no feeling?
I'll pinch you to the bones, then, my proud lady!
　　　　　　　　　　　　　[*Aside, and then exit.*

[b] *Good madam, be not so rough with repentance*] " This line Mr. Seward gives to *Leon* very absurdly." WEBER.

Marg. See you preserve him thus, upon my favour;
You know his temper, tie him to the grindstone.
The next rebellion I'll be rid of him:
I'll have no needy rascals I tie to me
Dispute my life. Come in, and see all handsome.
 Altea. I hope to see you so too; I have wrought ill else.
 [*Aside. Exeunt.*

SCENE II.—*A room in a mean house.*

Enter PEREZ.

Perez. Shall I never return to mine own house again?
We are lodg'd here in the miserablest dog-hole!
A conjuror's circle gives content above it;
A hawk's mew is a princely palace to it:
We have a bed no bigger than a basket,
And there we lie like butter clapt together,
And sweat ourselves to sauce immediately.
The fumes are infinite inhabit here too,
And to that so thick, they cut like marmalet;
So various too, they'll pose a gold-finder.
Never return to mine own paradise?—
Why, wife, I say! why, Estefania!
 Estef. [*within*] I am going presently.
 Perez. Make haste, good jewel!
I am like the people that live in the Sweet Islands [c]:
I die, I die, if I stay but one day more here;
My lungs are rotten with the damps that rise,
And I cough nothing now but stinks of all sorts.
The inhabitants we have are two starv'd rats
(For they are not able to maintain a cat here),
And those appear as fearful [d] as two devils;
They have eat a map of the whole world up already,

---

[c] *the Sweet Islands*] "i. e. the Sugar-islands, Barbadoes, St. Kitts, &c., the heat and unwholesomeness of which, at particular seasons, is well known. Mr. Theobald, not seeing this, reads 'sweat *islands.*'" SEWARD.

[d] *fearful*] i. e. dreadful, terrible.

And, if we stay a night, we are gone for company.
There's an old woman that's now grown to marble,
Dried in this brick-kiln[d], and she sits i' the chimney
(Which is but three tiles, rais'd like a house of cards)
The true proportion of an old smok'd sibyl;
There is a young thing too, that nature meant
For a maid-servant, but 'tis now a monster;
She has a husk about her like a chesnut
With laziness [e], and living under the line here;
And these two make a hollow sound together,
Like frogs, or winds between two doors that murmur.
Mercy deliver me!

Enter ESTEFANIA.

Oh, are you come, wife?
Shall we be free again?

Estef. I am now going,
And you shall presently to your own house, sir:
The remembrance of this small vexation
Will be argument [f] of mirth for ever.
By that time you have said your orisons,
And broke your fast, I shall be back, and ready
To usher you to your old content, your freedom.

Perez. Break my neck rather: is there any thing here to eat
But one another, like a race of cannibals?
A piece of butter'd wall you think is excellent.
Let's have our house again immediately;
And, pray you, take heed unto the furniture,
None be embezzled.

Estef. Not a pin, I warrant you.

Perez. And let 'em instantly depart.

Estef. They shall both,
(There's reason in all courtesies,) they must both,
For by this time I know she has acquainted him,
And has provided too; she sent me word, sir,
And will give over gratefully unto you.

[d] *brick-kiln*] Both the old eds. "*brick* hill."

[e] *laziness*] The 4to "bassinesse". The second folio "basiness".

[f] *be argument*] Seward silently printed "*be an argument*".

Perez. I 'll walk i' the church-yard;
The dead cannot offend more than these living.
An hour hence I 'll expect you.
   Estef. I 'll not fail, sir.
   Perez. And, do you hear, let 's have a handsome dinner;
And see all things be decent as they have been;
And let me have a strong bath to restore me,
I stink like a stale fish-shambles, or an oil-shop [g].
   Estef. You shall have all—which some interpret nothing.—
                                                            [*Aside.*
I 'll send you people for the trunks aforehand,
And for the stuff.
   Perez. Let 'em be known and honest;
And do my service to your niece.
   Estef. I shall, sir:
But, if I come not at my hour, come thither,
That they may give you thanks for your fair courtesy.
And, pray you, be brave [h], for my sake.
   Perez. I observe you.   [*Exeunt severally.*

SCENE III.—*A street.*

     Enter JUAN, SANCHIO, *and* CACAFOGO.
   Sanc. Thou art very brave.
   Cac. I have reason; I have money.
   Sanc. Is money reason?
   Cac. Yes, and rhyme too, captain:
If you have no money, you 're an ass.

---

   [g] *I stink like a stale fish-shambles, or an oil-shop*] Both the old eds. have "*I stink like a* stall-fish *shambles, or an* oile *shop.*"—Seward printed " *I stink like a stale-fish shambles, or an oil-shop.*"—The Editors of 1778 gave " *I stink like a* stall-fish, *shambles, or an oil-shop* ",—i. e., they say, "I smell as strong as a fish-stall, a butcher's shambles, or an oil-shop." Weber retained their punctuation, explaining, however, " stall-fish " to mean—" a fish which has long lain upon a stall for show, and has not been kept fresh in water."

   [h] *brave*] " i. e. *well-dressed;* a request peculiarly humorous; Estefania having pillaged Perez's trunks, and left him but that ' one civil suit ' which was upon his back. *J. N.*" *Ed.* 1778.

Sanc. I thank you.

Cac. You have manners; ever thank him that has money.

Sanc. Wilt thou lend me any?

Cac. Not a farthing, captain;
Captains are casual things.

Sanc. Why, so are all men:
Thou shalt have my bond.

Cac. Nor bonds nor fetters, captain:
My money is mine own; I make no doubt on 't.

Juan. What dost thou do with it?

Cac. Put it to pious uses,
Buy wine and wenches, and undo young coxcombs
That would undo me.

Juan. Are those hospitals?

Cac. I first provide to fill my hospitals
With creatures of mine own, that I know wretched,
And then I build; those are more bound to pray for me:
Besides, I keep th' inheritance in my name still.

Juan. A provident charity! Are you for the wars, sir?

Cac. I am not poor enough to be a soldier,
Nor have I faith enough to ward [1] a bullet:
This is no lining for a trench, I take it.

Juan. You have said wisely.

Cac. Had you but my money,
You would swear it, colonel: I had rather drill at home
A hundred thousand crowns, and with more honour,
Than exercise ten thousand fools with nothing:
A wise man safely feeds, fools cut their fingers.

Sanc. A right state-usurer! Why dost thou not marry,
And live a reverend justice?

Cac. Is 't not nobler
To command a reverend justice, than to be one?
And for a wife, what need I marry, captain,
When every courteous fool that owes me money,
Owes me his wife too, to appease my fury?

Juan. Wilt thou go to dinner with us?

Cac. I will go,

---

[1] *ward*] "i. e. ward off." WEBER.

And view the pearl of Spain, the orient fair one[j],
The rich one too; and I will be respected;
I bear my patent here: I will talk to her;
And, when your captainships shall stand aloof
And pick your noses, I will pick the purse
Of her affection.

Juan. The Duke dines there to-day too,
The Duke of Medina.

Cac. Let the king dine there;
He owes me money, and so far's my creature;
And certainly I may make bold with mine own, captain.

Sanc. Thou wilt eat monstrously.

Cac. Like a true-born Spaniard;
Eat as I were in England, where the beef grows:
And I will drink abundantly, and then
Talk ye as wantonly as Ovid did,
To stir the intellectuals of the ladies;
I learnt it of my father's amorous scrivener.

Juan. If we should play now, you must supply me.

Cac. You must pawn a horse-troop,
And then have at you, colonel!

Sanc. Come, let's go.—
This rascal will make rare sport: how the ladies
Will laugh at him! Leave anger [k].

Juan. If I light on him,
I'll make his purse sweat too.

Cac. Will ye lead, gentlemen?   [*Exeunt.*

SCENE IV.—*Another street; before a mean house.*

Enter PEREZ, *an* Old Woman, *and* Maid.

Perez. Nay, pray you, come out, and let me understand you;
And tune your pipe a little higher, lady:

---

[j] *the pearl of Spain, the orient fair one*] See note, p. 403.

[k] *Leave anger*] The 4to " *leave* ager".—Omitted in the second folio; and by Seward and the Editors of 1778.

I'll hold you fast. Rub! how came my trunks open?
And my goods gone? what pick-lock spirit——
　Old Wom. Ha! what would you have?
　Perez. My goods again: how came my trunks all open?
　Old Wom. Are your trunks open?
　Perez. Yes, and [my] clothes gone,
And chains, and jewels.—How she smells, like hung beef!—
The palsy and pick locks! fie, how she belches!
The spirit of garlic!　　　　　　　　　　　　　[*Aside.*
　Old Wom. Where's your gentlewoman?
The young fair woman?
　Perez. What's that to my question?
She is my wife, and gone about my business.
　Maid. Is she your wife, sir?
　Perez. Yes, sir[1]; is that wonder?
Is the name of wife unknown here?
　Old Wom. Is she truly,
Truly your wife?
　Perez. I think so, for I married her;
It was no vision, sure.
　Maid. She has the keys, sir.
　Perez. I know she has; but who has all my goods, spirit?
　Old Wom. If you be married to that gentlewoman,
You are a wretched man; she has twenty husbands.
　Maid. She tells you true.
　Old Wom. And she has cozen'd all, sir.
　Perez. The devil she has!—I had a fair house with her,
That stands hard by, and furnish'd royally.
　Old Wom. You are cozen'd too; 'tis none of hers, good
　　　　gentleman [m];
It is a lady's.—What's the lady's name, wench?
　Maid. The Lady Margarita: she was her servant,
And kept the house, but going from her, sir,
For some lewd tricks she play'd—

---

[1] *sir*] See note, p. 420.

[m] '*tis none of hers, good gentleman*] "Mr. Seward chooses to read '*good gentlewoman*'." *Ed.* 1778. Seward,—(who compares what the same speaker says presently, "She may go bare, *good gentlewoman*," p. 436),—was probably right: it must be observed, however, that the Old Woman calls Perez "gentleman" at p. 437.

Perez. Plague o' the devil!
Am I, i' the full meridian of my wisdom,
Cheated by a stale quean? [*Aside.*]—What kind of lady
Is that that owes [n] the house?
  Old Wom. A young sweet lady.
  Perez. Of a low stature?
  Old Wom. She is indeed but little,
But she is wondrous fair.
  Perez. I feel I am cozen'd;
Now I am sensible I am undone!
This is the very woman, sure, that cousin,
She told me would entreat but for four days
To make the house hers: I am entreated [o] sweetly! [*Aside.*
  Maid. When she went out this morning, (that I saw, sir,)
She had two women at the door attending,
And there she gave 'em things, and loaded 'em;
But what they were——I heard your trunks too open,
If they be yours.
  Perez. They were mine while they were laden,
But now they have cast their calves, they are not worth
    owning.
Was she her mistress, say you?
  Old Wom. Her own mistress,
Her very mistress, sir, and all you saw
About and in that house was hers.
  Perez. No plate,
No jewels, nor no hangings?
  Maid. Not a farthing;
She is poor, sir, a poor shifting thing.
  Perez. No money?
  Old Wom. Abominable poor, as poor as we are,
Money as rare to her, unless she steal it:
But for one civil [p] gown her lady gave her,
She may go bare, good gentlewoman.
  Perez. I am mad now!

---

  [n] *owes*] i. e. owns.
  [o] *entreated*] "i. e. treated, used." WEBER.
  [p] *civil*] i. e. sober, not shewy.

SCENE IV.] RULE A WIFE AND HAVE A WIFE. 437

I think I am as poor as she; I am wide ^q else:
One civil suit I have left too, and that's all,
And, if she steal that, she must flay me for it.— [*Aside.*
Where does she use ^r?
Old Wom. You may find truth as soon:
Alas, a thousand conceal'd corners, sir, she lurks in!
And here she gets a fleece, and there another,
And lives in mists and smokes where none can find her.
Perez. Is she a whore too?
Old Wom. Little better, gentleman;
I dare not say she is so, sir, because she is yours, sir;
But these five years she has firk'd a pretty living ^s,
Until she came to serve.——I fear he will knock
My brains out for lying ^t. [*Aside.*
Perez. She has serv'd me faithfully;
A whore and thief! two excellent moral learnings
In one she-saint! I hope to see her legend.
Have I been fear'd for my discoveries,
And courted by all women to conceal 'em?
Have I so long studied the art of this sex,
And read the warnings to young gentlemen?
Have I profess'd to tame the pride of ladies,
And make 'em bear all tests, and am I trick'd now?
Caught in mine own noose? Here's a rial ^u left yet.—[*Aside.*
There's for your lodging and your meat for this week:
A silk-worm lives at a more plentiful ordinary, [*Gives rial.*

^q *wide*] "i. e. wide of the mark." WEBER.

^r *use*] "i. e. frequent, lodge." WEBER.

^s *firk'd a pretty living*] i. e. picked up a pretty livelihood by all sorts of roguish tricks. See note, p. 379.

^t *for lying*] "Seward strikes out the words '*for lying*', because, as he says, most of the things that the old woman said were true, with a little exaggeration; and because they destroy all appearance of measure. But no measure was intended [—in this assertion Mason is certainly wrong—], and exaggeration is lying. Some part of the old woman's story was true; but it does not appear that Estefania was a whore, or had twenty husbands." MASON. "Mr. Seward had his brains out. The humour lies in Estefania's having ordered the Old Woman to tell these tales of her; for though an intriguer, she is not represented as other than chaste; and as to the metre, it is perfectly correct." Coleridge's *Remains*, ii. 305.

^u *rial*] Here both the old eds. "royal"; but previously (p. 410) they have "rial".

And sleeps in a sweeter box. Farewell, great-grandmother :
If I do find you were an accessary,
('Tis but the cutting off two smoky minutes)
I 'll hang you presently.
   Old Wom. An I deserve it [v].
I tell but truth.
   Perez. Nor[w] I,—I am an ass, mother.
   [*Exit* PEREZ. *Exeunt* Old Woman *and* Maid *into the house.*

      SCENE V.—*A hall in the house of* MARGARITA.

Enter the DUKE OF MEDINA, JUAN, ALONZO, SANCHIO, CACAFOGO, *and* Attendants.

   Duke. A goodly house!
   Juan. And richly furnish'd too, sir.
   Alon. Hung wantonly : I like that preparation ;
It stirs the blood unto a hopeful banquet,
And intimates the mistress free and jovial :
I love a house where pleasure prepares welcome.
   Duke. Now, Cacafogo, how like you this mansion ?
'Twere a brave pawn.
   Cac. I shall be master of it ;
'Twas built for my bulk, the rooms are wide and spacious,
Airy and full of ease, and that I love well.
I 'll tell you when I taste the wine, my lord,
And take the height of her table with my stomach,
How my affections stand to the young lady.

      Enter MARGARITA, ALTEA, Ladies, *and* Servants.

   Marg. All welcome to your grace, and to these soldiers !
You honour my poor house with your fair presence.
Those few slight pleasures that inhabit here, sir,
I do beseech your grace command ; they are yours ;
Your servant but preserves 'em to delight you.

---

   [v] *An I deserve it*] Both the old eds. "And *I deserve it*"; and so Seward and the Editors of 1778.—Mason (not perceiving that "And" is merely the old spelling of "*An*") proposed to read "And I'd *deserve it*"; which was adopted by Weber, who calls it "a correction that needs no defence."—See note, p. 418.
   [w] *Nor*] So the 4to.—The second folio "Not".

SCENE V.] RULE A WIFE AND HAVE A WIFE. 439

Duke. I thank you, lady. I am bold to visit you,
Once more to bless mine eyes with your sweet beauty:
'T has been a long night since you left the court,
For, till I saw you now, no day broke to me.
　Marg. Bring in the duke's meat!
　Sanc. She is most excellent.
　Juan. Most admirable fair as e'er I look'd on;
I had rather command her than my regiment.
　Cac. I'll have a fling; 'tis but a thousand ducats,
Which I can cozen up again in ten days,
And some few jewels, to justify my knavery.
Say I should marry her, she'll get more money
Than all my usury, put my knavery to it:
She appears the most infallible way of purchase ^x.
I could wish her a size or two stronger for the encounter,
For I am like a lion where I lay hold;
But these lambs will endure a plaguy load,
And never bleat neither; that, sir, time has taught us ^y.
I am so virtuous now, I cannot speak to her;
The arrant'st shamefac'd ass! I broil away too.　[*Aside.*
　　　　　　　Enter LEON.
　Marg. Why, where's this dinner?
　Leon. 'Tis not ready, madam,
Nor shall not be until I know the guests too;
Nor are they fairly welcome till I bid 'em.
　Juan. Is not this my alferez ^z? he looks another thing:
Are miracles afoot again?
　Marg. Why, sirrah!
Why, sirrah, you!
　Leon. I hear you, saucy woman;

---

^x *way of purchase*] i. e. means of acquiring gain.

^y *that, sir, time has taught us*] The Editors of 1778 silently printed "*that* Sir Time *has taught us*"; and so Weber.—Of "sir" and similar improprieties, occurring *in soliloquies and speeches spoken aside*, I have collected examples from Shakespeare and other early dramatists in my *Remarks on Mr. Collier's and Mr. Knight's editions of Shakespeare*, p. 102; and the following passage may be added to them from Fletcher's *Woman's Prize*, (act iii. sc. 2, vol. vii. 162); it is spoken by Petruchio while *solus*;
　　　　　"'Tis hard dealing,
　　Very hard dealing, *gentlemen*, strange dealing!"

^z *alferez*] See note, p. 397.

And, as you are my wife, command your absence!
And know your duty; 'tis the crown of modesty.
   Duke. Your wife!
   Leon. Yes, good my lord, I am her husband;
And, pray, take notice that I claim that honour,
And will maintain it.
   Cac. If thou be'st her husband,
I am determin'd thou shalt be my cuckold;
I 'll be thy faithful friend.
   Leon. Peace, dirt and dunghill!
I will not lose my anger on a rascal;
Provoke me more, I will beat thy blown body
Till thou rebound'st again like a tennis-ball.
   Alon. This is miraculous.
   Sanc. Is this the fellow
That had the patience to become a fool,
A flurted fool, and on a sudden break
(As if he would shew a wonder to the world)
Both into bravery, and fortune too?
I much admire the man; I am astonish'd.
   Marg. I 'll be divorc'd immediately.
   Leon. You shall not;
You shall not have so much will to be wicked:
I am more tender of your honour, lady,
And of your age. You took me for a shadow,
You took me to gloss over your discredit,
To be your fool; you had thought you had found a coxcomb:
I am innocent of any foul dishonour I mean to you;
Only I will be known to be your lord now,
And be a fair one too, or I will fall for 't.
   Marg. I do command you from me, thou poor fellow,
Thou cozen'd fool!
   Leon. Thou cozen'd fool! 'tis not so;
I will not be commanded; I am above you:
You may divorce me from your favour, lady,
But from your state[z] you never shall; I 'll hold that,
And hold it to my use; the law allows it:
And then maintain your wantonness; I 'll wink at it.
   Marg. Am I brav'd thus in mine own house?

---

[z] *state*] "i. e. estate." WEBER.

Leon. 'Tis mine, madam;
You are deceiv'd; I am lord of it, I rule it
And all that's in 't: you have nothing to do here, madam,
But as a servant to sweep clean the lodgings,
And at my farther will to do me service;
And so I'll keep it.
  Marg. As you love me, give way!
  Leon. It shall be better,—I will give none, madam [a]:
I stand upon the ground of mine own honour,
And will maintain it. You shall know me now
To be an understanding feeling man,
And sensible of what a woman aims at,
A young proud woman, that has will to sail with,
An itching woman, that her blood provokes too.
I cast my cloud off, and appear myself,
The master of this little piece of mischief:
And I will put a spell about your feet, lady;
They shall not wander but where I give way now.
  Duke. Is this the fellow that the people pointed at
For the mere sign of man, the walking image?
He speaks wondrous highly.
  Leon. As a husband ought, sir,
In his own house; and it becomes me well too.
I think your grace would grieve, if you were put to it,
To have a wife or servant of your own
(For wives are reckon'd in the rank of servants)
Under your own roof to command you.
  Juan. Brave!
A strange conversion! Thou shalt lead in chief now.
  Duke. Is there no difference betwixt her and you, sir?
  Leon. Not now, [my] lord; my fortune makes me even;
And, as I am an honest man, I am nobler.
  Marg. Get me my coach!

---

[a] *It shall be better,—I will give none, madam*] Seward printed;
  " *Mar.* As you love me, give way, it shall be better——
    Leon. I will give none, Madam,
       I stand ", &c.
And Mason approves of the alteration.—" Leon may very properly say, 'he will do better than give way, by opposing her'." Ed. 1778.—" The meaning is: 'It shall be a better way, first;—as it is, I will not give it, or any that you in your present mood would wish'." Colcridge's *Remains*, ii. 306.

Leon. Let me see who dare get it
Till I command; I'll make him draw your coach too [b],
And eat your coach (which will be hard diet),
That executes your will.   Or, take your coach, lady;
I give you liberty; and take your people,
Which I turn off, and take your will abroad with you;
Take all these freely, but take me no more:
And so, farewell.
    Duke. Nay, sir, you shall not carry it   [*Draws his sword.*
So bravely off; you shall not wrong a lady
In a high huffing strain, and think to bear it:
We stand not by as bawds to your brave fury,
To see a lady weep.
    Leon. They are tears of anger,
(I beseech [c] ye note 'em) not worth pity,
Wrung from her rage, because her will prevails not
(She would swound [d] now, if she could not cry);
Else they were excellent, and I should grieve too;
But falling thus, they shew nor sweet nor orient.
Put up, my lord; this is oppression,
And calls the sword of justice to relieve me,
The law to lend her hand, the king to right me;
All which shall understand how you provoke me.
In mine own house to brave me! is this princely?
Then to my guard! and, if I spare your grace,
                          [*Draws his sword.*
And do not make this place your monument,
Too rich a tomb for such a rude behaviour,—
I have a cause will kill a thousand of ye,—
Mercy forsake me!
    Juan. Hold, fair sir, I beseech you!
The gentleman but pleads his own right nobly.
    Leon. He that dares strike against the husband's freedom,

---

    [b] *too*] Would seem to be misplaced by a mistake of the transcriber or printer; and Seward was probably right in giving the passage as follows;
                "I'll make him draw your coach,
      And eat your coach *too* (which will be hard diet)", &c.
    [c] *I beseech*] Seward silently printed "*I do beseech*".
    [d] *swound*] So both the old eds.—Altered by the modern editors to "swoon" (Seward printing "e'en swoon"). See note, vol. i. 422.

The husband's curse stick to him, a tam'd cuckold!
His wife be fair and young, but most dishonest,
Most impudent, and have no feeling of it,
No conscience to reclaim her from a monster!
Let her lie by him like a flattering ruin,
And at one instant kill both name and honour!
Let him be lost, no eye to weep his end,
Nor find no earth that's base enough to bury him!—
Now, sir, fall on! I am ready to oppose you.
    Duke. I have better thought. I pray, sir, use your wife well.
    Leon. Mine own humanity will teach me that, sir.—
And now you are all welcome, all, and we 'll to dinner:
This is my wedding-day.
    Duke. I 'll cross your joy yet.   [*Aside.*
    Juan. I have seen a miracle. Hold thine own, soldier!
Sure, they dare fight in fire that conquer women.
    Sanc. H 'as beaten all my loose thoughts out of me,
As if he had thresh'd 'em out o' the husk.

Enter PEREZ.

    Perez. Save ye!
Which is the lady of the house?
    Leon. That 's she, sir,
That pretty lady, if you would speak with her.
    Juan. Don Michael!
    Leon. Another darer come [e]!
    Perez. Pray, do not know me; I am full of business:
When I have more time I 'll be merry with ye.—
It is the woman [*Aside*].—Good madam, tell me truly,
Had you a maid call'd Estefania?
    Marg. Yes, truly, had I.
    Perez. Was she a maid, do you think?
    Marg. I dare not swear for her;
For she had but a scant fame.

---

[e] *Juan. Don Michael!*
    Leon. Another darer come!] So Heath (*MS. Notes*), and rightly, beyond all doubt.—Both the old eds. have (with a slight variation of pointing),—
        "*Juan.* Don Michael, Leon, another darer come?"
and so the modern editors.

Perez. Was she your kinswoman?

Marg. Not that I ever knew. Now I look better,
I think you married her: give you much joy, sir!
You may reclaim her; 'twas a wild young girl.

Perez. Give me a halter!—Is not this house mine, madam?
Was not she owner of it? pray, speak truly.

Marg. No, certainly; I am sure my money paid for it;
And I ne'er remember yet I gave it you, sir.

Perez. The hangings and the plate too?

Marg. All are mine, sir,
And every thing you see about the building:
She only kept my house when I was absent,
And so ill kept it, I was weary of her.

Sanc. What a devil ails he?

Juan. He's possess'd, I'll assure you.

Perez. Where is your maid?

Marg. Do not you know that have her?
She is yours now; why should I look after her?
Since that first hour I came, I never saw her.

Perez. I saw her later.—Would the devil had had her!
It is all true, I find; a wild-fire take her! [*Aside.*

Juan. Is thy wife with child, Don Michael? thy excellent
wife?
Art thou a man yet?

Alon. When shall we come and visit thee?

Sanc. And eat some rare fruit? thou hast admirable
orchards.
You are so jealous now! pox o' your jealousy,
How scurvily you look!

Perez. Prithee, leave fooling;
I am in no humour now to fool and prattle.—
Did she ne'er play the wag with you?

Marg. Yes, many times,
So often that I was asham'd to keep her;
But I forgave her, sir, in hope she would mend still;
And, had not you o' th' instant married her,
I had put her off.

Perez. I thank you.—I am blest still!
Which way soe'er I turn, I am a made man!
Miserably gull'd beyond recovery! [*Aside.*

Juan. You'll stay and dine?

Perez. Certain I cannot, captain.
Hark in thine ear; I am the arrant'st puppy,
The miserablest ass! but I must leave you;
I am in haste, in haste!—Bless you, good madam,
An you[e] prove as good as my wife! [*Exit.*

Leon. Will you come near, sir? will your grace but honour
    me,
And taste our dinner? you are nobly welcome:
All anger's past, I hope, and I shall serve you.

Juan. Thou art the stock of men, and I admire thee.
[*Exeunt.*

ACT IV.

SCENE I.—*Seville.*—*A street.*

Enter PEREZ.

Perez. I'll go to a conjuror but I'll find this polecat,
This pilfering whore. A plague of veils, I cry,
And covers for the impudence of women!
Their sanctity in show will deceive devils.

Enter ESTEFANIA, *with a casket.*

It is my evil angel; let me bless me! [*Aside.*

Estef. 'Tis he; I am caught; I must stand to it stoutly,
And shew no shake of fear; I see he is angry,
Vex'd at the uttermost. [*Aside.*

Perez. My worthy wife,
I have been looking of your modesty
All the town over.

Estef. My most noble husband,
I am glad I have found you; for, in truth, I am weary,
Weary and lame, with looking out your lordship.

Perez. I have been in bawdy-houses.

---

[e] *An you*] Both the old eds. "And *you*".—Seward and his successors give
"And may *you*". See notes, p. 418, 438.

Estef. I believe you,—
And very lately too.
　Perez. Pray you, pardon me ;—
To seek your ladyship. I have been in cellars,
In private cellars, where the thirsty bawds
Hear your confessions : I have been at plays,
To look you out amongst the youthful actors :
At puppet-shows (you are mistress of the motions [f]) :
At gossipings I hearken'd after you,
But amongst those confusions of lewd tongues
There's no distinguishing beyond a Babel :
I was amongst the nuns, because you sing well ;
But they say yours are bawdy songs, they mourn for you :
And last I went to church to seek you out ;
'Tis so long since you were there, they have forgot you.
　Estef. You have had a pretty progress : I'll tell mine now.
To look you out, I went to twenty taverns——
　Perez. And are you sober ?
　Estef. Yes, I reel not yet, sir ;——
Where I saw twenty drunk, most of 'em soldiers ;
There I had great hope to find you disguis'd too :
From hence to the dicing-house ; there I found quarrels
Needless and senseless, swords, and pots, and candlesticks,
Tables, and stools, and all in one confusion,
And no man knew his friend : I left this chaos,
And to the chirurgeon's went ; he will'd me stay,
" For," says he learnedly, " if he be tippled,
Twenty to one he whores, and then I hear of him ;
If he be mad, he quarrels, then he comes too " :
I sought you where no safe thing would have ventur'd,
Amongst diseases base and vild, vild [g] women,
For I remember'd your old Roman axiom,—
The more the danger, still the more the honour :
Last, to your confessor I came, who told me,
You were too proud to pray : and here I have found you.

　[f] *motions*] i. e. puppets (used with a quibble).
　[g] *vild, vild*] i. e. vile : see note, vol. i. 331. So the 4to here, as also in the next speech but two.—The second folio " vile " in both places ; and so the modern editors.

Perez. She bears up bravely, and the rogue is witty;
But I shall dash it instantly to nothing.— [*Aside.*
Here leave we off our wanton languages,
And now conclude we in a sharper tongue.
Why am I cozen'd h ?
　Estef. Why am I abus'd?
　Perez. Thou most vild, base, abominable——
　Estef. Captain!
　Perez. Thou stinking, over-stew'd, poor, pocky——
　Estef. Captain!
　Perez. Do you echo me?
　Estef. Yes, sir, and go before you,
And round about you! Why do you rail at me
For that that was your own sin, your own knavery?
　Perez. And brave me too?
　Estef. You had best now draw your sword, captain!
Draw it upon a woman, do, brave captain!
Upon your wife, oh, most renownèd captain!
　Perez. A plague upon thee! answer me directly;
Why didst thou marry me?
　Estef. To be my husband;
I had thought you had had infinite, but I'm cozen'd.
　Perez. Why didst thou flatter me, and shew me wonders,
A house and riches, when they are but shadows,
Shadows to me?
　Estef. Why did you work on me
(It was but my part to requite you, sir)
With your strong soldier's wit, and swore you would bring me
So much in chains, so much in jewels, husband,
So much in right rich clothes?
　Perez. Thou hast 'em, rascal;
I gave 'em to thy hands, my trunks and all,
And thou hast open'd 'em, and sold my treasure.
　Estef. Sir, there's your treasure; sell it to a tinker
To mend old kettles: is this noble usage?
Let all the world view here the captain's treasure!

　h *Why am I cozen'd ?*] These words are given in both the old eds. to Estefania; and so Seward.

A man would think now, these were worthy matters :
[*Opens the casket.*
Here's a shoeing-horn-chain gilt over,—how it scenteth !
Worse than the mouldy dirty heel it serv'd for ;
And here's another of a lesser value,
So little I would shame to tie my dog in 't :
These are my jointure ! Blush, and save a labour,
Or these else will blush for you.
   Perez. A fire subtle you !
Are you so crafty ?
   Estef. Here's a goodly jewel ;
Did not you win this at Goletta[1], captain ?
Or took it in the field from some brave bashaw ?
How it sparkles—like an old lady's eyes !
And fills each room with light—like a close lanthorn !
This would do rarely in an abbey window,
To cozen pilgrims.
   Perez. Prithee, leave prating.
   Estef. And here's a chain of whitings' eyes for pearls ;
A muscle-monger would have made a better.
   Perez. Nay, prithee, wife, my clothes, my clothes !
   Estef. I'll tell you ;
Your clothes are parallels to these,—all counterfeit :
Put these and them on, you are a man of copper,
A kind of candlestick : these you thought, my husband,
To have cozen'd me withal, but I am quit with you.
   Perez. Is there no house, then, nor no grounds about it ?
No plate nor hangings ?
   Estef. There are none, sweet husband ;
Shadow for shadow is an equal justice.
Can you rail now ? pray, put your fury up, sir,
And speak great words ; you are a soldier ; thunder !
   Perez. I will speak little ; I have play'd the fool,
And so I am rewarded.
   Estef. You have spoke well, sir ;

---

[1] *Goletta*] " The memorable siege of Goletta, on the coast of Barbary, is well known from the immortal work of Cervantes, where the captive gives a very animated account of it. See *Don Quixote*, Ed. Madrid, 1788, 8vo, vol. III. p. 234." WEBER.

And, now I see you are so conformable,
I 'll heighten you again : go to your house,
They are packing to be gone; you must sup there ;
I 'll meet you, and bring clothes and clean shirts after,
And all things shall be well.—I 'll colt^j you once more,
And teach you to bring copper!   [*Aside.*

  Perez. Tell me one thing,
I do beseech thee tell me, tell me truth, wife,
(However, I forgive thee,) art thou honest ?
The beldame swore——
  Estef. I bid her tell you so, sir;
It was my plot. Alas, my credulous husband!
The lady told you too——
  Perez. Most strange things of thee.
  Estef. Still 'twas my way, and all to try your sufferance :
And she denied the house ?
  Perez. She knew me not,
No, nor no title that I had.
  Estef. 'Twas well carried.
No more; I am right and straight.
  Perez. I would believe thee,
But Heaven knows how my heart is. Will you follow me ?
  Estef. I 'll be there straight.
  Perez. I am fool'd, yet dare not find it.
    [*Aside, and then exit.*
  Estef. Go, silly fool! thou mayst be a good soldier
In open field, but for our private service
Thou art an ass; I 'll make thee so, or miss else.
Here comes another trout that I must tickle,
And tickle daintily, I have lost my end else.

    Enter CACAFOGO.

May I crave your leave, sir ?
  Cac. Prithee, be answer'd, thou shalt crave no leave ;
I am in my meditations; do not vex me.—
A beaten thing, but this hour a most bruis'd thing,
That people had compassion on, it look'd so;

---

^j *colt*] " i. e. fool, trick." REED.

The next, Sir Palmerin [k]: here's fine proportion!
An ass, and then an elephant; sweet justice!
There's no way left to come at her now; no craving;
If money could come near, yet I would pay him;
I have a mind to make him a huge cuckold,
And money may do much: a thousand ducats?
'Tis but the letting blood of a rank heir. [*Aside.*
   Estef. Pray you, hear me.
   Cac. I know thou hast some wedding-ring to pawn now,
Of silver and gilt, with a blind posy in 't,
Love and a mill-horse should go round together,
Or thy child's whistle, or thy squirrel's chain:
I'll none of 'em.—I would she did but know me,
Or would this fellow had but use of money,
That I might come in any way! [*Aside.*
   Estef. I am gone, sir;
And I shall tell the beauty sent me to you,
The Lady Margarita——
   Cac. Stay, I prithee;
What is thy will? I turn me wholly to you;
And talk now till thy tongue ache; I will hear you.
   Estef. She would entreat you, sir——
   Cac. She shall command, sir [l]:
Let it be so, I beseech thee, my sweet gentlewoman;
Do not forget thyself.
   Estef. She does command, then,
This courtesy, because she knows you are noble——
   Cac. Your mistress, by the way?
   Estef. My natural mistress——
Upon these jewels, sir——they are fair and rich,
And, view 'em, right [m]——
   Cac. To doubt 'em is an heresy.
   Estef. A thousand ducats; 'tis upon necessity
Of present use; her husband, sir, is stubborn.
   Cac. Long may he be so!

---

  [k] *Sir Palmerin*] "Either Palmerin of England, or Palmerin de Oliva," &c. WEBER. See note, vol. ii. 145.

  [l] *sir*] See note, p. 420.

  [m] *right*] i. e. not counterfeit, real: compare a passage, p. 146.

Estef. She desires withal
A better knowledge of your parts and person;
And, when you please to do her so much honour——
  Cac. Come, let's despatch.
  Estef. In troth, I have heard her say, sir,
Of a fat man, she has not seen a sweeter.
But in this business, sir——
  Cac. Let's do it first,
And then dispute; the lady's use may long for 't.
  Estef. All secrecy she would desire: she told me
How wise you are.
  Cac. We are not wise to talk thus;
Carry her the gold; I'll look her out a jewel
Shall sparkle like her eyes, and thee another.
Come, prithee come; I long to serve thy lady,
Long monstrously.—Now, valour, I shall meet you,
You that dare dukes!   [*Aside.*
  Estef. Green goose, you are now in sippets.   [*Aside.*
                                                   [*Exeunt.*

SCENE II.—*Another street.*

Enter the DUKE OF MEDINA, SANCHIO, JUAN, *and* ALONZO.

  Duke. He shall not have his will, I shall prevent him;
I have a toy here that will turn the tide,
And suddenly, and strangely. Here, Don Juan,
Do you present it to him.   [*Gives a paper.*
  Juan. I am commanded.   [*Exit.*
  Duke. A fellow founded [n] out of charity,
And moulded to the height, contemn his maker,
Curb the free hand that fram'd him! this must not be.
  Sanc. That such an oyster-shell should hold a pearl,
And of so rare a price, in prison! Was she made
To be the matter of her own undoing,

---

[n] *founded*] "i. e. living upon a charitable foundation." WEBER. Here the word is equivalent to—raised, supported.

To let a slovenly unwieldy fellow,
Unruly and self-will'd, dispose her beauties?
We suffer all, sir, in this sad eclipse;
She should shine where she might shew like herself,
An absolute sweetness, to comfort those admire her,
And shed her beams upon her friends. We are gull'd all,
And all the world will grumble at your patience,
If she be ravish'd thus.
    Duke. Ne'er fear it, Sanchio;
We'll have her free again, and move at court
In her clear orb. But one sweet handsomeness
To bless this part of Spain, and have that slubber'd!
    Alon. 'Tis every good man's cause, and we must stir in it.
    Duke. I'll warrant he ° shall be glad to please us,
And glad to share too: we shall hear anon
A new song from him; let's attend a little.   [*Exeunt.*

SCENE III.—*An apartment in the house of* MARGARITA.

Enter LEON *with a paper, and* JUAN.

    Leon. Colonel, I am bound to you for this nobleness.
I should have been your officer, 'tis true, sir;
And a proud man I should have been to have serv'd you:
'T has pleas'd the king, out of his boundless favours,
To make me your companion; this commission
Gives me a troop of horse.
    Juan. I rejoice at it,
And am a glad man we shall gain your company:
I am sure the king knows you are newly married,
And out of that respect gives you more time, sir.
    Leon. Within four days I am gone, so he commands me,
And 'tis not mannerly for me to argue it;
The time grows shorter still. Are your goods ready?
    Juan. They are aboard.

    ° *I'll warrant he*] Seward silently printed "*I'll warrant* ye *he*".

Leon. Who waits there?

Enter Servant.

Serv. Sir?
Leon. Do you hear, ho!
Go, carry this unto your mistress, sir,
And let her see how much the king has honour'd me;
Bid her be lusty, she must make a soldier.
                    [*Exit* Servant *with paper*.
[Lorenzo!]

Enter LORENZO.

Lor. Sir?
Leon. Go, take down all the hangings,
And pack up all my clothes, my plate and jewels,
And all the furniture that's portable.—
Sir, when we lie in garrison, 'tis necessary
We keep a handsome port, for the king's honour.—
And, do you hear, let all your lady's wardrobe
Be safely plac'd in trunks; they must along too.
Lor. Whither must they go, sir?
Leon. To the wars, Lorenzo,
And you and all; I will not leave a turn-spit,
That has one dram of spleen against a Dutchman.
Lor. Why, then, St. Jaques, hey! you have made us all, sir;
And, if we leave you——Does my lady go too?
Leon. The stuff must go to-morrow towards the sea, sir;
All, all must go.
Lor. Why, Pedro, Vasco, Diego!
Come, help me; come, come, boys; soldadoes, comrades!
We'll flay these beer-bellied rogues: come away quickly!
                    [*Exit.*

Juan. H'as taken a brave way to save his honour,
And cross the duke; now I shall love him dearly:
By the life of credit, thou art a noble gentleman! [*Aside.*

Enter MARGARITA, *led by two* Ladies.

Leon. Why, how now, wife! what, sick at my preferment?
This is not kindly done.
Marg. No sooner love you,

Love you entirely, sir, brought to consider
The goodness of your mind and mine own duty,
But lose you instantly, be divorc'd from you!
This is a cruelty: I'll to the king,
And tell him 'tis unjust to part two souls,
Two minds so nearly mix'd.
  Leon. By no means, sweetheart.
  Marg. If he were married but four days, as I am——
  Leon. He would hang himself the fifth, or fly his country.
                                                                         [*Aside.*
  Marg. He would make it treason for that tongue that durst
But talk of war, or any thing to vex him.
You shall not go.
  Leon. Indeed, I must, sweet wife.
What, shall I lose the king for a few kisses?
We'll have enough.
  Marg. I'll to the duke my cousin;
He shall to the king.
  Leon. He did me this great office,
I thank his grace for 't; should I pray him now
To undo't again, fie, 'twere a base discredit!
  Marg. Would I were able, sir, to bear you company;
How willing should I be then, and how merry!
I will not live alone.
  Leon. Be in peace; you shall not.   [*Knocking within.*
  Marg. What knocking's this? Oh, Heaven, my head!—
    Why, rascals!—
I think the war's begun i' th' house already.
  Leon. The preparation is; they are taking down
And packing up the hangings, plate, and jewels,
And all those furnitures that shall befit me
When I lie in garrison.

                Enter Coachman.

  Coachman. Must the coach go too, sir?
  Leon. How will your lady pass to the sea else easily?
We shall find shipping for 't there to transport it.
  Marg. I go? alas!

Leon. I 'll have a main care of you;
I know you are sickly; he shall drive the easier,
And all accommodation shall attend you.
Marg. Would I were able!
Leon. Come, I warrant you;
Am not I with you, sweet?—Are her clothes pack'd up,
And all her linens?—Give your maids direction;
You know my time's but short, and I am commanded.
Marg. Let me have a nurse,
And all such necessary people with me,
And an easy bark.
Leon. It shall not trot, I warrant you;
Curvet it may sometimes.
Marg. I am with child, sir.
Leon. At four days' warning? this is something speedy.
Do you conceive, as our jennets do, with a west wind [P]?
My heir will be an arrant fleet one, lady:
I 'll swear you were a maid when I first lay with you.
Marg. Pray, do not swear; I thought I was a maid too;
But we may both be cozen'd in that point, sir.
Leon. In such a strait point, sure, I could not err, madam.
Juan. This is another tenderness to try him;
Fetch her up now. [*Aside.*
Marg. You must provide a cradle;
And what a trouble's that!
Leon. The sea shall rock it,
'Tis the best nurse; 'twill roar and rock together;
A swinging storm will sing you such a lullaby!
Marg. Faith, let me stay; I shall but shame you, sir.
Leon. An you were a thousand shames, you shall along
  with me;
At home I am sure you 'll prove a million:
Every man carries the bundle of his sins
Upon his own back; you are mine; I 'll sweat for you.

   Enter *the* DUKE OF MEDINA, ALONZO, *and* SANCHIO.

Duke. What, sir, preparing for your noble journey?
'Tis well, and full of care.

P *Do you conceive, as our jennets do, with a west wind?*] See note, vol. v. 273; and compare vol. vii. 140.

I saw your mind was wedded to the war,
And knew you would prove some good man for your
   country,—
Therefore, fair cousin, with your gentle pardon,
I got this place. What, mourn at his advancement?
You are to blame; he will come again, sweet cousin;
Mean time, like sad Penelope and sage,
Amongst your maids at home, and huswifely——

Leon. No, sir, I dare not leave her to that solitariness;
She is young, and grief, or ill news from those quarters,
May daily cross her; she shall go along, sir.

Duke. By no means, captain.

Leon. By all means, an't please you.

Duke. What, take a young and tender-bodied lady,
And expose her to those dangers, and those tumults;
A sickly lady too?

Leon. 'Twill make her well, sir;
There's no such friend to health as wholesome travel.

Sanc. Away! it must not be.

Alon. It ought not, sir:
Go hurry her? it is not humane, captain.

Duke. I cannot blame her tears: fright her with tempests,
With thunder of the war?
I dare swear, if she were able——

Leon. She is most able;
And, pray you, swear not; she must go, there's no remedy;
Nor greatness, nor the trick you had to part us,
Which I smell too rank, too open, too evident,—
And, I must tell you, sir, 'tis most unnoble,—
Shall hinder me : had she but ten hours' life,
Nay, less, but two hours', I would have her with me;
I would not leave her fame to so much ruin,
To such a desolation and discredit,
As her weakness and your hot will would work her to.

Enter PEREZ.

What masque is this now?
More tropes and figures to abuse my sufferance?
What cousin's this?

Juan. Michael Van Owl, how dost thou?

In what dark barn, or tod^q of agèd ivy,
Hast thou lien hid?
 Perez. Things must both ebb and flow, colonel,
And people must conceal, and shine again.—
You are welcome hither, as your friend may say, gentlemen^r;
A pretty house, ye see, handsomely seated,
Sweet and convenient walks, the waters crystal.
 Alon. He's certain mad.
 Juan. As mad as a French tailor,
That has nothing in's head but ends of fustians.
 Perez. I see you are packing now, my gentle cousin,
And my wife told me I should find it so;
'Tis true I do. You were merry when I was last here,
But 'twas your will to try my patience, madam.
I am sorry that my swift occasions
Can let you take your pleasure here no longer;
Yet I would have you think, my honour'd cousin,
This house and all I have are all your servants.
 Leon. What house, what pleasure, sir? what do you mean?
 Perez. You hold the jest so stiff, 'twill prove discourteous:
This house I mean, the pleasures of this place.
 Leon. And what of them?
 Perez. They are mine, sir, and you know it;
My wife's, I mean, and so conferr'd upon me:
The hangings, sir, I must entreat your servants,
That are so busy in their offices,
Again to minister to their right uses;
I shall take view o' the plate anon, and furnitures
That are of under place. You are merry still, cousin,
And of a pleasant constitution;
Men of great fortunes make their mirths *ad placitum.*
 Leon. Prithee, good stubborn wife, tell me directly,
Good evil wife, leave fooling, and tell me honestly,
Is this my kinsman?
 Marg. I can tell you nothing.
 Leon. I have many kinsmen; but so mad a one,
And so fantastic——All the house?

^q *tod*] "i. e. bush." WEBER.
^r *gentlemen*] Both the old eds. "gentleman."

Perez. All mine,
And all within it: I will not bate you an ace on 't.
Can you not receive a noble courtesy,
And quietly and handsomely, as you ought, coz,
But you must ride o' the top on 't?
Leon. Canst thou fight?
Perez. I 'll tell you presently; I could have done, sir.
Leon. For you must law and claw before you get it.
Juan. Away; no quarrels!
Leon. Now I am more temperate,
I 'll have it prov'd if you were never yet in Bedlam,
Never in love (for that 's a lunacy),
No great state [r] left you that you never look'd for
Nor cannot manage (that 's a rank distemper),
That you were christen'd, and who answer'd for you;
And then I yield.
Perez. H 'as half persuaded me I was bred i' the moon:
I have ne'er a bush [s] at my breech. Are not we both mad?
And is not this a fantastic house we are in,
And all a dream we do? Will you walk out, sir?
And, if I do not beat thee presently
Into a sound belief as sense can give thee,
Brick me into that wall there for a chimney-piece,
And say I was one o' the Cæsars, done by a seal-cutter.
Leon. I 'll talk no more; come, we 'll away immediately.
Marg. Why, then, the house is his, and all that 's in it;—
I 'll give away my skin, but I 'll undo you!—   [*Aside.*
I gave it to his wife: you must restore, sir,
And make a new provision.
Perez. Am I mad now,
Or am I christen'd? You, my pagan cousin,
My mighty Mahound [t] kinsman, what quirk now?—
You shall be welcome all; I hope to see, sir,
Your grace here, and my coz; we are all soldiers,
And must do naturally for one another.

---

[r] *state*] i. e. estate.

[s] *a bush*] "An allusion to the bush, one of the attributes of the man in the moon", &c. WEBER.

[t] *Mahound*] i. e. Mahomet,—Mahometan.

SCENE III.] RULE A WIFE AND HAVE A WIFE. 459

Duke. Are you blank at this? then I must tell you, sir,
You have no command: now you may go at pleasure,
And ride your ass-troop: 'twas a trick I us'd
To try your jealousy, upon entreaty,
And saving [u] of your wife.
 Leon. All this not moves me,
Nor stirs my gall, nor alters my affections.—
You have more furniture, more houses, lady,
And rich ones too; I will make bold with those;
And you have land i' th' Indies, as I take it;
Thither we'll go, and view a while those climates,
Visit your factors there, that may betray you:
'Tis done; we must go.
 Marg. Now thou art a brave gentleman,
And, by this sacred light, I love thee dearly!—
The house is none of yours, I did but jest, sir; [*To* PEREZ.
Nor you are no coz of mine; I beseech you vanish;
I tell you plain, you have no more right than he has;
That, senseless thing, your wife has once more fool'd you [v]:
Go you, and consider!

 [u] *saving*] " Perhaps we should read ' craving '." *Ed.* 1778. I think not.
 [v] *I tell you plain, you have no more right than he has;*
  That, senseless thing, your wife has once more fool'd you] Stands thus in both
the old eds. ;
  " *I tell you plaine, you have no more right then he*
  Has, that senselesse thing, your wife has once more foold ye".
Seward printed ;
  " *I tell you plain, you've no more right than has*
  That senseless thing. Your wife has once more fool'd ye ",—
Margarita, at the words " *that senseless thing,*"—" pointing to a chair, table, or
any thing near her."—I have given the passage according to the punctuation of
the Editors of 1778 (which was adopted also by Weber) : " It is Perez ", they
observe, " whom she calls ' *senseless thing,*' and tells him his wife has duped
him again ; and that he has no more right ' *than he has,*' pointing to any indifferent person in company."—Mason remarks, " I am inclined to read ' Thou
senseless thing '; and suppose that, when Margarita says ' *you've no more right
than he has* ', she points to some uninterested person of the company. The use
of the word ' *ye* ' at the end of the [last] line confirms this conjecture. She
had used the word ' *you* ' twice in the preceding line, in speaking to Perez ; and
could not, with propriety, have changed it to ' *ye* ' at the end of the last, if the
word ' thou ' had not been introduced in the beginning of it." I am not sure
that I understand the latter part of Mason's note : but there can be no doubt
that he makes a distinction between ' *you* ' and ' *ye* ' which was never dreamed
of by our early poets, transcribers, or printers.

Leon. Good morrow, my sweet cousin!
I should be glad, sir——
   Perez. By this hand, she dies for 't,
Or any man that speaks for her!   [*Exit.*
   Juan. These are fine toys.
   Marg. Let me request you stay but one poor month,
You shall have a commission, and I'll go too;
Give me but will so far.
   Leon. Well, I will try you.—
Good morrow to your grace; we have private business.
   Duke. If I miss thee again, I am an arrant bungler.
                                       [*Aside.*
   Juan. Thou shalt have my command, and I'll march under thee;
Nay, be thy boy, before thou shalt be baffled,
Thou art so brave a fellow.
   Alon. I have seen visions.   [*Exeunt.*

ACT V.

SCENE I.—*Seville.*—*A garden belonging to the house of* MARGARITA.

Enter LEON *with a letter, and* MARGARITA.

   Leon. Come hither, wife; do you know this hand?
   Marg. I do, sir;
'Tis Estefania's, that was once my woman.
   Leon. She writes to me here, that one Cacafogo,
An usuring jeweller's son (I know the rascal),
Is mortally faln in love with you——
   Marg. He's a monster:
Deliver me from mountains!
   Leon. Do you go a-birding for all sorts of people?—[*Aside.*
And this evening will come to you and shew you jewels,

And offers any thing to get access to you:
If I can make or sport or profit on him
(For he is fit for both), she bids me use him;
And so I will, be you conformable,
And follow but my will.

  Marg. I shall not fail, sir.

  Leon. Will the duke come again, do you think?

  Marg. No, sure, sir,
He has now no policy to bring him hither.

  Leon. Nor bring you to him, if my wit hold fair, wife [w].
Let's in to dinner.   [*Exeunt.*

SCENE II.—*A street.*

Enter PEREZ.

  Perez. Had I but lungs enough to bawl sufficiently,
That all the queans in Christendom might hear me,
That men might run away from [the] contagion,
I had my wish: would it were most high treason,
Most infinite high, for any man to marry!
I mean, for any man that would live handsomely,
And like a gentleman, in his wits and credit.
What torments shall I put her to? Phalaris' bull now?
Pox, they love bulling too well, though they smoke for't:
Cut her a-pieces? every piece will live still,
And every morsel of her will do mischief:
They have so many lives, there's no hanging of 'em [x];
They are too light to drown, they are cork and feathers;
To burn too cold, they live like salamanders:
Under huge heaps of stones to bury her,
And so depress her as they did the giants?
She will move under more than built old Babel.
I must destroy her.

---

  [w] *hold fair, wife*] The modern editors (the old eds. having no point except at the end of the line) very absurdly print " *hold, fair wife.*"

  [x] *there's no hanging of 'em*] Weber silently printed " *there is no hanging 'em*".

Enter CACAFOGO, *with a casket.*

Cac. Be cozen'd by a thing of clouts, a she-moth,
That every silk-man's shop breeds! to be cheated,
And of a thousand ducats, by a whim-wham!
Perez. Who's that is cheated? speak again, thou vision!
But art thou cheated? minister some comfort;
Tell me directly, art thou cheated bravely?
Come, prithee, come; art thou so pure a coxcomb
To be undone? do not dissemble with me;
Tell me, I conjure thee.
Cac. Then keep thy circle,
For I am a spirit wild that flies about thee,
And, whoe'er thou art, if thou be'st human,
I'll let thee plainly know, I am cheated damnably.
Perez. Ha, ha, ha!
Cac. Dost thou laugh? Damnably, I say, most damnably.
Perez. By whom, good spirit? speak, speak! ha, ha, ha!
Cac. I will utter—laugh till thy lungs crack—by a rascal woman,
A lewd, abominable, and plain woman.
Dost thou laugh still?
Perez. I must laugh; prithee, pardon me;
I shall laugh terribly.
Cac. I shall be angry,
Terrible angry; I have cause.
Perez. That's it,
And 'tis no reason but thou shouldst be angry,
Angry at heart; yet I must laugh still at thee.
By a woman cheated? art sure it was a woman?
Cac. I shall break thy head; my valour itches at thee.
Perez. It is no matter. By a woman cozen'd?
A real woman?
Cac. A real devil;
Plague of her jewels, and her copper chains,
How rank they smell!
Perez. Sweet cozen'd sir, let me see them;
I have been cheated too, (I would have you note that,)
And lewdly cheated, by a woman also,

A scurvy woman; I am undone, sweet sir,
Therefore I must have leave to laugh.
 Cac. Pray you, take it;
You are the merriest undone man in Europe:
What need we fiddles, bawdy songs, and sack,
When our own miseries can make us merry?
 Perez. Ha, ha, ha!   [*Looking into the casket.*
I have seen these jewels: what a notable pennyworth
Have you had next your heart! You will not take, sir,
Some twenty ducats——
 Cac. Thou art deceiv'd; I will take——
 Perez. To clear your bargain now?
 Cac. I'll take some ten,
Some any thing, some half ten, half a ducat.
 Perez. An excellent lapidary set these stones, sure;
Do you mark their waters?
 Cac. Quick-sand choke their waters,
And hers that broughtʸ 'em too! but I shall find her.
 Perez. And so shall I, I hope; but do not hurt her;
You cannot find in all this kingdom, if
You had need of cozening (as you may have,
For such gross natures will desire it often,
It is at some time too a fine variety),
A woman that can cozen you so neatly.—
She has taken half mine anger off with this trick.
         [*Aside, and then exit.*
 Cac. If I were valiant now, I would kill this fellow;
I have money enough lies by me, at a pinch,
To pay for twenty rascals' lives that vex me.
I'll to this lady; there I shall be satisfied.   [*Exit.*

   ʸ *brought*] Both the old eds. "bought".

SCENE III.—*An apartment in the house of* MARGARITA.

Enter LEON *and* MARGARITA.

Leon. Come, we 'll away unto your country-house,
And there we 'll learn to live contently [a] :
This place is full of charge, and full of hurry;
No part of sweetness dwells about these cities.
  Marg. Whither you will, I wait upon your pleasure;
Live in a hollow tree, sir, I 'll live with you.
  Leon. Ay, now you strike a harmony, a true one,
When your obedience waits upon your husband,
And your sick will aims at the care [b] of honour.
Why, now I dote upon you, love you dearly,
And my rough nature falls, like roaring streams,
Clearly and sweetly into your embraces.
Oh, what a jewel is a woman excellent,
A wise, a virtuous, and a noble woman!
When we meet such, we bear our stamps on both sides,
And through the world we hold our current virtues;
Alone, we are single medals, only faces,
And wear our fortunes out in useless shadows.
Command you now, and ease me of that trouble;
I 'll be as humble to you as a servant :
Bid whom you please, invite your noble friends,
They shall be welcome all; visit acquaintance,
Go at your pleasure, now experience
Has link'd you fast unto the chain of goodness!
  [*Clashing of swords within, and a cry,* Down with their swords!
What noise is this? what dismal cry?
  Marg. 'Tis loud too :
Sure, there 's some mischief done i' the street.—Look out there!
  Leon. Look out, and help!

---

[a] *contently*] The modern editors silently print "contentedly",—and rightly perhaps, though both in Todd's *Johnson's Dict.* and in Richardson's *Dict.* the present passage is cited for the word "*contently.*"

[b] *care*] Altered, most unnecessarily, to "cure" by Seward.

Enter Servant.

Serv. Oh, sir, the Duke Medina——
Leon. What of the Duke Medina?
Serv. Oh, sweet gentleman,
Is almost slain!
Marg. Away, away, and help him!
All the house help!   [*Exit with* Servant.
Leon. How! slain!—Why, Margarita! why, wife!—Sure,
Some new device they have afoot again,
Some trick upon my credit; I shall meet it.
I had rather guide a ship imperial
Alone, and in a storm, than rule one woman.

Enter the DUKE *of Medina, led by* MARGARITA, SANCHIO, ALONZO, *and* Servant.

Marg. How came you hurt, sir?
Duke. I fell out with my friend, the noble colonel;
My cause was naught, for 'twas about your honour,
And he that wrongs the innocent ne'er prospers;
And he has left me thus. For charity,
Lend me a bed to ease my tortur'd body,
That, ere I perish, I may shew my penitence:
I fear I am slain.
Leon. Help, gentlemen, to carry him.—
There shall be nothing in this house, my lord,
But as your own.
Duke. I thank you, noble sir.
Leon. To bed with him; and, wife, give your attendance.

Enter JUAN.

Juan. Doctors and surgeons!
Duke. Do not disquiet me,
But let me take my leave in peace.
   [*Exeunt* DUKE, SANCHIO, ALON., MARG., *and* Serv.
Leon. Afore me,
'Tis rarely counterfeited!
Juan. True, it is so, sir;
And take you heed this last blow do not spoil you.
He is not hurt, only we made a scuffle,

As though we purpos'd anger; that same scratch on 's hand
He took, to colour all, and draw compassion,
That he might get into your house more cunningly.
I must not stay. Stand now, and you 're a brave fellow.
   Leon. I thank you, noble colonel, and I honour you.
                                               [*Exit* JUAN.
Never be quiet?
                 Re-enter MARGARITA.
   Marg. He's most desperate ill, sir;
I do not think these ten months will recover him.
   Leon. Does he hire my house to play the fool in,
Or does it stand on fairy ground, we are haunted [b]?
Are all men and their wives troubled with dreams thus?
   Marg. What ail you, sir?
   Leon. Nay, what ail you, sweet wife,
To put these daily pastimes on my patience?
What dost thou see in me, that I should suffer thus?
Have not I done my part like a true husband,
And paid some desperate debts you never look'd for?
   Marg. You have done handsomely, I must confess, sir.
   Leon. Have I not kept thee waking like a hawk?
And watch'd thee with delights to satisfy thee,
The very tithes of which had won a widow?
   Marg. Alas, I pity you!
   Leon. Thou wilt make me angry:
Thou never saw'st me mad yet.
   Marg. You are always;
You carry a kind of Bedlam still about you.
   Leon. If thou pursu'st me further, I run stark mad;
If you have more hurt dukes or gentlemen
To lie here on your cure, I shall be desperate:
I know the trick, and you shall feel I know it.
Are you so hot that no hedge can contain you?
I 'll have thee let blood in all the veins about thee,
I 'll have thy thoughts found too, and have them open'd,

---

  [b] *Or does it stand on fairy ground, we are haunted?*] The modern editors, not catching the meaning of the line (which is—Or does it stand on fairy ground, *that* we are haunted), point " *Or does it stand on fairy ground?* We 're haunted ".

SCENE III.]   RULE A WIFE AND HAVE A WIFE.   467

Thy spirits purg'd, for those are they that fire you;
Thy maid shall be thy mistress, thou the maid,
And all those servile labours that she reach'd[c] at,
  * * * * * *
And go through cheerfully, or else sleep empty;
That maid shall lie by me, to teach you duty,
You in a pallet by, to humble you,
And grieve for what you lose.
 Marg. I have lost myself, sir,
And all that was my base self, disobedience; [*Kneels.*
My wantonness, my stubbornness, I have lost too;
And now, by that pure faith good wives are crown'd with,
By your own nobleness——
 Leon. [*raising her*] I take you up,
And wear you next my heart; see you be worth it.

     Enter ALTEA.
Now, what with you?
 Altea. I come to tell my lady,
There is a fulsome fellow would fain speak with her.
 Leon. 'Tis Cacafogo: go, and entertain him,
And draw him on with hopes.
 Marg. I shall observe you.
 Leon. I have a rare design upon that gentleman;
And you must work too.
 Altea. I shall, sir, most willingly.
 Leon. Away, then, both, and keep him close in some place
From the duke's sight; and keep the duke in too;
Make 'em believe both: I'll find time to cure 'em. [*Exeunt.*

 [c] *reach'd*] Both the old eds. "reach".—Seward gave the passage thus,—
    "thou the maid,
   And all her servile labours thou shalt reach *at,*
   And go through cheerfully," &c.
and so the Editors of 1778.—Weber printed,—
    "*thou the maid*
   To *all those servile labours that she* reaches *at,*
   And go thro' cheerfully," &c.
But there cannot be the smallest doubt that here (as in an earlier part of the play, p. 419) a line is wanting.

H H 2

SCENE IV.—*A street.*

Enter, severally, Perez *and* Estefania.

Perez. Why, how dar'st thou meet me again, thou rebel,
 [*Draws his sword.*
And know'st how thou hast us'd me thrice, thou rascal?
Were there not ways enough to fly my vengeance,
No holes nor vaults to hide thee from my fury,
But thou must meet me face to face to kill thee?
I would not seek thee to destroy thee willingly,
But now thou com'st to invite me, and com'st upon me:
How like a sheep-biting rogue, taken i' the manner [d],
And ready for the halter, dost thou look now!
Thou hast a hanging look, thou scurvy thing!
Hast ne'er a knife,
Nor never a string, to lead thee to Elysium?
Be there no pitiful 'pothecaries in this town,
That have compassion upon wretched women,
And dare administer a dram of rats-bane,
But thou must fall to me?

Estef. I know you have mercy [e].

Perez. If I had tons of mercy, thou deserv'st none.
What new trick is now afoot, and what new houses
Have you i' th' air? what orchards in apparition?
What canst thou say for thy life?

Estef. Little or nothing;
I know you'll kill me, and I know 'tis useless
To beg for mercy. Pray, let me draw my book out,
And pray a little.

Perez. Do; a very little,
For I have farther business than thy killing;
I have money yet to borrow. Speak when you are ready.

---

[d] *taken i' the manner*] "*Taken in the manner,* or with the manner, means, in the language of the law, taken with the thing stolen about you." Mason. Seward proposed altering "*manner*" to "*matter*"!

[e] *I know you have mercy*] After these words Weber added a stage-direction "*Kneels*": but see the next speech of Estefania.

Estef. Now, now, sir, now! [*Shews a pistol.*]—Come on! do you start off from me?
Do you sweat, great captain? have you seen a spirit?
Perez. Do you wear guns?
Estef. I am a soldier's wife, sir,
And by that privilege I may be arm'd.
Now, what's the news? and let's discourse more friendly,
And talk of our affairs in peace.
Perez. Let me see,
Prithee, let me see thy gun; 'tis a very pretty one.
Estef. No, no, sir; you shall feel.
Perez. Hold, you villain ᶠ!
What, thine own husband?
Estef. Let mine own husband, then,
Be in's own wits.—There, there's a thousand ducats—
[*Shews a purse.*
Who must provide for you?—and yet you'll kill me.
Perez. I will not hurt thee for ten thousand millions.
Estef. When will you redeem your jewels? I have pawn'd 'em,
You see for what: we must keep touch ᵍ.
Perez. I'll kiss thee,
And, get as many more, I'll make thee famous.
Had we the house now!
Estef. Come along with me;
If that be vanish'd, there be more to hire, sir.
Perez. I see I am an ass when thou art near me. [*Exeunt.*

SCENE V.—*Ante-room to a bed-chamber in the house of* MARGARITA.

Enter LEON, MARGARITA, *and* ALTEA *with a taper.*
Leon. Is the fool come?
Altea. Yes, and i' the cellar fast,
And there he stays his good hour till I call him;

ᶠ *Hold, you villain*] Seward silently printed "*Hold,* hold," &c.; and so his successors.

ᵍ *keep touch*] See note, p. 92.

He will make dainty music among the sack-butts:
I have put him just, sir, under the duke's chamber.
  Leon. It is the better.
  Altea. He has given me royally,
And to my lady a whole load of portigues [h].
  Leon. Better and better still.—Go, Margarita,
Now play your prize [i]: you say you dare be honest;
I 'll put you to your best [j].
  Marg. Secure yourself, sir;
Give me the candle; pass away in silence.
            [*Exeunt* LEON *and* ALTEA.   MARG. *knocks.*
  Duke. [*within*] Who 's there? oh, oh!
  Marg. My lord!
  Duke. [*within*] Have you brought me comfort?
  Marg. I have, my lord:
Come forth; 'tis I; come gently out; I 'll help you;
Come softly too.
            Enter the DUKE *of Medina in a gown.*
                How do you?
  Duke. Are there none here?
Let me look round; we cannot be too wary. [*Noise below.*
Oh, let me bless this hour! Are you alone, sweet friend?
  Marg. Alone, to comfort you.   [*Noise below.*
  Duke. What 's that you tumble [k]?—
I have heard a noise this half hour under me,
A fearful noise.
  Marg. The fat thing 's mad i' the cellar,
And stumbles from one hogshead to another;
Two cups more, and he ne'er shall find the way out.—
                                          [*Aside.*
What do you fear? come, sit down by me cheerfully;
My husband 's safe. How do your wounds?

  [h] *portigues*] See note, vol. viii. 312.
  [i] *play your prize*] See note, vol. vi. 529.
  [j] *I 'll put you to your best*] Seward (citing from *The False One*, act i. sc. 2, "I 'll put you to the test") altered here "*best*" to "test"; and so the Editors of 1778. But I think, with Weber, that the old reading is right; it refers to "play your prize" in the preceding line.
  [k] *What 's that you tumble?*] Seward, at Sympson's suggestion, printed, "*What 's that* rumble?"

Duke. I have none, lady;
My wounds I counterfeited cunningly,
And feign'd the quarrel too, to enjoy you, sweet:
Let's lose no time. [*Noise below.*] Hark, the same noise again!
    Marg. What noise? why look you pale? I hear no stirring.——
This goblin in the vault will be so tippled!—— [*Aside.*
You are not well, I know by your flying fancy;
Your body's ill at ease; your wounds——
    Duke. I have none;
I am as lusty, and as full of health,
High in my blood——
    Marg. Weak in your blood, you would say.
How wretched is my case, willing to please you,
And find you so disable!
    Duke. Believe me, lady——
    Marg. I know you will venture all you have to satisfy me,
Your life, I know; but is it fit I spoil you?
Is it, my love, do you think?
    Cac. [*below*] Here's to the duke!
    Duke. It nam'd me certainly;
I heard it plainly sound.
    Marg. You are hurt mortally,
And fitter for your prayers, sir, than pleasure.
What starts you make! I would not kiss you wantonly,
For the world's wealth. Have I secur'd my husband,
And put all doubts aside, to be deluded?
    Cac. [*below*] I come, I come.
    Duke. Heaven bless me!
    Marg. And bless us both, for, sure, this is the devil!
I plainly heard it now; he will come to fetch you;
A very spirit, for he spoke under ground,
And spoke to you just as you would have snatch'd me.
You are a wicked man, and, sure, this haunts you:
Would you were out o' th' house!
    Duke. I would I were,
O' that condition I had leap'd a window!
    Marg. And that's the least leap, if you mean to scape, sir.

Why, what a frantic man were you to come here,
What a weak man to counterfeit deep wounds,
To wound another deeper!
   Duke. Are you honest, then?
   Marg. Yes, then, and now, and ever, and excellent honest;
And exercise this pastime but to shew you,
Great men are fools sometimes as well as wretches.
Would you were well hurt, with any hope of life,
Cut to the brains, or run clean through the body,
To get out quietly as you got in, sir!
I wish it like a friend that loves you dearly;
For, if my husband take you, and take you thus
A counterfeit, one that would clip his credit,
Out of his honour he must kill you presently;
There is no mercy, nor an hour of pity;
And for me to entreat in such an agony,
Would shew me little better than one guilty.
Have you any mind to a lady now?
   Duke. Would I were off fair!
If ever lady caught me in a trap more——
   Marg. If you be well and lusty—fie, fie, shake not!—
You say you love me; come, come bravely now;
Despise all danger; I am ready for you.
   Duke. She mocks my misery.—Thou cruel lady!
   Marg. Thou cruel lord! wouldst thou betray my honesty,
Betray it in mine own house, wrong my husband,
Like a night-thief, thou dar'st not name by daylight?
   Duke. I am most miserable.
   Marg. You are, indeed;
And, like a foolish thing, you have made yourself so.
Could not your own discretion tell you, sir,
When I was married I was none of yours?
Your eyes were then commanded to look off me;
And I now stand in a circle and secure,—
Your spells nor power can never reach my body.
Mark me but this, and then, sir, be most miserable;
'Tis sacrilege to violate a wedlock,
You rob two temples, make yourself twice guilty,
You ruin hers, and spot her noble husband's.

Duke. Let me be gone; I'll never more attempt you.
Mary. You cannot go; 'tis not in me to save you:
Dare you do ill, and poorly then shrink under it?
Were I the Duke Medina, I would fight now,
For you must fight, and bravely, it concerns you;
You do me double wrong, if you sneak off, sir,
And all the world would say I lov'd a coward;
And you must die too, for you will be kill'd,
And leave your youth, your honour, and your state,
And all those dear delights you worshipp'd here.
Duke. The noise again! [*Noise below.*
Cac. [*below*] Some small beer, if you love me!
Mary. The devil haunts you, sure; your sins are mighty;
A drunken devil too, to plague your villany.
Duke. Preserve me but this once!
Mary. There's a deep well
In the next yard, if you dare venture drowning:
It is but death.
Duke. I would not die so wretchedly.
Mary. Out of a garret-window I'll let you down, then;
But say the rope be rotten? 'tis huge high too.
Duke. Have you no mercy?
Mary. Now you are frighted throughly,
And find what 'tis to play the fool in sin,
And see with clear eyes your detested folly [1],
I'll be your guard.

---

[1] *And find what 'tis to play the fool in sin,*
And see with clear eyes your detested folly] Both the old eds.;
"*And find what 'tis to play the foole in folly,*
And see with cleere eyes your detested folly";
and so Seward, who observes; "If the reader thinks '*playing the fool in folly*' not a justifiable expression, he will choose to discard it from the first [line], and then 'sin' or 'vice' may supply the vacancy; but, as I think the expression not unjustifiable, the following seems to me to bid fairest for having been the original;
'*And find what 'tis to play the fool in folly,*
And see with clear eyes your detested crime'."
The Editors of 1778 gave,—
"——————— *the fool in* vice,
——————— *your detested* folly".
Weber printed,—
"——————— *the fool in* folly,
——————— *your detested* vice".

Duke. And I'll be your true servant,
Ever from this hour virtuously to love you,
Chastely and modestly to look upon you;
And here I seal it.   [*Kisses her.*
  Marg. I may kiss a stranger [m],
For you must now be so.

        Re-enter LEON, *with* JUAN, ALONZO, *and* SANCHIO.
  Leon. How do you, my lord?
Methinks you look but poorly on this matter:
Has my wife wounded you? you were well before.
Pray, sir, be comforted; I have forgot all,
Truly forgiven too.—Wife, you are a right one,
And now with unknown nations I dare trust you.
  Juan. No more feign'd fights, my lord; they never prosper.

        Re-enter ALTEA, *with* CACAFOGO *drunk, and* Servant.
  Leon. Who's this? the devil in the vault?
  Altea. 'Tis he, sir,
And as lovingly drunk as though he had studied it.
  Cac. Give me a cup of sack!—and kiss me, lady;
Kiss my sweet face, and make thy husband cuckold!—
An ocean of sweet sack!—Shall we speak treason?
  Leon. He is devilish drunk.
  Duke. I had thought he had been a devil;
He made as many noises, and as horrible.
  Leon. Oh, a true lover, sir, will lament loudly.—
Which of the butts is your mistress?

---

  [m] *kiss a stranger*] "Marston, a very severe satirist, lashes this custom in the following words, which he puts into the mouth of a lady: 'By the faith and trust I beare to my face, 'tis grown one of the most vnsauorie ceremonies; boddy a' beautie, 'tis one of the most vnpleasing iniurious customes to ladyes: any fellow that has but one nose on his face, and standing collor and skirtes also linde with taffety sarcenet, must salute vs on the lipps as familierly! Soft skins saue us, there was a stubbearded John-a-stile with a Ploydens face saluted me last day, and stroke his bristles through my lippes: I ha' spent 10 shillings in pomatum since to skinne them againe. Marry, if a nobleman or a knight with one locke vissit us, though his vncleane goose-turnd-greene teeth ha' the palsy, his nostrells smell worse then a putrified maribone, and his loose beard drops into our bosome, yet wee must kisse him with a cursy,—a curse!' *The Dutch Courtesan,* act III. scene I." WEBER.

www.ingramcontent.com/pod-product-compliance
Lightning Source LLC
Chambersburg PA
CBHW031225170426
43191CB00030B/85